CAMBRIDGE GREEK AND LATIN CLASSICS

XENOPHON ON
GOVERNMENT

EDITED BY
VIVIENNE J. GRAY

Professor of Classics and Ancient History
University of Auckland

CAMBRIDGE
UNIVERSITY PRESS

CAMBRIDGE UNIVERSITY PRESS
Cambridge, New York, Melbourne, Madrid, Cape Town, Singapore, São Paulo

Cambridge University Press
The Edinburgh Building, Cambridge CB2 8RU, UK

Published in the United States of America by Cambridge University Press, New York

www.cambridge.org
Information on this title: www.cambridge.org/9780521588591

© Cambridge University Press 2007

First published 2007

Printed in the United Kingdom at the University Press, Cambridge

A catalogue record for this publication is available from the British Library

Library of Congress Cataloging-in-Publication data
Xenophon.
[Selections. 2007]
Xenophon on government / edited By Vivienne J. Gray.
p.   cm. – (Cambridge Greek and Latin classics)
Greek text with introduction and commentary in English.
Includes bibliographical references and index.
ISBN-13: 978-0-521-58154-7 (hardback)
ISBN-13: 978-0-521-58859-1 (pbk.)
1. Xenophon. Hieron.   2. Xenophon. Lacedaemoniorum respublica.   3. Constitution
of Athens.   I. Gray, Vivienne.   II. Title.   III. Title: On government.   IV. Series.
PA4494.A25   2007
321.9–dc22
2006033313

ISBN 978-0-521-58154-7 hardback
ISBN 978-0-521-58859-1 paperback

CONTENTS

PREFACE

The three works in this collection have been chosen for their common focus on government. Xenophon of Athens wrote two of them. They present analyses of three types of government: the personal rule of Hiero of Syracuse, the laws of Lycurgus of Sparta, and the practices of Athenian democracy. A general introduction surveys Xenophon's thought on government in order to establish common principles behind the three works and then reads his life in relation to that thought. The focus on government continues in the separate introductions to each work and the commentaries, which also address as a priority the literary manner in which this thought is presented.

The University of Auckland was my employer for the period of writing, and the Faculty of Arts provided a Summer Scholarship for a student assistant, Jessica Priestley. I thank Jessica for proofing the original typescript, checking references and correcting errors. In this part of the world there are few Xenophontic experts, but I have had much encouragement from Bill Barnes, otherwise a specialist in the epic. The general and detailed assistance from the editors, Richard Hunter and Pat Easterling, has been so great that no acknowledgement could express my gratitude to them, but I would like to single out their generous production of the *apparatus criticus*.

REFERENCES AND ABBREVIATIONS

References are to Oxford Classical Texts where available. Teubner texts were used for Aeschines: M. R. Dilts (1997); Andocides: F. Blass (1913); Antiphon: F. Blass (1914); Athenaeus: G. Kaibel (1887); Demetrius: L. Radermacher (1967); Diogenes Laertius: M. Marcovich (1999); Dionysius of Halicarnassus: H. Usener and L. Radermacher (1965); Isocrates: B. G. Mandilaras (2003); Plutarch: Lindskog/ Ziegler (1914–69). References are made to the Budé text for Asclepiodotus: L. Poznanski (1992) and the Loeb Classical Library text for *Lyric Poetry*: D. A. Campbell (1982–93).

The needs of undergraduates are considered in referencing and abbreviating, with common English titles for the plays of Aristophanes and the speeches of the orators, Thuc. (not Th.), Dem. (not D.). I use transliterated Greek titles for Xenophon's works. Where not specified the author is Xenophon.

Ancient names are spelled for ease of recognition.

Collections of texts and works of reference are abbreviated as follows:

AJP	*American Journal of Philology*
C&M	*Classica et Mediaevalia*
CJ	*Classical Journal*
CMR	Raeder, I. *Collectionum Medicarum Reliquiae* (Amsterdam 1964)
CQ	*Classical Quarterly*
CR	*Classical Review*
DK	Diels, H. and Kranz, W. *Die Fragmente der Vorsokratiker¹²* (Dublin–Zurich 1966–7)
FGH	Jacoby, F. *Die Fragmente der griechischen Historiker* (Leiden 1950–99)
GG	Goodwin, W. W. *Greek Grammar* (London 1984)
GHI	Meiggs, R. and Lewis, D. *A Selection of Greek Historical Inscriptions to the End of the Fifth Century* BC (Oxford 1969, 2nd edn. 1988)
GL	Campbell, D. A. *Greek Lyric*, 5 vols. (Cambridge, Mass. 1982–93)
GP	Denniston, J. D. *The Greek Particles* (Oxford 1954)
GRBS	*Greek, Roman and Byzantine Studies*
HSCP	*Harvard Studies in Classical Philology*
IEG	West, M.L. *Iambi et Elegi Graeci* (Oxford 1989, 1992)
IG	*Inscriptiones Graecae*, vol. 1³ (Berlin 1981–8) by D. Lewis, vol. 2² (Berlin 1913) by I. Kirchner
JHS	*Journal of Hellenic Studies*
KG	Kühner, R. and Gerth, B. *Ausführliche Grammatik der griechischen Sprache³* (Darmstadt 1966)
LCL	*Loeb Classical Library*
LCM	*Liverpool Classical Monthly*

LSJ	H. G. Liddell, R. Scott, H. Stuart Jones, R. Mackenzie, *A Greek–English Lexicon*[9] (Oxford 1968)
M&T	Goodwin, W. W. *Syntax of Greek Moods and Tenses* (London 1897)
Mus. Helv.	*Museum Helveticum*
PCG	Kassel, R. and Austin, C. *Poetae Comici Graeci* (Berlin 1983–2001)
PMG	Page, D. L. *Poetae Melici Graeci* (Oxford 1962)
QUCC	*Quaderni Urbinati di Cultura Classica*
Rev. de Phil.	*Revue de Philologie, de Littérature et d'Histoire Anciennes*
RFIC	*Rivista di Filologia e d' Istruzione Classica*
SEG	*Supplementum Epigraphicum Graecum*
SIFC	*Studi Italiani di Filologia Classica*
Smyth	Smyth, H. W. *Greek Grammar*, revised by Gordon M. Messing (Harvard 1956)

GENERAL INTRODUCTION

Similarities and differences

These three texts share an important common focus, but there is an equal attraction in their differences.[1]

Their common focus is the problem of government. Aristotle defined this at the beginning of his *Politics* as how to organize and direct the *polis* (or any other κοινωνία or association of interests) with a view to securing its success (εὐδαιμονία)[2] through promotion of the common good. Yet these texts treat this common problem from very different perspectives, use very different political systems as illustrations, have very different literary forms, and differ even in their authorship and consequently also in their style.[3]

Hiero is the first work we have that is entirely devoted to rulership, and is in the form of a dialogue between a wise man and a tyrant about the relative happiness of the ruler and the non-ruler. The tyrant proves to be a suffering human being whose tyranny prevents him achieving personal εὐδαιμονία, but the wise man shows him that he can achieve it through service to the εὐδαιμονία of those he rules. *Respublica Lacedaemoniorum* (*Lac.*) is the first comprehensive account we have of the laws that Lycurgus created for the εὐδαιμονία of the Spartans. It contains the earliest description of his eugenic programme, his educational system, his various other arrangements for the promotion of virtue, his army practices, and the customs for the Spartan kings, and it provokes questions about the function of law and the relationship of law to custom. *Respublica Atheniensium* (*Ath.*) is the first extant analysis of how the Athenian democracy secured the happiness of its members, and the only extant analysis of democracy from the point of view of the *demos*; it contains among other things the first account of the theory of imperial sea power. Indeed, *Ath.* offers starting points to the reader for a full examination of the realities of the Athenian democracy and empire in all its aspects,

---

[1] I therefore thank P. E. Easterling, a foundation editor of this series, for suggesting them to me.

[2] In discussing *eudaimonia*, I tend to say 'happiness' when thinking of the experiences of individuals, and 'success' when speaking of the experience of the community of individuals. So, by ensuring the 'success' of the *polis* in *Hiero* (11.5), the ruler will achieve personal 'happiness' (2.4); and by ensuring the 'success' of the *polis* in *RL*, Lycurgus brought his citizens the individual happiness of conquering enemies such as is described at *Hiero* 2.14–16.

[3] Xenophon of Athens is the author of *Hiero* and *Lac.* Anderson (1974) gives a balanced and accessible account of the life. Diogenes Laertius (third century AD) wrote an account of his life and works (2.48–59), drawing on writers such as Ephorus and Dinarchus (fourth to third centuries BC) and Diocles and Demetrius of Magnesia (first century BC); these supplement the information Xenophon gives about himself in *Anabasis*. The author of *Ath.* is unknown, but is commonly referred to as the 'Old Oligarch'. Diogenes lists *Ath.* among Xenophon's works, but he surely did not write it; see pp. 19–20 below.

1

political, social, cultural, administrative, and *Lac.* offers a similar range of Spartan historical realities, as well as their 'mirage'.[4] Their different perspectives enrich their contribution to political thought. The author of *Ath.* challenges the idea that success depends on securing the common good when he shows that the Athenian *demos* rules in its own interests, but still prospers. In contrast, Xenophon connects success and happiness with the common good in both his works. Nevertheless *Hiero* focuses on the happiness of the ruler in such an arrangement, whereas *Lac.* focuses more directly on the success of the community.[5] As paradigms of successful communities, they could even appear polarized: *Hiero* secures the success of his community through personal rule, *Lac.* through the rule of law. *Hiero* envisages a society in which the brave and wise and just find their place, warriors as well as the farmers and traders, thus addressing the twin needs of peace-time prosperity and of wartime, while *Lac.* educates a small population in mainly military virtues to give leadership to others in war, barely mentioning the economy, which we know was left in the hands of helots and other inferiors. *Lac.* reflects historical realities to some extent, which may partly explain the difference, but both governments are presented as positive paradigms, so it is hard for the student of political thought to decide at first glance whether, in Xenophon's view, the rule of law is preferable to personal rule or whether dedication to military virtue is preferable to economic development. Similar kinds of questions are raised about the relationship between Plato's *Republic* and *Laws*, the one offering the paradigm of the philosopher-king, the other a programme of legislation, the one a blueprint for the best society, the other an avowedly second-best constitution.[6]

Fortunately, Xenophon provides a wider framework of political thought in his many other works within which *Hiero* and *Lac.* can be better understood. These works are *Anabasis*, *Cyropaedia*, *Hellenica*, the Socratic works *Memorabilia*, *Symposium*, *Oeconomicus* and *Apologia Socratis*, and the so-called 'minor' works apart from *Hiero* and *Lac.*: *De Re Equestri*, *Hipparchicus*, *Cynegeticus*, *Agesilaus* and *Poroi*. They represent a variety of literary traditions: history, autobiography and encomium, the dialogue, the technical handbook, even a speech to the leaders of democratic Athens telling them how to improve the Athenian economy and make her 'more just' toward her allies (*Poroi*). What they all have in common, however, is an interest in paradigms of government, from Cyrus the Great in *Cyropaedia* down to the Athenian householder Ischomachus and his wife in *Oeconomicus*. Xenophon has liberal and inclusive views on government that are not well represented in the scholarly literature, but they span gender and race

---

[4] A phrase used to describe the idealized Sparta, from Ollier (1933/43).

[5] The division between the rulers and the ruled may be unpalatable to modern tastes in politics, but was a regular feature of Greek political thought, and obedience to rulers was a requirement in all associations, whether the rulers were the poor majority or their elected representatives, or a hereditary monarch (Arist. *Pol.* 1332b12–15).

[6] Schofield (1999) 31–50 describes the various views of the relations between Plato's *Republic*, *Statesman* and *Laws*. Laks (2000) has argued that *Republic* is to *Laws* as Paradigm is to Best Approximation.

and all types of human organization. As a much older commentator said of him: 'On s'attend à trouver un auteur, on est ravi de trouver un homme.'[7]

Paradigms of political thought

Xenophon was a philosopher, well placed to make a contribution to political thought because political thought was a branch of philosophy. Diogenes presents him as a prominent philosopher,[8] one of the chief pupils of Socrates, alongside Plato and Antisthenes (2.47).[9] Socrates becomes for Xenophon a major mouthpiece of political thought, one through whom he may voice his master's authentic beliefs as well as some of his own.[10] His views give a firm context for *Hiero* and *Lac*. It is convenient to divide these views into those concerning personal rule and those concerning the rule of law; though they have much in common.

Universal rules

Xenophon's Socrates maintains that the principles on which communities should be organized are universal. Aristotle considered the government of a *polis* different from that of households (*Pol.* 1252a7–16), on the grounds that the *polis* was a community of equals whereas the household included natural inferiors (women and slaves), but Socrates found common principles behind all kinds of κοινωνίαι, from empire to *polis* and down through its infrastructures. Xenophon makes him say: 'The management of private affairs is different from the management of public affairs only in point of numbers' (*Mem.* 3.4.12); 'whatever association a man takes charge of, if he knows what is necessary and can supply the goods, he would be a good manager (προστάτης) whether he manages a chorus, a household, a *polis* or an army' (*Mem.* 3.4.6).

Because the principles of leadership were universal, Socrates presents the administration of his provinces by Cyrus the Younger (*Oec.* 4.4–25) as a model for the administration of the householders in that work, and *Memorabilia* shows Socrates using common principles to heal dysfunctional relationships within associations both personal and political, between rulers and the ruled who include mothers and sons, brothers, friends, masters and slaves (2.2–10), elected military commanders and their

---

[7] Croiset (1873) 421.

[8] He says, presumably of *Cyropaedia, Hellenica, Anabasis*: 'first among the philosophers he *also* wrote history' (2.48). Marcovich (Teubner 1999) notes the correct translation of the words in his *apparatus criticus*, against Suda, which understands 'he was the first who wrote a history of the philosophers'; cf. also Hicks (*LCL*, 1925).

[9] Antisthenes is a major character of Xenophon's *Symposium* and figures in *Memorabilia* (2.5). Xenophon's only reference to Plato is his observation that neither Plato nor the rest of his family were able to prevent their young relative Glaucon from trying to advise the Athenian *demos* at a very young age, and completely without knowledge (*Mem.* 3.6.1 and *passim*). This may be gently critical of Plato's failure at 'leading' his relatives in the right direction.

[10] Fortunately, eliciting political thought from this paradigm does not involve the 'Socratic problem', which attempts to discover what Socrates really thought, since it is only Xenophon's representation that matters. See the bibliography on the Socratic works (*Memorabilia, Oeconomicus, Symposium* and *Apologia Socratis*) in Morrison (1988).

men (3.1–5), the masses and their champions (3.6–7).[11] Leadership of many different types of communities indeed defined the achievement of those who sought through their education under Socrates to be worthy of the description καλοί τε κἀγαθοί. They are described as those who 'were able to use well i.e. manage their household and householders and relatives and friends and city and citizens' (*Mem.* 1.2.48). Women and slaves were capable of the same achievement. The householder Ischomachus, maintaining that he and his wife contribute equally to the knowledgeable administration of their estate, refers to their partnership in the rule of their common enterprise (κοινωνοί, κοινωνία: *Oec.* 7.11, 13, 18, 30). He goes so far as to tell Socrates that he invites his wife to prove herself 'better' than he is in contributing to their common good and thus rule him as she would a slave (7.42).[12] He even teaches his leading slaves to rule other slaves (*Oec.* 12.3–4, 13.3–5, 14.1).

PERSONAL RULE

Definition of the leader

Xenophon's Socrates defines the ideal personal ruler in the paradigm of Agamemnon as one who secures the εὐδαιμονία of his community.[13] This is the calling to which Hiero is asked to respond (*Hiero* 11.7) as well as the purpose of Lycurgus' laws (*Lac.* 1.1–2). Socrates had asked: 'What is rule over men? What is a ruler over men?' (*Mem.* 1.1.16: τί ἀρχὴ ἀνθρώπων, τί ἀρχικὸς ἀνθρώπων). He found an answer in Homer's descriptions of Agamemnon as the paradigm 'shepherd of his people' and as 'both a good king and a doughty warrior too' (*Mem.* 3.2.2), which he interpreted as proof that the ruler served the happiness of his people, securing their lives and livelihood, and making them good warriors like himself. 'For a king is elected [sic] not to take care of himself, but to ensure that those who elected him do well through him; and people go to war to secure the best possible livelihood and they elect generals for this, to lead them toward that' (*Mem.* 3.2.3). 'By his reflections on what is the virtue of a good leader, he stripped away the rest and left the definition that he made those he ruled happy' (*Mem.* 3.2.4: τὸ εὐδαίμονας ποιεῖν ὧν ἂν ἡγῆται).

The common good

Agamemnon served the common good (τὸ κοινὸν ἀγαθόν) in order to achieve εὐδαιμονία. Socrates recognized different types of government (kingship and tyranny,

---

[11] Gray (1998) surveys the contents and general thrust of this work.
[12] There is a lot of interest in the wife of Ischomachus: Pomeroy (1994).
[13] See Schofield (1999) 3–30 for comment on Homer's paradigms of Greek political thought. Since Antisthenes, Socrates' close associate, was a leading interpreter of Homer, Agamemnon's paradigm may represent the interests of the authentic Socrates in Homeric interpretation; see Richardson (1975); Navia (2001) 39–52. Plato saw Homer of course as a major source of instruction for the young, editing out the corruption and leaving only the positive paradigms, including that of obedience: *Rep.* 389d–391a.

aristocracy, plutocracy, democracy: *Mem.* 4.6.12), but judged them all by that standard. Hiero is encouraged to serve this common good (11.1), and the *eudaimonia* of the Spartans is the evident focus of Lycurgus' laws. The definition of the good proved slippery when subjected to dialectical investigation, which challenged the validity of even the most obvious 'goods' (*Mem.* 4.2.31–6), but the power to 'increase' the 'greatness' of the community is a basic constituent. This 'increase' might take various forms: improving the economy, or enhancing the virtues and abilities of the membership – their military capacity or their justice toward one another. The shorthand for improvement of the people themselves was to make them 'as they should be' (οἵους δεῖ: *Mem.* 2.3.10, *Cyr.* 1.6.7, *Lac.* 2.13). Agamemnon made his army great by preserving their lives, securing their livelihood, improving their warrior qualities and giving them success in war (*Mem.* 3.2). Ischomachus and his wife teach their woman housekeeper justice, and also to take her share of the success and the failure of the household, so that she will 'increase the household' in partnership with them (συναύξειν τὸν οἶκον: *Oec.* 9.11–16). The laws of Lycurgus increased the power of Sparta by improving the quality of the citizens in ensuring that they acquired 'all the virtues', making them as they should be to secure their prosperity (10.4). Hiero considers that his citizens derive great satisfaction from 'increasing' their *polis* through war, while he is obliged to 'diminish' it as tyrant because of his fear of the citizens, reducing it both in terms of their numbers and their quality (*Hiero* 2.15–17; 5, 6.12–16); in response, Simonides shows him how he can achieve success by 'increasing' it without fear in military and other ways (11.13). Xenophon's Socrates criticized Critias and Charicles as leaders of the Thirty, for diminishing the *polis* of Athens – killing innocent citizens, forcing the rest to commit injustice, and thus making the citizens both 'fewer and worse', since the elimination of the good reduced the population and left only the worse to flourish (*Mem.* 1.2.32). The improvement of other members is an act of leadership even in an 'association' of brothers (*Mem.* 2.3): Socrates encourages one to make the other 'as he should be', i.e. fit to secure the many benefits that arise from the association of brothers, by becoming 'more leaderly in securing his friendship' (*Mem.* 2.3.10, 14). In contrast, the *demos* in *Ath.* seeks only to 'increase the democracy' (*Ath.* 1.4), and entirely eschew the promotion of the good, which perverts this ideal.

Knowledge

Xenophon was of course at one with Plato that to secure the common εὐδαιμονία, the ruler needed superior knowledge. His Socrates concluded that his brightest pupils would produce success for themselves and their households, and for fellow citizens and entire *poleis* – 'if they were properly educated' (*Mem.* 4.1.2). 'Kings and rulers', his Socrates said, 'were not those who held the sceptre of power, nor those elected by sundry persons nor those who won it in the ballot or used force or deceit, but those who understood how to rule' (*Mem.* 3.9.10). The wise poet Simonides teaches Hiero this knowledge in *Hiero*. Lycurgus is wise even though no instruction is recorded (*Lac.* 1.2).

Xenophon came to think of rulers as those who take the initiative from knowledge in creating success in any partnership and the ruled as those who benefit from it and give willing obedience as a result:

> When a person agreed that the function of the ruler was to give orders about what to do, and the function of the ruled to obey, he showed how in a ship the one who understood how to rule was the captain, and the owners and all others in the ship obeyed the one who understood; and that in farming those who had estates, and in disease those who were sick, and in exercise those who were in training, and all the rest who did anything that needed care and attention, that these people took the care and attention themselves if they thought they understood, but otherwise they obeyed those who did understand, not only in their presence, but sending for them in their absence, so that they could obey them and do what was necessary.

He adds as his final example of rulership that women because of their superior knowledge 'rule' men in wool-work (*Mem.* 3.9.11).

Various 'orders' of knowledge were required for rule. When Socrates educates Euthydemus (*Mem.* 4.2–3 and 5–6) in 'the kingly art' of being a man of the *polis* and of the household, able to rule, able to assist oneself and others (4.2.11), he shows that the highest order of knowledge is dialectical. Socrates used dialectical definitions to show Euthydemus how ignorant he was (4.2 passim), then encouraged him to be pious (4.3), just (4.4), and in possession of the self-control needed for practical leadership and for the further practice of dialectic (4.5.11–12). As a culmination, he made him 'dialectical' by teaching him how to define the good so as to avoid the bad (4.6). This gave him a vision of the common good and the personal qualities to implement it. Even at the most basic level, dialectic allowed a commander to recognize which men were good and which were bad, so that the good could be stationed both in front of and behind the cowards, so as to contain them (*Mem.* 3.1.8–9).

Socrates endorsed the need for another kind of knowledge in a series of conversations with elected leaders of the democracy (*Mem.* 3.1–7). This was implementation of the good through 'man-management', the art of knowing how to 'use men', without which human affairs could make no progress (*Mem.* 3.4.12). The art was to win their obedience and make them as they should be for the part they would play in securing the good. This is the skill that the brother is asked to develop in handling his sibling (cf. p. 5) and that Simonides teaches to Hiero.

The ruler also had to have the required technical knowledge for rule or the ability to muster second-order expertise, and to be able to communicate. So that in conversation with an elected cavalry leader, Socrates stresses the need for him to make technical improvements in the horses and their riders, as well as secure obedience by demonstrating the greatest knowledge about horsemanship and communicating the benefits of obedience (*Mem.* 3.3).

Willing obedience

'Willing obedience' was the outcome of successful personal rule and an essential ingredient of the success of the association. Those with superior knowledge were invited to rule because they were recognized as a source of benefit in the various associations at *Mem.* 3.9.11. *Mem.* 3.9.12–13 shows that disobedience meant failure even within the association of the wise and the powerful; the man of power could disobey his wise advisers, but was automatically punished by not having the wisdom to make the right decision. Willing obedience was necessary for the ruler's happiness too. Ischomachus contrasts the happiness of the ruler who secures assent (τὸ ἐθελόντων ἄρχειν) with the unhappiness of ruling without it (τὸ ἀκόντων τυραννεῖν: *Oec.* 21.12). The inability to win willing obedience proves to be the main obstacle to Hiero's personal happiness, and the winning of it the main solution to his dilemma. Lycurgus also wins assent to his laws (*Lac.* 8.5) and the Spartans as a community enjoy the willing obedience of other Greeks in *Lac.* 14.6 because of the virtues that his laws instilled in them.

To secure willing obedience was not just a matter of serving the common good in the cold sense of supplying its needs. The ruler needed also to be a servant of those he ruled, looking to their emotional, as well as their physical and moral welfare. In this he shared the προθυμία of the ideal friend. Socrates makes the connection between friendship and politics explicit when he observes that 'friendship slips through and unites the best people'; they renounce those desires that stand in the way of harmony, share the goods on offer, and assist one another, competing only for their mutual improvement, considering their own wealth as their friends', and eventually sharing political office as partners in power rather than competitors (*Mem.* 2.6.21–6, esp. 26). Cyrus the Younger was so intent as a ruler on winning the friendship of those he ruled that Xenophon found no man who was more 'beloved' (*An.* 1.9.28: οὐδένα κρίνω ὑπὸ πλειόνων πεφιλῆσθαι). Hiero also seeks friendship as a remedy to his personal unhappiness as a ruler, and like Cyrus, who won more friends from small kindnesses than from his large wealth, he is also encouraged to begin with these (*Hiero* 8.1–3; cf. *An.* 1.9.24–7). The ideal friend took as much pleasure in his friends' achievements as his own, worked constantly for their good, and sought to win the paradoxical victory over them in serving their interests (*Mem.* 2.6.35).[14] Hiero also recognizes that one friend 'willingly serves another without compulsion' in a free and equal partnership (1.37), envies the emotional support and the protection that comes of the friendship between citizens (3.1), and is encouraged to the paradoxical victory of service over those he rules (*Hiero* 11.14). The Spartan King Agesilaus is another friend to his people

---

[14] Socrates found this friendship even in the oldest profession, in the association of courtesan and client: 'You . . . know how to best please him with your glances or cheer him with your words, how to receive gladly one who cares for you, but shut out the pleasure-seeker, take special thought for a sick friend and share his great pleasure when he does something fine, and be a delight in all your soul to one who cares strongly about you' (*Mem.* 3.11.10).

(*Ages.* 7.3). Even Lycurgus' laws produce friendly *homonoia* among the Spartans 'living together at home on moderate means' (*Lac.* 14.1), training citizens to 'assist their companions' (*Lac.* 7.4).

The ruler's happiness

Because sensual and material pleasures (food and drink, sex and sleep, wealth) were a potential source of corruption and could distract the ruler from pursuit of the common good, he had to guard against any indulgence in them, but his pursuit of friendship brought other rewards. Aristippus takes a negative view of the experience of a leader in the democracy as no pleasures for himself and constant service to the pleasures of the *demos* (*Mem.* 2.1), but Socrates concludes that the pleasure lies in acquiring the goods that are the common desire of all men: many friends, and no enemies, the ability to benefit these friends and the entire *polis*, and to earn praise and envy (*Mem.* 2.1.18–19). The renunciation of sensual and material pleasures also made the ruler more appealing to those he ruled. Lycurgus cultivated austerity in his Spartans to such an extent that the Greeks sought their leadership as a result (*Lac.* 7,14.2, 6). Pleasures were empty without successful relations with others in the community. Hiero had all the pleasures he could wish for, but was unable to enjoy them without friendship; yet once he acquired friends, he would have the greatest pleasures that came from friendship, and they would willingly give him in addition the wealth he won them as a ruler of excellence (*Hiero* 11.13; cf. also *Cyr.* 8.2.13–23).

Personal rule could not of course achieve complete utopia. Xenophon's Socrates was not so naïve as to think that the ruler would secure from everyone the positive reciprocal response he deserved. He recognized that the competitive side of human nature was a barrier to successful friendship, that there were rogues who did not know how to respond (*Mem.* 2.6.19–20) and that even a brother's kindness might not be repaid (*Mem.* 2.3.17). The best paradigms use punishment and force alongside reward and praise. For this reason, Simonides encouraged Hiero to use different methods with rogues from those he used with men of virtue (*Hiero* 10.1–2). Another non-utopian aspect of the theory was that it was not possible for just any person to become a ruler of an association such as the *polis*, not even in a democracy. Leadership there was the privilege of those who had traditional access to power through birth. Nevertheless, this was not necessarily unwelcome to those they ruled. Socrates considers that Callias has special appeal to the Athenian people precisely because of his ancestors and their achievements, his ancestral priesthood, and his impressive physique (*Symp.* 8.40).

The pambasileia

Xenophon clearly extends his notion of leadership beyond those great men who lead the larger associations of *polis* or empire, but he does envisage praise for Hiero's sole rule of his *polis* after his reform, and it is important to understand the qualifications he places on sole rule. They are in short what we find in *Hiero*: superior knowledge, dedication to the common good, rule by willing assent and so on. Xenophon is not alone in his endorsement. Aristotle recognized the claims of 'complete kingship' or *pambasileia* and subjected it to the same qualifications (*Pol.* 1284a3–15). He argues that if there is a man whose virtue and political competency to produce justice is so great that it is not comparable with the others in his association, it would be unjust to consider him their equal and therefore unjust to subject him to their law, on the grounds that law is set up for those who are equals, but he is 'like a god among men'. Others would not think it fit to rule him in any case, for that would be like claiming to rule Zeus. Rather they give him their willing obedience because that is 'in accordance with nature'. Aristotle later returns to the proposition that it is unjust for one man to rule others in a *polis* because all are equal, and that the law should therefore rule, because it allows for ruling and being ruled alike. However, he continues to argue the case for the rule of the man whose virtue is so great that it eclipses all the rest (1288a 15–29). Nature does not let the part overtop the whole. The man of virtue represents more of the whole than the part. It is therefore not seemly to make him subject to other parts in any way. The community more or less has an obligation to obey his wishes.

THE RULE OF LAW

Xenophon found personal rule compatible with the rule of law. The holder of the *pambasileia* is above the law in the strict sense, but Xenophon's paradigms indicate that even he created and implemented practices to which those he ruled gave assent; these had the force of law, as the example of Cyrus the Great will show below. Xenophon's Socrates certainly found no tension between the rule of law and the personal techniques of rule because he worked within the Athenian democracy, instructing among others office-holders who had been formally elected by law to implement the laws in their 'rule' of the people. They needed to learn the personal techniques as much as any one-man ruler. The same need is found in Spartan society, in the paradigm King Agesilaus, who put his personal leadership at the service of law (*Ages.* 1.36, 7.2–3).

Socrates endorses obedience to the laws and their officers as the secret of political and personal success within the *polis* in his conversation with the sophist Hippias in *Memorabilia* 4.4.[15] This is prefaced with an account of his own obedience to the laws and their officers even in the face of fearful opposition both oligarchic and democratic (4.4.1–4). Law as he saw it was an education in virtue, making the citizens 'as they should be' for their own prosperity, telling them 'what to do and what not to do',

---

[15] This has been subject to an attempt to find tension between Socrates' support for positive written law in the first part of the dialogue and his support for unwritten law in the second: Morrison (1995), Johnson (2003), but cf. de Romilly (1971) 32, 120–7. It is hard to imagine that the instances of unwritten law mentioned in the dialogue (respect for gods and parents, taboos against incest and ingratitude) could ever be in conflict with the laws that communities write for themselves.

encouraging virtuous practice as well as discouraging vice (*Mem.* 1.2.42, 4.4.13). In this respect it had the same effect as his teaching in philosophy: to promote the good and deter the bad. This educational function underpins the laws of *Lac.* and of the Persians, which are contrasted with laws that merely punish wrongdoing (*Cyr.* 1.2.3). The rule of law ideally produced the same 'increase' of virtue as the sole ruler.

Willing obedience was as important for the rule of law as for personal rule and takes the form of assent to its implementation. Socrates thus endorses law as 'whatever the citizens write down after consultation', which means that law should be subject to the assent of those who live under it. Alcibiades pushed the need for assent to extremes (*Mem.* 1.2.45) when he argued that, because it did not persuade the wealthy, the rule of the poor majority was based on force and therefore invalid in law (cf. *Mem.* 4.6.12). *Lac.* shows how even Lycurgus ensured assent to his laws (8.1–5). Socrates of course also recognizes the special category of divine or natural laws that do not need to be written down because transgression incurs automatic penalties (*Mem.* 4.4.19–25). One of the purposes of other law was to prescribe penalties.

The laws as Socrates defined them also preserved the harmony of the community as the personal ruler did. Indeed they arise from this harmony since they take the form of the consultative process above. Xenophon's Socrates praises Lycurgus for securing the obedience to his laws that brought the Spartans their *homonoia* (*Mem.* 4.4.15) and extends this praise to personal leaders in other *poleis* for getting the message across that obedience to law ensured success through unity. Those who obeyed the laws enjoyed the personal benefits of social harmony as well as the success of their community as a whole. These are the 'goods' that he endorses elsewhere as the product of friendship, such as Hiero misses: the confidence of fellow citizens, praise rather than blame, benefit rather than harm, being trusted rather than distrusted (*Mem.* 4.4.17). The desire for these 'goods' was a private incentive to obedience to law, just as the desire for community success was a public one.

Political thought in Cyropaedia

Xenophon's ideas about how to organize and direct the community come together in his longest work: *Cyropaedia.*[16] In the introduction, he exhibits the universality of his principles and his basic thoughts on leadership when he observes that associations of all kinds, from democracies, monarchies and tyrannies down to households, have collapsed because they failed to win willing support from the ruled, but that many *poleis* and entire nations gave Cyrus the Great their 'willing obedience' (ἐθελήσαντας πείθεσθαι), which proved that rulership could succeed if a man had knowledge of the art (ἐπισταμένως 1.1.3). This partnership between the ruler and the ruled allowed him

---

[16] Due (1989) 147–206 surveys the ideal leadership of *Cyropaedia*. This is shaped by his own thought even though it is based on Persian traditions (1.2.1, 1.4.25). Gera (1993) 13–22 discusses the Persian sources for *Cyropaedia*. Xenophon could have heard these while he was on the expedition with Cyrus the Younger.

to defend Persia against its enemies and form the greatest empire that the world had known, bringing success to his people beyond their dreams. Cyrus in effect embodies Aristotle's *pambasileia* (above pp. 8–9). He held power as a result of his royal birth, but he had a natural superiority: superlative beauty, superlative love of other people (φιλανθρωπία), superlative love of knowledge and honour (1.2.1). These gave him a head start in winning willing obedience. He needed only to enhance them with life-long learning of the art of rule in order to succeed.

Cyrus was educated in virtue in obedience to ancestral Persian laws (*Cyr.* 1.2.2–16), but he gained his knowledge about personal rule from his father, and they rehearse this in a Socratic type of conversation on the eve of his first military expedition. He has learned that though it was a great achievement to improve himself and his household, it was greater to know how to rule others so as to make them 'as they should be' (οἵους δεῖ) for success (1.6.7). He acknowledges that to secure success he must win the willing obedience of his army by preserving and feeding them, caring for them in sickness and in health, rejoicing in their success and commiserating in their failure, and generally working for their benefit (1.6.12–25). His mature definition of leadership in the context of his own government is the same as Socrates' definition of the government of Agamemnon, as that of the good shepherd who makes his flocks prosper and serves their common good (*Cyr.* 8.2.14, *Mem.* 3.2).

The ideal ruler improved the abilities of those he led and thus 'increased' their capabilities; Cyrus is no exception. A special feature of his early leadership is his development and promotion of the Persian commoners to equality with their former superiors, producing an entire community of warrior equals dedicated to the military rule of others – such as we find in *Lac*. The original Persian laws gave all citizens access to power and privilege through education, but poverty limited this to those who could afford it. The result was a division into two classes: the privileged 'equals' who formed an army to defend the land, and the commoners who produced the goods to maintain them. It was a successful 'association' as it stood, but a pressing need for more men to defend the land against invasion encouraged Cyrus to make both classes militarily 'useful' (*Cyr.* 2.1.1–19).[17] He therefore armed them alike and translated their theoretical equality into practice by making the commoners 'as they should be', i.e. as good as their former superiors, through training programmes, competitions, rewards and punishment, and a sense of humour (2.1.20–31, 2.2.1–31). He offered them what would in modern society be called 'equal outcomes' – equal shares of the profits of their campaigns regardless of their contribution to the common good – but they chose 'equal opportunity' – reward according to their contribution in competition with the elite (2.2.18ff., 2.3.1–16).[18] The commoner Pheraulas leads the move toward this 'democratic competition' (2.3.7–16, esp. 2.3.15). His subsequent story uncovers the benefits of Cyrus' leadership for the commoners. He acquires wealth as reward for

[17] Another paradigm, Theramenes of Athens, arguing against the tyranny of Critias, also proposed to enfranchise those who could use their arms to assist the community (*Hell.* 2.3.48).
[18] Harvey (1965) defined these two types of equality in political thought.

his contribution, but, thanks to Cyrus, his values are not material, and he delegates its management to others, modelling himself on Cyrus in this too (8.3.35–48; cf. 8.2.15–23). As a ruler in his own right now, he concludes that men are very easy to rule, thus again (like Cyrus) disproving the view in the preface (8.3.49–50, cf. 1.1–3) – because they respond so readily to kindness. He even finds an acceptable way of making the former elite accept through him the orders that he now brings from Cyrus (8.3.5–8). This promotion of the commoner was possible only because of the growth of the empire, which both required their military service and relieved them of the need to grow their own food.

In his development of a successful military machine, Cyrus routinely establishes and enforces customs for success that have the force of law, in the same manner as Lycurgus in *Lac.* (e.g. 6.1.27–30, 7.1.45–7). The later part of the work describes the customs he laid down to preserve the empire he had created and make his associates 'as they should be' (8.1.16). He secures their implementation through punishment and reward and develops his role as a model for others to imitate (this is surprisingly absent from *Hiero*, but found in *Lac.* in the model of obedience set by the kings: 8.1–2). Like the ideal ruler too, he wins the friendship of those who would be naturally inclined to oppose him because of their own superior qualities, but who, for the same reason, would be most useful to him as partners in his administration (*Cyr.* 8.1.47–8.2.28). He honours them, empathizes in their success and failure, and employs the usual methods to make himself a more desirable friend to them than others with whom they might conspire. Ideal leaders do not take wealth for themselves, but encourage justice in their companies by enriching the just more than those who sought wealth unjustly (Ischomachus in *Oec.* 14.4–7, Cyrus the Younger in *An.* 1.9.16–17). Cyrus the Great goes further and evokes such a positive response from those he enriched that whenever he needs resources they become his 'treasure chests', giving him freely whatever he wants of the wealth, since he was the source of it (*Cyr.* 8.2.15–19). Hiero is asked to cultivate these same important people in order to receive exactly this same display of friendship (*Hiero* 11.13).

It is in making these important people 'as they should be' that Xenophon directly addresses the relative merits of the rule of law and personal rule. He credits Cyrus with the belief that 'men were made better through written laws', but that 'the good ruler had the advantage of being a law with eyes – since he was able to give orders and see those who disobeyed and punish them' (*Cyr.* 8.1.24). In holding this view he resembles Ischomachus, who combines personal rule with the rule of law over his household slaves, using the written laws of Solon and Dracon to punish wrong, as well as those of the Persian king, on the grounds that they both punish wrong and reward right. He sums up the importance of personal supervision in the Persian story of how the eyes of the master fatten the horse (*Oec.* 12.20).

Personal supervision of the law gave the ruler flexibility to achieve justice. In the homeland from which he had set out to create his empire, Cyrus swore an oath to respect the ancestral laws within those precincts (*Cyr.* 8.5.25), but though these developed virtue in the Persians (*Cyr.* 1.2.2–3), their criminal laws had already proven unable to achieve perfect justice without skilled interpretation.[19] As a boy in school, Cyrus showed that the law was inadequate when, in the course of a mock trial, he refused to punish the big boy with the tunic too small, who took from a smaller boy a tunic that was too big, on the grounds that the theft produced a situation that was 'fitting' for both (1.3.16–17). His teacher punished him for not following the law, but he produced a justice that was larger than written law. In his maturity, Cyrus showed the same flexibility when he refused to press the strict justice of the death penalty against the king of Armenia, on the grounds that his mercy would make the man a better friend than he was before (*Cyr.* 3.1.31). *Cyropaedia* thus confirms the need for a personal dimension in the application of the unyielding boundaries of written laws of this detailed kind.

IMPORTANCE OF THE PARADIGMS

Hiero and *Lac.* are more comprehensible in the context of Xenophon's other paradigms of government, because they are variations on the basic principles. The rule of law is not so divorced from personal rule as it seemed, since both of them can achieve prosperity and increase. Both are indeed to some extent necessary. Lycurgus educated the citizens to virtue and harmony and success through law, but introduced personal rule in the form of the Spartan ephors; they represent the 'law with eyes' because they have power to punish transgressions without consultation (8.3–4, 13.5). Hiero seems likely to become the law with eyes, rewarding those who do good (*Hiero* 9.1–11), but he may also win assent to written law that will prolong the success of his *polis* beyond his lifetime, since he already envies the protection the citizens have thanks to written laws for their most intimate friendships and even their lives (3.1–3, 4.3–5). The two sorts of government increase their community in different ways, but these are not so far apart as they seemed either. Lycurgus produces an increase of mainly military fame and power through the promotion of military and communal virtues, while Hiero is encouraged to develop a flourishing economy as well as a flourishing army, but this difference may be put down to the size of their populations. Lycurgus needs to include every citizen in the military effort because the Spartans had such a small population, but Hiero had sufficient numbers to achieve increase in both areas. Nevertheless, in producing good warriors Lycurgus merely makes compulsory the competitions in military and communal excellence that Hiero is asked to encourage in his citizens through the reward of honour. And both of them see honour and dishonour as incentives (*Hiero* 9.6–11; *Lac.* 4.3–4, 9.4–6). The tyrannical stereotype means that there is also a bodyguard for Hiero to use in the armed forces, and he thus turns to his credit what the citizens saw to his discredit when he used it for his personal security.

[19] Plato, *Politicus* 294a–b mentions one of the main weaknesses of written laws: that they were inflexible and could never accommodate the infinite variety of people and their actions. *Oeconomicus* 14.4–7 addresses another difficulty in Greek law as opposed to Persian: that the laws punished vice but did not promote virtue. *Memorabilia* 4.4.14 addresses the need for laws to change and how that affects their status.

These paradigms assist understanding in other ways as well. *Lac.* 14 appears to point to weaknesses in Lycurgus' original arrangements when it indicates that the Spartans had lost their success at the time of its composition because the harmosts had succumbed to their desires for wealth and flattery and escaped the control of the laws while residing abroad. Yet the paradigm of the 'laws' of Xenophon's teacher Socrates in *Memorabilia* shows that such lapses do not make his arrangements defective, but actually reinforce their worth. For Socrates also controlled the desires of Critias and Alcibiades while they associated with him and obeyed his laws, but they were corrupted through their desires when they escaped his control, just like the harmosts (*Mem.* 1.2.24–8, esp. 19–23). And Xenophon is not arguing there that their lapses make the paradigm of Socrates any less compelling, but actually more so, since such desires as these evidently took some powerful force to control in the first place, for no matter how long. The same must apply to Lycurgus. His laws had after all produced perfection since the time of the Heraclids (10.8). In contrast, *Hiero*'s paradigm is not yet tested in time, and the collapse of Cyrus' empire soon after his death (*Cyr.* 8.8) suggests that personal rule remained fallibly attached to a person no matter how effective it was in securing success for a generation.

Finally, the paradigms, by their multiplication of the positive faces of good government, may begin to counter the 'ironist' interpretations that read so much negativity into them, driven by scepticism about the possibility of such goodness.[20] Sinister interpretations have been proposed for the apparently positive relations between the ruler and the ruled in both *Hiero* and *Cyropaedia*, *Lac.* has been read as a 'most ably disguised satire on Spartan lack of education' rather than the endorsement it appears to be, while passages from *Memorabilia* come in for the same treatment.[21] Suspicion may already be aroused in readers by the sheer number of works that Xenophon is alleged to ironize, and the degree to which the surface meaning must in most cases be rejected to accommodate them, but Appendix 1 will demonstrate further that there is no irony in the positive image of rulership described by Simonides in *Hiero*, and Appendix 3 will elucidate the confirming rhetoric behind the praise of the laws of Lycurgus in *Lac.*

XENOPHON'S LIFE

Xenophon's life is intimately connected with the development of his political thought and his writings on leadership. Luccioni (1946) explored the connection to negative

---

[20] Strauss finds critical subtexts in *Lac.* (1939) and *Hiero* (1947/1963/2000) (see Appendix 1). Higgins (1977) confirms these (60–75 on *Hiero* and *Lac.*) and other ironic readings. Tatum (1989) finds a subtext of criticism of Cyrus' leadership in *Cyropaedia*, and is followed by Nadon (2001). *Memorabilia* 4.4 has been interpreted as an examination of the conflict of written and unwritten law rather than the harmony it purports to be: Johnson (2003). Azoulay (2004) has questioned all positive manifestations of relations between rulers and followers. Yet voices are raised in protest. Due (1989) gives a straight reading of *Cyropaedia*. Cartledge in Hodkinson and Powell (eds.) (1999) 320 does not accept the ironic reading of *Lac.* Schofield (1999) 34 refers in a not entirely complimentary way to 'the Straussians' who subscribe to excessively ironic interpretations of Plato. See also my reviews of Nadon (2004.2), Johnson (2004.3), and Azoulay (2006).

[21] For the quotation: Strauss (1939) 531.

effect,[22] for instance in his assessments of Xenophon's approval of autocracy over democracy.[23] Different conclusions can be reached, however, if the life is read more sensitively in the light of the paradigms.

Xenophon was born to Gryllus of Erchia, an Athenian, in the early years of the Peloponnesian War and he died some time after 355 BC.[24] The first thing we know about him is his connection with Socrates. Diogenes (2.48) tells a story of his recruitment to the cause: that Socrates barred his way in an alley and questioned him until he stumped him with an inquiry about where to find men who were good and true, inviting him then, 'Follow me and learn.' This phase of his life as he presents it in his Socratic works laid the foundations of his interest in leadership.

It was against Socrates' advice that Xenophon joined the expedition he describes in *Anabasis*, in which Cyrus the Younger led the Ten Thousand Greek mercenaries into the heart of Asia in order to depose his brother, the ruling king of Persia (*An.* 3.1.5). He presents his decision to go as the result of an opportunity to acquire Cyrus' friendship. We might assume that he hoped to make his name and fortune, like his friend Proxenus (*An.* 2.6.17), and that like others who joined Cyrus because they heard of his virtue, he was not driven by poverty, and always intended to return home, either to parents or to children (*An.* 6.4.8). This expedition at any rate gave him the first opportunity we know he had to observe a range of highly talented leaders in action and put his observations into literary form. The obituaries for Cyrus and the Greek mercenary generals (*An.*1.9, 2.6) reveal his special interest in their leadership, particularly how they secured obedience.[25] He characterizes the Spartan Clearchus as a leader who loved war and could inspire men to follow him through fear, but had none of the human sympathy that the best leader required; he never smiled or rewarded; and he punished on principle (*An.* 2.6.9–14). The Boeotian in contrast failed in his leadership because he relied on praising the good and not praising the rogues; as a result they just laughed at him and took advantage (*An.* 2.6.20). Thessalian Menon's leadership

---

[22] Luccioni (1946) 139–74 alleges for example that Xenophon praised the Spartans in *Lac.* in order to repay them for giving him his residence at Scillus (see p. 19), and at the same time to get revenge on the Athenians for exiling him (see p. 17); but that events then made him change his mind and add the fourteenth chapter in order to withdraw the praise and save his reputation among the other Greeks. His effort is summed up as that of 'un panégyriste sincère' (141) but 'maladroit' (152) who was 'dupe de sa propre admiration' (160) for Spartans. This diminishes the paradigmatic value of the work and ignores its stated aim, which is to praise the laws rather than the Spartans. It also invites reconsideration of the relationship between Xenophon's life and thought.

[23] Gray in Rowe and Schofield (eds.) (2000) 142–54 and (2004a) has attempted to produce a more balanced appreciation of his thought.

[24] A birth-date no earlier than 430 BC can be deduced. Xenophon implies that he was too young for military command in 401 BC (*An.* 3.1.14, 25), and this probably means he was under thirty. It seems that those under thirty were called 'young' (*Mem.* 1.2.35). Proxenus was thirty years old at that time of his military command and it is significant that Xenophon does not call him too young (*An.* 2.6.20). He could even have been under twenty; his Alcibiades challenged the wisdom of Pericles at this early age, and his Glaucon tried (unwisely) to advise the Athenians about the management of their affairs (*Mem.* 1.2.40, 3.6.1). Proof that he lived at least until 355/354 BC is found in the reference he makes to the Sacred War (*Poroi* 5.9; cf. D.S. 16.23).

[25] See Momigliano (1971) for Xenophon's pioneering role in Greek biography.

is a deliberate perversion of friendship practices, and he secures willing obedience by partnering his men in crime (*An.* 2.6.21–9). Cyrus combined the styles of Clearchus and Proxenus, punishing terribly those who did not serve him, but rewarding good service with his constant friendship. The result was enthusiastic service, such as the Persian nobles display when they rush headlong in all their finery in order to dig the waggons out of the mud (*An.* 1.5.7–8) and such as his sceptre-bearing subordinate shows even unto death, committing suicide over his dead body with the dagger that Cyrus had given him in recognition of his previous good service (*An.* 1.8.28–9). Later in the expedition Xenophon also observed the rule that Seuthes exercised over his Thracians (*An.* 7.2.10–31; 7.3.4–47; 7.4.1–23; 7.5.2–16; 7.6.2–44; 7.7.1–55).

Xenophon relates his personal experience to his political thought about rulership when he describes his own association with Cyrus as a friendship. Insisting that he did not join Cyrus 'as general or brigade commander or ordinary soldier' (*An.* 3.1.4), he describes how his 'long-time friend' Proxenus, who had studied philosophy with Gorgias of Leontini, introduced him to Cyrus as a 'friend'. These are guest-friendships,[26] but the 'enthusiasm' that Cyrus and Proxenus showed for Xenophon (προθυμουμέ-νου δὲ τοῦ Προξένου καὶ ὁ Κῦρος συμπρουθυμεῖτο μεῖναι αὐτὸν 3.1.9) is also typical of Xenophon's other paradigms of friendships, including those between rulers and followers. Cyrus' enthusiasm is explicable in terms of his desire to surround himself with those who could serve him, but the nature of Xenophon's appeal is unclear. He must have undergone the normal Athenian ephebic military service and service in the Peloponnesian War, but he makes nothing of his military role in the beginning and records only his service as an interpreter and go-between in the main battle (*An.* 1.8.15–16). Perhaps we are asked to imagine that a bright young Socratic might give a young ruler such as Cyrus wise advice, in the paradigmatic relationship of wise man and ruler that is found in *Hiero*. Plato played out this paradigm in his *Seventh Letter*, in his friendship with the tyrants of Syracuse, which was arranged through the invitation of his own friend in philosophy, Dion.[27] Alexander the Great took the philosophers Callisthenes and Anaxarchus with him on his eastern expeditions. Anaxarchus advised him about the powers of kings and Callisthenes recorded his exploits – as Xenophon recorded those of Cyrus in *Anabasis*.[28] The young Persian prince might have thought that Xenophon would assist him in a variety of ways that included such reportage.

Xenophon became his own paradigm of leadership in his promotion to command in the crisis after the murder of the Greek generals (*An.* 3.1ff.). His success in leading them back to the coast ('The sea! The sea!') in spite of his relative youth confirms that he was able to translate into action the practical training and experience he must have gained from his Athenian military service, the theories of leadership that he

---

[26] Herman (1987) 47, 97–101 on the guest-friendships of Xenophon and Cyrus, and *passim* for other guest-friendships in Xenophon. Luccioni (1946) 27–8 gives no prominence to this friendship with Cyrus.

[27] See Schofield (2000) 293–303 on this episode in Plato's experience. The evidence for it is [Plato] *Epistle* 7 and Plutarch, *Dion*.

[28] Arrian, *An.* 4.9.7–12.

credits to Socrates, and subsequent observation of rulers. His widespread reputation as one who seemed 'too much a friend of the ordinary soldier' indicates an excess of ideal rulership (*An.* 7.6.4, 39). Yet he justifies the worth of this style of leadership when he describes how his approachability at any time of the day or night secured the common good in the crossing of a river (*An.* 4.3.10–14). His harsh treatment of a man who abandoned his sick colleague during a march through the snow is in contrast a classic case of securing unwilling obedience from those who did not serve the common good (*An.* 5.8). His idea for founding a *polis* in the east is his most ambitious political project – one that met with suspicion and was abandoned before the details could be assessed (5.6.15ff.).

Yet Socrates had warned him there that the Athenians would blame him for his association with Cyrus, on the grounds that he had been their enemy in the Peloponnesian War. For this reason, it appears, the Athenians did exile him, even though Diogenes says that he was exiled for his association with the Spartans (2.51). Xenophon indicates that the sentence had not yet been passed at the end of the expedition when he was preparing to return home (*An.* 7.7.57).

His exile raises the question of his view of democracy. It is possible to say that he joined Cyrus out of disaffection with democracy in Athens, but that is unlikely by his own account because he says he was intending to return home after the expedition ended. It is possible that his subsequent exile made him bitter, but there is no evidence of this in his works either, and indeed a lot of evidence to the contrary.[29] He seems to have resigned himself to his exile, even blaming himself for it when, in the persona of his younger self, he foolishly ignores Socrates' prediction that the Athenians would blame him for his friendship with Cyrus (*An.* 3.1.5). *Anabasis* 7.7.57 mentions the exile only in order to evoke sympathy as he plans his homecoming in happy ignorance of his fate. *Hellenica* 2.4 is actually very generous in its portrayal of Thrasybulus and of the democracy he put in place after the overthrow of the tyrannical regime that the Spartans had imposed on Athens at the end of the Peloponnesian War – even though this was the democracy from which Xenophon took his leave and which exiled him.

Thrasybulus perfectly fits Socrates' description of the 'best men' who administer oaths to secure the *homonoia* that comes from the rule of law (*Mem.* 4.4.15–16). His speeches (*Hell.* 2.4.40–2) indicate that the only valid claim to rule others is that of superior courage and other virtue, and that the *demos* possesses this while their opponents do not.[30] Nevertheless he reconciles both the *demos* and their opponents with an oath (*Hell.* 2.4.43). Xenophon indeed thinks that the behaviour of the *demos* was so exemplary that he breaks the chronological order of his narrative to indicate that even down to his own times it had remained true to the oaths it swore on that occasion (*Hell.* 2.4.43). The *demos* does send those cavalrymen who served the tyrants overseas on service in the hope that they may perish as a 'profit to the *demos*'

---

[29] Luccioni (1946) 17 explains some of this away as the product of his gratitude to the democracy when it eventually recalled him from exile.

[30] Luccioni (1946) 15 dismisses his approval of Thrasybulus as a result of his connection with the Spartans, but that is not at all prominent in his characterization.

(*Hell.* 3.1.4); but these are the criminals who regularly stand in the way of good government in Xenophon's theory (see p. 8).[31] Thrasybulus remains a positive paradigm, endorsing the decision of the Athenians to repay greater favour to the Thebans than they deserved (*Hell.* 3.5.16), and 'having a reputation as a good man' on his death after further excellent service to the democracy in the Aegean (*Hell.* 4.8.25–31).[32] Xenophon reveals in contrast in *Hellenica* 2.3.11–2.4.42 how much he detested the tyrannical regime of Critias, which overthrew democracy. Socrates also detested Critias and his colleagues, because they made the population fewer and worse as a result of their bad government (*Mem.* 1.2.12–48).

Xenophon was also working to increase the prosperity of that democracy when he wrote *Hipparchicus* to improve the leadership of democratically elected Athenian cavalry commanders, and *Poroi* to improve the Athenian economy. In these works he plays the role of Socrates, who is also found in *Memorabilia* advising those recently elected to cavalry command (3.3) and those who wish to improve the resources of the Athenians (3.7). *Poroi* remedied the complaint made by the leaders of the *demos* at Athens that they were unable to feed the *demos* without exploiting the empire, by suggesting reforms to make Athens economically self-sufficient, so that it might provide for the *demos* from its own resources and rule an empire based on assent rather than exploitation. This provides an effective contrast to *Ath.*

Xenophon joined up with the Spartans after the expedition with Cyrus was over, and at first enjoyed uneasy relations with them. This led him to reject the sole command of the Ten Thousand; they viewed him with hostility as an Athenian, their old enemy (*An.* 6.1.25–33). He eventually earned their respect, but his intention to return home to Athens before his exile indicates that it was not his deliberate choice to continue serving the Spartans. After his exile, his service to them was a matter of opportunity and survival. More importantly, he found both negative and positive paradigms in their leaders. So, he observes that Dercylidas was a more disciplined commander than Thibron in Asia, and that this is why the men were more disciplined (*Hell.* 3.2.7), and that Thibron is defeated because he does not control his desires (4.8.18–19), whereas Diphridas succeeds because he is 'no less charming, but a more disciplined and self-controlled general, for the pleasures of his body did not control him, but he always attended to the task in hand' (4.8.22). He calls the enthusiasm that the Spartan Teleutias elicited from his men 'an achievement most worthy of a man' and asks what he did to achieve it (*Hell.* 5.1.4); his answer is his sympathy, his sharing of their difficulties, and his strategy to secure their supplies (14–24). But he criticizes him at a later time for his folly in giving in to emotion and securing his own death and the annihilation of his army (5.3.7). The other evaluations in *Hellenica*

---

[31] The interest that Xenophon shows in horses (*Hipparchicus* etc.) indicates that he probably served in the Athenian cavalry (as his sons did after him), but he need not have served the tyrants. He refers himself to cavalrymen on the side of the democrats: *Hell.* 2.4.25.

[32] Irony has been detected in δοκῶν εἶναι, but other similar phrases are used of valid 'reputations', in which 'seeming' merely presents the perspective of those who shared the evaluation; cf. how Dercylidas 'seemed to be' cunning (*Hell.* 3.1.8); his reputation is certainly validated in the narrative.

(6.2.32, 39; 6.5.51–2; 7.5.8, 19) sufficiently praise and blame leaders of other *poleis* to balance any impression of prejudice.

Xenophon's association with the Spartans and their King Agesilaus gave him a special advantage in breaking through the secrecy for which Thucydides says the Spartans were famed (2.39.1; 5.68.1–2). It advanced the knowledge of their system that had begun with Socrates (*Mem.* 4.4.15–16) and gave him special access to the laws he purports to describe in *Lac.*, since the king swore an oath to the people to maintain their integrity (*Lac.* 15.7). Plutarch presents Xenophon's relationship with Agesilaus as that between a wise man and a ruler (*Ages.* 20.2) such as is found in *Hiero*, but this could also have been a form of guest-friendship; he does not, however, find Xenophon entirely wise.[33] The acquaintance also produced *Agesilaus* as another study in leadership and an appropriate expression of personal friendship. The King's piety, justice, self-control, bravery, wisdom, patriotism, affability and simplicity complement the austere virtues developed by the laws in *Lac.* and remind us that *Lac.* is only a partial paradigm of virtue overall.

The Spartans eventually gave Xenophon an estate at Scillus in the Peloponnese (*An.* 5.3.4–13) and that gave him a chance to become his own paradigm of peacetime leadership. He used the tithe to Artemis from his eastern expedition to establish a sanctuary and a temple on the model of Artemis of Ephesus (*An.* 5.3.6–7) and he increased the common good of his local community by organizing a festival and a hunt.[34] His exile is sometimes said to have isolated him from the mainstream, but his estate was close to Olympia, which was a hive of activity, intellectual, artistic and athletic. From here he witnessed the end of Spartan leadership, even over the Peloponnese. According to Diogenes (2.53), he lived in Corinth after leaving Scillus, but according to Pausanias (5.6.6), he was buried in Scillus. At all events his contact with Athens was subsequently restored, since they say that his son Gryllus died fighting in the Athenian cavalry as an ally of the Spartans at the battle of Mantinea in 362 BC. Xenophon describes this engagement without naming his son (*Hell.* 7.5.15–17), but many paid tribute to the son in order to 'please' the father, who evidently was famous (D.L. 2.54–5). In exile he wrote his works (D.L. 2.52) – the fruits of his long association with leaders and leadership theory.

AUTHORSHIP

Manuscripts credit all three works in this collection to 'Xenophon Rhetor' (whom we know as Xenophon of Athens), but Diogenes Laertius raised doubts about *Lac.* and

---

[33] See n. 26 on guest-friendship. The interpretation of Plutarch's anecdote favours Agesilaus rather than Xenophon. In it, Xenophon is called 'the wise', but the point seems to be that Agesilaus is wiser. Xenophon is described as a zealous supporter of the king, but Agesilaus tells him to send his sons to be trained in Spartan ways, which are both to rule and be ruled, as if he senses that Xenophon is too keen on rulership. Nevertheless, it is characteristic that Xenophon is introduced in a context about rulership.

[34] Purvis (2003) shows how unique his evidence is for private cult by spending a large part of her book on this episode.

Ath. when he listed among his works a Λακεδαιμονίων καὶ Ἀθηναίων πολιτείαν, and added ἥν φησιν οὐκ εἶναι Ξενοφῶντος ὁ Μάγνης Δημήτριος (2.57). Richards (1897) 232–3 surmised that the original objection must have been only to *Ath.*, since *Ath.* is not written in the style of Xenophon,[35] whereas nothing about *Lac.* indicates that Xenophon did not write it.[36] Moreover, *Ath.* does not reflect Xenophon's political thought about democracy,[37] and is almost certainly a product of the second half of the fifth century,[38] whereas Xenophon was composing his major works in the period 362–354 BC.[39] Manuscripts probably included *Ath.* alongside *Lac.* because of their focus on political thought. The author of *Ath.* is traditionally called 'The Old Oligarch', but he cannot be identified. Diogenes' apparent conflation of *Lac.* and *Ath.* could be his own error or that of Demetrius, the critic from Magnesia (1st century BC): Frisch (1942) 38f.

TEXTUAL TRADITION

I have followed Denyer, *Plato Alcibiades* (Cambridge 2001) 26–7 in referring to the textual tradition in the *apparatus criticus* (D, d, i, c), but in the following description the normal designations are used.

Because of their shortness, manuscripts regularly collect a number of Xenophon's *opuscula* together in various orders, by themselves, alongside his longer works, either complete or excerpted, or in the company of the works of other authors, such as Plutarch and Arrian. This means that conclusions on the textual tradition of any one of them need not be the same for all. However, Vaticanus 1335 (A and α), Vaticanus 1950 (B), Marcianus 511 (M), Mutinensis 145 (C) have been considered important for all three works. A, now dated to the tenth century, is the best for *Hiero* and *Lac.* It is marked with erasures, obliterations and numerous marginal variants and interlinear corrections in different hands (α) that are of variable worth (Jackson 1988). One level of annotation dated to the fifteenth century includes the completion of *Lac.*,

---

[35] Xenophon writes in so many different genres that require different styles that it is impossible to speak of any one style as characteristic, but none of them is consistently like *Ath.* There is no study of his style that is satisfactory. Norden, vol. 1 (1971) 101–3 is very brief. See pp. 22–9 for comments on the style of *Hiero*, and *Lac.* and *Ath.*

[36] Richards (1897) examines the differences between the language of *Ath.* and *Lac.* and finds all the characteristics of his style in *Lac.* Lana (1992) 17–26 finds that the most frequently occurring words in *Lac.* and *Ath.* are not the most frequent in *Hellenica*, but this is not surprising, given their very different content. Jessica Priestley, a student of advanced statistics as well as Greek, comments to this editor that his article is 'an interesting reminder of how misleading graphs can be' (17 November 2002). He finds the use of particles and conjunctions similar.

[37] See the comments on *Ath.*, pp. 56–7.

[38] I comment more fully on the date of *Ath.* on pp. 57–8.

[39] *Poroi* 5.9 indicates a date of composition in 355/354 BC (D.S. 16.23 on the Sacred War); *Hell.* 6.4.37 was written after the accession to power of Tisiphonus in 357/6 BC (D.S. 16.14.1–2); *Agesilaus* after Agesilaus' death, in 362/1 BC (D.S. 15.93.6 and Plut. *Ages.* 40.3); *Cyr.* 8.8.4 after the Satraps' Revolt c. 361 BC (D.S. 15.90–3).

which the original scribe had copied only up to 15.5, and the entire text of *Ath.* (this is what is referred to as α or a rather than A). B is the better manuscript for *Ath.* Serra (1979) 89 compared good readings in B with some egregiously inferior ones in α.

Editors had already recognized other fourteenth-century manuscripts (called *deteriores*) as occasionally valuable (e.g. in *Hiero* 2.17 αὔξει against ἄξει ACM, and 5.4 συγχαίρει against συγχωρεῖ ACM), but Haltinner-Schmoll (1980) 236 went further and concluded that ABCM represent a single family for *Hiero*, and that the *deteriores* Laurentianus 55.21 (F), Laurentianus 80.13 (H) and Lipsiensis 9 (D – which lacks *Ath.*) represent another separate family worthy of equal attention, so that 'only by combining the reconstructed source of DFH with its gemellus A can we arrive at the archetype'. Jackson's investigations of *Hipparchicus* (1990) and *Poroi* (1990) confirmed this second family of *opuscula* manuscripts. Of interest is the view that DFH have contaminated the A family (Haltinner-Schmoll, Jackson). For *Lac.*, Muratore (1997) 172 calls for the use of a wider range of manuscripts apart from A in the foundation of a new text, including F, H, D.

B, belonging to the fourteenth century, is close to A, but it is unclear whether it is a copy of A, or derived from an ancestor of A. To a large extent it looks like A without much of its subsequent annotation. C is now thought to be a descendant of A for all three works, with a great deal of scribal improvement: Haltinner-Schmoll (1980) 231 n. 4, Muratore (1997), Bowersock (1968), Serra (1979). For example, C supplies missing connectives at *Hiero* 1.26 and 2.1. However, C omits ἄλυπον at *Hiero* 9.9 even though the word is characteristic of Xenophon. It fills the lacuna in *Ath.* 2.5, but modern editors transpose the addition to make better sense of it. M, again of the fourteenth century, has been considered independent of ABC for all three works, which gives it special status, but this independence has been challenged for *Hiero* (above).

Other ancient writers provide valuable readings because they had access to earlier texts. In the fifth century AD, Stobaeus made extensive excerpts from *Hiero* and *Lac.* and one from *Ath.* (*Florilegium* 4.1.50–1; 4.2.23; 4.5.109, 4.8.30). He inspires no confidence when he paraphrases loosely in his version of *Hiero* 6.6, which seems to import vocabulary from 3.3 and 9.8 (Stobaeus: συμπαρομαρτῶν λυμαντήρ ἐστιν, codd.: συμπαρακολουθῶν λυμεὼν γίγνεται), and he omits not only words but entire phrases and sentences; moreover, his manuscripts (ASM) do not date back earlier than the eleventh century. Yet some of his readings carry serious weight, for example his ὀφθαλμοῖς in *Lac.* 3.5 (which follows Longinus, *On Sublimity* 4.4 = 181v., against the manuscripts), his ἀλκίμους for κοσμίους in *Hiero* 5.1, his ὁπλιτικῶν in *Lac.* 11.4 and πολιτικὰ in *Hiero* 9.5; even some of his omissions have been championed, such as the phrase [ἀνυπόδητον . . . ὑποδεδεμένον] in *Lac.* 2.3. In the third century, Athenaeus made extensive excerpts from *Hiero* (1.17–20 = *Deipnosophistae* 4.144c–e; 1.22–3 = 3.121d–e; 4.2 = 4.171e–f). His value for *Lac.* can be seen in his reading ἀγρευομένων (codd. ἀργευομένων) and ἄρτον (codd. ἀργὸν) in *Lac.* 5.3. Plutarch's paraphrases of Xenophon's works, particularly his *Lycurgus*, can also assist in settling problems in *Lac.*

XENOPHON'S LANGUAGE AND STYLE

Xenophon's writing drew favourable ancient comment for its use of words and the ideas they express, but no critics take their examples from the *opuscula*.[40] Dionysius of Halicarnassus called his vocabulary 'pure' (καθαρός: *Ad Pomp.* 4.3 = 778, meaning by Attic prose standards), but he does use words, and some constructions too, such as final ὡς and ὡς for ὥστε (*M&T* 608–9, with Appendix IV), that are not normal in Attic prose of his time. Others called his vocabulary poetic, but words found in poetry sometimes also occur in prose in non-Attic dialects, so Xenophon may use them as part of a normal vocabulary enriched by his life abroad rather than for special poetic effect. Some do occur in passages where there is no obvious special effect, but others seem more deliberate.[41] Thus, Hiero uses unusual words to enhance the solemnity of the law against seduction, which shows how important friendship is to the citizens (3.3–4: λυμαντῆρας 'spoilers': Gautier (1911) 45–7, ἀκήρατος 'undefiled'). He also uses the poetic λυμεών to enhance the grim metaphor of the fear in the heart of the tyrant as a 'courtier' in a passage of intense emotion (6.6). Simonides uses a poetic epithet (ἐκπαγλοτάτοις) to describe the armour of the tyrant in a passage where he is striving for a splendid effect, and where perhaps there is a suggestion of old-fashioned epic values (11.3).[42]

As for his style and the power of his ideas, Suda s.v. 'Xenophon' called him the 'Attic Muse' and the 'Attic Bee' because of its sweetness, but Demetrius (*On Style* 2.37) said that he blended μεγαλοπρεπεία, δεινότης, and χάρις ('elevation, force, charm'), and Dionysius of Halicarnassus called his ideas 'fine, magnificent, appropriate for a philosopher': καλὰς καὶ μεγαλοπρεπεῖς καὶ ἀνδρὶ φιλοσόφωι προσηκούσας, projecting a character that was 'pious and just and enduring and affable, decorated in a word with all the virtues' (*Pomp.* 4.1–2 = 777–8). [Longinus], *On Sublimity* 8.1 (= 182 v.) implies that he had a 'powerful grasp of ideas': τὸ περὶ τὰς νοήσεις ἀδρεπήβολον.

Hiero

The short account in Luccioni (1947) 8–10 is the fullest modern assessment of the language and style of *Hiero*, but the work could be said to exhibit all the above features. Even the plain introduction: Σιμωνίδης ὁ ποιητὴς ἀφίκετό ποτε πρὸς Ἱέρωνα τὸν τύραννον might be analysed as a piece of artistic writing in the same way as the introduction to *Republic*: κατέβην χθὲς εἰς Πειραιᾶ μετὰ Γλαύκωνος τοῦ Ἀρίστωνος,

---

[40] The ancient critics exemplify mainly from *Anabasis* and *Cyropaedia*. This is also characteristic of Gautier (1911). Demetrius (*On Style* 5.297) does not use Xenophon's Socratic works even in describing the Socratic style.

[41] See Gautier (1911) 11–21 for general description of this problem.

[42] Other examples call for fine judgement: for instance whether γεραίρειν makes the honour done to the benefactor grander than τιμᾶν (*Hiero* 7.2 uses both), whether γαυροῦσθαι makes the pride of the citizens grander than, say, ἐπαίρεσθαι (2.15). Richards (1897) 135 lists non-Attic vocabulary from *Lac*. Poetic effects there, because of the nature of the work, seem mostly unlikely.

on which Plato is said to have meditated so long. Denniston (1952) 41 divides this *colon* into two *commata* of about equal length, and says that the barely perceptible pause between them makes for ease and grace. *Hiero*'s introduction could be divided into three units of almost equal length for the same effect. The central statement of Simonides' arrival separates but binds the poet and the tyrant in the partnership that will be the theme of the dialogue. The rhythm is iambic/trochaic. Xenophon was rhythmical in the manner appropriate to prose, capturing echoes of poetic rhythm rather than entire lines (Demetr. *On Style* 3.180–1).

The conclusion is another piece of artful simplicity: εὐδαιμονῶν γὰρ οὐ φθο-νηθήσηι. The sentence could be envisaged as two *commata* of equal length, with four-syllable words marking the important concepts of 'happiness' and 'hatred' and flanking the two monosyllables in *chiasmus*. *Republic*'s opening unit κατέβην χθὲς εἰς Πειραιᾶ has two trisyllables flanking two monosyllables without *chiasmus*, but *Hiero*'s arrangement brings attention to the connection between happiness and the absence of hatred which has been a central focus of the thought.

One challenge to the writer of dialogue was to characterize the participants and their moods. Tentative expressions such as 'I seem to have learned' (e.g. 1.4) and invitations to 'investigate' this or that idea (e.g. 3.1) capture the spirit of philosophical inquiry and seem designed to emphasize the process of reflection rather than con-vey any real uncertainty. Simonides and Hiero both use such expressions, even when they are totally convinced of what they say, as Hiero is at 1.33. Simonides' meticu-lous classification of the pleasures of the senses (1.4–6) gives him further philosophic characterization, but Hiero is capable of close analysis too, and is able to recall the precise order of Simonides' classification (1.10). The participants use more dogmatic expressions when they have the upper hand in the argument, as when Hiero claims knowledge of the tyrant's life based on experience in the first part of the dialogue (e.g. 1.10, 2.6), and when Simonides uses imperatives to mark the beginning (8.3–4) and the end of his teaching (11.1, 13–15).

Word order is of interest. Frequently, the characters employ what seems to be an unnatural order of words, which conveys an impression of forcefulness. To give one illustration: τῶι δὲ ὕπνωι ὅτι μὲν ἡδόμεθα δοκῶ μοι αἰσθάνεσθαι, ὅπως δὲ καὶ ὧιτινι καὶ ὁπότε, ταῦτα μᾶλλόν πῶς, ἔφη, δοκῶ μοι ἀγνοεῖν (In sleep, that we take pleasure, I seem to know; but how and by what means and when, about these, somehow, he said, I seem to be in greater ignorance: 1.6). Yet such word order is regularly found in the conversation of *Hiero* (see note on 1.6), and occurs quite frequently in *Lac.* and in *Ath.* too, so that this impression of force may need to be moderated. Key words are regularly brought to the front of the sentence, and phrases are regularly placed before the demonstrative that sums them up. Of much more force in the illustration from 1.6 is the parenthetical 'he said', which creates a pause before the significant admission of ignorance. The use of the assertive demonstrative to sum up the three preceding clauses is also forceful, regardless of where it is placed.

Another contrived type of word order is *anaphora*. This is frequently employed when the content seems emotional, but it also gives order to unemotional content, and it emphasizes the repeated words. Thus, Hiero uses *anaphora* to express his memories of his happiness as a non-ruler, and his current experience of unhappiness as ruler (e.g. 1.35, 6.1–4) and other pleasures that he misses (3.1, 4.1). He also marshals less pleasant experiences in *anaphora*, such as the contradictory sources of fear that produce such confusion in his heart (6.4): 'To fear a crowd, to fear isolation, to fear a lack of guards, to fear the guards themselves, not to be willing to have unarmed men around one nor to gaze upon those who have been armed in pleasure, how is this not a harrowing condition?' Yet Simonides uses *anaphora* to give a clear order to unemotional content (1.4). Frequently, the elements in *anaphora* convey a vivid sequence of phases of actions, such as Hiero's passionate memory of sexual flirtation, which moves from glances to questions to answers to lovers' quarrels: 'From one who loves you in return, sweet are the glances, sweet the questions, sweet the answers, but sweetest and most full of love the quarrels and the fights' εὐθὺς γὰρ παρὰ τοῦ ἀντιφιλοῦντος ἡδεῖαι μὲν αἱ ἀντιβλέψεις, ἡδεῖαι δὲ αἱ ἐρωτήσεις, ἡδεῖαι δὲ αἱ ἀποκρίσεις, ἥδισται δὲ καὶ ἐπαφροδιτόταται αἱ μάχαι τε καὶ ἔριδες (1.35). The final element in this instance is expanded, substituting the superlative degree of the adjective, two forms indeed of superlative, and two synonymous nouns. This sentence may also exemplify Xenophon's famous charm, since love is charming and fights and quarrels have a charming unexpectedness.[43] Another instance of action-phase *anaphora* (2.15) is found in his description of the joyous pleasures that the citizens have in their community war. The understanding of Xenophon's arrangements in *anaphora* can be crucial in establishing the meaning, as is the case with his expression of his fear of the wise (5.1–2; see the note on that passage). He uses *chiasmus* less often, but still effectively, as in the conclusion to the work, and when he separates out the special lack of sexual pleasure from other deprivations at 2.1: μειονεκτοῦντας καὶ σίτων καὶ ποτῶν και ὄψων καὶ ἀφροδισίων γε ἀπεχομένους.

Xenophon was also admired for his rounded thoughts: περίοδοι,[44] and there is a tour de force in Hiero's description of the honoured man (7.9), which uses ten *cola* to build up a sequence of the ways in which he is honoured. As other sentences do in *anaphora*, this sentence presents a progressive sequence of actions. It observes the general rule to keep the *cola* relatively short, and to keep the reader informed of the overall shape of the sentence; for this reason οἱ ἄνθρωποι in the first *colon* is picked up at the end in οἱ αὐτοὶ οὖτοι.

The dialogue generally also displays that richness of ideas for which Xenophon was noted. For example, *Hiero* 2.7–11 systematically compares the pleasures and pains of rulers and non-rulers when there are no wars, on campaign, when they are attacked, when they make peace or arrange truces. The comparisons are nuanced; the citizens

---

[43] Charm came generally from compression, arrangement, and an element of surprise. Demetr., *On Style* 3.137–9 cites the classic example: 'As presents he gave him a horse, a robe, a linked collar – and the assurance that his land would not be plundered' (derived from *An.* 1.2.27, which has a longer and more impressive list: horse, gold collar, bracelets, a gold sword, a robe, then the assurance).

[44] Demetr. *On Style* 1.3 finds a classic and simple example in the opening of *Anabasis*.

can go wherever they want in time of peace without fear of being killed, but all tyrants proceed everywhere as if through enemy country; citizens *think* that they are safe when they come home, but tyrants *know* that they are then among the greatest numbers of enemies; citizens think they are safe when they are inside the walls of their *polis*, but the tyrant does not think he is out of danger even when inside his own *house*. And so on.

Xenophon produces some effective images to support his ideas in *Hiero*, not only the central image of the war that the tyrant conducts against his citizens, but also more localized images of the tyrant as professional athlete competing with amateurs (4.6), of fear as a courtier in his heart (6.6), and the men of virtue as horses, whom the tyrant cannot control, but must use in his administration (6.15–16).[45] The idea that desire will not wish to live in the heart of the tyrant because it will so quickly be satisfied is rich in implications, since the attendant death of desire is inevitable in the midst of such availability (1.30). The description of the citizens as 'bodyguards' for each other, and of the laws as 'standing guard' over the guards and the citizens, are further examples that draw attention to the tyrant's concern for his security (4.3, 6.10).

Lac.

Lac. has some of the same traits of language and style. Its authenticity has been challenged on the basis of the language, but Richards (1897) 134–5 demonstrates its authenticity by pointing to the normal range of Xenophon's vocabulary and constructions; cf. Lipka (2002) 46–53. *Lac.* uses some Spartan dialect, but *Hellenica* has more extended passages (1.1.23, 4.4.11; cf. τὼ σιώ in *Hell.* 4.4.11 and *An.* 6.6.34). Spartan words naturally describe Spartan institutions; apart from the obvious 'polemarch' and 'ephor', we have γεροντία (10.1), and φιλίτιον (3.5, 5.6, also at *Hell.* 5.4.28) and δαμοσίαν alongside δημοσίαν (13.7, 15.4). Some words describe technical or semi-scientific content: ἀραιός for the packing of a phalanx (11.6), ὑδαρής for watered wine (1.3) and ῥαδινός for 'slender' (2.5). In other cases unusual words have a special effect; ἀκίνητοι is fittingly used in *Lac.* 14.1 of Lycurgus' sacred laws; ἐμπεδορκοῦντος (found in poetry and inscriptions and in Hdt. 4.201 in a legal context) and the poetic ἀστυφέλικτον capture the solemnity of the oath that the kings and the ephors swear (15.7). However, non-Attic μάσσω (12.5) has no such effect, and must be just part of Xenophon's normal vocabulary – or perhaps that of the Spartans.

There is as little ancient opinion on the style of *Lac.* as on *Hiero*, but it has the same artistry.[46] The introduction (1.1–2) is marked by ring composition, where 'Sparta emerged most powerful and famous' is restated at the end as the achievement of Lycurgus: 'he made his fatherland pre-eminent in prosperity'. The initial wonder at Spartan success is replaced by wonder for its architect, and the restatement explains

---

[45] Demetr. *On Style* 2.80, 89 cites him for his 'poetical comparison' (cf. Longinus 32.5): 'as a well-bred hound rushes at a boar without thought of the future' (*Cyr.* 1.4.21).

[46] Lipka (2002) 53–5 is critical of the style, calling 9.5 'a tedious syntax of enumeration' and 11.8–10 'jejune'; but he is trying to prove that *Lac.* is an unfinished draft.

the cause of success in the uniqueness of his arrangements. The conclusion to the work as a whole, describing honours for dead kings, is not only artful but almost a complete hexameter (15.9). *Isocolon* in this final section marks the separation, but also the equality of the king and his people in the oath: 'The oath is for the king to exercise kingship according to the established laws of the *polis*, and for the *polis* to keep the kingship undisturbed while he remained true to that.' Lycurgus' motives for the compact have a similar balance: 'neither to provide kings with a tyrant's pride, nor to implant envy of his power in the citizens' (15.8).

Anaphora (1.5, 2.2, 3.1, 3.2, 5.4, 5.6, 9.3 etc.) frequently marks the qualities that are central to the educative purpose of the laws, and some instances effectively demonstrate the expanded third element, such as: ἥκιστα μὲν ὕβριν, ἥκιστα δὲ παροινίαν, ἥκιστα δὲ αἰσχουργίαν καὶ αἰσχρολογίαν (5.6). The long sentence with ten verbal adjectives to describe the compulsion on the coward effectively conveys the multiple penalties that accrue to his disgrace (*Lac.* 9.5); *Hiero* 8.9 uses the same device for the long list of unpopular things that the tyrant is compelled to do. Even the loose participial subordination describing the intentions of Lycurgus in developing his laws aptly conveys his multi-faceted reasoning (5.2: 'Lycurgus, finding . . . realizing . . . , brought the dining into the open, thinking . . .'). Xenophon is also the master of the sequence of effective short sentences, as in 10.8.

Analysis reveals that same subtle richness of ideas as in *Hiero*. So in the sentence in 4.7, Lycurgus' arrangements for those past the ephebic age are contrasted with those of other Greeks. The age group is announced in the initial dative, and the relative clause spells out the expectation that they will fill the major offices of state, then come the contradictory actions of other Greeks in 'removing' the need for them to cultivate physical condition on the one hand, but 'commanding' them nevertheless to continue in the army on the other. The inconsistent actions of other states are then replaced by the reasoned and purposeful actions of Lycurgus. Lycurgus passed a law that hunting be the finest pursuit for such age groups 'unless some public duty intervened'. He did this precisely in order to give them the condition to undertake military duties. The phrase 'unless some public duty intervened', which refers back to the earlier expectation of public office, captures the subtle difference from other *poleis*: that physical condition was the main activity of the Spartans, and that public offices (much pursued in other states?) were merely something necessary that occasionally intervened.

Xenophon expresses the contrast between Lycurgus' arrangements and those of other *poleis* in a variety of ways. In the case above, the contrast is captured in one sentence. In the case of the regime for the boys, other arrangements for their supervision, shoes, clothing and food come first, then Lycurgus' different measures are introduced for each category: ἀντὶ μὲν . . . ἀντί γε μὴν . . . καὶ ἀντί γε . . . then σῖτόν γε μήν (2.2–5). Lycurgus' laws about the privileges of the kings have a similar blend of consistency and variety (15.2ff.): ἔθηκε . . . ἔδωκε . . . ἀπέδειξεν.

There are few similes or metaphors, but the one that is mentioned by ancient critics: the comparison of Spartan boys with girls in respect of their modesty (*Lac.* 3.5) is discussed in full in the commentary.

Ath.

Caballero López (1997) provides an extensive analysis of the language and style of *Ath.* The language is different from Xenophon's (Richards [1897] 229–31), more apparently representative of early Attic prose-writing (though Richards [1897] 231f. was cautious). It exhibits elements familiar from fifth-century Attic inscriptions, as well as the Ionic of Herodotus and the Hippocratics.[47] So (allowing for 'corrections' to the manuscript by well-meaning scribes) σμικρὸς (2.7) sits alongside μικρὸς (3.9), θαλασσοκράτορες (2.2) and ἄσσα (2.17) alongside Attic -ττ- forms (πράττειν 1.1, 1.4 etc.), and ἐπιμισγόμενοι (2.7), also occurs. 1.1 uses ἔδοξεν αὐτοῖς in formulating the will of the *demos*, 1.1 and 3.3 use διαπράττειν and διαπράττεσθαι of transacting business and section 3 is full of technical language for judicial business.

In the area of style, Palmer (1980) 160–2 refers to *Ath.*'s 'untidy arrangement, the awkward syntax, and above all the monotonous diction', exemplifying the author's 'untutored and unpractised hand' from the opening sentence, in particular his verbal repetitions (cf. Richards [1897] 231f.). Yet this style can produce some very effective writing. The sentences are often constructed on the principles of *lexis eiromene* ('speech strung together'), in which short units are 'strung together' with basic connectives such as καί and δέ and οὖν, and repetitions of key words reinforce the key ideas, while they also isolate and highlight phrases that are not repeated. The introduction uses this style:

περὶ δὲ τῆς Ἀθηναίων πολιτείας, ὅτι μὲν εἴλοντο τοῦτον τὸν τρόπον τῆς πολιτείας οὐκ ἐπαινῶ διὰ τόδε, ὅτε ταῦθ' ἑλόμενοι εἴλοντο τοὺς πονηροὺς ἄμεινον πράττειν ἢ τοὺς χρηστούς· διὰ μὲν οὖν τοῦτο οὐκ ἐπαινῶ. ἐπεὶ δὲ ταῦτα ἔδοξεν οὕτως αὐτοῖς, ὡς εὖ διασώιζονται τὴν πολιτείαν καὶ τἆλλα διαπράττονται ἃ δοκοῦσιν ἁμαρτάνειν τοῖς ἄλλοις Ἕλλησι, τοῦτ' ἀποδείξω.

In the first statement, the ideas of 'constitution' and 'deliberate choice' and the author's insistence on his withdrawal of praise are very important for the treatise as a whole. In the second, the idea of 'resolution' varies the reference to 'choice', and the new important ideas of preservation and error make their entrance.

The conclusion uses this same style, with effective short sentences that reinforce the theme of just or unjust deprivation of rights:

Ὑπολάβοι δέ τις ἂν ὡς οὐδεὶς ἄρα ἀδίκως ἠτίμωται Ἀθήνησιν. ἐγὼ δὲ φημί τινας εἶναι οἳ ἀδίκως ἠτίμωνται. ὀλίγοι μέντοι τινές. ἀλλ'... οὕτως ἔχει, οὐδὲν ἐνθυμεῖσθαι ἀνθρώπους οἵτινες δικαίως ἠτίμωνται, ἀλλ' εἴ τινες ἀδίκως. πῶς ἂν οὖν ἀδίκως οἴοιτό τις ἂν τοὺς πολλοὺς ἠτιμῶσθαι Ἀθήνησιν ... (3.12)

Another example of significant repetition is the use of eleven διαδικ- words referring to the judicial process that is essential to the success of the democracy (3.6–7). Perhaps this is meant to reflect the speech of the plain man. *Cynegeticus* uses similar short sentences and repetitions to reflect such speech, distinguishing it from that of the

---

[47] Frisch (1942) 164–84 and Caballero López (1997).

sophists: 'Perhaps I do not speak sophistically in my words. Nor do I seek this. What those well educated for virtue need, correctly opined, I seek to say. Words would not educate, but opinions, if they are correct' (13.5).

However, alongside this style, there is the complex type of sentence which contains several integrated ideas, such as the denial that the democracy can be changed for the better and still be preserved (3.9 ὥστε μὲν γὰρ βέλτιον ἔχειν τὴν πολιτείαν . . .). The comparison of the advantages of sea power and land power exhibits antithesis:

ἔπειτα δὲ τοῖς μὲν κατὰ θάλατταν ἄρχουσιν οἷόν τ᾽ ἀποπλεῦσαι ἀπὸ τῆς σφετέρας αὐτῶν ὁπόσον βούλει πλοῦν, τοῖς τε κατὰ γῆν (sc. ἄρχουσι) οὐχ οἷόν τε ἀπὸ τῆς σφετέρας αὐτῶν ἀπελθεῖν πολλῶν ἡμερῶν ὁδόν.   (2.5)

There is antithesis indeed in almost every section, such as 1.13: χορηγοῦσι μὲν οἱ πλούσιοι, χορηγεῖται δὲ ὁ δῆμος, where the contrast perfectly captures the passive role of the *demos* and the active role of their betters, or 2.19: διὰ τὴν κτῆσιν τὴν ἐν τοῖς ὑπερορίοις καὶ διὰ τὰς ἀρχὰς τὰς εἰς τὴν ὑπερορίαν. Sometimes, the natural balance is deliberately avoided in order to bring emphasis to a point, as in the contrast of the noun τὸν μὲν δῆμον with the adverb ἰδίαι δὲ (2.18), when τοὺς δὲ ἰδίους would have been the obvious mechanical choice. ἐν οὐδεμίαι γὰρ πόλει τὸ βέλτιστον εὔνουν ἐστὶ τῶι δήμωι, ἀλλὰ τὸ κάκιστον ἐν ἑκάστηι ἐστὶ πόλει εὔνουν τῶι δήμωι (3.10) has the opposed elements in different orders. In the first clause, the emphatic phrase 'in no *polis*' occupies first place, whereas in the second this is occupied by the emphatic 'the worst element'. These emphasize their opposing numbers in the other clause. The innocuous verb splits the natural integrity of 'well-disposed to the *demos*' in the first and 'in each *polis*' in the second, so as to bring further attention to these elements. The overall effect is one of maximum emphasis and force.

The author uses *anaphora* and *asyndeton* for special effect. The rhetorical question ποῖ διαθήσεται, ἐὰν μη πείσηι is repeated in *anaphora* to capture the inevitable transportation of all the wealth of the world toward Athens in 2.11. Five instances of *anaphora* mark the long list of the materials they secure: παρὰ μὲν τοῦ ξύλα, παρὰ δὲ τοῦ σίδηρος . . . . and another five, involving πολλά, mark the great number of other items of business they conduct (3.2). *Asyndeton* conveys the rapidity with which the *demos* has acquired new buildings for bathing (2.10). There is deliberate variety in the descriptions of the great numbers of festivals, trials and other business: ὅσας οὐδεμία τῶν Ἑλληνίδων πόλεων . . . ὅσας οὐδ᾽ οἱ σύμπαντες ἄνθρωποι ἐκδικάζουσι (3.2).

Ath. uses the traditional device of 'ring-composition' to structure the analysis. The restatement of the introduction at 3.1 reinforces key points. References to the numbers of festivals frame the description of administration (3.2–8), and this is relevant to the rhetoric (see the note on 3.8). The *demos'* monopoly of office at 1.2–3 is picked up again at the close of the work (3.13). Cf. Herodotus 6.121 and 123 for the same kind of ring-composition:

It is a wonder to me and I do not accept the story that the Alcmaeonids would ever have shown the signal to the Persians as a result of complicity, out of a wish that Athens be subject to foreigners and to Hippias, men who were evidently tyrant-haters if anything more than Callias . . .

And the Alcmaeonids were at least no less than this man tyrant-haters. So it is a wonder to me and I do not admit the slander . . .

INTRODUCTION TO *HIERO*

Hiero develops Xenophon's paradigms of personal rule, calling particular attention to the need for friendship in the partnership of rulers and the ruled (above pp. 7–8, 12). It represents Simonides, who was one of the most celebrated poets of the first half of the fifth century, discussing the relative happiness of the ruler and the non-ruler with his contemporary Hiero, one of the most celebrated of the early tyrants of Syracuse.[1] In arguing that the ruler is much less happy, Hiero refers to 'the ruler' in the third person, but some first-person statements reveal that it is his own condition of which he speaks. He is ignorant of how to be happy or to make his citizens happy because he is compelled to make them fear rather than love him. His misery arises from his lack of their friendship. Simonides solves his problem by showing him the happiness that will come when he serves the interests of those he rules as a *prostates* of their common good (11.1), competing with other rulers to make his *polis* the happiest among them (εὐδαιμονεστάτην 11.7). His citizens will willingly give him their friendship in recognition of his service; so that in securing their happiness he will become happy himself (εὐδαιμονῶν γὰρ οὐ φθονηθήσηι 11.15).

As a piece of political thought, *Hiero* could be considered a response to the suggestion in Plato, *Laws* 710d, that the best constitution, which would combine knowledge and power, would emerge most easily and quickly from a tyranny, through a first-rate counsellor and an orderly tyrant. Plato's suggestion has been thought ironic, in view of the impossibility of an orderly tyrant, or one who remains orderly for very long,[2] but *Hiero* explores the possibility that a tyrant might not like the disorder in his soul and that the very basic human desire for a positive reception from other human beings might still triumph over the inevitable corruption of the desires. Xenophon's Socrates also believes that the positive desire to be loved unites men of good sense in successful political and personal partnerships (*Mem.* 2.6.21–6).

Hiero endorses the government of one man, but Simonides' reform has broadly democratic implications because it changes Hiero from a tyrant, who serves his own interests, to a king, who serves the common good. Aristotle (*Pol.* 1279a22–1288b15) recognizes kingship among three constitutions that serve the 'common good' as opposed to deviant forms like tyranny that serve the interests only of the rulers. So Hiero in effect creates Aristotle's *pambasileia* (pp. 8–9). Simonides (and Xenophon) could then make the same claim as Isocrates when he defended his instruction of the sole ruler Nicocles to his democratic audience as that of a free man in defence of freedom and the common good (*Antidosis* 15.70: '[I was] defending those he rules and trying to secure for them the mildest constitution possible.'

---

[1] The significant commentaries are Holden (1888) and Luccioni (1947); Strauss (2000) produces a virtual commentary on his own translation.

[2] See Schofield (1999) 31–50 esp. 44–50.

In keeping with his concern for the common good, Xenophon elsewhere gives negative accounts of sole rulers who served their own good. He magnificently condemns the tyranny of the Thirty at Athens (*Hell.* 2.3.11–56, 4.1–43, *Mem.* 1.2.12–39). Critias, called the most grasping and violent member of an oligarchy that thrived on murder (*Mem.* 1.2.12), is quite as lawless as the stereotyped tyrant (*Mem.* 4.6.12), making his own law to silence Socrates (*Mem.* 1.2.33–8), and ignoring his own law to silence Theramenes (*Hell.* 2.3.50–6). Cleocritus also condemns them for destroying the natural associations within the *polis* that were part of its *homonoia* (*Hell.* 2.4.20–2). Jason of Pherae inspired such fear that his assassins were honoured throughout Greece, and his brothers continued the dynasty amidst international piracy, fratricide and murder (*Hell.* 6.4.27–37). The exiles who assassinated Euphron of Sicyon were acquitted when they told the Thebans who had the jurisdiction that tyrants had no protection in law (*Hell.* 7.3.4–12). Euphron was honoured by his citizens (7.3.12) but he evidently did not win the exiles. Mania is the exception that proves the rule about the importance of friendship in the ideal association in giving loyal service to Pharnabazus when she inherited the tyranny of Aeolis (*Hell.* 3.1.10–14), and she has good relations with her subjects as well. Her only failing was to put too much trust in the goodwill of her family members, since she was strangled by her trusted but jealous son-in-law.

THE LITERARY TRADITION

Hiero comes from a literary tradition of meetings between the wise and powerful.[3] [Plato] *Epistle* 2, 310e5–311b6 summarizes the tradition, identifying Simonides among the wise, and Hiero as the man of power, in a letter addressed to Dionysius II, the tyrant of Syracuse:

> Wisdom and great power were born to come together. These pursue and seek and cohabit with each other. People enjoy discussing them and hearing about them from others in private gatherings and in literature. So that when men discuss Hiero and Pausanias the Spartan, they like to introduce Simonides, indicating what he did, and said to them. And their custom is to hymn Periander of Corinth alongside Thales of Miletus, Pericles and Anaxagoras, and Croesus and Solon as wise men and Cyrus as ruler. And in imitation, the poets bring together Creon and Tiresias, Polyeidus and Minos, Agamemnon and Nestor, Odysseus and Palamedes – and, as it seems to me, the first men brought together Prometheus with Zeus in this kind of way – and they sing of some of them entering into conflicts, some into friendships, some into friendship and enmity in turn, in harmony on some points, in conflict on others.

---

3 The genre is still with us, but sometimes in debased form. Orizio (2003) has a colourful cast of modern despots, but lacks any theory of government.

Hiero fits into this tradition. Other partnerships, such as the instruction of Neoptolemus by Nestor, could easily be added.[4] Xenophon's Socrates addresses the association of wise and powerful when he observes that the ruler ignores the advice of the wise to his automatic detriment (*Mem.* 3.9.12–13), and when he uses the partnerships of Daedalus and Minos, Palamedes and Odysseus to demonstrate to Euthydemus that even wisdom was not the unqualified 'good thing' that he thought it was, since Minos' possessive desire for Daedalus' wisdom deprived him of his freedom, his fatherland and his family, and Odysseus killed Palamedes out of envy of his wisdom (*Mem.* 4.2.33; cf. *Ap.* 26). The question will arise soon whether *Hiero* represents friendly or unfriendly relations between Simonides and Hiero.

The relative happiness of the ruler and the non-ruler was also a standard philosophical question. Xenophon has Socrates discuss it with Aristippus, and conclude that the ruler can be happier (*Mem.* 2.1), but it had a particular literary history as the topic of discussion (explicit or otherwise) between the ruler and a wise man. The most famous example is Herodotus' account of the meeting between Solon and Croesus (1.29–33). In the first of a sequence of 'wise adviser' scenes in which happiness is the issue, Solon tried to dispel Croesus' ignorant belief that his wealth and power meant happiness. He failed but the deposed Croesus was made wise through suffering the loss of these goods, and passed on this lesson to the ruler Cyrus in the dramatic scene in which he stands burning on the pyre Cyrus has built for his immolation (1.86–7). Xenophon rewrote their meeting (Hdt. 1.86–91) to prove Croesus happier as a non-ruler (*Cyr.* 7.2.9–29).[5] His Cyrus too, when he passes on his kingdom to his sons, has the same view, explaining that the *eudaimonia* of the son who does not rule will be 'less painful' than the *eudaimonia* of the son who will be king (*Cyr.* 8.7.11–12). In proving the ruler happier, *Hiero* seems to swim against the current.

The motive for Simonides' visit to the court of Hiero is not stated. He could have come to produce his poetic performances, but the literary tradition suggests something else. Herodotus 1.29–30 says that Solon went abroad to avoid being asked to change his laws, but adopted the pretence of 'sightseeing' (κατὰ θεωρίης πρόφασιν). Yet this was not an entire pretence. He did visit the court of Croesus and 'sight' his tyrannical wealth, but as a philosopher with an interest in ethics, he also 'saw' through the appearance and tried to assist Croesus toward a better perception of happiness; and on looking similarly into the condition of the tyrant Philokypris, he praised him as the best of men (5.113.2). This captures a double meaning in θεωρία, a tension between the sights that are seen with the eyes, and those perceptions that are gained through

---

4 Plato confirms his interest in the association of wisdom and power of course in his paradigm of the philosopher-king, his introduction of a wise judge into the heart of his monster-tyrant (*Rep.* 577a–b) and his attempt to reform the tyrants of Syracuse through a marriage of their power and his wisdom. *Rep.* 568a–b confirms that 'tyrants are wise because of their partnership with the wise' ὡς ἄρα σοφοὶ τύραννοί εἰσι τῶν σοφῶν συνουσίαι. The tradition continues in the works of advice that Isocrates as wise man wrote to the Cyprian ruler Nicocles: *Or.* 2–3.

5 Lefèvre (1971) examines this rewriting.

the intellect into matters of the soul.[6] In *Hiero* too, Simonides sees the sights of Hiero's tyrannical court and describes his wealth in glowing terms (2.1–2), and Hiero agrees that it is an object of the gaze (2.4: θεᾶσθαι φανερά). However, Hiero expects wise men to 'see' through appearances to where true happiness resides (2.5: διὰ τῆς γνώμης . . . θεᾶσθαι), and Simonides meets this expectation in the course of the dialogue. His motive for his visit could then be the sights that are seen with the eyes (1.11–13), or the production of such sights in performance, but, like Solon, his eventual achievement is perception of the reality behind appearances and encouragement toward a happier reality.

THE CHARACTERS

Poets were of course the traditional wise men of archaic Greece. The divine wisdom of the Muses made Homer, Hesiod and Pindar omniscient (see the description of the singer Demodocus: Homer, *Od.* 8.487–97). Parmenides and Empedocles expressed their philosophies about the nature of the world in verse, and Solon and Tyrtaeus used verse to express their ideas for the political and military success of Athens and Sparta. Simonides was a poet of great prestige who wrote epigrams, elegies and choral lyric,[7] and he was noted for his ethical wisdom. In *Protagoras* 339a–347a, Plato has Socrates and his interlocutors discuss Simonides fr. 542 (Campbell), allegedly written for Scopas, tyrant of Thessaly, which considers whether a man can be truly good. Simonides' answer was pragmatic, that goodness is impossible because man is at the mercy of circumstance; the best he can do is avoid things that are base. Moralizing is also an integral part of Pindar's poetic celebrations of the victories of Hiero in the crown games (*Olympian* 1, *Pythians* 1–3). So, in making Simonides wise in *Hiero*, Xenophon recognizes the traditional characterization of the poet.

In making Simonides travel, Xenophon also follows a recognized tradition about poets. Arion performed at the court of Periander in Corinth and grew wealthy from his visit to Tarentum (Hdt. 1.24). Pausanias lists a series of poets who spent time at the courts of kings, including Aeschylus and Pindar at Syracuse (Paus. 1.2.3). Plato also makes the tyrant Hipparchus of Athens retain the services of Simonides 'to teach the citizens, so that he (the tyrant) might rule over them as being better men' (*Hipparchus* 228c). Philosophers inherited the poets' mantle when they continued to visit tyrants in order to educate them for rule. The sorry saga of Plato's failed mission to the court of the fourth-century tyrants of Syracuse is told in Plato's *Seventh Letter* and Plutarch's *Dion*.

---

[6] Goldhill in Goldhill and Osborne (eds.) (1999) 5–8 considers θεωρία in the context of performance culture, noting the connection between the wise man's 'viewing' of material things and his intellectual 'contemplation'.

[7] See Campbell *GL* vol. 3 (1991) for the *testimonia* and the poetry of Simonides including the record of his success in training a chorus for the dithyramb at Athens in 476 BC: *testimonium* 5; Bell (1978), Lefkowitz (1981) 49–56, Molyneux (1992) for his life and works; Boedeker and Sider (eds.) (2001) for recent discoveries that have transformed our understanding of his poetic range.

Yet Simonides loses his historical identity in *Hiero*. He does not mention his poetry or his travels, even if he does know as much about choral production as the next man (9.4). There is no sign either of the anecdotal tradition that focused on his avarice, even though it put him at the court of Hiero.[8] Instead, Xenophon modernizes Simonides, having him teach Hiero the principles of political thought that we associate with Xenophon, and use the dialogue method we associate with Socrates, rather than the didactic mode of his actual poems. Some teachings never changed. Socrates in conversation with Aristippus (*Mem.* 2.1) shows how the instruction on toil remained the same down the ages: Hesiod taught it didactically, the sophist Prodicus made an epideictic display of it, while Socrates himself expressed it dialectically. But Greeks regularly made characters from the past reflect contemporary interests. So Plato subjects Simonides' poems to dialectical examination and proves that they contain Socratic ideas (*Rep.* 331e–334b, *Prot.* 339a–347a). And Xenophon's Socrates interprets the reputation of Homer's Odysseus as a 'safe orator' as a reference to his use of dialectic, which also proceeds safely because it takes care to win the assent of its audience (*Mem.* 4.6.15). There are further examples of such modernization at *Mem.* 1.2.58–9, 1.3.7, 2.6.11–12. He also uses Homer's epithets for Agamemnon to provide a modern definition of good rule (*Mem.* 3.2), and Ganymede's name as an indication that Zeus' love for him was spiritual (*Symp.* 8.30).

Hiero has also lost his historical identity. He plays the generic tyrant to Simonides' generic wise man, with the wise man representing knowledge of rule on the one hand and the ruler representing the power of rule on the other. Diodorus Siculus says that he ruled Gela while his brother Gelon ruled Syracuse, then inherited the tyranny of Syracuse and ruled the east of Sicily, 478–467 BC,[9] but though Simonides recognizes that Hiero was once a non-ruler, Gelon is not mentioned, not even where this would be appropriate, such as in the discussion about tyrants' family relations (1.27–8, 3.7–9, 11.14). Hiero's great achievements against the Etruscans and Carthaginians are also missing: his foundation of the strategic military colony at Aetna (Pindar, *Pythian* 1.60–8), and his defeat of the Etruscans in the sea battle off Cumae in 474 BC (lines 71–5).[10] Perhaps the dialogue is meant to take place before these events, but Hiero must have assisted Gelon to defeat the Carthaginians at Himera in 480 BC before he became

---

[8] When asked whether it was better to be wise or rich, he told Hiero's wife that he preferred to be rich, since the wise had to wait at the gates of the rich (Arist. *Rhet.* 1391a8–12). He was also asked to write a poem for a victory in the mule race but refused to praise 'half-beasts' until his fee was raised; he then praised them as 'daughters of storm-footed steeds' (Arist. *Rhet.* 1405b23–6). Hunter (1996) 98–100 suggests that Simonides' avarice is reflected in *Hiero* 11.8, where he may expect that his own hymns will secure fame for the reformed Hiero (in return of course for payment). Avoiding excessive expenditure is presented, however, as a concern of Hiero, for whom revenues are a larger problem than for the poet, who, as a private individual, will have only moderate needs in comparison with tyrants: 4.6–11.

[9] Berve (1967) I.147–52, II.603–7 discusses the tyranny and the evidence. The main narrative is D.S. 11.38, 48–53, 66. Hdt. 7.155–6 gives supplementary evidence. See for general background: Finley (1968).

[10] There is no mention either of the story that Simonides reconciled Hiero with his other brother Polyzelos: scholiast on Pindar, *O.* 2.29; D.S. 11.48.3–8.

tyrant of Syracuse, yet this goes unmentioned too. There is only a general impression of the external wars that tyrants conduct and the need for revenues to support these. Diodorus does describe his employment of a bodyguard to secure himself against the hatred of his people (cf. *Hiero* 10.1–2), but their identity and numbers remain vague. Chariot victories are mentioned (11.5–8), but not specified as those of Pindar's *Olympian* 1, *Pythians* 1–3, and Bacchylides' *Odes* 3 to 5 (the Olympic horse race in 476 BC, the Pythian chariot race in 470 BC, the Olympic chariot race in 468 BC). Simonides could reflect Pindar's encouragement in *Pythian* 1.90 that Hiero be more generous with his expenditures (11.1), but the picture again remains largely generic.

The literary tradition adequately explains Xenophon's choice of Hiero and Simonides as his characters, and Plato's interest in Simonides in *Protagoras* indicates that he was an appropriate focus of interest for a Socratic, but Xenophon's particular reason for fixing on Hiero as the tyrant has been explained in terms of his desire to reform the tyrants of Syracuse (405–357 BC); he chose an earlier tyrant from Syracuse to make the work relevant to them while avoiding the possible offence of the direct approach.[11] *Hiero* may indeed have reached those tyrannical ears, with effects that we can only guess at, but the work was of equal relevance for philosophers interested in how to reform a tyrant. Perhaps Xenophon's awareness of the Sicilian tyrants stimulated his interest in their predecessor, as his interest in Cyrus the Younger was matched by his interest in Cyrus the Great;[12] but perhaps *Hiero* needed no specific historical impetus, but, for no other reason than its intrinsic cultural and political significance, addressed a literary tradition about rulership in which Hiero and Simonides already figured, in an age when tyrants were still a common phenomenon in Greece, and rulership was a continuing focus of philosophic interest. Wise men might use the work as a blueprint for reform, and rulers might see themselves in the mirror, but the general audience would be as they always were, intrigued by the relations of power and wisdom and the question of happiness. The reason why Xenophon did not choose Socrates as the wise man would have been the sheer implausibility of having Socrates conversing with a tyrant; he never left Athens to visit tyrants and no tyrant ever visited Athens in his time. The wise man also had to trim the sails of his free speech in dealing with an actual tyrant, and that might damage Socrates' philosophic integrity too much.

THE STRUCTURE

The dialogue is in two parts. Simonides drives Hiero to despair (ἀθύμως ἔχειν: 8.1) by making him reveal his ignorance about how to achieve happiness as a ruler in the

---

[11] The work has been dated on this kind of speculation to the years following the participation by Dionysius I in the Olympic Festival of 388 BC (D.S. 14.109): Sordi (1980).

[12] Xenophon was very aware of the Dionysii. He notes the beginning of their tyranny and refers to the later assistance they gave the Spartans: *Hell.* 2.2.24 and 2.3.5, 6.2.4, 33, and 7.1.20, 22. Athenaeus *Deipnosophistae* 10.427f–428a tells an anecdote in which Xenophon complains to the tyrant about being forced to eat too much, thus illustrating the Socratic teaching about consumption. This looks like a story that has been created on the basis of *Hiero*.

first part of the work (1–7), and follows this with positive instruction about how his condition can be made happy in the second (8–11). The first part is perhaps designed to deter those who were inclined to seek a tyranny, and the second to reform those still undeterred,[13] but their responsion reflects the 'aporetic' style of instruction in Socrates' dialogue with Euthydemus in *Memorabilia*, where Socrates drove Euthydemus to despair (ἀθύμως ἔχειν: 4.2.23, πάνυ ἀθύμως ἔχων: 4.2.39) by making him reveal his ignorance of 'the kingly art', then gave him more positive instruction after that (4.2.40).

Another description of the movement, but still in the Socratic mode, is as an account of modern therapeutic 'on the couch' counselling, in which the 'doctor' provokes the 'patient' to diagnose his own difficulties before attempting a cure. Hiero indeed describes the tyrant as a sick man at 1.23. Simonides first provokes Hiero to despairing self-diagnosis by pretending that he thinks that tyrants are the happiest men in the world, then proceeds to the cure on the basis of this diagnosis. Simonides needs the diagnosis in order to produce a cure that addresses the patient's concerns and to develop a vision to which he can respond. The therapeutic role of the wise man is made explicit in *Mem.* 2.7.1, where Socrates attempts to 'cure the dilemmas of ignorance' of his friends in conversation (καὶ μὴν τὰς ἀπορίας γε τῶν φίλων τὰς μὲν δι' ἄγνοιαν ἐπειρᾶτο γνώμῃ ἀκεῖσθαι). There too, his method is to provoke them to reveal their miseries with a comment about how glum they look (*Mem.* 2.7.1), and then to 'cure' the difficulties that they diagnose in their lives (*Mem.* 2.8–10). The difference is that Simonides is dealing with a ruler rather than a private citizen, and must show more deference.

This straightforward reading would make *Hiero* one of those meetings that bring the wise and the powerful into a partnership of friendship, since friendship consists in offering support to those in distress. The stories that Xenophon's Socrates tells about Daedalus and Minos and Palamedes and Odysseus represent in contrast unfriendly relationships, like the stories in which the tyrant Dionysius I of Syracuse imprisons the wise man for not telling him what he wanted to hear (D.S. 15.6–7). It was a commonplace that some encounters were so unfriendly that the wise should use veiled language in their reforms (Plato, *Ep.* 7, 332d, Demetr. *On Style* 5.289–90). Simonides' comment that no one is willing to criticize Hiero to his face (1.14) could explain his own lack of criticism in these terms, but his ultimate contribution is to advise Hiero as a friend who is concerned for his happiness as well as that of his citizens.

The question of the irony of the wise man is significant in a dialogue in which the instruction is Socratic. There is an expectation that the wise man will pretend to a view that is morally inferior in order to facilitate his instruction. Simonides' initial indication that Hiero will know the answer to the central question better than he does is certainly ironic, since he does later disprove Hiero's assertion that tyranny has the disadvantage in happiness. His irony also consists in pressing inferior grounds for his

---

[13] This is implied in Luccioni (1947) 21–8. For *Hiero* as a study of the transition from tyranny to royalty: Luccioni (1946) 256–68.

view that tyranny has the advantage. Hiero points to this irony when he expresses amazement that Simonides is adopting the view of the 'masses' on the happiness of tyranny (2.3–5). The reason why he conceals his true wisdom is to avoid the preaching style and to involve the pupil, which was the best pedagogy, but also, in the Socratic process of therapeutics, to hear the patient out and make him receptive to the cure that he offers. This is a kind of a deceit, but Xenophon believed that it was just to deceive even those who were your friends if this was in their better interests (*Mem.* 4.2.14–19). The reason why Simonides wishes to help Hiero is evidently because this improvement is what the wise contrive.

Strauss and others have detected much more extensive irony in *Hiero* in the wise man's advice about government, and even in Hiero's own diagnosis of the miseries of tyranny. For arguments against, refer to Appendix 1.

THE CONTENT

Simonides maintains that the tyrant has a greater share of the 'good things' that give pleasure to body or to soul, or both body and soul, in respect of the senses (1), power and wealth (2–6), honour (7). Within these large categories, the more detailed constituents of happiness emerge for both rulers and non-rulers as those that ordinary people enjoy: security rather than danger, freedom as opposed to slavery, peace as opposed to war, friendship rather than enmity, trust as opposed to distrust, honour in preference to dishonour, praise rather than blame, sympathy rather than enmity, and so on. Hiero declares the tyrant deprived of all these because he lacks the friendship of his citizens. Simonides accepts his diagnosis (8.1, 11.8).

On the matter of sensual pleasures, Hiero complains first that the tyrant cannot see the sights abroad for fear of assassination or deposition while the shows he sees at home are as pricey as they are tawdry because he is a captive audience. No one dares to blame him to his face, but the praise he hears is a cover for hostility. His food and drink do not please him; pleasure comes from anticipation, whereas he has everything all the time, and is quickly sated; his perfumes are enjoyed more by those around him. He cannot find a wife of suitable rank unless he takes a foreigner – which as a patriot he is loath to do; he has to marry below his station if he marries from within the city. The boys are enslaved as much as everyone else – no true friendship or loving glances – just the sexual compliance that comes from fear. In response to the idea that he has superior material pleasures, he locates happiness and unhappiness in the soul. He considers peace a much better thing than war, but the tyrant is in a permanent state of war against the citizens, constantly fearful, never enjoying the pleasures of the private man's war. He lacks friendship or trust. His greater possessions win him a hollow victory over the private man; for wealth is relative and he is compelled to spend large amounts on his security. His fear leads him to eliminate the best men and have to use the inferior types. He loves his city, but the nature of his rule is to make it weak rather than strong. He can have no security from his bodyguards as citizens do; they work for pay, and would get more for killing him than guarding him. The belief that he has the power to help his friends and harm his enemies is illusory. He has no friends and can never adequately punish his enemies without emptying the city. In response to the idea that it must be honour in which the tyrant enjoys the advantage, he replies that it is as insincere as the praise; he knows the happiness of the truly honoured man, but he is incapable of attaining it. When Simonides asks why he does not lay tyranny aside, he says that tyrants could never account for their crimes. The only profit he can see is to hang himself (7.13).

Hiero could sound insincere were it not for the passionate quality of his utterances, which persuade the reader that here is a man in genuine torment, and were it not for Xenophon's other paradigms, such as Cyrus the Great, which also place such importance on friendship. He wins the argument then, but his 'victory' proves that he does not know how to be happy or make his subjects happy.

Simonides then sets out to treat Hiero's ignorance and prove that tyrants can secure friendship, and through this, have a share of those good things that Hiero said they lacked. Almost everything he says responds to what Hiero has told him, as the commentary will show. To offer small services costs nothing and puts him on a level of equality with his citizens, which is the best setting for friendship; and yet the kind word, the word of praise, the small gift have far greater impact if they come from a ruler. And if he achieves the goodwill he desires by doing what anyone can do, how much more so with his greater possessions? Hiero objects. He has to do some things such as raising taxes and punishing criminals that will never win friends. Simonides advises delegation of these areas of administration. He goes on to recommend competitions to secure revenues and promote bravery and justice and wisdom. These will secure goodwill as well as prosperity and increase. Hiero asks for advice about his bodyguards. Simonides surprises him by recommending that he must keep them, but use them to guard the common interest of the citizens rather than his own. He should look to the interests of the city rather than his own in every way, down to the last chariot victory, and if he does that, he will achieve that happiness and love he desires.

The dialogue is open-ended, and the wise man will presumably continue to assist the ruler in his transition to good government. Simonides has proposed the reform of an existing constitution, according to the requirements of Aristotle (*Pol.* 1289a1–5). He has not produced a philosopher king or a blueprint for perfection, but he has moved Hiero onward and upward. *Mem.* 3.9.12–13 suggests that if he ignores the wise man, it will be to his own detriment.

INTRODUCTION TO *RESPUBLICA LACEDAEMONIORUM*

LITERARY TRADITION AND POLITICAL THOUGHT

Lac. belongs to the broad tradition of literature that describes political constitutions and how they secure success.[1] It attributes the success of the Spartans to their obedience to the laws of Lycurgus, who had the wisdom required of the ideal ruler to create laws that produced the habits of success in the population. The account begins:

> Reflecting once that Sparta, though one of the *poleis* with the smallest populations, emerged most powerful and famous in Greece, I wondered how on earth this came about; but when I grasped the customs (ἐπιτηδεύματα) of the citizens, I wondered no more. As for Lycurgus who laid down the laws (νόμους) for them, in obedience to which they prospered (ηὐδαιμόνησαν), I wonder at this man and think him wise in the extreme (εἰς τὰ ἔσχατα σοφόν). He, not by imitating the other *poleis* but by going against the majority of them in his determinations, made his homeland pre-eminent in success (προέχουσαν εὐδαιμονίαι).

Xenophon was not the first to produce such an account of the Spartan constitution,[2] but his introduction suggests that his originality lies in explaining Spartan success as the single-minded and coherent purpose of the law-giver, and in contrasting his customs so uniformly with those of other Greeks.

Lycurgus' laws are the substance of the Spartan *politeia* and they provide an education through custom,[3] making the Spartans 'as they should be' by developing 'all the virtues' and 'complete political virtue' in them (10.4–7).[4] Their improvement in quality made up for their small citizen numbers. Through their obedience to the laws, they acquired internal harmony and leadership of Greece. The Greeks 'asked' for their leadership, offering them the willing obedience that was due to good leaders; they withdrew their support only when the Spartans abandoned their obedience to the laws and became corrupt (14.6).

---

[1] Bordes (1982) 13–29 describes the parameters.

[2] Critias wrote two studies before him, one in verse and one in prose, now extant only in fragments, and *Lac.* echoes some of these. Critias' prose version of the constitution begins with diet and exercise for parents, as *Lac.* does (DK, Critias, fr. 32; cf. *Lac.* 1.3–4), mentions their avoidance of 'compulsory drinking rounds', as *Lac.* does (DK, fr. 6 on προπόσεις; cf. *Lac.* 5.4, where ἀναγκαίας πόσεις 'ruin bodies, ruin minds') and their security measures against helots, as *Lac.* does (DK, fr. 37: τὸ δόρυ ἔχων ἀεὶ περιέρχεται; cf. τὸ δὲ ἔχοντας τὰ δόρατα ἀεὶ περιιέναι *Lac.* 12.4). This gives rise to the idea that Xenophon borrowed from Critias, but Tigerstedt, vol. 1 (1965) 163 n. 495 does not accept that because *Hell.* 2.3.11–56 and *Mem.* 1.2.31–8 show how he detested Critias. Cf. Bordes (1982) 206–10.

[3] Xenophon similarly defines the '*politeia*' of the Persians (*Cyr.* 1.2.15) as the laws governing their education in virtue.

[4] de Romilly (1971) 227–50 has an excellent treatment of this function of law.

The focus on education means that *Lac.* is not a complete catalogue of Spartan laws. There is no Great Rhetra,[5] nor mention of administrative laws such as the law against electing the same man twice as nauarch (*Hell.* 2.1.7), the law about the succession to the kingship (*Hell.* 3.3.1–3) or the ἀρχαῖον νόμιμον that allowed a commander to act on his own authority for the good of Sparta (*Hell.* 5.2.32). Laws that punish wrongdoers, such as those against bribery (*Hell.* 5.4.24–33) are also missing, but the punishment of cowards is included because they lack the main virtues developed by the system and threaten its entire success (*Lac.* 9, 10.6). The roles of the elders and the ephors are seen only in relation to this education. So, we hear that the elders compete for admission to the Gerousia in order to acquire the honour of judging cases involving the death penalty (*Lac.* 10.1–3) because it provided an educational incentive that kept them virtuous in old age; but we do not hear about the specific criminal laws they judged. The ephors likewise are the enforcers of obedience to the laws of Lycurgus, but only those laws that confirm their wide authority to enforce that obedience are mentioned in detail (8.3–4). The domestic role of the kings is also limited to the laws that ensured their virtue and continuance (15).

Lac. is of course not a constitutional history because the laws of Lycurgus have remained the same since their introduction (10.8), nor does it mention helots or other inferior classes in Sparta, evidently because political thought is about the happiness of the free community: the Spartiates. Slaves are introduced only in relation to their education in virtue: *doulai* do the wool-work to release free girls from this menial task in order to develop virtue (1.4), men show their *homonoia* when they share the use of their *oiketai* (6.3), *oiketai* detect illicit wealth in their masters' houses (7.5), citizens protect their weapons against *douloi* (12.4). *Lac.* takes no account of the *perioikoi* even when it notes that some of their lands went to the king (15.3).

Success was often attributed to educational laws and customs. Pericles' Funeral Speech urges the Athenians to investigate: 'from what kinds of habits of life we came to (greatness) and with what kind of constitution and from what characteristics this greatness arose' (Thuc. 2.36.4).[6] Xenophon's Socrates urges Pericles the Younger to recover the ancestral glory of the Athenians by discovering and practising their ancestors' ἐπιτηδεύματα, or imitating the 'practices' of those who lead Greece, such as the Spartans (*Mem.* 3.5.14). Laws and customs were regularly credited to 'founding fathers'.[7] The success of the empire of Cyrus the Great was also the result of customs he put in place (above pp. 10–13). The interest in the causes of a rise of a *polis* to greatness is found in Isocrates (*Peace*, 8.116–19), who urges a 'philosophic inquiry' into why Athens and Sparta rose to first place in Greece from obscure beginnings and then collapsed, and why Thessaly with its fertile plains did not achieve success, whereas stony Megara flourished.

---

[5] Plut. *Lyc.* 6 gives the text of the Great Rhetra; see MacDowell (1986) 3–5.

[6] Loraux (1986) is the standard work on this genre.

[7] Solon of Athens, and Zaleucus and Charondas of Catana are instances. See Plutarch's *Solon*, Aristotle, *Ath. Pol.* 5–12 on Solon, Aristotle, *Pol.* 1274a23–b26 for other lawgivers. See further: Ruschenbusch, (1958) 398–424, Szegedy-Maszak (1978) 199–209, Gagarin (1986) 51–80.

Lac. makes claims for the uniqueness and excellence of the laws that were regular features of these traditions, but often denied to the Spartans. Thucydides' Pericles claimed originality and excellence for the Athenians: 'We have a constitution that does not vie with the laws of our neighbours; we are ourselves more a model for some of them rather than imitating others' (2.37.1); he found Spartan virtue inferior, because it was too dependent on training (2.39). Isocrates said that Lycurgus had copied the customs of the Athenian ancestors rather than initiating his own (*Panath.* 12.153–4). The Spartans had not 'discovered the finest habits, used them and revealed them to the rest of the world', he said, because they had been in the Peloponnese for only 700 years and many wise men had existed before then (202–7). They were too ignorant of philosophy to invent good laws (as was proven by their custom of teaching boys to steal and making magistrates of those who were the best thieves: 208–14; cf. *Lac.* 2.6–9), and though their military customs were good (217), they perverted them for unjust use against other Greeks (219–20). The debate about the uniqueness of the law continued in the fourth-century historian Ephorus, who argued that Lycurgus postdated the Cretan lawgiver Epimenides, and so must have imitated his laws, but refined them to an extent that made them unique.[8] Herodotus of course had said that Lycurgus received the constitution ready-made from Delphi, or imported it from Crete – which the Spartans themselves endorsed (1.65.4). Plato's *Laws* took the arrangements devised by the lawgivers of the Spartans and Cretans as an excellent basis for an ideal code,[9] but he criticized their systems for relying on warfare and enforced abstinence rather than justice and voluntary self-control. The Spartan constitution survived only because it was 'mixed' (going to neither extreme of freedom or enslavement: *Laws* 691c–692a). Aristotle also thought they were too dedicated to warfare, and was able to point out that the Spartans had declined while actually remaining true to their laws, which showed how defective they were (*Pol.* 1333b5–1334a10).

THE STRUCTURE

Lac. systematically praises the laws of Lycurgus in contrast to those of other Greeks. First, the laws governing the education of the individual in virtue are presented as a chronological progression from birth to old age (1–10). The laws of other *poleis* are described for each age-group, then Lycurgus is praised for producing different and better laws, with an accompanying description of his motivation and the effects he intended to produce: ἡγήσατο . . . νομίσας . . . ἔταξεν . . . ἐποίησε . . . νομίζων (1.4); ὁρῶν . . . ἔγνω . . . ἔθηκε (1.5); ἀποπαύσας . . . ἔταξεν . . . νομίζων (1.6); ὁρῶν . . . ἐνόμισεν . . . ἐποίησεν (1.7). The chronological order seems natural, but Aeschines claims that his chronological presentation of Solon's legislation for education through the different ages (*Or.* 1.7–36) made it 'easy to understand' (8), and Xenophon implies

---

[8] *FGH* 70.149 = Strabo, 10.4.18; cf. Aristotle, *Pol.* 1271b20–30.
[9] See Laks in Rowe and Schofield (2000) 258–92 for an exploration of *Laws*.

that the chronological order of his account of Persian education clarifies the great pains they took to improve the citizens (*Cyr.* 1.2.5). Both could apply to *Lac.*

After concluding this initial section with the remark that though all the Greeks praise these customs, none is willing to imitate them (10.8), Xenophon turns to the practices of the army on campaign (11–12). This section is one of the earliest technical accounts of warfare, and is also presented as a chronological progression, from the call-up and related matters such as equipment and uniform, on to formations and tactics, then camp life. The laws determining the duties and privileges of the king on campaign account for his military leadership (13). An explanation intervenes of how the Spartans have at the time of writing lost their success because they have lapsed from the laws (14). The work closes with the laws that determine the customs of the kings at home, explaining the stability of the kingship in these terms (15).

The account is also structured as a debate with an imagined audience, particularly in opening or closing discussions of particular significance. After early invitations to 'anyone who wants' to investigate the points raised (1.10, 2.14), the account of the practice of teaching boys to steal and their chaste form of homosexuality assumes a hostile audience ('a man might say, then why . . . ? . . . because, I reply' 2.8; 'I am not astonished that this is disbelieved by some': 2.14). Yet Xenophon eventually assumes that his audience is disposed to accept his argument when he says that *all poleis* admire the Spartan ways (10.8) and it follows that he can then imagine that they will next inquire about military laws (11.1). This new inquiry merely assumes an ignorant 'majority' who think that Spartan military manoeuvres are hard to learn (11.5). He represents the audience as accepting his account entirely when he poses the final challenge they might make: 'if someone should ask me whether these laws seem to me to be still unchanged' (14.1); he declares in response that he would have to deny the proposition.

THE PROBLEM OF CHAPTER 14

Questions have been raised about the fourteenth chapter of *Lac.* The view taken in this edition is that the chapter is authentic, is properly placed between chapters 13 and 15 and confirms the praise of Lycurgus' laws. Those interested in my views are directed to Appendix 3.

THE DATE

The references to νῦν and to the rejection of Spartan leadership in the fourteenth chapter are the only indications of the date of composition of *Lac.* Some have favoured a specific date, but the use of νῦν in the epilogue of *Cyropaedia*, in which Xenophon systematically contrasts past excellence with present decline in the same way as he does in *Lac.* 14, suggests that it refers loosely to 'nowadays in the present generation'. In *Cyropaedia*, νῦν does describe the treachery of Mithridates (8.8.4), which we can date to 361 BC, but another passage (8.8.12) dates the decline from the reign of Artaxerxes (from 405/4 BC), and another indicates that it had already set in by the time of the treachery done to the generals of the Ten Thousand in 401 BC (8.8.3). So νῦν in *Cyropaedia* covers a forty-year period.[10] This should also be the time-span of νῦν in *Lac*. 14. Its opinions about Spartan leadership fit this span. The time at which the other *poleis* ask the Spartans to be their leaders is the period of the Peloponnesian War, in which the Spartans led willing allies against the Athenians. The time at which they became corrupt is at the end of this War. Plutarch, who is adapting the explanation of corruption in *Lac*., dates its beginning to the activities of Lysander as harmost in the later years of the War: *Lyc*. 30.1. The time at which the Greeks rejected their leadership and made efforts to prevent them ruling (or ruling again, for which see the note in the commentary on 14.6 on the translation of πάλιν) begins formally with the time that they banded together against them in the Corinthian War in 395 BC and continues after the battle of Leuctra in 371 BC when the Peloponnesians desert them. A date in the 360s BC is probable. Xenophon was writing other major works in the 360s too (above p. 20). Leuctra destroyed their hegemony, but their desire for hegemony persisted. Isocrates is still describing that desire in the present tense in *Panathenaicus* (12.188) in 339 BC: 'But the Spartans have never given a thought to this. They look to nothing other than to secure as many of the goods of others as is possible.'

THE PURPOSE

Lac. is the first systematic account we have of the laws of Lycurgus, and its first aim was evidently to demonstrate the secret of their political success; this was of interest to those of a political and philosophical cast of mind. It has also seemed to offer an implicit challenge to other Greeks to adopt the laws ('all praise such practices, but no *polis* is willing to imitate them': 10.8). This remark, which closes the main account of Spartan customs, sounds very similar to that which closes a section of advice to the cavalry commander: 'almost everyone knows these things, but not many are willing to persist in their implementation' (*Hipp*. 4.5). It could seem merely to be a device for closure, but in fact reinforces the paradigmatic nature of what has preceded. Accepting that Xenophon is offering a paradigm for imitation, then, and not just indicating closure, who is a possible audience? The challenge is not to the Spartans, since they are a lost cause.[11] Ollier (1934) suggested that it challenged the Athenians,[12] Chrimes (1948) 30–2 narrowed this down to Athenian laconizers. But other small *poleis* are also candidates for reform. Agesilaus himself encouraged his supporters among the Phliasians to imitate the Spartan public dining system (*syssitia*) during a period of internal conflict (*Hell*. 5.3.16–17) and their new laws may also have imitated Spartan

---

[10] *Cyr*. 8.8.3 also uses νῦν with the past tense to mean 'in reality': νῦν δὲ δὴ τῆι πρόσθεν αὐτῶν δοξῆι πιστεύσαντες ἐνεχείρισαν ἑαυτούς.

[11] Cf. Luppino-Manes (1988).

[12] Ollier (1934) xxviii: Xenophon was bitter about his exile and indulged 'le coeur gros de rancune' in praising the rivals of Athens.

precedent (*Hell.* 5.3.25). His reform is responsible for their superb achievement in the service of the Spartans against the most powerful Greeks in their region, which Xenophon praises so highly (*Hell.* 7.2). Phlius had a small population, like Sparta, and needed to develop quality to succeed. Their leader Procles, emphasizing their small size, nevertheless points to the strength that the Athenians would find in many numbers of such small *poleis* (*Hell.* 6.5.38–48).

However, there is evidence in Xenophon's other works that imitation of the Spartan model is not restricted to small *poleis*, but offered to all those who could profit from it. His Socrates urges the son of Pericles to discover and imitate the customs not only of the ancestors of the Athenians (τὰ τῶν προγόνων ἐπιτηδεύματα) in order to improve the military forces, but also the customs of others who are pre-eminent in their own time, whom Pericles takes to be the Spartans (*Mem.* 3.5.14–15). Imitation is of course an essential part of Socratic education too; the imitation of the personal 'customs' of Socrates was the way to individual excellence for Euthydemus as well (*Mem.* 4.2.40).

LE MIRAGE SPARTIATE

Lac. is at the heart of the debate about 'le mirage spartiate'.[13] Lycurgus was legendary, one of those father figures to whom *poleis* attributed their laws.[14] Tigerstedt (1965) 72 describes him as 'a vehicle for political propaganda and philosophical doctrine' because he was made to serve various agenda at various stages in the development of his 'mirage'. Plutarch (*Lyc.* 1.1) begins his life with the comment: 'about Lycurgus the lawgiver, in general, nothing can be said which is not disputed.'

Xenophon certainly makes him a vehicle for his own political thought. He does not bother with biographical detail except where it enhances this thought. He therefore omits the story he tells in his *Apologia Socratis* 15, in which Socrates mentions Lycurgus' reception by Delphi as more of a god than a man (cf. Hdt. 1.65.2–3). Yet he attributes the laws to Lycurgus' wisdom, rejecting the tradition that he received them from Delphi or Crete (Herodotus 1.65.4), because this makes him the ideal ruler who by his own qualities secures the common good. He does date Lycurgus' achievement to the time of the Heraclids (*Lac.* 10.8), but this is also only to enhance the challenge to other Greeks to imitate the laws: they were 'most ancient', but still 'most novel' in that they were unimitated.[15] He also reveals his own special interest when he emphasizes the various measures Lycurgus took to win the willing obedience of the Spartans:

---

[13] See Tigerstedt, vol. 1 (1965) 70–3 on Lycurgus.

[14] Solon is perhaps the most documented. Herodotus 1.29.1 says that Solon 'made laws for the Athenians at their bidding'; Xenophon describes him in similar terms to Lycurgus, calling to mind (*Symp.* 8.39) 'how Solon once after philosophical inquiry set down excellent laws for his *polis*'; other fourth-century sources call him ὁ παλαιὸς νομοθέτης, 'the one who ordered the democracy by means of the finest laws' and 'the ancient law-giver' (Aesch. 3.175, 257).

[15] MacDowell (1986) 1–2 gives a range of dates for Lycurgus' reforms. Ephorus, *FGH* 70.118 = Strabo 8.5.5 says that Hellanicus chose the early date too, when he attributed the laws to Eurysthenes and Procles. Herodotus makes Lycurgus a regent for Leobotes 870–40 BC.

presenting the obedience of the most powerful Spartans as a model for imitation, creating the ephors to implement the law, and securing the religious sanction of Delphi. The religious sanction is overtly said to be among 'many other fine devices for securing willing obedience' (8.5 πολλῶν δὲ καὶ ἄλλων ὄντων μηχανημάτων καλῶν . . . εἰς τὸ πείθεσθαι τοῖς νόμοις ἐθέλειν). This characteristic focus on willing obedience develops the tradition in which founding fathers secured their laws against change (Solon and Lycurgus in Herodotus 1.29 and 1.65.5).

THE LAWS

Lycurgus' 'laws' have been denied proper legal status on the grounds that they are mere customs, and therefore not subject to the specified penalties that are considered an attribute of law in the strict sense.[16] Yet Xenophon seems to differentiate ἐπιτήδευμα ('custom') from νόμος ('law') in his introduction, and then to define customs as the product of law when he says that Lycurgus 'laid down law' that produced 'such-and-such a custom' (5.1 ἐνομοθέτησεν . . . ἐπιτηδεύματα; 6.4: ἐποίησεν ἐπιτηδεύεσθαι). He also makes the laws subject to legal process, if not to specified penalties. He has the elders hold trials (10.1–3) and the ephors punish transgressors, imposing fines and deposing magistrates (8.3–4). The *paidonomos* has his own jurisdiction, and brings before the ephors those boys who have not obeyed his instructions to stop fighting (4.6). The possessor of silver and gold is also punished by unnamed parties (7.6). The *hippagretes* adopts a process similar to *dokimasia* in Athens (cf. *Mem.* 2.2.13) when he explains the reasons for choosing some ephebes as *hippeis* and rejecting others (*Lac.* 4.3–4). Those who were not chosen also looked for lapses from the law in those who were chosen – evidently in order to report them to the authorities for punishment. In a military system, moreover, failure to wear the right uniform (*Lac.* 11.3) or perform the prescribed exercises (12.6–7) would be subject to procedures instigated by officers at every level. Not observing standard military manoeuvres (*Lac.* 11.5–10) might incur the penalties that the ephors imposed for taking an unauthorized initiative, as in the case of Phoebidas (*Hell.* 5.2.32).

Some also suggest that unwritten law does not have the same status as written law, though there are opinions on both sides in this debate.[17] Plutarch (*Lyc.* 13.1–2)

---

[16] Greeks often used the same word for law and custom: νόμοι. De Romilly (1971) 51–71 has an excellent treatment of their relations. Gagarin (1986) 57f. concludes that the Spartans did not have laws in the strict sense outside the *rhetras* until the fourth century, only customs and traditions.

[17] Thomas champions the status of unwritten law in Foxhall and Lewis (eds.) (1996) 9–31, against Gagarin (1986), who nevertheless does recognize exceptions to the rule that laws are by definition written: 9–10. This type of unwritten law is to be distinguished from the unwritten 'natural law' that Greeks regularly endorsed (Thuc. 2.37.3, Xen. *Mem.* 4.4.19–24). That law was dictated by the divine order and transgressions carried their own automatic penalty, such as the law against incest, with the 'god-given' penalty of a weak baby, or against ingratitude, which brought social ostracism (*Mem.* 4.4.19–24). The tyrant's refusal to obey the wise is another instance of a transgression with an automatic penalty (*Mem.* 3.9.12–14). The type of law adopted by Lycurgus was in contrast dictated by a man but remained oral.

raises the issue when he says that Lycurgus actually decreed that the laws be left unwritten (μὴ χρῆσθαι νόμοις ἐγγράφοις). One reason was that they developed a positive *prohairesis* for virtue that was deeply implanted in the citizens and needed no written enforcement. Lycurgus also recognized the inflexibility of written law when he decreed that even business law remain unwritten because people educated in virtue needed freedom to make their own just decisions. Xenophon never suggests that Lycurgus' laws were unwritten, however, and certainly never questions their status. He puts them alongside the written laws of the Athenians and other *poleis*, as if he discerns no difference between their force (*Mem.* 4.4.15–16).

A separate question is whether the laws described in *Lac.* ever were in force or whether they are indeed just 'mirage'. Xenophon was well placed to know the answer to this because of his association with Agesilaus, whose oath to maintain the laws in his compacts with his citizens begs his certain and detailed knowledge of them (*Lac.* 15.7). Against this there is their location in the distant past, their literary tradition, and their conformity with other ideal legislation, for instance, on eugenic arrangements (*Lac.* 1.3–10).[18]

Xenophon nevertheless inspires confidence by confirming Spartan realities against the mirage, speaking for example as if Spartans inherited private property from their fathers rather than communal allotments (*Lac.* 1.9), assuming private ownership as a background to their communal use of property (*Lac.* 6.3.1–3), and countering the usual impression that Lycurgus broke the power of the family by making the authorities and the families work together in educating their boys (*Lac.* 3.3). Moreover, *Hellenica* and *Anabasis* have no idealizing agenda, yet they confirm the laws about age-group education and chaste homosexual relationships (*Hell.* 5.4.24–33 mentions both; cf. *Lac.* 2–4), boys' thefts (*An.* 4.6.14–16, *Lac.* 2.6–9), tough training (*An.* 4.8.25–6), the ephors' power to suspend officials in mid-office (*An.* 2.6.3 and the implication in *Hell.* 3.2.6–7, *Lac.* 8.4) and their sobering effect on their citizens (*Hell.* 6.4.16, *Lac.* 8.3–4, 13.5). Lycurgus' laws have an authentic individuality even in comparison with the similar laws that govern Persian education (*Cyr.* 1.2): the Persians do not adopt Spartan eugenics, nor does *Lac.* train the boys in Persian justice through mock trials.[19]

Xenophon does exaggerate the uniqueness of Lycurgus' laws in insisting that they were contrary to those of other *poleis*, but this was a natural extension of the literary

---

[18] Aristotle, *Politics* 1334b29–38 begins his construction of the ideal constitution with measures for marriage and marital relations designed to produce the strongest infants – as does *Lac*. Plato's *Laws* confirm the Spartan arrangements for women as midway between the housebound life of the Athenians and the martial life of the legendary Sauromatides (804d–806c), but go on to construct a life for women that includes military service. Other legislation fosters communality (*Laws* 739c–d; cf. *Lac.* 6), bans profiteering and the possession of gold and silver (*Laws* 741c–742c; cf. *Lac.* 7), and exposure to foreign influences through travel abroad or through the admission of strangers to the community (*Laws* 949e–953e; cf. *Lac.* 14). There are similar provisions about education in Aristophanes' old education, *Clouds* 961–1035, Socrates' personal regime (*Mem.* 1.6.2–3, 6), and Isocrates' old constitution in *Areopagiticus* (for example, on discipline 7.37–45).

[19] Tuplin in Powell and Hodkinson (1994) esp. 150–61.

tradition of constitutional praise.[20] The similarity of other laws in actual operation is in fact an argument in favour of their authenticity. It was in no utopia, but as evidence in an Athenian law court that Solon's 'customs' for boys: ἃ χρὴ τὸν παῖδα τὸν ἐλεύθερον ἐπιτηδεύειν καὶ ὡς δεῖ αὐτὸν τραφῆναι were adduced (Aesch. 1.7–36). Aristotle's account of legislation for the education of Athenian ephebes mentions supervisors (*sophronistai*) who control their diet, their common dinners, their training, their dress, and replace paternal with state control (Arist. *Ath. Pol.* 42) – as in *Lac.* The importance of obedience to these laws is shown in decrees that honour these supervisors.[21] The 'Law of the Gymnasiarch' from Beroia resembles the laws for boys and ephebes in *Lac.*, particularly the supervision of their discipline by the gymnasiarch and his officials.[22] The privileges of the kings (*Lac.* 15) look entirely like the 'hereditary kingships on fixed privileges' as defined by Thucydides 1.13, and are paralleled in other laws about the duties and privileges of a priest,[23] which was one of the main roles of the Spartan king. Other laws also prescribe customs for funerals such as those for the kings,[24] legislate against cowardice (Aesch. 3.175; cf. *Lac.* 9.4–6), regulate coinage and trade,[25] and even liability for injuries to animals, which might explain the requirement that borrowed animals be returned 'in good condition' at Sparta;[26] regulations are also found for brawls between adolescents.[27]

Xenophon's predecessors also attribute the same laws to the Spartans as he does, and while this could just show how pervasive the 'myth' was, it was difficult to fool all of the people all of the time. The similarities with Critias have been mentioned at the beginning of this chapter. Herodotus' Lycurgus produced *eunomia* out of *kakonomia*, changing τὰ νόμιμα πάντα and creating the military divisions of the *enomotia* and *syssitia*, as well as the ephorate and gerousia, securing these against change and enabling the Spartans to conquer the Peloponnese (1.65.1–5). Xenophon's Lycurgus does the same: *Lac.* 5, 11.4 on the *syssitia* and *enomotia*, 8.3–4 and 10.1–3 on the ephors and *gerousia*, 8.1–2, 5 on how he secured his laws against change. Xenophon also confirms Herodotus in his account of the γερέα of the kings (6.56–60; cf. *Lac.* 13, 15), their laws against cowardice (7.231; cf. *Lac. passim*), in favour of long hair and exercise (1.82.8, 7.209.3; cf. *Lac.* 11.3, 12.5–6) and his view that their freedom is guaranteed by δεσπότης νόμος (7.104.4; cf. *Lac.* 10.4–7) – even if Herodotus does not attribute these laws to Lycurgus or give them an overt educational purpose from infancy.

---

[20] Gagarin (1986) challenges the communality of Greek law, but Osborne in Mitchell and Rhodes (1997) suggests that inscribed laws require a common background in order to make sense; the literary evidence also assumes communality when it emphasizes the original contributions of the great lawgivers.

[21] Reinmuth (1971).

[22] Gauthier and Hatzopoulos (1993).

[23] Sokolowski (1955) no. 37, translated in Arnaoutoglou (1998) no. 107.

[24] Sokolowski (1969) no. 97, translated in Arnaoutoglou (1998) no. 109; and (1955) no. 16, translated in Arnaoutoglou (1998) no. 110; cf. *Lac.* 15.8–9.

[25] *SEG* XXVI. 72; *IC* 4.62, translated in Arnaoutoglou (1998) nos. 50–1; cf. *Lac.* 7.1–6.

[26] Guarducci (1950) 4.41.1 translated in Arnaoutoglou (1998) no. 55; cf. *Lac.* 6.3.

[27] Guarducci (1935) 1.11.2 translated in Arnaoutoglou (1998) no. 32; cf. *Lac.* 4.6.

The consensus of modern scholarship is also that *Lac.* describes realities of some kind; it is only Xenophon's interpretations that are sometimes seen as 'mirage'. So, he has been said to misinterpret as a system of *education* what was a random accretion of practices from religious ritual.[28] And the later age of marriage, the restriction on sex in the first part of marriage, and the wife-sharing in his account of the customs concerning women (*Lac.* 1.3–9) are seen as measures to control birthrate and stabilize land tenure rather than as the eugenic measures that Xenophon says they were.[29]

Therefore, *Lac.* may be part of the Spartan 'mirage', but there are no grounds to dismiss all its evidence *en bloc*, and though the status of its laws may be debated, similar laws from other *poleis* and the general ancient consensus confirm their plausibility. For those who seek to understand realities then, a law by law approach is in order.

---

[28] See Kennell (1995) 123–37 after Jeanmaire (1939/1975) 463–588. Burkert (1985) 260–2 connects ritual with education and notes (260): 'The formation of the rising generation appears almost the principal function of religion, where ritual concentrates on the introduction of adolescents into the world of adults.' Calame (1997) 141–206, 235–7 concludes that eugenically inspired athletics overlaid the ritual foot races for Spartan girls or developed alongside them.

[29] See Cartledge (1981) 84–105 and Hodkinson in Powell (ed.) (1989) 79–121.

INTRODUCTION TO *RESPUBLICA ATHENIENSIUM*

POLITICAL THOUGHT

Ath. is our earliest extant analysis of the Athenian democracy, just as *Lac.* is our first comprehensive account of the laws of Lycurgus. The introduction also puts the work in the same tradition of constitutional praise and blame as *Lac.*[1]

> Concerning the constitution of the Athenians, their choice of this form of constitution I do not praise for this reason, that in making this choice, they chose to have the unworthy (πονηρούς) do better than the worthy (χρηστούς).[2] For this reason I do not praise it. But since they have resolved on this constitution, that the Athenians preserve it securely and administer well those other areas in which they seem to the other Greeks to be in error, this will I reveal.

The constitution is the radical democracy of the Athenian empire, founded on the power of her fleets, and defined as the rule of the *demos*. This lasted in its radical form from the time of the reforms of Ephialtes down to the end of the Peloponnesian War. It has been noted that most ancient analyses of this form of democracy exhibit the 'politics of dissent' (which simply means an opposing point of view) and criticize democracy on three main counts: for not restraining the *demos*, when it is in need of restraint, but allowing it to do what it likes instead; for not honouring the best people in the community but the worst; and for replacing the rule of law with rule in its own interests.[3]

Some aspects of this negative view can already be found in Herodotus' 'constitutional debate' (3.80–2), which purports to be a discussion that took place when Darius and his fellow Persian conspirators were contemplating the best form of government for Persia.[4] Otanes argues in favour of democracy against monarchy that it implies equal shares for all (ἰσονομίη) and has none of the drawbacks of monarchy, that offices are allotted to citizens at random, that the officers are accountable, and decisions are made in common (3.80.6), but Megabyzus argues in favour of oligarchy against democracy that the many are useless, ignorant, insolent and unrestrained;

---

[1] Bordes (1982) 139–63 analyses *Ath.* in the genre of the literature of *politeiai*.

[2] *Ath.* assumes the inferiority of the *demos* throughout calling them: . . . τοῖς πονηροῖς καὶ πένησι καὶ δημοτικοῖς . . . οἱ μὲν γὰρ πένητες καὶ οἱ δημόται καὶ οἱ χείρους . . . (1.4–5) and claiming: ἐν δὲ τῶι δήμωι ἀμαθία τε πλείστη καὶ ἀταξία καὶ πονηρία.

[3] Jones (1957) 43–52 discovers positive democratic theory by examining these main criticisms. Ober (1998) considers *Ath.* as the starting point for the politics of dissent. Aristotle alone, it seems, among ancient authors justifies the rule of the base over their betters on the moral grounds that they can pool their many scattered parts of virtue to match the whole virtues of the good few: *Pol.* 1281a39–b22.

[4] See most recently, with full bibliography: Pelling (2002).

that they rush at things like a river in spate: 'The tyrant at least, if he does something, does it with deliberation, but the *demos* does not even have deliberation in it: τῶι δὲ οὐδὲ γιγνώσκειν ἔνι' (3.81.2). His view is that oligarchy is the best form of government because the 'best men give best counsel' (3.81.3). Darius defeats them both when he argues that nothing could be better than the rule of one best man; that neither oligarchy nor democracy last, but both lead inevitably to monarchy; since, among the few, competitions arise which lead to the sole rule of the leading competitor; the rule of the many on the other hand produces friendships in public crime, and a single man must then arise to protect the *demos*, who wins their admiration and makes himself sole ruler.

Ath. exhibits these politics of dissent when it characterizes the *demos* as uneducated and unrestrained to the point of being 'madmen' (1.4–9). They certainly do not honour the best people, who are the rich, but pursue profit through deliberate exploitation of the rich, driven by the need to remedy their poverty, which is their defining characteristic. Indeed they are engaged in a class struggle that is presented as a battle of the elements: 'The best element is hostile to democracy in every land' (1.5). 'In no *polis* is the best element well disposed to the *demos*' (3.10). They do deliberate, but in order to promote the interests of their own kind through democracy in the type of partnership in crime to which Darius referred. Their rule is not the 'best' because they are not the 'best' people and do not pursue the 'best' interests, but *Ath.* aims a shaft at this idea by saying that they counsel 'best' by allowing the 'worst' to counsel (1.6; cf. the view of Megabyzus above). The democracy fits Alcibiades' description as the tyranny of the many over the few through the force of numbers: 'so then, whatever the masses as a whole write down as law, using their power over the property-owners without persuading them, all that would also be force rather than law?' (*Mem.* 1.2.45).

Yet *Ath.* offers a paradox: that the rule of the worst produced a best constitution, in the sense that it ensured its continuance. Aristotle said that the greatest achievement of a nomothete was not to produce a constitution, but one that lasted: ἔστι δὲ ἔργον τοῦ νομοθέτου . . . οὐ τὸ καταστῆσαι (sc. τὴν πολιτείαν) μέγιστον ἔργον οὐδὲ μόνον, ἀλλ' ὅπως σώιζεται μᾶλλον (*Pol.* 1319b33–35). This was indeed a rarity. Herodotus in his constitutional debate, *Cyropaedia* and *Agesilaus* in their introductions, and *Lac.* 15.1 envisage constant change from one constitution to another as the norm. Plato's review of the types of constitutions in *Republic* 8–9 shows how change inevitably occurs from within the ruling class in its education of the next generation. Aristotle's entire fifth book of *Politics* is dedicated to why the different types of constitutions are destroyed and how they can be preserved. Only the best lasted.

The paradox therefore challenges traditional political thought about the connection between the quality of a regime and its continuance, rather than just suggesting ambivalence of praise and blame in the author.[5] The same paradox can be found in

---

[5] Jones (1957) 41 found only bitter hostility to the democracy in the work, but Ober (1998) 43 and (1996) 156–7 found an ironic use of democratic discourse that had an unintended effect: it was too plausible and led to the collapse of the criticism it was meant to convey. Richards (1897) 234f.

Isocrates, who has imaginary opponents respond to his criticism of democracy (*Peace* 8.57): how come the democracy survives and has a power inferior to no other if it is such a bad constitution? His short answer is that the Athenians survive because of the blunders of others, but *Ath.* takes a completely different course by arguing that their constitutional arrangements have deliberately secured this preservation.[6] The author systematically examines the workings of the democracy from this point of view. His often ingenious and unrelenting argument detracts from the value of *Ath.* as a historical source, but not as an illustration of political thought.

Ober (1998) 23–6 notes the *aporia* of the author of *Ath.*, who can see no possibility of reform or overthrow for the democracy. He concludes: 'The elite author . . . leads his newly enlightened reader smack into a brick wall and abandons him there . . . There is simply nowhere to go from here, and not surprisingly, the text itself terminates' (25). This is entirely true. The disillusion is particularly apparent in the conclusion to the work, where he proves that there is no threat to the democracy even from the exiles. Aristotle, *Pol.* 1304b19–1305a7 cites cases where democracy was overthrown by exiles, but *Ath.* argues that the *demos* does not produce sufficient numbers. Moreover the author ignores the idea in Herodotus' constitutional debate that the democracy could be overthrown, not by revolutionaries, but by the sole ruler whom the democracy would inevitably throw up as its champion against power cliques, or who would deceive them into accepting him, as Pisistratus does in Herodotus.[7] *Ath.* offers blanks where quite interesting arguments could be developed, perhaps because he thought that the *demos* had too much dislike of those who sought to rise higher than anyone else (*Ath.* 2.18).

THE STRUCTURE AND CONTENT

Ath. begins with δέ, but need not suggest continuity from a previous work.[8] It addresses a second person singular, but need not suggest a conversation.[9] It could be incorporated into a larger discourse, as if it were just one of the speeches from Herodotus' constitutional debate,[10] but it can also stand alone, since the abrupt beginning is characteristic of a range of other works and the second person is a device that enlivens and structures even non-conversational narrative. Here it represents those who hold the view expressed in the introduction that the *demos* is in error in its arrangements, and who then raise a series of criticisms, which the author refutes in terms of the *demos'*

---

indicates that the impression of irony has a long history, but he does not entertain it himself. There is a possible parallel for an ironic reading of *Ath.* in the Spartan sympathizer's perverse reading of Isocrates' apparently blunt criticism of the Spartans as veiled praise (λανθάνειν ἐπαινῶν) in *Panath.* 12.239, but Isocrates does not endorse this as a true reading: Gray (1994).

[6] Their deliberations are constantly emphasized in words such as γιγνώσκειν and even ἀντιλογίζονται: 1.7, 11,13; 14.18; 2.9, 16, 19, 20; 3.10.

[7] Hdt. 1.59–64. Solon also charged the *demos* with bringing the tyranny of Pisistratus upon themselves through ignorance of the dangers of great men: fr. 9 and 11, West, *IEG* vol. 2.

[8] Caballero-López (1997) 108–112 discusses the inceptive use.

[9] Compare e.g. *Lac.* 3.5.

[10] See Raaflaub in Connor (ed.) (1990). See also Canfora (1980) 79–90.

deliberate pursuit of profit. His engagement with the audience marks passages of special controversy, such as the hot topic of *eunomia* (1.8–9), the freedom of slaves (1.10–12), the vast number of judicial processes that the *demos* needs to undertake (3.6–7). The readers in fact assume various identities apart from the second person; the objections also come from 'some people', 'a person' (1.4, 6, 7, 11, 3.6–7). In the end the author raises his own criticism, and then answers it, representing the debate as an internal monologue (3.10).

Ath. follows the introduction to the work with a justification of the rule of the *demos*, which is their importance to the naval enterprise that is the foundation of Athenian power (1.2). The author does not explain its origins. Isocrates, *Panath.* 12.114–18 says that those who introduced the radical democracy wanted sea power to defend themselves against the Spartans. They saw that this meant relying on the masses to row the ships, and recognizing their contribution by giving them power in politics to exploit the empire, which would ruin the ancestral constitution, but they preferred, he says, to rule others unjustly than be ruled by Sparta. *Ath.* in contrast, presents naval power not as a tool to be used against the Spartans, but one that secures the profits of the *demos* at home and abroad.

The first sections concentrate on the *demos'* control of the magistracies, assembly and council through the ballot and the vote and the freedom to speak. They let the rich hold the military offices that preserve their security, while they hold those that carry payment (1.3). They 'increase' their own numbers and remedy their poverty in this way, on the understanding that like supports like, whereas the rich and good are their enemies (1.4–7). Their political domination preserves their freedom to do what they like (a pleasure), and wards off enslavement to the few (a pain), which would be the outcome under the *eunomia* of a 'best' constitution (1.8–9).

Their rejection of the possibility of being enslaved to the 'best' under *eunomia* raises their own excessively generous treatment of real slaves (and other non-citizens: 1.10–12). The paradox is that they rely on them for their personal profit to the point where they become slaves of these inferiors even though they refused to become slaves of their betters. Their pursuit of profit continues in their abolition of the private practice of gymnastics and athletics, in which they cannot participate because of their poverty and ignorance. Instead they promote the liturgies, in which they are supervised by the wealthy and secure profit from them through paid participation (1.13).

The sections summarized so far already reveal a problematic feature of *Ath.*: that the author describes the will of the *demos*, so that he indicates what they 'allow' and do not allow or what 'is possible' and what is not, rather than specifying the laws they introduce. Often, as in their measures about comic writers (2.18), there is the impression that the author is speaking of the pressure of their public opinion rather than law. References to νόμος can indicate general 'custom' rather than legislation (1.10, 18). There is the same kind of tension between custom and law as in *Lac.*

The profits that the *demos* secures from their allied *poleis* are next addressed (1.14–20). They increase the power of the *demoi* in these *poleis* just as they increase their own, securing profit for themselves by misappropriating the farms of the wealthy through judicial extortion, and forcing their original owners to work them on their behalf. They make the rich come to Athens for trial and add to their own judicial burden, but they secure profits from their 'visitors', renting out accommodation and other 'tourist' services, and enjoying their flattery in the law courts (1.18). Some further incidental profits arise. Because of their personal supervision of their overseas properties, they have learned to manage ships without formal learning, and this has assisted them in their naval domination (1.19–20).

Their treatment of the allies gives rise to consideration of their cultivation of sea power, the general advantages of sea power over land power in controlling allies, and how they use it to coerce their allies into paying the tribute (their major cash crop: 2.1–5). This is the earliest analysis we have of the connection between democracy and sea power and empire. Thucydides develops many of the same ideas in Pericles' contrast of the land and sea powers' strengths and weaknesses (1.141–4, 2.62–5), but from the perspective of the war with Sparta, while *Ath.* develops them solely to prove their profit for the *demos*.[11] So that whereas in Thucydides the Athenians gained their naval expertise only through hard training, the *demos* of *Ath.* has gained it merely through constant visits to their overseas properties (1.19–20). And whereas in Thucydides the inferiority of Athenian hoplites is an accident of history, the *demos* of *Ath.* has deliberately diminished them (2.1), calculating only what they need to control their allies. Nor does *Ath.* connect sea power with the need for capital expenditure as Thucydides does; rather the profits of empire go to the poor (1.15), and they avoid the expense of sending out the fleet if they can (1.16).

This section ends with the advantage they have through sea power in surviving local famine, and in enjoying imported food and other luxuries (2.6–8). The author then explains how they organize religion to secure access to sacrificial feasts, and establish public baths for their own pleasure (2.9–10). Their enjoyment of world-market commodities, particularly the materials for shipbuilding, is another advantage of their domination of the seas (2.11–12). Pericles famously indicates the advantage for a sea power to be based on an island and urges the Athenians to evacuate their land and become such an island, so that they will not need to face the Spartans on land (Thuc. 1.143.5), but the *demos* of *Ath.* gain their advantage even out of the prospect of enemy invasion (2.13–16); for while the lands of the rich remain subject to invasion the *demos* lives without fear by evacuating its possessions offshore. Thucydides 2.65.2 confirms in this case that the wealthy classes did suffer greater losses than the *demos*, since they had more property to begin with.

Their attitude to alliances and sworn agreements is next addressed, and is followed by an account of their restrictions on comic writers. The link between these apparently disparate topics is that they escape blame for renouncing alliances that they subsequently do not like by putting the blame for the original agreement on the individuals who proposed the motion and put it to the vote, just as they escape the censure of comic writers by turning their attacks against rich individuals (2.17–18).

---

[11] See Frisch (1942) 63–87 on sea power and defensive theory.

Their deliberate attacks on the rich indicate that they recognize the good, but prefer to suppress them. An analysis follows of four types of political preferences: the natural preference of the *demos* for democracy, and of their enemies for their own kinds of constitution, and the perverted preferences of those who do not run true to their own kind (2.19–20).

The final section of the work addresses the vast amount of administration necessary to secure the 'goods' that have been described (3.1–9). The introduction suggests a division within the work between the 'preservation' of the constitution and 'administration' of it, but the administration of the *demos* also secures its preservation. The impossibility of reforming the system without destroying it leads to consideration of the *demos*' good sense in supporting *demoi* in allied *poleis*. Their occasional support for the rich in other *poleis* has meant the enslavement of the *demoi* and loss of their own advantage (3.10–11). The work ends with the demonstration that there is no threat from their own ἄτιμοι (3.12–13); this is a logical conclusion to a work that focuses on the *demos*' preservation.

THE AUTHOR

The author cannot be identified, but his rhetorical *persona* can be reconstructed. He twice expresses his *prohairesis* (i.e. his deliberate moral and intellectual preference for the better over the worse): 'I do not praise the democracy' (1.1, 3.1), and he admires *eunomia* because it restrains the freedom of the many (1.8–9). This has earned him the name 'The Old Oligarch'. He seems to be an Athenian, since he knows his naval terminology as they are said to do (1.2, 2.19), uses the technical language of Attic official business (3 *passim*), and, although he refers mostly to the *demos* as 'them' (1.1), in a series of passages, he merges his identity with theirs and accepts responsibility for their practices (1.10–12, 2.10–12). He thus refers to how 'we' have given rights to metics because of their value in securing the power of the fleet (1.12), and he continues in his own voice the argument started by the Athenians when they 'reason out an answer in response' to their critics (1.16). He seems to identify himself with the *demos* again when he says that the Athenians have great wealth because they control the sea and its exchange, particularly building materials for ships (timber, pitch, linen, metals): 'There are ships *for me*' from these materials, and 'though making nothing from the land, I have all these materials through the sea' (2.11–12 οὐδὲν ποιῶν ἐκ τῆς γῆς πάντα ταῦτα ἔχω διὰ τὴν θάλατταν) – whereas no single land naturally produces even two of them. This statement could be pressed to say that he owns ships, merchant or military, that he does not possess land or that it fails to produce, and that he makes his living from ships, possibly as a *naukleros*. But another meaning of 'making nothing from the land' in the context of shipbuilding materials is that he 'produces' none of these (*Mem.* 2.7.2: λαμβάνομεν δὲ οὔτε ἐκ τῆς γῆς οὐδέν), and since it would be absurd for one individual to produce all such materials from his own private land, he must be speaking as a member of the collective, and the land to which he refers is the whole of Attica.[12] The ships are not merchant vessels, but those triremes that constitute the naval power on which the security and the prosperity of Athens are based, and which are such an important focus of parts of the work. His possession is public rather than private; each individual Athenian such as he enjoys what no other entire city enjoys. *Ath.* often stresses the profit that accrues to the individual within the collective (1.15; 2.9–10). The identification of our upright author with the base collective must of course carry a degree of irony, but he seems to be still an Athenian.

His references to Athens as αὐτόθι (1.2, 10, 11, 13; 3.1, 6) could indicate that he was living outside Athens, but in other contexts the word can mean either 'here' or 'there' equally.[13] Ar. *Knights* 118–120 uses φέρ' ἴδω τί ἄρ' ἔνεστιν αὐτόθι to mean 'here' of something very near at hand. *Mem.* 2.8.1 uses αὐτόθεν to mean 'here' in the mouth of a man who is resident in Athens, as opposed to 'overseas'. In *Cyr.* 6.2.31 it means 'on the spot'. Sometimes it is used with a place-name, as in αὐτόθι ἐν Σπάρτηι; *Ath.* also uses it near Ἀθήνηισιν: 1.10. Herodotus contrasts αὐτόθι with other places: 4.192.2 'there are the same beasts in this land as in any other': ταῦτά τε δὴ αὐτόθι ἐστὶ θηρία καὶ τά περ τῆι ἄλληι. *Ath.* 2.7 also contrasts Athens with ἄλλοθι. Thucydides uses οἱ αὐτόθεν for 'the people of the locality' (2.25.3).

The author's integrity has also been questioned, on the grounds that he should not be living in a democracy if he cannot praise it. Indeed, critics hoist him with his own petard when he withdraws sympathy from one who though 'not being of the *demos*' has 'chosen' (εἵλετο) to 'live in' (οἰκεῖν) a democratic *polis* rather than an oligarchic *polis* (2.19–20); this man, he says, has deliberately prepared himself for a life of base pursuits, hoping to escape attention among the many others who are base in the democracy. To rescue the Old Oligarch from a life abroad, or from his own charge of being a deliberate criminal, the infinitive 'live in' has been interpreted as active participation in the democracy, but this restricts the meaning too far. The weight seems rather to fall on the positive preference of such a person for democracy. *Prohairesis* is the issue, the deliberate moral and intellectual preference for the better over the worse. This 'choice' is the aim of the pursuit of virtue through dialectical categorization of the better and worse (*Mem.* 4.5.11). The author has shown his preference in the introduction in refusing to praise the democracy. The criminal to whom he refers has to the contrary demonstrated the *prohairesis* of men like those who, for example, positively preferred the criminal system of tyranny to freedom (*Hiero* 5.2). The author confirms that he does not share this criminal preference when he immediately follows his condemnation with a restatement of his own deliberate choice: 'I do not praise this constitution.' So that it is respectable for the author to live under the democratic constitution, as long as he issues pamphlets against it and advertises its corruption to the wider world.

---

[12] Frisch (1942) on 2.12 prefers this interpretation, and de Romilly (1962) 236 n.2.
[13] Frisch (1942) 92–4.

IN CONTRAST TO XENOPHON

Luccioni (1947) 108–36 makes a case to support his claim that Xenophon is 'adversaire de la démocratie athénienne', but his works offer such a favourable representation of democracy that he could never be this Old Oligarch (see pp. 17–18). This is borne out by the comparison of *Ath.* with Xenophon's *Poroi* on imperialism. *Ath.* had indicated that the *demos* knew the good, but deliberately chose the bad (2.19), and ruled the allied *poleis* in their own interests to remedy their poverty. *Poroi* 1.1 presents this as the policy that their champions (προστάται) were compelled to adopt: 'they recognize justice no less than other men, but said that they were compelled by the poverty of the masses to be more unjust toward the allied cities.' The compulsion makes their injustice less deliberately criminal than in *Ath.* The other difference is that whereas *Ath.* could see no other remedy for their poverty, and the *demos* desired none, Xenophon proposes a range of practical suggestions designed to make Athens economically self-sufficient and no longer needing to practise injustice against the allies. He will not tolerate the idea in *Ath.* that class conflict is the inevitable product of poverty; his best paradigm, Cyrus, promotes the common good and enriches the common man (see pp. 11–12). *Poroi* endorses this when it concludes that the wealthy few, who will enjoy the economic miracle alongside the *demos*, will willingly put their increased resources at the disposal of the *polis*:

> If nothing of these arrangements is impossibly difficult, if they are achieved, we will be more beloved by the Greeks, live in greater security, have better repute, and the *demos* will have an abundance of food, and the rich will be relieved of their expenditure on war, and with a great excess of capital, we as a community will be able to conduct festivals even more magnificent than now, built temples, erect walls and shipyards, and give their ancestral rights back to priests and council and magistrates and cavalry. (6.1)

In main outline then, while Xenophon sees the injustice of the democracy as the product of the ignorance of its leaders, *Ath.* sees it as the deliberate engineering of the masses, and whereas *Ath.* can see no alternative, Xenophon is full of ideas and optimism for a just society, as much with this democracy as with the tyrant in *Hiero*. He becomes a Socrates, taking in hand the limitations of those like the young Glaucon, who also wished to govern the Athenians but did not have the economic knowledge required for the job (*Mem.* 3.6).

In matters of detail too, the differences arise. *Ath.* 1.12 deplores the generous treatment given to metics for the profit of the *demos*, but *Poroi* 2.1–7 champions their cause, not for the profit of the *demos*, but of the entire *polis*. It suggests that they share in honour as far as is good for the *polis*, be spared military service and allowed to buy up vacant land, and that an immigration office be set up to see to their recruitment and well-being. It recognizes that they cost the *polis* nothing, bring in business and actually pay tax for the privilege. *Ath.* does not mention this tax, but is intent only on those profits that come to individuals or that degrade the *demos*.

There is a difference too in their explanations of how Athens enjoys the wealth of the world as a market for export and import. *Ath.* 2.3, 11–12 says that she exploits by force her total dominion of the seas, Xenophon mentions the attraction of her location and her facilities (*Poroi* 1.6–8, 3.1–5). And whereas of course *Ath.* assumes that the *demos* does not abide by its sworn agreements (2.17), Xenophon insists that they remained true to these down to his own times (*Hell.* 2.4.42).

Poroi is in short a monument to Xenophon's good intentions and a sample of his creative thinking about the improvement of constitutions. His Socrates may not have been a complete democrat. He did not approve of the use of the ballot to choose the officers of the democracy (*Mem.* 1.2.9), but he saw, contrary to *Ath.* 1.5–6, that election and public debate often produced a wise choice (*Mem.* 3.4 for example, where he defends the *demos*' election to military office of a businessman rather than a warrior, and *Mem.* 3.6, where the *demos* has rightly laughed the young Glaucon off the speaker's platform). He was capable of calling the masses 'most weak and silly', but only when in conversation with one who needed to have his fear of their opinion of him dismissed (*Mem.* 3.7, where he encourages a man to serve the *demos* though he fears their ridicule). However, he was strictly obedient to the laws and their officers (*Mem.* 4.4.1–4) and, as the sequence of conversations shows in *Mem.* 3.1–7, strictly positive in encouraging those he educated to serve the democracy rather than merely to express the 'politics of dissent'.[14] Xenophon offers such service himself in *Poroi*.

THE DATE

Apart from the impression that the prose style is early (pp. 27–9), internal evidence has suggested a range of dates of composition, from before the Peloponnesian War (Bowersock (1966) 33–55) to the period of the War (Gomme: (1940)), down even to the fourth century (Roscalla (1995)).[15] The constant reference to Athenian control of the sea suggests the fifth century (1.11,15; 2.1–7, 2.11), references to events that occurred in the middle of the fifth century (3.11) bring the date down to the 440s BC and a strict interpretation of the reference to the imperial tribute (2.1; 3.2, 5) dates it to before 413 BC when this was abolished (Thuc. 7.28.4).

The evidence for a more precise date is open to debate because it relies mainly on implications in discussions that seem to be theoretical. The reference to the theoretical advantages of occupying headlands (2.13) has suggested specific events such as the Athenian occupation of the headland of Pylos in 425 BC; the theoretical idea that long journeys overland are impossible for land powers (2.5) has suggested that the author did not know of the march of Brasidas through Thrace in 424 BC. But the author of *Ath.* might have ignored isolated instances that failed to uphold his theory, just as Xenophon in *Cyropaedia* ignored the seventy years of Athenian democracy when he

---

[14] See Gray (2004a).
[15] Frisch (1942) 47–62 surveys the main arguments for dating. Hornblower (2000) also favours a fourth-century date.

maintained that no democracies have lasted any significant time. In the discussion of comedy, the ban on attacking the *demos* has suggested the time Aristophanes was reprimanded for satirizing the *demos* in *Babylonians* (426 BC) or *Knights* (424 BC), but the ban could simply represent the informal attitude of the *demos* or a theoretical stance over a longer time.

Ath. gives the general impression of peacetime conditions, and certainly no clear impression of a war in progress. Attempts to find the Peloponnesian War in references to 'the enemies' or 'the war' (2.4, 2.12, 3.2) have proven unconvincing. The lack of reference to the plague suggests a situation before the War, but the author might not mention this because it countered his view that the *demos* had arranged everything to secure their profit. The plague proved that their sea power brought its own disadvantages, because it came to Athens by sea (Thuc. 2.48.1). The remark that the rich are obliged to court the enemy for fear of invasion and that the *demos* transfers their goods to the islands in the face of invasion and 'looks on while their land is laid waste' sounds more like a description of wartime reality (2.16). Thucydides says that Athenians en masse evacuated the countryside and 'looked on' while the Spartans invaded (2.18.5, 20.2, 21.2) in the first part of the Peloponnesian War. However, these tactics may have been thought by the author of *Ath.* to be manifest during the Persian invasions and occupation of Attica, or the troubled times of the First Peloponnesian War, when invasion again became a reality (Thuc. 1.114.2). The Spartans are said to have merely 'looked on' in the Persian invasions of Attica in the Persian Wars (Hdt. 9.6–7) – which makes this a *topos*.

XENOPHON
HIERO

Note on text

Information about the readings of the manuscripts and the majority of conjectures comes from Marchant's edition. The apparatus that accompanies the text is extremely selective, and silence should never be assumed to imply that the tradition is unanimous; those seeking more detailed information should consult Persson (1915), Marchant (1920), Pierleoni (1937) and Bowersock (1966/1968).

The sigla adopted are as follows:

D The only reading found in the manuscripts that provide our direct evidence for the text.

d One of two or more readings found in the manuscripts that provide our direct evidence of the text.

i A reading found in the quotations, or suggested by the paraphrases and allusions, that provide our indirect evidence for the text.

c A reading found neither in our direct nor in our indirect evidence, but conjectured out of dissatisfaction with the readings found there.

ΙΕΡΩΝ
Η ΤΥΡΑΝΝΙΚΟΣ

Σιμωνίδης ὁ ποιητὴς ἀφίκετό ποτε πρὸς Ἱέρωνα τὸν τύραννον. **1**
σχολῆς δὲ γενομένης ἀμφοῖν εἶπεν ὁ Σιμωνίδης· Ἆρ' ἄν μοι ἐθελήσαις,
ὦ Ἱέρων, διηγήσασθαι ἃ εἰκὸς εἰδέναι σε βέλτιον ἐμοῦ; Καὶ ποῖα
ταῦτ' ἐστίν, ἔφη ὁ Ἱέρων, ὁποῖα δὴ ἐγὼ βέλτιον ἂν εἰδείην σοῦ οὕτως
5 ὄντος σοφοῦ ἀνδρός; Οἶδά σε, ἔφη, ἐγὼ καὶ ἰδιώτην γεγενημένον καὶ **2**
νῦν τύραννον ὄντα· εἰκὸς οὖν ἀμφοτέρων πεπειραμένον καὶ εἰδέναι
σε μᾶλλον ἐμοῦ πῆι διαφέρει ὁ τυραννικός τε καὶ ὁ ἰδιωτικὸς βίος
εἰς εὐφροσύνας τε καὶ λύπας ἀνθρώποις. Τί οὖν, ἔφη ὁ Ἱέρων, οὐχὶ **3**
καὶ σύ, ἐπεὶ νῦν γε ἔτι ἰδιώτης εἶ, ὑπέμνησάς με τὰ ἐν τῶι ἰδιωτικῶι
10 βίωι; οὕτως γὰρ ἄν σοι οἶμαι μάλιστα ἐγὼ δύνασθαι δηλοῦν τὰ
διαφέροντα ἐν ἑκατέρωι. οὕτω δὴ ὁ Σιμωνίδης εἶπεν· Τοὺς μὲν δὴ **4**
ἰδιώτας ἔγωγε, ὦ Ἱέρων, δοκῶ μοι καταμεμαθηκέναι διὰ μὲν τῶν
ὀφθαλμῶν ὁράμασιν ἡδομένους τε καὶ ἀχθομένους, διὰ δὲ τῶν ὤτων
ἀκούσμασι, διὰ δὲ τῶν ῥινῶν ὀσμαῖς, διὰ δὲ τοῦ στόματος σίτοις τε
15 καὶ ποτοῖς, τὰ δ' ἀφροδίσια δι' ὧν δὴ πάντες ἐπιστάμεθα· τὰ δὲ ψύχη **5**
καὶ θάλπη καὶ σκληρὰ καὶ μαλακὰ καὶ κοῦφα καὶ βαρέα ὅλωι τῶι
σώματί μοι δοκοῦμεν, ἔφη, κρίνοντες ἥδεσθαί τε καὶ λυπεῖσθαι ἐπ'
αὐτοῖς· ἀγαθοῖς δὲ καὶ κακοῖς ἔστι μὲν ὅτε δι' αὐτῆς τῆς ψυχῆς μοι
δοκοῦμεν ἥδεσθαι, ὁτὲ δ' αὖ λυπεῖσθαι, ἔστι δ' ὅτε κοινῆι διά τε τῆς
20 ψυχῆς καὶ διὰ τοῦ σώματος. τῶι δ' ὕπνωι ὅτι μὲν ἡδόμεθα δοκῶ μοι **6**
αἰσθάνεσθαι, ὅπως δὲ καὶ ὧιτινι καὶ ὁπότε, ταῦτα μᾶλλόν πως, ἔφη,
δοκῶ μοι ἀγνοεῖν. καὶ οὐδὲν ἴσως τοῦτο θαυμαστόν, εἰ τὰ ἐν τῶι
ἐγρηγορέναι σαφεστέρας ἡμῖν τὰς αἰσθήσεις παρέχεται ἢ τὰ ἐν τῶι
ὕπνωι. πρὸς ταῦτα δὴ ὁ Ἱέρων ἀπεκρίνατο· Ἐγὼ μὲν τοίνυν, ἔφη, **7**
25 ὦ Σιμωνίδη, ἔξω τούτων ὧν εἴρηκας σύγε οὐδ' ὅπως ἂν αἴσθοιτό
τινος ἄλλου ὁ τύραννος ἔχοιμ' ἂν εἰπεῖν, ὥστε μέχρι γε τούτου οὐκ
οἶδ' εἴ τινι διαφέρει ὁ τυραννικὸς βίος τοῦ ἰδιωτικοῦ βίου. καὶ ὁ **8**
Σιμωνίδης εἶπεν· Ἀλλ' ἐν τοῖσδε, ἔφη, διαφέρει· πολλαπλάσια μὲν
δι' ἑκάστου τούτων εὐφραίνεται, πολὺ δὲ μείω τὰ λυπηρὰ ἔχει.
30 καὶ ὁ Ἱέρων εἶπεν· Οὐχ οὕτως ἔχει, ὦ Σιμωνίδη, ταῦτα, ἀλλ' εὖ ἴσθ'
ὅτι μείω πολὺ εὐφραίνονται οἱ τύραννοι τῶν μετρίως διαγόντων
ἰδιωτῶν, πολὺ δὲ πλείω καὶ μείζω λυποῦνται. Ἄπιστα λέγεις, **9**

19 κοινῆι i: καὶ κοινῆι d: καὶ d

61

ἔφη ὁ Σιμωνίδης. εἰ γὰρ οὕτως ταῦτ' εἶχε, πῶς ἂν πολλοὶ μὲν
ἐπεθύμουν τυραννεῖν, καὶ ταῦτα τῶν δοκούντων ἱκανωτάτων
10 ἀνδρῶν εἶναι; πῶς δὲ πάντες ἐζήλουν ἂν τοὺς τυράννους; Ὅτι
ναὶ μὰ τὸν Δί, ἔφη ὁ Ἱέρων, ἄπειροι ὄντες ἀμφοτέρων τῶν ἔργων
σκοποῦνται περὶ αὐτοῦ. ἐγὼ δὲ πειράσομαί σε διδάσκειν ὅτι 5
ἀληθῆ λέγω, ἀρξάμενος ἀπὸ τῆς ὄψεως· ἐντεῦθεν γὰρ καὶ σὲ δοκῶ
11 μεμνῆσθαι ἀρξάμενον λέγειν. πρῶτον μὲν γὰρ ἐν τοῖς διὰ τῆς ὄψεως
θεάμασι λογιζόμενος εὑρίσκω μειονεκτοῦντας τοὺς τυράννους.
ἄλλα μέν γε ἐν ἄλληι χώραι ἐστὶν ἀξιοθέατα· ἐπὶ δὲ τούτων ἔκαστα οἱ μὲν
ἰδιῶται ἔρχονται καὶ εἰς πόλεις ἃς ἂν βούλωνται θεαμάτων ἔνεκα, 10
καὶ εἰς τὰς κοινὰς πανηγύρεις, ἔνθα γ' ἃ ἀξιοθεατότατα δοκεῖ εἶναι
ἀνθρώποις συναγείρεται. οἱ δὲ τύραννοι οὐ μάλα ἀμφὶ θεωρίας
12 ἔχουσιν. οὔτε γὰρ ἰέναι αὐτοῖς ἀσφαλὲς ὅπου μὴ κρείττονες τῶν
παρόντων μέλλουσιν ἔσεσθαι, οὔτε τὰ οἴκοι κέκτηνται ἐχυρά,
ὥστε ἄλλοις παρακαταθεμένους ἀποδημεῖν. φοβερὸν γὰρ μὴ ἅμα 15
τε στερηθῶσι τῆς ἀρχῆς καὶ ἀδύνατοι γένωνται τιμωρήσασθαι
13 τοὺς ἀδικήσαντας. εἴποις οὖν ἂν ἴσως σύ, ἀλλ' ἄρα ἔρχεται αὐτοῖς
τὰ τοιαῦτα καὶ οἴκοι μένουσι. ναὶ μὰ Δία, ὦ Σιμωνίδη, ὀλίγα γε
τῶν πολλῶν καὶ ταῦτα τοιαῦτα ὄντα οὕτω τίμια πωλεῖται τοῖς
τυράννοις ὥστε οἱ ἐπιδεικνύμενοι καὶ ὁτιοῦν ἀξιοῦσι πολλαπλάσια 20
λαβόντες ἐν ὀλίγωι χρόνωι ἀπιέναι παρὰ τοῦ τυράννου ἢ ὅσα ἐν
14 παντὶ τῶι βίωι παρὰ πάντων τῶν ἄλλων ἀνθρώπων κτῶνται. καὶ
ὁ Σιμωνίδης εἶπεν· Ἀλλ' εἰ ἐν τοῖς θεάμασι μειονεκτεῖτε, διά γέ τοι
τῆς ἀκοῆς πλεονεκτεῖτε. ἐπεὶ τοῦ μὲν ἡδίστου ἀκροάματος, ἐπαίνου,
οὔποτε σπανίζετε· πάντες γὰρ οἱ παρόντες ὑμῖν πάντα καὶ ὅσα 25
ἂν λέγητε καὶ ὅσα ἂν ποιῆτε ἐπαινοῦσι. τοῦ δ' αὖ χαλεπωτάτου
ἀκροάματος, λοιδορίας, ἀνήκοοί ἐστε· οὐδεὶς γὰρ ἐθέλει τυράννου
15 κατ' ὀφθαλμοὺς κατηγορεῖν. καὶ ὁ Ἱέρων εἶπε· Καὶ τί οἴει, ἔφη, τοὺς
μὴ λέγοντας κακῶς εὐφραίνειν, ὅταν εἰδῆι τις σαφῶς ὅτι οἱ σιω-
πῶντες οὗτοι πάντες κακὰ νοοῦσι τῶι τυράννωι; ἢ τοὺς ἐπαινοῦντας 30
τί δοκεῖς εὐφραίνειν, ὅταν ὕποπτοι ὦσιν ἕνεκα τοῦ κολακεύειν τοὺς
16 ἐπαίνους ποιεῖσθαι; καὶ ὁ Σιμωνίδης εἶπεν· Τοῦτο μὲν δὴ ναὶ μὰ τὸν
Δία ἔγωγέ σοι, Ἱέρων, πάνυ συγχωρῶ, τοὺς ἐπαίνους παρὰ τῶν
ἐλευθερωτάτων ἡδίστους εἶναι, ἀλλ', ὁρᾶις; ἐκεῖνό γε οὐκ ἂν ἔτι
πείσαις ἀνθρώπων οὐδένα ὡς οὐ δι' ὧν τρεφόμεθα οἱ ἄνθρωποι, πολὺ 35
17 πλείω ὑμεῖς ἐν αὐτοῖς εὐφραίνεσθε. Καὶ οἶδά γ', ἔφη, ὦ Σιμωνίδη,
ὅτι τούτωι κρίνουσιν οἱ πλεῖστοι ἥδιον ἡμᾶς καὶ πίνειν καὶ ἐσθίειν
τῶν ἰδιωτῶν, ὅτι δοκοῦσι καὶ αὐτοὶ ἥδιον ἂν δειπνῆσαι τὸ ἡμῖν

παρατιθέμενον δεῖπνον ἢ τὸ ἑαυτοῖς· τὸ γὰρ τὰ εἰωθότα ὑπερβάλ-
λον, τοῦτο παρέχει τὰς ἡδονάς. διὸ καὶ πάντες ἄνθρωποι ἡδέως 18
προσδέχονται τὰς ἑορτὰς πλὴν οἱ τύραννοι· ἔκπλεωι γὰρ αὐτοῖς
ἀεὶ παρεσκευασμέναι οὐδεμίαν ἐν ταῖς ἑορταῖς ἔχουσιν αἱ τράπεζαι
5 αὐτῶν ἐπίδοσιν· ὥστε ταύτηι πρῶτον τῆι εὐφροσύνηι τῆς ἐλπίδος
μειονεκτοῦσι τῶν ἰδιωτῶν. ἔπειτα δ᾽, ἔφη, ἐκεῖνο εὖ οἶδ᾽ ὅτι καὶ σὺ 19
ἔμπειρος εἶ ὅτι ὅσωι ἂν πλείω τις παραθῆται τὰ περιττὰ τῶν ἱκανῶν,
τοσούτωι καὶ θᾶττον κόρος ἐμπίπτει τῆς ἐδωδῆς· ὥστε καὶ τῶι
χρόνωι τῆς ἡδονῆς μειονεκτεῖ ὁ παρατιθέμενος πολλὰ τῶν
10 μετρίως διαιτωμένων. Ἀλλὰ ναὶ μὰ Δί᾽, ἔφη ὁ Σιμωνίδης, ὅσον ἂν 20
χρόνον ἡ ψυχὴ προσίηται, τοῦτον πολὺ μᾶλλον ἥδονται οἱ ταῖς
πολυτελεστέραις παρασκευαῖς τρεφόμενοι τῶν τὰ εὐτελέστερα
παρατιθεμένων. Οὐκοῦν, ἔφη ὁ Ἱέρων, ὦ Σιμωνίδη, τὸν ἑκάστωι 21
ἡδόμενον μάλιστα, τοῦτον οἴει καὶ ἐρωτικώτατα ἔχειν τοῦ ἔργου
15 τούτου; Πάνυ μὲν οὖν, ἔφη. Ἦ οὖν ὁρᾷς τι τοὺς τυράννους ἥδιον
ἐπὶ τὴν ἑαυτῶν παρασκευὴν ἰόντας ἢ τοὺς ἰδιώτας ἐπὶ τὴν ἑαυτῶν;
Οὐ μὰ τὸν Δί᾽, ἔφη, οὐ μὲν οὖν, ἀλλὰ καὶ ἀγλευκέστερον, ὡς πολλοῖς
ἂν δόξειεν. Τί γάρ, ἔφη ὁ Ἱέρων, τὰ πολλὰ ταῦτα μηχανήματα 22
κατανενόηκας ἃ παρατίθεται τοῖς τυράννοις, ὀξέα καὶ δριμέα καὶ
20 στρυφνὰ καὶ τὰ τούτων ἀδελφά; Πάνυ μὲν οὖν, ἔφη ὁ Σιμωνίδης,
καὶ πάνυ γέ μοι δοκοῦντα παρὰ φύσιν εἶναι ταῦτα ἀνθρώποις.
Ἄλλο τι οὖν οἴει, ἔφη ὁ Ἱέρων, ταῦτα τὰ ἐδέσματα εἶναι ἢ μαλακῆς 23
καὶ ἀσθενούσης ψυχῆς ἐπιθυμήματα; ἐπεὶ εὖ οἶδ᾽ ἔγωγε ὅτι οἱ ἡδέως
ἐσθίοντες καὶ σύ που οἶσθα ὅτι οὐδὲν προσδέονται τούτων τῶν
25 σοφισμάτων. Ἀλλὰ μέντοι, ἔφη ὁ Σιμωνίδης, τῶν γε πολυτελῶν 24
ὀσμῶν τούτων, αἷς χρίεσθε, τοὺς πλησιάζοντας οἶμαι μᾶλλον
ἀπολαύειν ἢ αὐτοὺς ὑμᾶς, ὥσπερ γε καὶ τῶν ἀχαρίτων ὀσμῶν οὐκ
αὐτὸς ὁ βεβρωκὼς αἰσθάνεται, ἀλλὰ μᾶλλον οἱ πλησιάζοντες. Οὕτω 25
μέντοι, ἔφη ὁ Ἱέρων, καὶ τῶν σίτων ὁ μὲν ἔχων παντοδαπὰ ἀεὶ οὐδὲν
30 μετὰ πόθου αὐτῶν λαμβάνει· ὁ δὲ σπανίσας τινός, οὗτός ἐστιν ὁ
μετὰ χαρᾶς πιμπλάμενος, ὅταν αὐτῶι προφανῆι τι. Κινδυνεύουσιν, 26
ἔφη ὁ Σιμωνίδης, αἱ τῶν ἀφροδισίων μόνον ὑμῖν ἀπολαύσεις τοῦ
τυραννεῖν τὰς ἐπιθυμίας παρέχειν· ἐν γὰρ τούτωι ἔξεστιν ὑμῖν
ὅ τι ἂν κάλλιστον ἴδητε τούτωι συνεῖναι. Νῦν δή, ἔφη ὁ Ἱέρων, 27
35 εἴρηκας ἐν ὧι γε, σάφ᾽ ἴσθι, μειονεκτοῦμεν τῶν ἰδιωτῶν. πρῶτον
μὲν γὰρ γάμος ὁ μὲν ἐκ μειζόνων δήπου καὶ πλούτωι καὶ δυνάμει
κάλλιστος δοκεῖ εἶναι καὶ παρέχειν τινὰ τῶι γήμαντι φιλοτιμίαν μεθ᾽

---

4 παρεσκευασμέναι i: -α D   9 ἡδονῆς i: ἐδωδῆς Di   17 ἀγλευκέστερον i: ἀγλυκέσ-
τερον D   23 ψυχῆς i: τρυφῆι ψυχῆς d: τρυφῆς ψυχῆς d   35 γε c: δὴ i: δὲ d:
om. d

64 ΞΕΝΟΦΩΝΤΟΣ

ἡδονῆς· δεύτερος δ' ὁ ἐκ τῶν ὁμοίων· ὁ δ' ἐκ τῶν φαυλοτέρων
28 πάνυ ἄτιμός τε καὶ ἄχρηστος νομίζεται. τῶι τοίνυν τυράννωι, ἂν
μὴ ξένην γήμηι, ἀνάγκη ἐκ μειόνων γαμεῖν, ὥστε τὸ ἀγαπητὸν
οὐ πάνυ αὐτῶι παραγίγνεται. πολὺ δὲ καὶ αἱ θεραπεῖαι αἱ ἀπὸ
τῶν μέγιστον φρονουσῶν γυναικῶν εὐφραίνουσι μάλιστα, αἱ 5
δ' ὑπὸ δούλων παροῦσαι μὲν οὐδέν τι ἀγαπῶνται, ἐὰν δέ τι
29 ἐλλείπωσι, δεινὰς ὀργὰς καὶ λύπας ἐμποιοῦσιν. ἐν δὲ τοῖς παιδικοῖς
ἀφροδισίοις ἔτι αὖ πολὺ μᾶλλον ἢ ἐν τοῖς τεκνοποιοῖς μειονεκτεῖ
τῶν εὐφροσυνῶν ὁ τύραννος. ὅτι μὲν γὰρ τὰ μετ' ἔρωτος ἀφροδίσια
30 πολὺ διαφερόντως εὐφραίνει πάντες δήπου ἐπιστάμεθα· ὁ δὲ ἔρως 10
πολὺ αὖ ἐθέλει ἥκιστα τῶι τυράννωι ἐγγίγνεσθαι. οὐ γὰρ τῶν
ἑτοίμων ἥδεται ὁ ἔρως ἐφιέμενος, ἀλλὰ τῶν ἐλπιζομένων. ὥσπερ
οὖν τις ἄπειρος ὢν δίψους τοῦ πιεῖν οὐκ ἂν ἀπολαύοι, οὕτω καὶ ὁ
ἄπειρος ὢν ἔρωτος ἄπειρός ἐστι τῶν ἡδίστων ἀφροδισίων. ὁ μὲν
31 οὖν Ἱέρων οὕτως εἶπεν. ὁ δὲ Σιμωνίδης ἐπιγελάσας, Πῶς λέγεις, ἔφη, 15
ὦ Ἱέρων; τυράννωι οὐ φὴις παιδικῶν ἔρωτας ἐμφύεσθαι; πῶς μὴν
32 σύ, ἔφη, ἐρᾶις Δαϊλόχου τοῦ καλλίστου ἐπικαλουμένου; Ὅτι μὰ
τὸν Δί', ἔφη, ὦ Σιμωνίδη, οὐ τοῦ ἑτοίμου παρ' αὐτοῦ δοκοῦντός
εἶναι τυχεῖν τούτου μάλιστα ἐπιθυμῶ, ἀλλὰ τοῦ ἥκιστα τυράννωι
33 προσήκοντος κατεργάσασθαι. ἐγὼ γὰρ δὴ ἐρῶ μὲν Δαϊλόχου 20
ὧνπερ ἴσως ἀναγκάζει ἡ φύσις ἀνθρώπου δεῖσθαι παρὰ τῶν καλῶν,
τούτων δὲ ὧν ἐρῶ τυχεῖν, μετὰ μὲν φιλίας καὶ παρὰ βουλομένου
πάνυ ἰσχυρῶς ἐπιθυμῶ τυγχάνειν, βίαι δὲ λαμβάνειν παρ' αὐτοῦ
34 ἧττον ἄν μοι δοκῶ ἐπιθυμεῖν ἢ ἐμαυτὸν κακόν τι ποιεῖν· παρὰ
μὲν γὰρ πολεμίων ἀκόντων λαμβάνειν πάντων ἥδιστον ἔγωγε 25
νομίζω εἶναι, παρὰ δὲ παιδικῶν βουλομένων ἥδισται οἶμαι αἱ
35 χάριτές εἰσιν. εὐθὺς γὰρ παρὰ τοῦ ἀντιφιλοῦντος ἡδεῖαι μὲν αἱ
ἀντιβλέψεις, ἡδεῖαι δὲ αἱ ἐρωτήσεις, ἡδεῖαι δὲ αἱ ἀποκρίσεις, ἥδισται
36 δὲ καὶ ἐπαφροδιτόταται αἱ μάχαι τε καὶ ἔριδες· τὸ δὲ ἀκόντων
παιδικῶν ἀπολαύειν λεηλασίαι, ἔφη, ἔμοιγε δοκεῖ ἐοικέναι μᾶλλον ἢ 30
ἀφροδισίοις. καίτοι τῶι μὲν ληιστῆι παρέχει τινὰς ὅμως ἡδονὰς τό τε
κέρδος καὶ τὸ ἀνιᾶν τὸν ἐχθρόν· τὸ δὲ οὗ ἂν ἐρᾶι τις τούτωι ἥδεσθαι
ἀνιωμένωι καὶ φιλοῦντα μισεῖσθαι καὶ ἅπτεσθαι ἀχθομένου, πῶς
37 οὐχὶ τοῦτο ἤδη δυσχερὲς τὸ πάθημα καὶ οἰκτρόν; καὶ γὰρ δὴ τῶι
μὲν ἰδιώτηι εὐθὺς τεκμήριόν ἐστιν, ὅταν ὁ ἐρώμενός τι ὑπουργῆι, 35
ὅτι ὡς φιλῶν χαρίζεται, διὰ τὸ εἰδέναι ὅτι οὐδεμιᾶς ἀνάγκης οὔσης
ὑπηρετεῖ, τῶι δὲ τυράννωι οὔποτ' ἔστι πιστεῦσαι ὡς φιλεῖται.
38 ἐπιστάμεθα γὰρ δὴ τοὺς διὰ φόβον ὑπηρετοῦντας ὡς ἧι μάλιστ'

1 δεύτερος c: δεύτερον D   13 τις c: εἴ τις D   38 δὴ τοὺς c: αὐτοὺς D

ἂν δύνωνται ἐξεικάζουσιν αὐτοὺς ταῖς τῶν φιλούντων ὑπουργίαις.
καὶ τοίνυν αἱ ἐπιβουλαὶ ἐξ οὐδένων πλέονες τοῖς τυράννοις εἰσὶν ἢ
ἀπὸ τῶν μάλιστα φιλεῖν αὐτοὺς προσποιησαμένων.

Πρὸς ταῦτα εἶπεν ὁ Σιμωνίδης· Ἀλλὰ ταῦτα μὲν πάνυ ἔμοιγε   2
5 μικρὰ δοκεῖ εἶναι ἃ σὺ λέγεις. πολλοὺς γάρ, ἔφη, ἔγωγε ὁρῶ τῶν
δοκούντων ἀνδρῶν εἶναι ἑκόντας μειονεκτοῦντας καὶ σίτων καὶ
ποτῶν καὶ ὄψων καὶ ἀφροδισίων γε ἀπεχομένους. ἀλλ᾽ ἐκείνηι   2
γε πολὺ διαφέρετε τῶν ἰδιωτῶν, ὅτι μεγάλα μὲν ἐπινοεῖτε, ταχὺ
δὲ κατεργάζεσθε, πλεῖστα δὲ τὰ περιττὰ ἔχετε, κέκτησθε δὲ
10 διαφέροντας μὲν ἀρετῆι ἵππους, διαφέροντα δὲ κάλλει ὅπλα,
ὑπερέχοντα δὲ κόσμον γυναιξί, μεγαλοπρεπεστάτας δ᾽ οἰκίας,
καὶ ταύτας κατεσκευασμένας τοῖς πλείστου ἀξίοις, ἔτι δὲ πλήθει
καὶ ἐπιστήμαις θεράποντας ἀρίστους κέκτησθε, ἱκανώτατοι δ᾽
ἐστὲ κακῶσαι μὲν ἐχθρούς, ὀνῆσαι δὲ φίλους. πρὸς ταῦτα δὲ ὁ   3
15 Ἱέρων εἶπεν· Ἀλλὰ τὸ μὲν τὸ πλῆθος τῶν ἀνθρώπων, ὦ Σιμωνίδη,
ἐξαπατᾶσθαι ὑπὸ τῆς τυραννίδος οὐδέν τι θαυμάζω· μάλα γὰρ
ὁ ὄχλος μοι δοκεῖ δοξάζειν ὁρῶν καὶ εὐδαίμονάς τινας εἶναι καὶ
ἀθλίους· ἡ δὲ τυραννὶς τὰ μὲν δοκοῦντα πολλοῦ ἄξια κτήματα εἶναι   4
ἀνεπτυγμένα θεᾶσθαι φανερὰ πᾶσι παρέχεται, τὰ δὲ χαλεπὰ ἐν
20 ταῖς ψυχαῖς τῶν τυράννων κέκτηται ἀποκεκρυμμένα, ἔνθαπερ καὶ
τὸ εὐδαιμονεῖν καὶ τὸ κακοδαιμονεῖν τοῖς ἀνθρώποις ἀπόκειται.
τὸ μὲν οὖν τὸ πλῆθος περὶ τούτου λεληθέναι, ὥσπερ εἶπον, οὐ   5
θαυμάζω· τὸ δὲ καὶ ὑμᾶς ταῦτ᾽ ἀγνοεῖν, οἳ διὰ τῆς γνώμης δοκεῖτε
θεᾶσθαι κάλλιον ἢ διὰ τῶν ὀφθαλμῶν τὰ πλεῖστα τῶν πραγμάτων,
25 τοῦτό μοι δοκεῖ θαυμαστὸν εἶναι. ἐγὼ δὲ πεπειραμένος σαφῶς οἶδα,   6
ὦ Σιμωνίδη, καὶ λέγω σοι ὅτι οἱ τύραννοι τῶν μεγίστων ἀγαθῶν
ἐλάχιστα μετέχουσι, τῶν δὲ μεγίστων κακῶν πλεῖστα κέκτηνται.
αὐτίκα γὰρ εἰ μὲν εἰρήνη δοκεῖ μέγα ἀγαθὸν τοῖς ἀνθρώποις εἶναι,   7
ταύτης ἐλάχιστον τοῖς τυράννοις μέτεστιν· εἰ δὲ πόλεμος μέγα
30 κακόν, τούτου πλεῖστον μέρος οἱ τύραννοι μετέχουσιν. εὐθὺς γὰρ   8
τοῖς μὲν ἰδιώταις, ἂν μὴ ἡ πόλις αὐτῶν κοινὸν πόλεμον πολεμῆι,
ἔξεστιν ὅποι ἂν βούλωνται πορεύεσθαι μηδὲν φοβουμένους μή
τις αὐτοὺς ἀποκτείνηι, οἱ δὲ τύραννοι πάντες πανταχῆι ὡς
διὰ πολεμίας πορεύονται. αὐτοί τε γοῦν ὡπλισμένοι οἴονται
35 ἀνάγκην εἶναι διάγειν καὶ ἄλλους ὁπλοφόρους ἀεὶ συμπεριάγεσθαι.
ἔπειτα δὲ οἱ μὲν ἰδιῶται, ἐὰν καὶ στρατεύωνταί που εἰς πολεμίαν,   9
ἀλλ᾽ οὖν ἐπειδάν γε ἔλθωσιν οἴκαδε, ἀσφάλειαν σφίσιν ἡγοῦνται
εἶναι, οἱ δὲ τύραννοι ἐπειδὰν εἰς τὴν ἑαυτῶν πόλιν ἀφίκωνται, τότε ἐν

15 τὸ c: om. D

10 πλείστοις πολεμίοις ἴσασιν ὄντες. ἐὰν δὲ δὴ καὶ ἄλλοι στρατεύωσιν
εἰς τὴν πόλιν κρείττονες, ἐὰν ἔξω τοῦ τείχους ὄντες οἱ ἥττονες ἐν
κινδύνωι δοκῶσιν εἶναι, ἀλλ᾽ ἐπειδάν γε εἴσω τοῦ ἐρύματος ἔλθωσιν,
ἐν ἀσφαλείαι πάντες νομίζουσι καθεστάναι, ὁ δὲ τύραννος οὐδ᾽ ἐπειδὰν εἴσω τῆς οἰκίας παρέλθηι ἐν ἀκινδύνωι ἐστίν, ἀλλ᾽ ἐνταῦθα δὴ   5
11 καὶ μάλιστα φυλακτέον οἴεται εἶναι. ἔπειτα τοῖς μὲν ἰδιώταις καὶ
διὰ σπονδῶν καὶ δι᾽ εἰρήνης γίγνεται πολέμου ἀνάπαυσις, τοῖς δὲ
τυράννοις οὔτε εἰρήνη ποτὲ πρὸς τοὺς τυραννευομένους γίγνεται
12 οὔτε σπονδαῖς ἄν ποτε πιστεύσας ὁ τύραννος θαρρήσειε. καὶ πόλε-
μοι μὲν δή εἰσιν οὕς τε αἱ πόλεις πολεμοῦσι καὶ οὓς οἱ τύραννοι πρὸς   10
τοὺς βεβιασμένους· τούτων δὴ τῶν πολέμων ὅσα μὲν ἔχει χαλεπὰ ὁ
13 σὺν ταῖς πόλεσι, ταῦτα καὶ ὁ τύραννος ἔχει· καὶ γὰρ ἐν ὅπλοις δεῖ
εἶναι ἀμφοτέρους καὶ φυλάττεσθαι καὶ κινδυνεύειν, καὶ ἄν τι πάθωσι
κακὸν ἡττηθέντες, λυποῦνται ἐπὶ τούτοις ἑκάτεροι. μέχρι μὲν δὴ τού-
14 του ἴσοι οἱ πόλεμοι· ἃ δὲ ἔχουσιν ἡδέα οἱ συνόντες ταῖς πόλεσι πρὸς   15
15 τὰς πόλεις, ταῦτα οὐκέτι ἔχουσιν οἱ τύραννοι. αἱ μὲν γὰρ πόλεις
δήπου ὅταν κρατήσωσι μάχηι τῶν ἐναντίων, οὐ ῥάιδιον εἰπεῖν
ὅσην μὲν ἡδονὴν ἔχουσιν ἐν τῶι τρέψασθαι τοὺς πολεμίους, ὅσην
δ᾽ ἐν τῶι διώκειν, ὅσην δ᾽ ἐν τῶι ἀποκτείνειν τοὺς πολεμίους, ὡς δὲ
γαυροῦνται ἐπὶ τῶι ἔργωι, ὡς δὲ δόξαν λαμπρὰν ἀναλαμβάνουσιν,   20
16 ὡς δ᾽ εὐφραίνονται τὴν πόλιν νομίζοντες ηὐξηκέναι. ἕκαστος δέ τις
προσποιεῖται καὶ τῆς βουλῆς μετεσχηκέναι καὶ πλείστους ἀπεκτονέναι, χαλεπὸν δὲ εὑρεῖν ὅπου οὐχὶ καὶ ἐπιψεύδονται, πλέονας φάσκοντες ἀπεκτονέναι ἢ ὅσοι ἂν τῶι ὄντι ἀποθάνωσιν· οὕτω καλόν τι
17 αὐτοῖς δοκεῖ εἶναι τὸ πολὺ νικᾶν. ὁ δὲ τύραννος ὅταν ὑποπτεύσηι καὶ   25
αἰσθανόμενος τῶι ὄντι ἀντιπραττομένους τινὰς ἀποκτείνηι, οἶδεν
ὅτι οὐκ αὔξει ὅλην τὴν πόλιν, ἐπίσταταί τε ὅτι μειόνων ἄρξει,
φαιδρός τε οὐ δύναται εἶναι οὐδὲ μεγαλύνεται ἐπὶ τῶι ἔργωι, ἀλλὰ
καὶ μειοῖ καθ᾽ ὅσον ἂν δύνηται τὸ γεγενημένον, καὶ ἀπολογεῖται ἅμα
πράττων ὡς οὐκ ἀδικῶν πεποίηκεν. οὕτως οὐδ᾽ αὑτῶι δοκεῖ καλὰ   30
18 τὰ ποιούμενα εἶναι. καὶ ὅταν ἀποθάνωσιν οὓς ἐφοβήθη, οὐδέν τι
μᾶλλον τοῦτο θαρρεῖ, ἀλλὰ φυλάττεται ἔτι μᾶλλον ἢ τὸ πρόσθεν.
καὶ πόλεμον μὲν δὴ τοιοῦτον ἔχων διατελεῖ ὁ τύραννος ὃν ἐγὼ
δηλῶ.

3   Φιλίας δ᾽ αὖ καταθέασαι ὡς κοινωνοῦσιν οἱ τύραννοι. πρῶτον   35
2 μὲν εἰ μέγα ἀγαθὸν ἀνθρώποις ἡ φιλία, τοῦτο ἐπισκεψώμεθα. ὃς
γὰρ ἂν φιλῆται δήπου ὑπό τινων, ἡδέως μὲν τοῦτον οἱ φιλοῦντες

παρόντα ὁρῶσιν, ἡδέως δ᾽ εὖ ποιοῦσι, ποθοῦσι δέ, ἤν που ἀπῆι,
ἥδιστα δὲ πάλιν προσιόντα δέχονται, συνήδονται δ᾽ ἐπὶ τοῖς αὐτοῦ
ἀγαθοῖς, συνεπικουροῦσι δέ, ἐάν τι σφαλλόμενον ὁρῶσιν. οὐ μὲν 3
δὴ λέληθεν οὐδὲ τὰς πόλεις ὅτι ἡ φιλία μέγιστον ἀγαθὸν καὶ ἥδισ-
5 τον ἀνθρώποις ἐστί· μόνους γοῦν τοὺς μοιχοὺς νομίζουσι πολλαὶ
τῶν πόλεων νηποινεὶ ἀποκτείνειν, δῆλον ὅτι διὰ ταῦτα ὅτι λυμαντῆρας αὐτοὺς νομίζουσι τῆς τῶν γυναικῶν φιλίας πρὸς τοὺς ἄνδρας
εἶναι. ἐπεὶ ὅταν γε ἀφροδισιασθῆι κατὰ συμφοράν τινα γυνή, οὐδὲν 4
ἧττον τούτου ἕνεκεν τιμῶσιν αὐτὰς οἱ ἄνδρες, ἐάνπερ ἡ φιλία δοκῆι
10 αὐταῖς ἀκήρατος διαμένειν· τοσοῦτον δέ τι ἀγαθὸν κρίνω ἔγωγε 5
τὸ φιλεῖσθαι εἶναι ὥστε νομίζω τῶι ὄντι αὐτόματα τἀγαθὰ τῶι
φιλουμένωι γίγνεσθαι καὶ παρὰ θεῶν καὶ παρὰ ἀνθρώπων· καὶ τού- 6
του τοίνυν τοῦ κτήματος τοιούτου ὄντος μειονεκτοῦσιν οἱ τύραννοι πάντων μάλιστα. εἰ δὲ βούλει, ὦ Σιμωνίδη, εἰδέναι ὅτι ἀληθῆ
15 λέγω, ὧδε ἐπίσκεψαι. βεβαιόταται μὲν γὰρ δήπου δοκοῦσι φιλίαι 7
εἶναι γονεῦσι πρὸς παῖδας καὶ παισὶ πρὸς γονέας καὶ ἀδελφοῖς πρὸς
ἀδελφοὺς καὶ γυναιξὶ πρὸς ἄνδρας καὶ ἑταίροις πρὸς ἑταίρους· εἰ 8
τοίνυν ἐθέλεις κατανοεῖν, εὑρήσεις τοὺς μὲν ἰδιώτας ὑπὸ τούτων
μάλιστα φιλουμένους, τοὺς δὲ τυράννους πολλοὺς μὲν παῖδας
20 ἑαυτῶν ἀπεκτονότας, πολλοὺς δ᾽ ὑπὸ παίδων αὐτοὺς ἀπολωλότας,
πολλοὺς δὲ ἀδελφοὺς ἐν τυραννίσιν ἀλληλοφόνους γεγενημένους,
πολλοὺς δὲ καὶ ὑπὸ γυναικῶν τῶν ἑαυτῶν τυράννους διεφθαρμένους
καὶ ὑπὸ ἑταίρων γε τῶν μάλιστα δοκούντων φίλων εἶναι. οἵτινες οὖν 9
ὑπὸ τῶν φύσει πεφυκότων μάλιστα φιλεῖν καὶ νόμωι συνηναγκασ-
25 μένων οὕτω μισοῦνται, πῶς ὑπ᾽ ἄλλου γέ τινος οἴεσθαι χρὴ αὐτοὺς
φιλεῖσθαι;
Ἀλλὰ μὴν καὶ πίστεως ὅστις ἐλάχιστον μετέχει, πῶς οὐχὶ μεγάλου 4
ἀγαθοῦ μειονεκτεῖ; ποία μὲν γὰρ ξυνουσία ἡδεῖα ἄνευ πίστεως τῆς
πρὸς ἀλλήλους, ποία δ᾽ ἀνδρὶ καὶ γυναικὶ τερπνὴ ἄνευ πίστεως
30 ὁμιλία, ποῖος δὲ θεράπων ἡδὺς ἀπιστούμενος; καὶ τούτου τοίνυν 2
τοῦ πιστῶς πρός τινας ἔχειν ἐλάχιστον μέτεστι τυράννωι· ὁπότε
γε οὐδὲ σιτίοις καὶ ποτοῖς πιστεύων διάγει, ἀλλὰ καὶ τούτων πρὶν
ἀπάρχεσθαι τοῖς θεοῖς τοὺς διακόνους πρῶτον κελεύουσιν ἀπογεύεσθαι διὰ τὸ ἀπιστεῖν μὴ καὶ ἐν τούτοις κακόν τι φάγωσιν ἢ πίωσιν·
35 ἀλλὰ μὴν καὶ αἱ πατρίδες τοῖς μὲν ἄλλοις ἀνθρώποις πλείστου 3
ἄξιαι. πολῖται γὰρ δορυφοροῦσι μὲν ἀλλήλους ἄνευ μισθοῦ ἐπὶ τοὺς
δούλους, δορυφοροῦσι δ᾽ ἐπὶ τοὺς κακούργους, ὑπὲρ τοῦ μηδένα τῶν
πολιτῶν βιαίωι θανάτωι ἀποθνήισκειν. οὕτω δὲ πόρρω προελη-
40 λύθασι φυλακῆς ὥστε πεποίηνται πολλοὶ νόμον τῶι μιαιφόνωι 4

1 ἀπῆι c: ἀπίηι D

μηδὲ τὸν συνόντα καθαρεύειν· ὥστε διὰ τὰς πατρίδας ἀσφαλῶς
5 ἕκαστος βιοτεύει τῶν πολιτῶν. τοῖς δὲ τυράννοις καὶ τοῦτο ἔμπαλιν
ἀνέστραπται. ἀντὶ γὰρ τοῦ τιμωρεῖν αἱ πόλεις αὐτοῖς μεγάλως
τιμῶσι τὸν ἀποκτείναντα τὸν τύραννον, καὶ ἀντί γε τοῦ εἴργειν ἐκ
τῶν ἱερῶν, ὥσπερ τοὺς τῶν ἰδιωτῶν φονέας, ἀντὶ τούτου καὶ εἰκόνας 5
ἐν τοῖς ἱεροῖς ἱστᾶσιν αἱ πόλεις τῶν τοιοῦτόν τι ποιησάντων.

6 Εἰ δὲ σὺ οἴει ὡς πλείω ἔχων τῶν ἰδιωτῶν κτήματα ὁ τύραννος διὰ
τοῦτο καὶ πλείω ἀπ᾽ αὐτῶν εὐφραίνεται, οὐδὲ τοῦτο οὕτως ἔχει, ὦ
Σιμωνίδη, ἀλλ᾽ ὥσπερ οἱ ἀθληταὶ οὐχ ὅταν ἰδιωτῶν γένωνται κρείττονες, τοῦτ᾽ αὐτοὺς εὐφραίνει, ἀλλ᾽ ὅταν τῶν ἀνταγωνιστῶν ἥττους, 10
τοῦτ᾽ αὐτοὺς ἀνιᾶι, οὕτω καὶ ὁ τύραννος οὐχ ὅταν τῶν ἰδιωτῶν
πλείω φαίνηται ἔχων, τότ᾽ εὐφραίνεται, ἀλλ᾽ ὅταν ἑτέρων τυράννων
ἐλάττω ἔχηι, τούτωι λυπεῖται· τούτους γὰρ ἀνταγωνιστὰς ἡγεῖται
7 αὑτῶι τοῦ πλούτου εἶναι. οὐδέ γε θᾶττόν τι γίγνεται τῶι τυράννωι
ἢ τῶι ἰδιώτηι ὧν ἐπιθυμεῖ. ὁ μὲν γὰρ ἰδιώτης οἰκίας ἢ ἀγροῦ ἢ οἰκέ- 15
του ἐπιθυμεῖ, ὁ δὲ τύραννος ἢ πόλεων ἢ χώρας πολλῆς ἢ λιμένων ἢ
ἀκροπόλεων ἰσχυρῶν, ἅ ἐστι πολὺ χαλεπώτερα καὶ ἐπικινδυνότερα
8 κατεργάσασθαι τῶν ἰδιωτικῶν ἐπιθυμημάτων. ἀλλὰ μέντοι καὶ πένητας ὄψει οὕτως ὀλίγους τῶν ἰδιωτῶν ὡς πολλοὺς τῶν τυράννων.
οὐ γὰρ τῶι ἀριθμῶι οὔτε τὰ πολλὰ κρίνεται οὔτε τὰ ὀλίγα, ἀλλὰ 20
πρὸς τὰς χρήσεις· ὥστε τὰ μὲν ὑπερβάλλοντα τὰ ἱκανὰ πολλά ἐστί,
9 τὰ δὲ τῶν ἱκανῶν ἐλλείποντα ὀλίγα. τῶι οὖν τυράννωι τὰ πολλαπλάσια ἧττον ἱκανά ἐστιν εἰς τὰ ἀναγκαῖα δαπανήματα ἢ τῶι
ἰδιώτηι. τοῖς μὲν γὰρ ἰδιώταις ἔξεστι τὰς δαπάνας συντέμνειν εἰς
τὰ καθ᾽ ἡμέραν ὅπηι βούλονται, τοῖς δὲ τυράννοις οὐκ ἐνδέχεται. αἱ 25
γὰρ μέγισται αὐτοῖς δαπάναι καὶ ἀναγκαιόταται εἰς τὰς τῆς ψυχῆς
10 φυλακάς εἰσι· τὸ δὲ τούτων τι συντέμνειν ὄλεθρος δοκεῖ εἶναι. ἔπειτα
δὲ ὅσοι μὲν δύνανται ἔχειν ἀπὸ τοῦ δικαίου ὅσων δέονται, τί ἂν
τούτους οἰκτίροι τις ὡς πένητας; ὅσοι δ᾽ ἀναγκάζονται δι᾽ ἔνδειαν
κακόν τι καὶ αἰσχρὸν μηχανώμενοι ζῆν, πῶς οὐ τούτους ἀθλίους 30
11 ἄν τις καὶ πένητας δικαίως νομίζοι; οἱ τύραννοι τοίνυν ἀναγκάζονται πλεῖστα συλᾶν ἀδίκως καὶ ἱερὰ καὶ ἀνθρώπους διὰ τὸ εἰς τὰς
ἀναγκαίας δαπάνας ἀεὶ προσδεῖσθαι χρημάτων. ὥσπερ γὰρ πολέμου ὄντος ἀεὶ ἀναγκάζονται στράτευμα τρέφειν ἢ ἀπολωλέναι.

5 Χαλεπὸν δ᾽ ἐρῶ σοι καὶ ἄλλο πάθημα, ὦ Σιμωνίδη, τῶν 35
τυράννων. γιγνώσκουσι μὲν γὰρ οὐδὲν ἧττον τῶν ἰδιωτῶν τοὺς
ἀλκίμους τε καὶ σοφοὺς καὶ δικαίους. τούτους δ᾽ ἀντὶ τοῦ ἄγασθαι

3 αἱ πόλεις αὐτοῖς D: αὐτοῖς, αἱ πόλεις c: αἱ πόλεις c   19 οὕτως c: οὐχ οὕτως D
20 ὀλίγα c: ἱκανά Di   37 ἀλκίμους i: κοσμίους D

φοβοῦνται, τοὺς μὲν ἀνδρείους, μή τι τολμήσωσι τῆς ἐλευθερίας
ἕνεκεν, τοὺς δὲ σοφούς, μή τι μηχανήσωνται, τοὺς δὲ δικαίους,
μὴ ἐπιθυμήσηι τὸ πλῆθος ὑπ' αὐτῶν προστατεῖσθαι. ὅταν δὲ   2
τοὺς τοιούτους διὰ τὸν φόβον ὑπεξαιρῶνται, τίνες ἄλλοι αὐτοῖς
5 καταλείπονται χρῆσθαι ἀλλ' ἢ οἱ ἄδικοί τε καὶ ἀκρατεῖς καὶ
ἀνδραποδώδεις; οἱ μὲν ἄδικοι πιστευόμενοι, διότι φοβοῦνται ὥσπερ
οἱ τύραννοι τὰς πόλεις μήποτε ἐλεύθεραι γενόμεναι ἐγκρατεῖς αὐτῶν
γένωνται, οἱ δ' ἀκρατεῖς τῆς εἰς τὸ παρὸν ἐξουσίας ἕνεκα, οἱ δ'
ἀνδραποδώδεις, διότι οὐδ' αὐτοὶ ἀξιοῦσιν ἐλεύθεροι εἶναι. χαλεπὸν
10 οὖν καὶ τοῦτο τὸ πάθημα ἔμοιγε δοκεῖ εἶναι, τὸ ἄλλους μὲν ἡγεῖσθαι
ἀγαθοὺς ἄνδρας, ἄλλοις δὲ χρῆσθαι ἀναγκάζεσθαι. ἔτι δὲ φιλόπολιν   3
μὲν ἀνάγκη καὶ τὸν τύραννον εἶναι· ἄνευ γὰρ τῆς πόλεως οὔτ'
ἂν σώιζεσθαι δύναιτο οὔτ' εὐδαιμονεῖν· ἡ δὲ τυραννὶς ἀναγκάζει
καὶ ταῖς ἑαυτῶν πατρίσιν ἐνοχλεῖν. οὔτε γὰρ ἀλκίμους οὔτ' εὐό-
15 πλους χαίρουσι τοὺς πολίτας παρασκευάζοντες, ἀλλὰ τοὺς ξένους
δεινοτέρους τῶν πολιτῶν ποιοῦντες ἥδονται μᾶλλον καὶ τούτοις χρῶνται δορυφόροις. ἀλλὰ μὴν οὐδ' ἂν εὐετηριῶν γενομένων   4
ἀφθονία τῶν ἀγαθῶν γίγνηται, οὐδὲ τότε συγχαίρει ὁ τύραννος.
ἐνδεεστέροις γὰρ οὖσι ταπεινοτέροις αὐτοῖς οἴονται χρῆσθαι.
20   Βούλομαι δέ σοι, ἔφη, ὦ Σιμωνίδη, κἀκείνας τὰς εὐφροσύνας   6
δηλῶσαι ὅσαις ἐγὼ χρώμενος ὅτ' ἦν ἰδιώτης, νῦν ἐπειδὴ τύραννος
ἐγενόμην, αἰσθάνομαι στερόμενος αὐτῶν. ἐγὼ γὰρ ξυνῆν μὲν   2
ἡλικιώταις ἡδόμενος ἡδομένοις ἐμοί, συνῆν δὲ ἐμαυτῶι, ὁπότε
ἡσυχίας ἐπιθυμήσαιμι, διῆγον δ' ἐν συμποσίοις πολλάκις μὲν μέχρι
25 τοῦ ἐπιλαθέσθαι πάντων εἴ τι χαλεπὸν ἐν ἀνθρωπίνωι βίωι ἦν,
πολλάκις δὲ μέχρι τοῦ ὠιδαῖς τε καὶ θαλίαις καὶ χοροῖς τὴν ψυχὴν
συγκαταμιγνύναι, πολλάκις δὲ μέχρι κοίτης ἐπιθυμίας ἐμῆς τε καὶ
τῶν παρόντων. νῦν δὲ ἀπεστέρημαι μὲν τῶν ἡδομένων ἐμοὶ διὰ   3
τὸ δούλους ἀντὶ φίλων ἔχειν τοὺς ἑταίρους, ἀπεστέρημαι δ' αὖ
30 τοῦ ἡδέως ἐκείνοις ὁμιλεῖν διὰ τὸ μηδεμίαν ἐνορᾶν εὔνοιαν ἐμοὶ
παρ' αὐτῶν· μέθην δὲ καὶ ὕπνον ὁμοίως ἐνέδραι φυλάττομαι.
τὸ δὲ φοβεῖσθαι μὲν ὄχλον, φοβεῖσθαι δ' ἐρημίαν, φοβεῖσθαι δὲ   4
ἀφυλαξίαν, φοβεῖσθαι δὲ καὶ αὐτοὺς τοὺς φυλάττοντας, καὶ μήτ'
ἀόπλους ἔχειν ἐθέλειν περὶ αὐτὸν μήθ' ὡπλισμένους ἡδέως θεᾶσθαι,
35 πῶς οὐκ ἀργαλέον ἐστὶ πρᾶγμα; ἔτι δὲ ξένοις μὲν μᾶλλον ἢ   5
πολίταις πιστεύειν, βαρβάροις δὲ μᾶλλον ἢ Ἕλλησιν, ἐπιθυμεῖν δὲ
τοὺς μὲν ἐλευθέρους δούλους ἔχειν, τοὺς δὲ δούλους ἀναγκάζεσθαι
ποιεῖν ἐλευθέρους, οὐ πάντα σοι ταῦτα δοκεῖ ψυχῆς ὑπὸ φόβων

14 ἐνοχλεῖν c: ἐγκαλεῖν D   18 συγχαίρει d: συγχωρεῖ d   27 κοίτης c: κοινῆς D

6 καταπεπληγμένης τεκμήρια εἶναι; ὅ γέ τοι φόβος οὐ μόνον αὐτὸς
ἐνὼν ταῖς ψυχαῖς λυπηρός ἐστιν, ἀλλὰ καὶ πάντων τῶν ἡδέων
7 συμπαρακολουθῶν λυμεών γίγνεται. εἰ δὲ καὶ σὺ πολεμικῶν
ἔμπειρος εἶ, ὦ Σιμωνίδη, καὶ ἤδη ποτὲ πολεμίαι φάλαγγι πλησίον
ἀντετάξω, ἀναμνήσθητι ποῖον μέν τινα σῖτον ἡιροῦ ἐν ἐκείνωι τῶι   5
8 χρόνωι, ποῖον δέ τινα ὕπνον ἐκοιμῶ. οἷα μέντοι σοὶ τότ᾿ ἦν τὰ
λυπηρά, τοιαῦτά ἐστι τὰ τῶν τυράννων καὶ ἔτι δεινότερα· οὐ γὰρ
ἐξ ἐναντίας μόνον, ἀλλὰ καὶ πάντοθεν πολεμίους ὁρᾶν νομίζουσιν οἱ
9 τύραννοι. ταῦτα δ᾿ ἀκούσας ὁ Σιμωνίδης ὑπολαβὼν εἶπεν· Ὑπέρευ
μοι δοκεῖς ἔνια λέγειν. ὁ γὰρ πόλεμος φοβερὸν μέν, ἀλλ᾿ ὅμως, ὦ   10
Ἱέρων, ἡμεῖς γε ὅταν ὦμεν ἐν στρατείαι, φύλακας προκαθιστάμενοι
10 θαρραλέως δείπνου τε καὶ ὕπνου λαγχάνομεν. καὶ ὁ Ἱέρων ἔφη·
Ναὶ μὰ Δία, ὦ Σιμωνίδη· αὐτῶν μὲν γὰρ προφυλάττουσιν οἱ
νόμοι, ὥστε περὶ ἑαυτῶν φοβοῦνται καὶ ὑπὲρ ὑμῶν· οἱ δὲ τύραννοι
11 μισθοῦ φύλακας ἔχουσιν ὥσπερ θεριστάς. καὶ δεῖ μὲν δήπου τοὺς   15
φύλακας μηδὲν οὕτω ποιεῖν δύνασθαι ὡς πιστοὺς εἶναι· πιστὸν δὲ
ἕνα πολὺ χαλεπώτερον εὑρεῖν ἢ πάνυ πολλοὺς ἐργάτας ὁποίου
βούλει ἔργου, ἄλλως τε καὶ ὁπόταν χρημάτων μὲν ἕνεκα παρῶσιν
οἱ φυλάττοντες, ἐξῆι δ᾿ αὐτοῖς ἐν ὀλίγωι χρόνωι πολὺ πλείω λαβεῖν
ἀποκτείνασι τὸν τύραννον ἢ ὅσα πολὺν χρόνον φυλάττοντες παρὰ   20
12 τοῦ τυράννου λαμβάνουσιν. ὃ δ᾿ ἐζήλωσας ἡμᾶς ὡς τοὺς μὲν φίλους
μάλιστα εὖ ποιεῖν δυνάμεθα, τοὺς δὲ ἐχθροὺς πάντων μάλιστα
13 χειρούμεθα, οὐδὲ ταῦθ᾿ οὕτως ἔχει. φίλους μὲν γὰρ πῶς ἂν νομίσαις
ποτὲ εὖ ποιεῖν, ὅταν εὖ εἰδῆις ὅτι ὁ τὰ πλεῖστα λαμβάνων παρὰ
σοῦ ἥδιστ᾿ ἂν ὡς τάχιστα ἐξ ὀφθαλμῶν σου γένοιτο; ὅ τι γὰρ ἄν τις   25
λάβηι παρὰ τυράννου, οὐδεὶς οὐδὲν ἑαυτοῦ νομίζει πρὶν ἂν ἔξω τῆς
14 τούτου ἐπικρατείας γένηται. ἐχθροὺς δ᾿ αὖ πῶς ἂν φαίης μάλιστα
τοῖς τυράννοις ἐξεῖναι χειροῦσθαι, ὅταν εὖ εἰδῶσιν ὅτι ἐχθροὶ αὐτῶν
εἰσι πάντες οἱ τυραννούμενοι, τούτους δὲ μήτε κατακαίνειν ἅπαντας
15 μήτε δεσμεύειν οἷόν τε ἦι (τίνων γὰρ ἔτι ἄρξει;) ἀλλ᾿ εἰδότα ὅτι   30
ἐχθροί εἰσι, τούτους ἅμα μὲν φυλάττεσθαι δέηι, καὶ χρῆσθαι δ᾿
αὐτοῖς ἀναγκάζηται; εὖ δ᾿ ἴσθι καὶ τοῦτο, ὦ Σιμωνίδη, ὅτι καὶ οὓς
τῶν πολιτῶν δεδίασι χαλεπῶς μὲν αὐτοὺς ζῶντας ὁρῶσι, χαλεπῶς
δ᾿ ἀποκτείνουσιν· ὥσπερ γε καὶ ἵππος εἰ ἀγαθὸς μὲν εἴη, φοβερὸς
δὲ μὴ ἀνήκεστόν τι ποιήσηι, χαλεπῶς μὲν ἄν τις αὐτὸν ἀποκτείναι   35
16 διὰ τὴν ἀρετήν, χαλεπῶς δὲ ζῶντι χρῶιτο, εὐλαβούμενος μή τι
ἀνήκεστον ἐν τοῖς κινδύνοις ἐργάσηται, καὶ τἆλλά γε κτήματα

11 γε c: τε D   29 κατακαίνειν c: κατακτείνειν D   32 ἀναγκάζηται c: ἀναγκάζεσθαι D
34 γε c: γὰρ D

ὅσα χαλεπὰ μὲν χρήσιμα δ᾽ ἐστίν, ὁμοίως ἅπαντα λυπεῖ μὲν τοὺς
κεκτημένους, λυπεῖ δὲ ἀπαλλαττομένους.

Ἐπεὶ δὲ ταῦτα αὐτοῦ ἤκουσεν ὁ Σιμωνίδης, εἶπεν· Ἔοικεν, 7
ἔφη, ὦ Ἱέρων, μέγα τι εἶναι ἡ τιμή, ἧς ὀρεγόμενοι οἱ ἄνθρωποι
5 πάντα μὲν πόνον ὑποδύονται, πάντα δὲ κίνδυνον ὑπομένουσι.
καὶ ὑμεῖς, ὡς ἔοικε, τοσαῦτα πράγματα ἐχούσης ὁπόσα λέγεις 2
τῆς τυραννίδος, ὅμως προπετῶς φέρεσθε εἰς αὐτήν, ὅπως τιμᾶσθε
καὶ ὑπηρετῶσι μὲν ὑμῖν πάντες πάντα τὰ προσταττόμενα
ἀπροφασίστως, περιβλέπωσι δὲ πάντες, ὑπανιστῶνται δ᾽ ἀπὸ
10 τῶν θάκων ὁδῶν τε παραχωρῶσι, γεραίρωσι δὲ καὶ λόγοις καὶ
ἔργοις πάντες οἱ παρόντες ἀεὶ ὑμᾶς· τοιαῦτα γὰρ δὴ ποιοῦσι
τοῖς τυράννοις οἱ ἀρχόμενοι καὶ ἄλλον ὄντιν᾽ ἂν ἀεὶ τιμῶντες
τυγχάνωσι. καὶ γάρ μοι δοκεῖ, ὦ Ἱέρων, τούτῳ διαφέρειν ἀνὴρ 3
τῶν ἄλλων ζῴων, τῶι τιμῆς ὀρέγεσθαι. ἐπεὶ σιτίοις γε καὶ ποτοῖς
15 καὶ ὕπνοις καὶ ἀφροδισίοις πάντα ὁμοίως ἥδεσθαι ἔοικε τὰ ζῶια·
ἡ δὲ φιλοτιμία οὔτ᾽ ἐν τοῖς ἀλόγοις ζώιοις ἐμφύεται οὔτ᾽ ἐν ἅπασιν
ἀνθρώποις· οἷς δ᾽ ἂν ἐμφύῃ τιμῆς τε καὶ ἐπαίνου ἔρως, οὗτοί
εἰσιν ἤδη οἱ πλεῖστον μὲν τῶν βοσκημάτων διαφέροντες, ἄνδρες
δὲ καὶ οὐκέτι ἄνθρωποι μόνον νομιζόμενοι. ὥστε ἐμοὶ μὲν εἰκότως 4
20 δοκεῖτε ταῦτα πάντα ὑπομένειν ἃ φέρετε ἐν τῇι τυραννίδι, ἐπείπερ
τιμᾶσθε διαφερόντως τῶν ἄλλων ἀνθρώπων. καὶ γὰρ οὐδεμία
ἀνθρωπίνη ἡδονὴ τοῦ θείου ἐγγυτέρω δοκεῖ εἶναι ἢ ἡ περὶ τὰς
τιμὰς εὐφροσύνη. πρὸς ταῦτα δὴ εἶπεν ὁ Ἱέρων· Ἀλλ᾽, ὦ Σιμωνίδη, 5
καὶ αἱ τιμαὶ τῶν τυράννων ὅμοιαι ἐμοὶ δοκοῦσιν εἶναι οἷάπερ
25 ἐγώ σοι τὰ ἀφροδίσια ὄντα αὐτῶν ἀπέδειξα. οὔτε γὰρ αἱ μὴ 6
ἐξ ἀντιφιλούντων ὑπουργίαι χάριτες ἡμῖν ἐδόκουν εἶναι οὔτε
τὰ ἀφροδίσια τὰ βίαια ἡδέα ἐφαίνετο. ὡσαύτως τοίνυν οὐδὲ αἱ
ὑπουργίαι αἱ ὑπὸ τῶν φοβουμένων τιμαί εἰσι. πῶς γὰρ ἂν φαίημεν 7
ἢ τοὺς βίαι ἐξανισταμένους θάκων διὰ τὸ τιμᾶν τοὺς ἀδικοῦντας
30 ἐξανίστασθαι, ἢ τοὺς ὁδῶν παραχωροῦντας τοῖς κρείττοσι διὰ
τὸ τιμᾶν τοὺς ἀδικοῦντας παραχωρεῖν; καὶ δῶρά γε διδόασιν οἱ 8
πολλοὶ τούτοις οὓς μισοῦσι, καὶ ταῦτα ὅταν μάλιστα φοβῶνται
μή τι κακὸν ὑπ᾽ αὐτῶν πάθωσιν. ἀλλὰ ταῦτα μὲν οἶμαι δουλείας
ἔργα εἰκότως ἂν νομίζοιτο· αἱ δὲ τιμαί ἔμοιγε δοκοῦσιν ἐκ τῶν ἐναν-
35 τίων τούτοις γίγνεσθαι. ὅταν γὰρ ἄνθρωποι ἄνδρα ἡγησάμενοι 9
εὐεργετεῖν ἱκανὸν εἶναι, καὶ ἀπολαύειν αὐτοῦ ἀγαθὰ νομίσαν-
τες, ἔπειτα τοῦτον ἀνὰ στόμα τε ἔχωσιν ἐπαινοῦντες, θεῶνταί
τ᾽ αὐτὸν ὡς οἰκεῖον ἕκαστος ἀγαθόν, ἑκόντες τε παραχωρῶσι τούτωι

12 ὄντιν᾽ ἂν c: ὄντινα D   14 γε c: τε D   28 αἱ c: om. D

ὁδῶν καὶ θάκων ὑπανιστῶνται φιλοῦντές τε καὶ μὴ φοβούμενοι, καὶ
στεφανῶσι κοινῆς ἀρετῆς καὶ εὐεργεσίας ἕνεκα, καὶ δωρεῖσθαι ἐθέλωσιν, οἱ αὐτοὶ οὗτοι ἔμοιγε δοκοῦσι τιμᾶν τε τοῦτον ἀληθῶς οἷ ἂν
τοιαῦτα ὑπουργήσωσι καὶ ὁ τούτων ἀξιούμενος τιμᾶσθαι τῶι ὄντι.

10 καὶ ἔγωγε τὸν μὲν οὕτω τιμώμενον μακαρίζω· αἰσθάνομαι γὰρ αὐτὸν   5
οὐκ ἐπιβουλευόμενον ἀλλὰ φροντιζόμενον μή τι πάθηι καὶ ἀφόβως
καὶ ἀνεπιφθόνως καὶ ἀκινδύνως καὶ εὐδαιμόνως τὸν βίον διάγοντα· ὁ
δὲ τύραννος ὡς ὑπὸ πάντων ἀνθρώπων κατακεκριμένος δι᾽ ἀδικίαν
ἀποθνήισκειν, οὕτως, ὦ Σιμωνίδη, εὖ ἴσθι, καὶ νύκτα καὶ ἡμέραν
11 διάγει. ἐπεὶ δὲ ταῦτα πάντα διήκουσεν ὁ Σιμωνίδης, Καὶ πῶς, ἔφη,   10
ὦ Ἱέρων, εἰ οὕτως πονηρόν ἐστι τὸ τυραννεῖν καὶ τοῦτο σὺ ἔγνωκας,
οὐχ ἀπαλλάττηι οὕτω μεγάλου κακοῦ, ἀλλ᾽ οὔτε σὺ οὔτε ἄλλος μὲν
δὴ οὐδεὶς πώποτε ἑκὼν εἶναι τυραννίδος ἀφεῖτο, ὅσπερ ἂν ἅπαξ
12 κτήσαιτο; Ὅτι, ἔφη, ὦ Σιμωνίδη, καὶ ταύτηι ἀθλιώτατόν ἐστιν ἡ
τυραννίς· οὐδὲ γὰρ ἀπαλλαγῆναι δυνατὸν αὐτῆς ἐστι. πῶς γὰρ ἂν   15
τίς ποτε ἐξαρκέσειε τύραννος ἢ χρήματα ἐκτίνων ὅσους ἀφείλετο ἢ
δεσμοὺς ἀντιπάσχων ὅσους δὴ ἐδέσμευσεν, ἢ ὅσους κατέκανε πῶς
13 ἂν ἱκανὰς ψυχὰς ἀντιπαράσχοιτο ἀποθανουμένας; ἀλλ᾽ εἴπερ τωι
ἄλλωι, ὦ Σιμωνίδη, λυσιτελεῖ ἀπάγξασθαι, ἴσθι, ἔφη, ὅτι τυράννωι ἔγωγε εὑρίσκω μάλιστα τοῦτο λυσιτελοῦν ποιῆσαι. μόνωι γὰρ   20
αὐτῶι οὔτε ἔχειν οὔτε καταθέσθαι τὰ κακὰ λυσιτελεῖ.

8   Καὶ ὁ Σιμωνίδης ὑπολαβὼν εἶπεν· Ἀλλὰ τὸ μὲν νῦν, ὦ Ἱέρων,
ἀθύμως ἔχειν σε πρὸς τὴν τυραννίδα οὐ θαυμάζω, ἐπείπερ ἐπιθυμῶν
φιλεῖσθαι ὑπ᾽ ἀνθρώπων ἐμποδών σοι τούτου νομίζεις αὐτὴν
εἶναι. ἐγὼ μέντοι ἔχειν μοι δοκῶ διδάξαι σε ὡς τὸ ἄρχειν οὐδὲν   25
ἀποκωλύει τοῦ φιλεῖσθαι, ἀλλὰ καὶ πλεονεκτεῖ γε τῆς ἰδιωτείας.
2 ἐπισκοποῦντες δὲ αὐτὸ εἰ οὕτως ἔχει μήπω ἐκεῖνο σκοπῶμεν, εἰ
διὰ τὸ μεῖζον δύνασθαι ὁ ἄρχων καὶ χαρίζεσθαι πλείω δύναιτ᾽
ἄν, ἀλλ᾽ ἂν τὰ ὅμοια ποιῶσιν ὅ τε ἰδιώτης καὶ ὁ τύραννος, ἐννόει
πότερος μείζω ἀπὸ τῶν ἴσων κτᾶται χάριν. ἄρξομαι δέ σοι ἀπὸ   30
3 τῶν μικροτάτων παραδειγμάτων. ἰδὼν γὰρ πρῶτον προσειπάτω
τινὰ φιλικῶς ὅ τε ἄρχων καὶ ὁ ἰδιώτης· ἐν τούτωι τὴν ποτέρου
πρόσρησιν μᾶλλον εὐφραίνειν τὸν ἀκούσαντα νομίζεις; ἴθι δὴ
ἐπαινεσάντων ἀμφότεροι τὸν αὐτόν· τὸν ποτέρου δοκεῖς ἔπαινον
ἐξικνεῖσθαι μᾶλλον εἰς εὐφροσύνην; θύσας δὲ τιμησάτω ἑκάτερος·   35
4 τὴν παρὰ ποτέρου τιμὴν μείζονος ἂν χάριτος δοκεῖς τυγχάνειν; κάμνοντα θεραπευσάτωσαν ὁμοίως· οὐκοῦν τοῦτο σαφὲς ὅτι αἱ ἀπὸ τῶν

13–14 ἂν ἅπαξ D: ἅπαξ c   14 καὶ c: ἐν D   17 ἀντιπάσχων c: ἀντιπαράσχοι D
κατέκανε c: κατέκτανε(ν) D   34 ἀμφότεροι c: ἀμφοτέρων D   36 παρὰ ποτέρου c:
παρ᾽ ὁποτέρου D

δυνατωτάτων θεραπεῖαι καὶ χαρὰν ἐμποιοῦσι μεγίστην; δότωσαν
δὴ τὰ ἴσα· οὐ καὶ ἐν τούτωι σαφὲς ὅτι αἱ ἀπὸ τῶν δυνατωτάτων ἡμίσειαι χάριτες πλέον ἢ ὅλον τὸ παρὰ τοῦ ἰδιώτου δώρημα δύνανται;
ἀλλ' ἔμοιγε δοκεῖ καὶ ἐκ θεῶν τιμή τις καὶ χάρις συμπαρέπεσθαι ἀνδρὶ   5
5 ἄρχοντι. μὴ γὰρ ὅτι καλλίονα ποιεῖ ἄνδρα, ἀλλὰ καὶ τὸν αὐτὸν
τοῦτον ἥδιον θεώμεθά τε ὅταν ἄρχηι ἢ ὅταν ἰδιωτεύηι, διαλεγόμενοί τε ἀγαλλόμεθα τοῖς προτετιμημένοις μᾶλλον ἢ τοῖς ἐκ τοῦ ἴσου
ἡμῖν οὖσι. καὶ μὴν παιδικά γε, ἐν οἷς δὴ καὶ σὺ μάλιστα κατεμέμψω   6
τὴν τυραννίδα, ἥκιστα μὲν γῆρας ἄρχοντος δυσχεραίνει, ἥκιστα δ'
10 αἶσχος, πρὸς ὃν ἂν τυγχάνηι ὁμιλῶν, τούτου ὑπολογίζεται. αὐτὸ
γὰρ τὸ τετιμῆσθαι μάλιστα συνεπικοσμεῖ, ὥστε τὰ μὲν δυσχερῆ
ἀφανίζειν, τὰ δὲ καλὰ λαμπρότερα ἀναφαίνειν. ὁπότε γε μὴν ἐκ τῶν   7
ἴσων ὑπουργημάτων μειζόνων χαρίτων ὑμεῖς τυγχάνετε, πῶς οὐκ
ἐπειδάν γε ὑμεῖς πολλαπλάσια μὲν διαπράττοντες ὠφελεῖν δύνησθε,
15 πολλαπλάσια δὲ δωρεῖσθαι ἔχητε, ὑμᾶς καὶ πολὺ μᾶλλον φιλεῖσθαι
τῶν ἰδιωτῶν προσήκει; καὶ ὁ Ἱέρων εὐθὺς ὑπολαβών, Ὅτι νὴ Δί',   8
ἔφη, ὦ Σιμωνίδη, καὶ ἐξ ὧν ἀπεχθάνονται ἄνθρωποι, ἡμᾶς πολὺ
πλείω τῶν ἰδιωτῶν ἀνάγκη ἐστὶ πραγματεύεσθαι. πρακτέον μέν γε   9
χρήματα, εἰ μέλλομεν ἕξειν δαπανᾶν εἰς τὰ δέοντα, ἀναγκαστέον δὲ
20 φυλάττειν ὅσα δεῖται φυλακῆς, κολαστέον δὲ τοὺς ἀδίκους, κωλυτέον
δὲ τοὺς ὑβρίζειν βουλομένους· καὶ ὅταν γε τάχους καιρὸς παραστῆι
ἢ πεζῆι ἢ κατὰ θάλατταν ἐξορμᾶσθαι, οὐκ ἐπιτρεπτέον τοῖς
ῥαιδιουργοῦσιν. ἔτι δὲ μισθοφόρων μὲν ἀνδρὶ τυράννωι δεῖ· τούτου   10
δὲ βαρύτερον φόρημα οὐδέν ἐστι τοῖς πολίταις. οὐ γὰρ τυράννοις
25 ἰσοτιμίας, ἀλλὰ πλεονεξίας ἕνεκα νομίζουσι τούτους τρέφεσθαι.
　　Πρὸς ταῦτα δὴ πάλιν εἶπεν ὁ Σιμωνίδης· Ἀλλ' ὅπως μὲν οὐ   9
πάντων τούτων ἐπιμελητέον, ὦ Ἱέρων, οὐ λέγω. ἐπιμέλειαι μέντοι
μοι δοκοῦσιν αἱ μὲν πάνυ πρὸς ἔχθραν ἄγειν, αἱ δὲ πάνυ διὰ χαρίτων
εἶναι. τὸ μὲν γὰρ διδάσκειν ἅ ἐστι βέλτιστα καὶ τὸν κάλλιστα ταῦτα   2
30 ἐξεργαζόμενον ἐπαινεῖν καὶ τιμᾶν, αὕτη μὲν ἡ ἐπιμέλεια διὰ χαρίτων
γίγνεται, τὸ δὲ τὸν ἐνδεῶς τι ποιοῦντα λοιδορεῖν τε καὶ ἀναγκάζειν
καὶ ζημιοῦν καὶ κολάζειν, ταῦτα δὲ ἀνάγκη δι' ἀπεχθείας μᾶλλον
γίγνεσθαι. ἐγὼ οὖν φημι ἀνδρὶ ἄρχοντι τὸν μὲν ἀνάγκης δεόμενον   3
ἄλλοις προστακτέον εἶναι κολάζειν, τὸ δὲ τὰ ἆθλα ἀποδιδόναι δι'
35 αὐτοῦ ποιητέον. ὡς δὲ ταῦτα καλῶς ἔχει μαρτυρεῖ τὰ γιγνόμενα.
καὶ γὰρ ὅταν χοροὺς ἡμῖν βουλώμεθα ἀγωνίζεσθαι, ἆθλα μὲν ὁ   4
ἄρχων προτίθησιν, ἀθροίζειν δὲ αὐτοὺς προστέτακται χορηγοῖς καὶ

ἄλλοις διδάσκειν καὶ ἀνάγκην προστιθέναι τοῖς ἐνδεῶς τι ποιοῦσιν.
οὐκοῦν εὐθὺς ἐν τούτοις τὸ μὲν ἐπίχαρι διὰ τοῦ ἄρχοντος ἐγένετο,
5 τὰ δ' ἀντίτυπα δι' ἄλλων. τί οὖν κωλύει καὶ τἆλλα τὰ πολιτικὰ
οὕτως περαίνεσθαι; διήιρηνται μὲν γὰρ ἅπασαι αἱ πόλεις αἱ μὲν
κατὰ φυλάς, αἱ δὲ κατὰ μόρας, αἱ δὲ κατὰ λόχους, καὶ ἄρχοντες ἐφ' 5
6 ἑκάστωι μέρει ἐφεστήκασιν. οὐκοῦν εἴ τις καὶ τούτοις ὥσπερ τοῖς
χοροῖς ἆθλα προτιθείη καὶ εὐοπλίας καὶ εὐταξίας καὶ ἱππικῆς καὶ
ἀλκῆς τῆς ἐν πολέμωι καὶ δικαιοσύνης τῆς ἐν συμβολαίοις, εἰκὸς καὶ
7 ταῦτα πάντα διὰ φιλονικίαν ἐντόνως ἀσκεῖσθαι. καὶ ναὶ μὰ Δία
ὁρμῶιντό γ' ἂν θᾶττον ὅποι δέοι, τιμῆς ὀρεγόμενοι, καὶ χρήματα 10
θᾶττον ἂν εἰσφέροιεν, ὁπότε τούτου καιρὸς εἴη, καὶ τὸ πάντων γε
χρησιμώτατον, ἥκιστα δὲ εἰθισμένον διὰ φιλονικίας πράττεσθαι, ἡ
γεωργία αὐτὴ ἂν πολὺ ἐπιδοίη, εἴ τις ἆθλα προτιθείη κατ' ἀγροὺς
ἢ κατὰ κώμας τοῖς κάλλιστα τὴν γῆν ἐξεργαζομένοις, καὶ τοῖς εἰς
τοῦτο τῶν πολιτῶν ἐρρωμένως τρεπομένοις πολλὰ ἂν ἀγαθὰ περ- 15
8 αίνοιτο· καὶ γὰρ αἱ πρόσοδοι αὔξοιντ' ἄν, καὶ ἡ σωφροσύνη πολὺ
μᾶλλον σὺν τῆι ἀσχολίαι συμπαρομαρτεῖ. καὶ μὴν κακουργίαι γε
9 ἧττον τοῖς ἐνεργοῖς ἐμφύονται. εἰ δὲ καὶ ἐμπορία ὠφελεῖ τι πόλιν,
τιμώμενος ἂν ὁ πλεῖστα τοῦτο ποιῶν καὶ ἐμπόρους ἂν πλείους
ἀγείροι. εἰ δὲ φανερὸν γένοιτο ὅτι καὶ ὁ πρόσοδόν τινα ἄλυπον 20
ἐξευρίσκων τῆι πόλει τιμήσεται, οὐδ' αὕτη ἂν ἡ σκέψις ἀργοῖτο.
10 ὡς δὲ συνελόντι εἰπεῖν, εἰ καὶ κατὰ πάντων ἐμφανὲς εἴη ὅτι ὁ
ἀγαθόν τι εἰσηγούμενος οὐκ ἀτίμητος ἔσται, πολλοὺς ἂν καὶ τοῦτο
ἐξορμήσειεν ἔργον ποιεῖσθαι τὸ σκοπεῖν τι ἀγαθόν. καὶ ὅταν γε
πολλοῖς περὶ τῶν ὠφελίμων μέληι, ἀνάγκη εὑρίσκεσθαί τε μᾶλ- 25
11 λον καὶ ἐπιτελεῖσθαι. εἰ δὲ φοβῆι, ὦ Ἱέρων, μὴ ἐν πολλοῖς ἄθλων
προτιθεμένων πολλαὶ δαπάναι γίγνονται, ἐννόησον ὅτι οὐκ ἔστιν
ἐμπορεύματα λυσιτελέστερα ἢ ὅσα ἄνθρωποι ἄθλων ὠνοῦνται.
ὁρᾶις ἐν ἱππικοῖς καὶ γυμνικοῖς καὶ χορηγικοῖς ἀγῶσιν ὡς
μικρὰ ἆθλα μεγάλας δαπάνας καὶ πολλοὺς πόνους καὶ πολλὰς 30
ἐπιμελείας ἐξάγεται ἀνθρώπων;

10 Καὶ ὁ Ἱέρων εἶπεν· Ἀλλὰ ταῦτα μέν, ὦ Σιμωνίδη, καλῶς μοι δοκεῖς
λέγειν· περὶ δὲ τῶν μισθοφόρων ἔχεις τι εἰπεῖν ὡς μὴ μισεῖσθαι δι'
αὐτούς; ἢ λέγεις ὡς φιλίαν κτησάμενος ἄρχων οὐδὲν ἔτι δεήσεται
2 δορυφόρων; Ναὶ μὰ Δία, εἶπεν ὁ Σιμωνίδης, δεήσεται μὲν οὖν. οἶδα 35
γὰρ ὅτι ὥσπερ ἐν ἵπποις οὕτως καὶ ἐν ἀνθρώποις τισὶν ἐγγίγνε-
ται, ὅσωι ἂν ἔκπλεα τὰ δέοντα ἔχωσι, τοσούτωι ὑβριστοτέροις

εἶναι. τοὺς μὲν οὖν τοιούτους μᾶλλον ἂν σωφρονίζοι ὁ ἀπὸ τῶν   3
δορυφόρων φόβος. τοῖς δὲ καλοῖς κἀγαθοῖς ἀπ' οὐδενὸς ἄν μοι δοκεῖς
τοσαῦτα ὠφελήματα παρασχεῖν ὅσα ἀπὸ τῶν μισθοφόρων. τρέ-   4
φεις μὲν γὰρ δήπου καὶ σὺ αὐτοὺς σαυτῶι φύλακας· ἤδη δὲ πολ-
5 λοὶ καὶ δεσπόται βίαι ὑπὸ τῶν δούλων ἀπέθανον. ἓν οὖν ἂν πρῶτον τοῦτ' εἴη τῶν προστεταγμένων τοῖς μισθοφόροις, ὡς πάντων
ὄντας δορυφόρους τῶν πολιτῶν βοηθεῖν πᾶσιν, ἄν τι τοιοῦτον
αἰσθάνωνται. γίγνονται δέ που, ὡς πάντες ἐπιστάμεθα, κακοῦρ-
γοι ἐν πόλεσιν· εἰ οὖν καὶ τούτους φυλάττειν εἶεν τεταγμένοι, καὶ
10 τοῦτ' ἂν εἰδεῖεν ὑπ' αὐτῶν ὠφελούμενοι. πρὸς δὲ τούτοις καὶ τοῖς ἐν   5
τῆι χώραι ἐργάταις καὶ κτήνεσιν οὗτοι ἂν εἰκότως καὶ θάρρος καὶ
ἀσφάλειαν δύναιντο μάλιστα παρέχειν, ὁμοίως μὲν τοῖς σοῖς ἰδίοις,
ὁμοίως δὲ τοῖς ἀνὰ τὴν χώραν. ἱκανοί γε μήν εἰσι καὶ σχολὴν παρέχειν τοῖς πολίταις τῶν ἰδίων ἐπιμελεῖσθαι, τὰ ἐπίκαιρα φυλάττον-
15 τες. πρὸς δὲ τούτοις καὶ πολεμίων ἐφόδους κρυφαίας καὶ ἐξαπιναίας   6
τίνες ἑτοιμότεροι ἢ προαισθέσθαι ἢ κωλῦσαι τῶν ἀεὶ ἐν ὅπλοις τε
ὄντων καὶ συντεταγμένων; ἀλλὰ μὴν καὶ ἐν τῆι στρατιᾶι τί ἐστιν
ὠφελιμώτερον πολίταις μισθοφόρων; τούτους γὰρ προπονεῖν καὶ
προκινδυνεύειν καὶ προφυλάττειν εἰκὸς ἑτοιμοτάτους εἶναι. τὰς δ'   7
20 ἀγχιτέρμονας πόλεις οὐκ ἀνάγκη διὰ τοὺς ἀεὶ ἐν ὅπλοις ὄντας καὶ
εἰρήνης μάλιστα ἐπιθυμεῖν; οἱ γὰρ συντεταγμένοι καὶ σώιζειν τὰ
τῶν φίλων μάλιστα καὶ σφάλλειν τὰ τῶν πολεμίων δύναιντ' ἄν.
ὅταν γε μὴν γνῶσιν οἱ πολῖται ὅτι οὗτοι κακὸν μὲν οὐδὲν ποιοῦσι   8
τὸν μηδὲν ἀδικοῦντα, τοὺς δὲ κακουργεῖν βουλομένους κωλύουσι,
25 βοηθοῦσι δὲ τοῖς ἀδικουμένοις, προνοοῦσι δὲ καὶ προκινδυνεύουσι
τῶν πολιτῶν, πῶς οὐκ ἀνάγκη καὶ δαπανᾶν εἰς τούτους ἥδιστα;
τρέφουσι γοῦν καὶ ἰδίαι ἐπὶ μείοσι τούτων φύλακας.

Χρὴ δέ, ὦ Ἱέρων, οὐδ' ἀπὸ τῶν ἰδίων κτημάτων ὀκνεῖν δαπανᾶν   11
εἰς τὸ κοινὸν ἀγαθόν. καὶ γὰρ ἔμοιγε δοκεῖ τὰ εἰς τὴν πόλιν ἀναλού-
30 μενα μᾶλλον εἰς τὸ δέον τελεῖσθαι ἢ τὰ εἰς τὸ ἴδιον ἀνδρὶ τυράννωι.
καθ' ἓν δ' ἕκαστον σκοπῶμεν. οἰκίαν πρῶτον ὑπερβαλλούσηι   2
δαπάνηι κεκαλλωπισμένην μᾶλλον ἡγῆι κόσμου ἄν σοι παρέχειν ἢ
πᾶσαν τὴν πόλιν τείχεσί τε καὶ ναοῖς καὶ παστάσι καὶ ἀγοραῖς καὶ
λιμέσι κατεσκευασμένην; ὅπλοις δὲ πότερον τοῖς ἐκπαγλοτάτοις   3
35 αὐτὸς κατακεκοσμημένος δεινότερος ἂν φαίνοιο τοῖς πολεμίοις ἢ
τῆς πόλεως ὅλης εὐόπλου σοι οὔσης; προσόδους δὲ ποτέρως ἂν   4
δοκεῖς πλείονας γίγνεσθαι, εἰ τὰ σὰ ἴδια μόνον ἐνεργὰ ἔχοις ἢ εἰ
τὰ πάντων τῶν πολιτῶν μεμηχανημένος εἴης ἐνεργὰ εἶναι; τὸ   5

δὲ πάντων κάλλιστον καὶ μεγαλοπρεπέστατον νομιζόμενον εἶναι
ἐπιτήδευμα ἁρματοτροφίαν, ποτέρως ἂν δοκεῖς μᾶλλον κοσμεῖν,
εἰ αὐτὸς πλεῖστα τῶν Ἑλλήνων ἅρματα τρέφοις τε καὶ πέμποις εἰς
τὰς πανηγύρεις, ἢ εἰ ἐκ τῆς σῆς πόλεως πλεῖστοι μὲν ἱπποτρόφοι
εἶεν, πλεῖστοι δ᾽ ἀγωνίζοιντο; νικᾶν δὲ πότερα δοκεῖς κάλλιον εἶναι 5
6 ἅρματος ἀρετῆι ἢ πόλεως ἧς προστατεύεις εὐδαιμονίαι; ἐγὼ μὲν γὰρ
οὐδὲ προσήκειν φημὶ ἀνδρὶ τυράννωι πρὸς ἰδιώτας ἀγωνίζεσθαι.
νικῶν μὲν γὰρ οὐκ ἂν θαυμάζοιο ἀλλὰ φθονοῖο, ὡς ἀπὸ πολλῶν
οἴκων τὰς δαπάνας ποιούμενος, νικώμενος δ᾽ ἂν πάντων μάλιστα
7 καταγελῶιο. ἀλλ᾽ ἐγώ σοί φημι, ὦ Ἱέρων, πρὸς ἄλλους προστάτας 10
πόλεων τὸν ἀγῶνα εἶναι, ὧν ἐὰν σὺ εὐδαιμονεστάτην τὴν πόλιν
ἧς προστατεύεις παρέχηις, κηρυχθήσηι νικῶν τῶι καλλίστωι καὶ
8 μεγαλοπρεπεστάτωι ἐν ἀνθρώποις ἀγωνίσματι. καὶ πρῶτον μὲν
εὐθὺς κατειργασμένος ἂν εἴης τὸ φιλεῖσθαι ὑπὸ τῶν ἀρχομένων,
οὗ δὴ σὺ ἐπιθυμῶν τυγχάνεις· ἔπειτα δὲ τὴν σὴν νίκην οὐκ ἂν 15
εἷς εἴη ὁ ἀνακηρύττων, ἀλλὰ πάντες ἄνθρωποι ὑμνοῖεν ἂν τὴν
9 σὴν ἀρετήν. περίβλεπτος δὲ ὢν οὐχ ὑπὸ ἰδιωτῶν μόνον ἀλλὰ καὶ
ὑπὸ πολλῶν πόλεων ἀγαπῶιο ἄν, καὶ θαυμαστὸς οὐκ ἰδίαι μόνον
10 ἀλλὰ καὶ δημοσίαι παρὰ πᾶσιν ἂν εἴης, καὶ ἐξείη μὲν ἄν σοι ἕνεκεν
ἀσφαλείας, εἴ ποι βούλοιο, θεωρήσοντι πορεύεσθαι, ἐξείη δ᾽ ἂν 20
αὐτοῦ μένοντι τοῦτο πράττειν. ἀεὶ γὰρ ἂν παρὰ σοὶ πανήγυρις
εἴη τῶν βουλομένων ἐπιδεικνύναι εἴ τίς τι σοφὸν ἢ καλὸν ἢ ἀγαθὸν
11 ἔχοι, τῶν δὲ καὶ ἐπιθυμούντων ὑπηρετεῖν. πᾶς δὲ ὁ μὲν παρὼν
σύμμαχος ἂν εἴη σοι, ὁ δὲ ἀπὼν ἐπιθυμοίη ἂν ἰδεῖν σε. ὥστε οὐ
μόνον φιλοῖο ἄν, ἀλλὰ καὶ ἐρῶιο ὑπ᾽ ἀνθρώπων, καὶ τοὺς καλοὺς οὐ 25
πειρᾶν, ἀλλὰ πειρώμενον ὑπ᾽ αὐτῶν ἀνέχεσθαι ἄν σε δέοι, φόβον
12 δ᾽ οὐκ ἂν ἔχοις ἀλλ᾽ ἄλλοις παρέχοις μή τι πάθηις, ἑκόντας δὲ τοὺς
πειθομένους ἔχοις ἂν καὶ ἐθελουσίως σου προνοοῦντας θεῶιο ἄν, εἰ
δέ τις κίνδυνος εἴη, οὐ συμμάχους μόνον ἀλλὰ καὶ προμάχους καὶ
προθύμους ὁρώιης ἄν, πολλῶν μὲν δωρεῶν ἀξιούμενος, οὐκ ἀπορῶν 30
δὲ ὅτωι τούτων εὐμενεῖ μεταδώσεις, πάντας μὲν συγχαίροντας ἔχων
ἐπὶ τοῖς σοῖς ἀγαθοῖς, πάντας δὲ πρὸ τῶν σῶν ὥσπερ τῶν ἰδίων
13 μαχομένους. θησαυρούς γε μὴν ἔχοις ἂν πάντας τοὺς παρὰ τοῖς
φίλοις πλούτους. ἀλλὰ θαρρῶν, ὦ Ἱέρων, πλούτιζε μὲν τοὺς φίλους·
σαυτὸν γὰρ πλουτιεῖς· αὖξε δὲ τὴν πόλιν· σαυτῶι γὰρ δύναμιν περι- 35
14 άψεις· κτῶ δὲ αὐτῆι συμμάχους· ... νόμιζε δὲ τὴν μὲν πατρίδα οἶκον,

12 κηρυχθήσηι c: εὖ ἐσῆι D: σὺ ἔσει c: εὖ ἴσθι ἔσει ὁ c   32 σῶν c: σῶν ἰδίων D
36 lacunam indicauit c (e.g. <σαυτῶι γὰρ ἕξεις συμμαχοῦντας>)

τοὺς δὲ πολίτας ἑταίρους, τοὺς δὲ φίλους τέκνα σεαυτοῦ, τοὺς δὲ παῖδας ὅ τιπερ τὴν σὴν ψυχήν, καὶ τούτους πάντας πειρῶ νικᾶν εὖ ποιῶν. ἐὰν γὰρ τοὺς φίλους κρατῆις εὖ ποιῶν, οὐ μή σοι δύνων-   15
ται ἀντέχειν οἱ πολέμιοι. κἂν ταῦτα πάντα ποιῆις, εὖ ἴσθι, πάντων
5 τῶν ἐν ἀνθρώποις κάλλιστον καὶ μακαριώτατον κτῆμα κεκτήσει·
εὐδαιμονῶν γὰρ οὐ φθονηθήσηι.

5 κεκτήσει c: κεκτῆσθαι d: κέκτησο d

XENOPHON
RESPUBLICA LACEDAEMONIORUM

ΛΑΚΕΔΑΙΜΟΝΙΩΝ ΠΟΛΙΤΕΙΑ

Ἀλλ' ἐγὼ ἐννοήσας ποτὲ ὡς ἡ Σπάρτη τῶν ὀλιγανθρωποτάτων   1
πόλεων οὖσα δυνατωτάτη τε καὶ ὀνομαστοτάτη ἐν τῆι Ἑλλάδι
ἐφάνη, ἐθαύμασα ὅτωι ποτὲ τρόπωι τοῦτ' ἐγένετο· ἐπεὶ μέντοι
κατενόησα τὰ ἐπιτηδεύματα τῶν Σπαρτιατῶν, οὐκέτι ἐθαύμαζον.
5 Λυκοῦργον μέντοι τὸν θέντα αὐτοῖς τοὺς νόμους, οἷς πειθόμενοι   2
ηὐδαιμόνησαν, τοῦτον καὶ θαυμάζω καὶ εἰς τὰ ἔσχατα σοφὸν ἡγοῦ-
μαι. ἐκεῖνος γὰρ οὐ μιμησάμενος τὰς ἄλλας πόλεις, ἀλλὰ καὶ ἐναντία γνοὺς ταῖς πλείσταις, προέχουσαν εὐδαιμονίαι τὴν πατρίδα
ἐπέδειξεν.
10 Αὐτίκα γὰρ περὶ τεκνοποιίας, ἵνα ἐξ ἀρχῆς ἄρξωμαι, οἱ μὲν ἄλλοι   3
τὰς μελλούσας τίκτειν καὶ καλῶς δοκούσας κόρας παιδεύεσθαι καὶ
σίτωι ἧι ἀνυστὸν μετριωτάτωι τρέφουσι καὶ ὄψωι ἧι δυνατὸν
μικροτάτωι· οἴνου γε μὴν ἢ πάμπαν ἀπεχομένας ἢ ὑδαρεῖ χρωμένας
διάγουσιν. ὥσπερ δὲ οἱ πολλοὶ τῶν τὰς τέχνας ἐχόντων ἑδραῖοί
15 εἰσιν, οὕτω καὶ τὰς κόρας οἱ ἄλλοι Ἕλληνες ἡρεμιζούσας ἐριουργεῖν
ἀξιοῦσι. τὰς μὲν οὖν οὕτω τρεφομένας πῶς χρὴ προσδοκῆσαι
μεγαλεῖον ἄν τι γεννῆσαι; ὁ δὲ Λυκοῦργος ἐσθῆτας μὲν καὶ δούλας   4
παρέχειν ἱκανὰς ἡγήσατο εἶναι, ταῖς δ' ἐλευθέραις μέγιστον νομίσας
εἶναι τὴν τεκνοποιίαν πρῶτον μὲν σωμασκεῖν ἔταξεν οὐδὲν ἧττον
20 τὸ θῆλυ τοῦ ἄρρενος φύλου· ἔπειτα δὲ δρόμου καὶ ἰσχύος, ὥσπερ
καὶ τοῖς ἀνδράσιν, οὕτω καὶ ταῖς θηλείαις ἀγῶνας πρὸς ἀλλήλας
ἐποίησε, νομίζων ἐξ ἀμφοτέρων ἰσχυρῶν καὶ τὰ ἔκγονα ἐρρωμενέστερα γίγνεσθαι. ἐπεί γε μὴν γυνὴ πρὸς ἄνδρα ἔλθοι, ὁρῶν τοὺς   5
ἄλλους τὸν πρῶτον τοῦ χρόνου ἀμέτρως ταῖς γυναιξὶ συνόντας, καὶ
25 τούτου τἀναντία ἔγνω· ἔθηκε γὰρ αἰδεῖσθαι μὲν εἰσιόντα ὀφθῆναι,
αἰδεῖσθαι δ' ἐξιόντα. οὕτω δὲ συνόντων ποθεινοτέρως μὲν ἀνάγκη
σφῶν αὐτῶν ἔχειν, ἐρρωμενέστερα δὲ γίγνεσθαι, εἴ τι βλάστοι
οὕτω, μᾶλλον ἢ εἰ διάκοροι ἀλλήλων εἶεν. πρὸς δὲ τούτοις καὶ   6
ἀποπαύσας τοῦ ὁπότε βούλοιντο ἕκαστοι γυναῖκα ἄγεσθαι, ἔταξεν
30 ἐν ἀκμαῖς τῶν σωμάτων τοὺς γάμους ποιεῖσθαι, καὶ τοῦτο συμφέρον
τῆι εὐγονίαι νομίζων. εἴ γε μέντοι συμβαίη γεραιῶι νέαν ἔχειν, ὁρῶν   7
τοὺς τηλικούτους φυλάττοντας μάλιστα τὰς γυναῖκας, τἀναντία καὶ
τούτου ἐνόμισε· τῶι γὰρ πρεσβύτηι ἐποίησεν, ὁποίου ἀνδρὸς σῶμά
τε καὶ ψυχὴν ἀγασθείη, τοῦτον ἐπαγαγομένωι τεκνοποιήσασθαι. εἰ   8

27 βλάστοι c: βλάστοιεν d: βλάπτοιεν d: βλαστάνοιεν i   34 ἐπαγαγομένωι c:
ἐπαγομένωι D: ἀπαγαγομένωι i

δέ τις αὖ γυναικὶ μὲν συνοικεῖν μὴ βούλοιτο, τέκνων δὲ ἀξιολόγων
ἐπιθυμοίη, καὶ τοῦτο νόμιμον ἐποίησεν, ἥντινα ἂν εὔτεκνον καὶ γεν-
9 ναίαν ὁρῴη, πείσαντα τὸν ἔχοντα ἐκ ταύτης τεκνοποιεῖσθαι. καὶ
πολλὰ μὲν τοιαῦτα συνεχώρει. αἵ τε γὰρ γυναῖκες διττοὺς οἴκους
βούλονται κατέχειν, οἵ τε ἄνδρες ἀδελφοὺς τοῖς παισὶ προσλαμ- 5
βάνειν, οἳ τοῦ μὲν γένους καὶ τῆς δυνάμεως κοινωνοῦσι, τῶν δὲ
10 χρημάτων οὐκ ἀντιποιοῦνται. περὶ μὲν δὴ τεκνοποιίας οὕτω τἀναντία γνοὺς τοῖς ἄλλοις εἴ τι διαφέροντας καὶ κατὰ μέγεθος καὶ κατ'
ἰσχὺν ἄνδρας τῆι Σπάρτηι ἀπετέλεσεν, ὁ βουλόμενος ἐπισκοπείτω.
2 Ἐγὼ μέντοι, ἐπεὶ καὶ περὶ γενέσεως ἐξήγημαι, βούλομαι καὶ τὴν 10
παιδείαν ἑκατέρων σαφηνίσαι. τῶν μὲν τοίνυν ἄλλων Ἑλλήνων οἱ
φάσκοντες κάλλιστα τοὺς υἱεῖς παιδεύειν, ἐπειδὰν τάχιστα αὐτοῖς
οἱ παῖδες τὰ λεγόμενα ξυνιῶσιν, εὐθὺς μὲν ἐπ' αὐτοῖς παιδαγωγοὺς
θεράποντας ἐφιστᾶσιν, εὐθὺς δὲ πέμπουσιν εἰς διδασκάλων μαθη-
σομένους καὶ γράμματα καὶ μουσικὴν καὶ τὰ ἐν παλαίστραι. πρὸς δὲ 15
τούτοις τῶν παίδων πόδας μὲν ὑποδήμασιν ἁπαλύνουσι, σώματα
δὲ ἱματίων μεταβολαῖς διαθρύπτουσι· σίτου γε μὴν αὐτοῖς γαστέρα
2 μέτρον νομίζουσιν. ὁ δὲ Λυκοῦργος, ἀντὶ μὲν τοῦ ἰδίαι ἕκαστον
παιδαγωγοὺς δούλους ἐφιστάναι, ἄνδρα ἐπέστησε κρατεῖν αὐτῶν
ἐξ ὧνπερ αἱ μέγισται ἀρχαὶ καθίστανται, ὃς δὴ καὶ παιδονόμος 20
καλεῖται, τοῦτον δὲ κύριον ἐποίησε καὶ ἀθροίζειν τοὺς παῖδας καὶ
ἐπισκοποῦντα, εἴ τις ῥαιδιουργοίη, ἰσχυρῶς κολάζειν. ἔδωκε δ' αὐτῶι
καὶ τῶν ἡβώντων μαστιγοφόρους, ὅπως τιμωροῖεν ὁπότε δέοι,
3 ὥστε πολλὴν μὲν αἰδῶ, πολλὴν δὲ πειθὼ ἐκεῖ συμπαρεῖναι. ἀντί γε
μὴν τοῦ ἁπαλύνειν τοὺς πόδας ὑποδήμασιν ἔταξεν ἀνυποδησίαι 25
κρατύνειν, νομίζων, εἰ τοῦτ' ἀσκήσειαν, πολὺ μὲν ῥᾶιον ἂν ὀρθιάδε
ἐκβαίνειν, ἀσφαλέστερον δὲ πρανῆ καταβαίνειν, καὶ πηδῆσαι δὲ
καὶ ἀναθορεῖν καὶ δραμεῖν θᾶττον ἀνυπόδητον, εἰ ἠσκηκὼς εἴη τοὺς
4 πόδας, ἢ ὑποδεδεμένον. καὶ ἀντί γε τοῦ ἱματίοις διαθρύπτεσθαι
ἐνόμιζεν ἑνὶ ἱματίωι δι' ἔτους προσεθίζεσθαι, νομίζων οὕτως καὶ πρὸς 30
5 ψύχη καὶ πρὸς θάλπη ἄμεινον ἂν παρεσκευάσθαι. σῖτόν γε μὴν
ἔταξε τοσοῦτον ἔχοντα συμβολεύειν τὸν εἴρενα ὡς ὑπὸ πλησμονῆς
μὲν μήποτε βαρύνεσθαι, τοῦ δὲ ἐνδεεστέρως διάγειν μὴ ἀπείρως
ἔχειν, νομίζων τοὺς οὕτω παιδευομένους μᾶλλον μὲν ἂν δύνασθαι, εἰ
δεήσειεν, ἀσιτήσαντας ἐπιπονῆσαι, μᾶλλον δ' ἄν, εἰ παραγγελθείη, 35
ἀπὸ τοῦ αὐτοῦ σίτου πλείω χρόνον ἐπιταθῆναι, ἧττον δ' ἂν ὄψου
δεῖσθαι, εὐχερέστερον δὲ πρὸς πᾶν ἔχειν βρῶμα, καὶ ὑγιεινοτέρως

31 παρεσκευάσθαι c: παρασκευάσασθαι D   32 συμβολεύειν d: συμβουλεύειν d εἴρενα
c: ἄρρενα D

δ' ἂν διάγειν· καὶ εἰς μῆκος ἂν τὴν αὐξάνεσθαι ῥαδινὰ τὰ σώματα
ποιοῦσαν τροφὴν μᾶλλον συλλαμβάνειν ἡγήσατο ἢ τὴν διαπλατύνουσαν τῶι σίτωι. ὡς δὲ μὴ ὑπὸ λιμοῦ ἄγαν αὖ πιέζοιντο, ἀπραγ-   6
μόνως μὲν αὐτοῖς οὐκ ἔδωκε λαμβάνειν ὧν ἂν προσδέωνται, κλέπτειν
5 δ' ἐφῆκεν ἔστιν ἃ τῶι λιμῶι ἐπικουροῦντας. καὶ ὡς μὲν οὐκ ἀπορῶν ὅ τι   7
δοίη ἐφῆκεν αὐτοῖς γε μηχανᾶσθαι τὴν τροφήν, οὐδένα οἶμαι τοῦτο
ἀγνοεῖν· δῆλον δ' ὅτι τὸν μέλλοντα κλωπεύειν καὶ νυκτὸς ἀγρυπ-
νεῖν δεῖ καὶ μεθ' ἡμέραν ἀπατᾶν καὶ ἐνεδρεύειν, καὶ κατασκόπους δὲ
ἑτοιμάζειν τὸν μέλλοντά τι λήψεσθαι. ταῦτα οὖν δὴ πάντα δῆλον
10 ὅτι μηχανικωτέρους τῶν ἐπιτηδείων βουλόμενος τοὺς παῖδας ποιεῖν
καὶ πολεμικωτέρους οὕτως ἐπαίδευσεν. εἴποι δ' ἂν οὖν τις, τί δῆτα,   8
εἴπερ τὸ κλέπτειν ἀγαθὸν ἐνόμιζε, πολλὰς πληγὰς ἐπέβαλλε τῶι
ἁλισκομένωι; ὅτι, φημὶ ἐγώ, καὶ τἆλλα, ὅσα ἄνθρωποι διδάσκ-
ουσι, κολάζουσι τὸν μὴ καλῶς ὑπηρετοῦντα. κἀκεῖνοι οὖν τοὺς
15 ἁλισκομένους ὡς κακῶς κλέπτοντας τιμωροῦνται. καὶ ὡς πλείστους   9
δὴ ἁρπάσαι τυροὺς παρ' Ὀρθίας καλὸν θείς, μαστιγοῦν τούτους
ἄλλοις ἐπέταξε, τοῦτο δηλῶσαι καὶ ἐν τούτωι βουλόμενος ὅτι ἔστιν
ὀλίγον χρόνον ἀλγήσαντα πολὺν χρόνον εὐδοκιμοῦντα εὐφραί-
νεσθαι. δηλοῦται δὲ ἐν τούτωι ὅτι καὶ ὅπου τάχους δεῖ ὁ βλακεύων
20 ἐλάχιστα μὲν ὠφελεῖται, πλεῖστα δὲ πράγματα λαμβάνει. ὅπως δὲ   10
μηδ' εἰ ὁ παιδονόμος ἀπέλθοι, ἔρημοί ποτε οἱ παῖδες εἶεν ἄρχοντος,
ἐποίησε τὸν ἀεὶ παρόντα τῶν πολιτῶν κύριον εἶναι καὶ ἐπιτάτ-
τειν τοῖς παισὶν ὅ τι ἂν ἀγαθὸν δοκοίη εἶναι, καὶ κολάζειν, εἴ τι
ἁμαρτάνοιεν. τοῦτο δὲ ποιήσας διέπραξε καὶ αἰδημονεστέρους εἶναι
25 τοὺς παῖδας· οὐδὲν γὰρ οὕτως αἰδοῦνται οὔτε παῖδες οὔτε ἄνδρες
ὡς τοὺς ἄρχοντας. ὡς δὲ καὶ εἴ ποτε μηδεὶς τύχοι ἀνὴρ παρών,   11
μηδ' ὡς ἔρημοι οἱ παῖδες ἄρχοντος εἶεν, ἔθηκε τῆς ἴλης ἑκάστης τὸν
τορώτατον τῶν εἰρένων ἄρχειν· ὥστε οὐδέποτε ἐκεῖ οἱ παῖδες ἔρημοι
ἄρχοντός εἰσι.
30   Λεκτέον δέ μοι δοκεῖ εἶναι καὶ περὶ τῶν παιδικῶν ἐρώτων· ἔστι   12
γάρ τι καὶ τοῦτο πρὸς παιδείαν. οἱ μὲν τοίνυν ἄλλοι Ἕλληνες ἢ
ὥσπερ Βοιωτοὶ ἀνὴρ καὶ παῖς συζυγέντες ὁμιλοῦσιν, ἢ ὥσπερ
Ἠλεῖοι διὰ χαρίτων τῆι ὥραι χρῶνται· εἰσὶ δὲ καὶ οἳ παντάπασι τοῦ
διαλέγεσθαι τοὺς ἐραστὰς εἴργουσιν ἀπὸ τῶν παίδων. ὁ δὲ Λυκοῦρ-   13
35 γος ἐναντία καὶ τούτοις πᾶσι γνούς, εἰ μέν τις αὐτὸς ὢν οἷον δεῖ
ἀγασθεὶς ψυχὴν παιδὸς πειρῶιτο ἄμεμπτον φίλον ἀποτελέσασθαι
καὶ συνεῖναι, ἐπήινει καὶ καλλίστην παιδείαν ταύτην ἐνόμιζεν· εἰ
δέ τις παιδὸς σώματος ὀρεγόμενος φανείη, αἴσχιστον τοῦτο θεὶς

---

1 τὴν αὐξάνεσθαι c: αὐξάνεσθαι τὴν Di   28 εἰρένων c: ἀρρένων D

ἐποίησεν ἐν Λακεδαίμονι μηδὲν ἧττον ἐραστὰς παιδικῶν ἀπέχεσθαι
ἢ γονεῖς παίδων ἢ καὶ ἀδελφοὶ ἀδελφῶν εἰς ἀφροδίσια ἀπέχονται.

14 τὸ μέντοι ταῦτα ἀπιστεῖσθαι ὑπό τινων οὐ θαυμάζω· ἐν πολλαῖς
γὰρ τῶν πόλεων οἱ νόμοι οὐκ ἐναντιοῦνται ταῖς πρὸς τοὺς παῖδας
ἐπιθυμίαις. 5

Ἡ μὲν δὴ παιδεία εἴρηται ἥ τε Λακωνικὴ καὶ ἡ τῶν ἄλλων Ἑλ-
λήνων· ἐξ ὁποτέρας δ' αὐτῶν καὶ εὐπειθέστεροι καὶ αἰδημονέστεροι
καὶ ὧν δεῖ ἐγκρατέστεροι ἄνδρες ἀποτελοῦνται, ὁ βουλόμενος καὶ
ταῦτα ἐπισκοπείσθω.

3 Ὅταν γε μὴν ἐκ παίδων εἰς τὸ μειρακιοῦσθαι ἐκβαίνωσι, τηνικαῦτα 10
οἱ μὲν ἄλλοι παύουσι μὲν ἀπὸ παιδαγωγῶν, παύουσι δὲ ἀπὸ
διδασκάλων, ἄρχουσι δὲ οὐδένες ἔτι αὐτῶν, ἀλλ' αὐτονόμους
2 ἀφιᾶσιν· ὁ δὲ Λυκοῦργος καὶ τούτων τἀναντία ἔγνω. καταμαθὼν
γὰρ τοῖς τηλικούτοις μέγιστον μὲν φρόνημα ἐμφυόμενον, μάλιστα
δὲ ὕβριν ἐπιπολάζουσαν, ἰσχυροτάτας δὲ ἐπιθυμίας τῶν ἡδονῶν 15
παρισταμένας, τηνικαῦτα πλείστους μὲν πόνους αὐτοῖς ἐπέβαλε,
3 πλείστην δὲ ἀσχολίαν ἐμηχανήσατο. ἐπιθεὶς δὲ καὶ εἴ τις ταῦτα
φύγοι, μηδενὸς ἔτι τῶν καλῶν τυγχάνειν, ἐποίησε μὴ μόνον τοὺς
ἐκ δημοσίου ἀλλὰ καὶ τοὺς κηδομένους ἑκάστων ἐπιμελεῖσθαι, ὡς μὴ
4 ἀποδειλιάσαντες ἀδόκιμοι παντάπασιν ἐν τῆι πόλει γένοιντο. πρὸς 20
δὲ τούτοις τὸ αἰδεῖσθαι ἰσχυρῶς ἐμφῦσαι βουλόμενος αὐτοῖς καὶ ἐν
ταῖς ὁδοῖς ἐπέταξεν ἐντὸς μὲν τοῦ ἱματίου τὼ χεῖρε ἔχειν, σιγῆι δὲ
πορεύεσθαι, περιβλέπειν δὲ μηδαμοῖ, ἀλλ' αὐτὰ τὰ πρὸ τῶν ποδῶν
ὁρᾶν. ἔνθα δὴ καὶ δῆλον γεγένηται ὅτι τὸ ἄρρεν φῦλον καὶ εἰς τὸ
5 σωφρονεῖν ἰσχυρότερόν ἐστι τῶν τῆς θηλείας φύσεως. ἐκείνων γοῦν 25
ἧττον μὲν ἂν φωνὴν ἀκούσαις ἢ τῶν λιθίνων, ἧττον δ' ἂν ὄμματα
στρέψαις ἢ τῶν χαλκῶν, αἰδημονεστέρους δ' ἂν αὐτοὺς ἡγήσαιο καὶ
αὐτῶν τῶν ἐν τοῖς ὀφθαλμοῖς παρθένων. καὶ ἐπειδὰν εἰς τὸ φιλίτιόν
γε ἀφίκωνται, ἀγαπητὸν αὐτῶν καὶ τὸ ἐρωτηθὲν ἀκοῦσαι. καὶ τῶν
μὲν αὖ παιδίσκων οὕτως ἐπεμελήθη. 30

4 Περί γε μὴν τῶν ἡβώντων πολὺ μάλιστα ἐσπούδασε, νομίζων
τούτους, εἰ γένοιντο οἵους δεῖ, πλεῖστον ῥέπειν ἐπὶ τὸ ἀγαθὸν τῆι
2 πόλει. ὁρῶν οὖν, οἷς ἂν μάλιστα φιλονικία ἐγγένηται, τούτων καὶ
χοροὺς ἀξιακροατοτάτους γιγνομένους καὶ γυμνικοὺς ἀγῶνας ἀξιοθεατοτάτους, ἐνόμιζεν, εἰ καὶ τοὺς ἡβῶντας συμβάλλοι εἰς ἔριν περὶ 35
ἀρετῆς, οὕτως ἂν καὶ τούτους ἐπὶ πλεῖστον ἀφικνεῖσθαι ἀνδρα-
3 γαθίας. ὡς οὖν τούτους αὖ συνέβαλεν, ἐξηγήσομαι. αἱροῦνται τοίνυν

25 τῶν τῆς D: τῆς c   27 στρέψαις i: μεταστρέψαις D: στρεψάντων i
28 ὀφθαλμοῖς i: θαλαμοῖς D   30 παιδίσκων c: παιδικῶν D

αὐτῶν οἱ ἔφοροι ἐκ τῶν ἀκμαζόντων τρεῖς ἄνδρας· οὗτοι δὲ ἱππαγρέται καλοῦνται. τούτων δ' ἕκαστος ἄνδρας ἑκατὸν καταλέγει,
διασαφηνίζων ὅτου ἕνεκα τοὺς μὲν προτιμᾶι, τοὺς δὲ ἀποδοκιμάζει.
οἱ οὖν μὴ τυγχάνοντες τῶν καλῶν πολεμοῦσι τοῖς τε ἀποστείλασιν   4
5 αὐτοὺς καὶ τοῖς αἱρεθεῖσιν ἀνθ' αὑτῶν καὶ παραφυλάττουσιν
ἀλλήλους, ἐάν τι παρὰ τὰ καλὰ νομιζόμενα ῥαιδιουργῶσι.
Καὶ αὕτη δὴ γίγνεται ἡ θεοφιλεστάτη τε καὶ πολιτικωτάτη ἔρις,   5
ἐν ἧι ἀποδέδεικται μὲν ἃ δεῖ ποιεῖν τὸν ἀγαθόν, χωρὶς δ' ἑκάτεροι
ἀσκοῦσιν ὅπως ἀεὶ κράτιστοι ἔσονται, ἐὰν δέ τι δέηι, καθ' ἕνα
10 ἀρήξουσι τῆι πόλει παντὶ σθένει. ἀνάγκη δ' αὐτοῖς καὶ εὐεξίας   6
ἐπιμελεῖσθαι. καὶ γὰρ πυκτεύουσι διὰ τὴν ἔριν ὅπου ἂν συμβάλ-
ωσι· διαλύειν μέντοι τοὺς μαχομένους πᾶς ὁ παραγενόμενος κύριος.
ἢν δέ τις ἀπειθῆι τῶι διαλύοντι, ἄγει αὐτὸν ὁ παιδονόμος ἐπὶ τοὺς
ἐφόρους· οἱ δὲ ζημιοῦσι μεγαλείως, καθιστάναι βουλόμενοι εἰς τὸ
15 μήποτε ὀργὴν τοῦ μὴ πείθεσθαι τοῖς νόμοις κρατῆσαι.
Τοῖς γε μὴν τὴν ἡβητικὴν ἡλικίαν πεπερακόσιν, ἐξ ὧν ἤδη καὶ αἱ   7
μέγισται ἀρχαὶ καθίστανται, οἱ μὲν ἄλλοι Ἕλληνες ἀφελόντες αὐτῶν
τὸ ἰσχύος ἔτι ἐπιμελεῖσθαι στρατεύεσθαι ὅμως αὐτοῖς ἐπιτάττουσιν,
ὁ δὲ Λυκοῦργος τοῖς τηλικούτοις νόμιμον ἐποίησε κάλλιστον εἶναι
20 τὸ θηρᾶν, εἰ μή τι δημόσιον κωλύοι, ὅπως δύναιντο καὶ οὗτοι μηδὲν
ἧττον τῶν ἡβώντων στρατιωτικοὺς πόνους ὑποφέρειν.
Ἃ μὲν οὖν ἑκάστηι ἡλικίαι ἐνομοθέτησεν ὁ Λυκοῦργος ἐπιτηδεύ-   5
ματα σχεδὸν εἴρηται· οἵαν δὲ καὶ πᾶσι δίαιταν κατεσκεύασε, νῦν
πειράσομαι διηγεῖσθαι. Λυκοῦργος τοίνυν παραλαβὼν τοὺς Σπαρ-   2
25 τιάτας ὥσπερ τοὺς ἄλλους Ἕλληνας οἴκοι σκηνοῦντας, γνοὺς ἐν τούτοις πλεῖστα ῥαιδιουργεῖσθαι, εἰς τὸ φανερὸν ἐξήγαγε τὰ συσκήνια,
οὕτως ἡγούμενος ἥκιστ' ἂν παραβαίνεσθαι τὰ προσταττόμενα. καὶ   3
σῖτόν γε ἔταξεν αὐτοῖς ὡς μήτε ὑπερπληροῦσθαι μήτε ἐνδεεῖς γίγνεσθαι. πολλὰ δὲ καὶ παράλογα γίγνεται ἀπὸ τῶν ἀγρευομένων·
30 οἱ δὲ πλούσιοι ἔστιν ὅτε καὶ ἄρτον ἀντιπαραβάλλουσιν· ὥστε οὔτε
ἔρημός ποτε ἡ τράπεζα βρωτῶν γίγνεται, ἔστ' ἂν διασκηνῶσιν,
οὔτε πολυδάπανος. καὶ μὴν τοῦ πότου ἀποπαύσας τὰς ἀναγκαίας   4
πόσεις, αἳ σφάλλουσι μὲν σώματα, σφάλλουσι δὲ γνώμας, ἐφῆκεν
ὁπότε διψώιη ἕκαστος πίνειν, οὕτω νομίζων ἀβλαβέστατόν τε καὶ
35 ἥδιστον ποτὸν γίγνεσθαι. οὕτω γε μὴν συσκηνούντων πῶς ἄν τις
ἢ ὑπὸ λιχνείας ἢ οἰνοφλυγίας ἢ αὑτὸν ἢ οἶκον διαφθείρειεν; καὶ   5
γὰρ δὴ ἐν μὲν ταῖς ἄλλαις πόλεσιν ὡς τὸ πολὺ οἱ ἥλικες ἀλλήλοις

10 σθένει c: σθένει ἂν D   28 γε c: τε D   30 ἄρτον c: ἀργὸν D   32 ἀναγκαίας c:
οὐκ ἀναγκαίας D

σύνεισι, μεθ' ὧνπερ καὶ ἐλαχίστη αἰδὼς παραγίγνεται· ὁ δὲ Λυκοῦργος ἐν τῆι Σπάρτηι ἀνέμειξε . . . παιδεύεσθαι τὰ πολλὰ τοὺς
6 νεωτέρους ὑπὸ τῆς τῶν γεραιτέρων ἐμπειρίας. καὶ γὰρ δὴ ἐπιχώριον
ἐν τοῖς φιλιτίοις λέγεσθαι ὅ τι ἂν καλῶς τις ἐν τῆι πόλει ποιήσηι·
ὥστ' ἐκεῖ ἥκιστα μὲν ὕβριν, ἥκιστα δὲ παροινίαν, ἥκιστα δὲ αἰσ-   5
7 χουργίαν καὶ αἰσχρολογίαν ἐγγίγνεσθαι. ἀγαθά γε μὴν ἀπεργάζε-
ται καὶ τάδε ἡ ἔξω σίτησις· περιπατεῖν τε γὰρ ἀναγκάζονται ἐν τῆι
οἴκαδε ἀφόδωι, καὶ μὴν τοῦ ὑπὸ οἴνου μὴ σφάλλεσθαι ἐπιμελεῖσθαι,
εἰδότες ὅτι οὐκ ἔνθαπερ ἐδείπνουν καταμενοῦσι καὶ τῆι ὄρφνηι ὅσα
ἡμέραι χρηστέον· οὐδὲ γὰρ ὑπὸ φανοῦ τὸν ἔτι ἔμφρουρον ἔξεστι   10
πορεύεσθαι.
8 Καταμαθών γε μὴν ὁ Λυκοῦργος καὶ ὅτι ἀπὸ τῶν σίτων οἱ μὲν
διαπονούμενοι εὔχροί τε καὶ εὔσαρκοι καὶ εὔρωστοί εἰσιν, οἱ δ'
ἄπονοι πεφυσημένοι τε καὶ αἰσχροὶ καὶ ἀσθενεῖς ἀναφαίνονται, οὐδὲ
τούτου ἠμέλησεν, ἀλλ' ἐννοῶν ὅτι καὶ ὅταν αὐτός τις τῆι ἑαυτοῦ   15
γνώμηι φιλοπονῆι, ἀρκούντως τὸ σῶμα ἔχων ἀναφαίνεται, ἐπέταξε
τὸν ἀεὶ πρεσβύτατον ἐν τῶι γυμνασίωι ἑκάστωι ἐπιμελεῖσθαι ὡς μὴ
9 πόνους αὐτοῖς ἐλάττους τῶν σιτίων γίγνεσθαι. καὶ ἐμοὶ μὲν οὐδ' ἐν
τούτωι σφαλῆναι δοκεῖ. οὐκ ἂν οὖν ῥαιδίως γέ τις εὕροι Σπαρτιατῶν
οὔτε ὑγιεινοτέρους οὔτε τοῖς σώμασι χρησιμωτέρους· ὁμοίως γὰρ   20
ἀπό τε τῶν σκελῶν καὶ ἀπὸ χειρῶν καὶ ἀπὸ τραχήλου γυμνάζονται.
6 Ἐναντία γε μὴν ἔγνω καὶ τάδε τοῖς πλείστοις. ἐν μὲν γὰρ
ταῖς ἄλλαις πόλεσι τῶν ἑαυτοῦ ἕκαστος καὶ παίδων καὶ οἰκετῶν
καὶ χρημάτων ἄρχουσιν· ὁ δὲ Λυκοῦργος, κατασκευάσαι βουλόμενος ὡς ἂν μηδὲν βλάπτοντες ἀπολαύοιέν τι οἱ πολῖται ἀλλήλων   25
ἀγαθόν, ἐποίησε παίδων ἕκαστον ὁμοίως τῶν ἑαυτοῦ καὶ τῶν
2 ἀλλοτρίων ἄρχειν. ὅταν δέ τις εἰδῆι ὅτι οὗτοι πατέρες εἰσὶ τῶν
παίδων, ὧν αὐτὸς ἄρχει ἀνάγκη οὕτως ἄρχειν ὥσπερ ἂν καὶ
τῶν ἑαυτοῦ ἄρχεσθαι βούλοιτο. ἢν δέ τις παῖς ποτε πληγὰς
λαβὼν ὑπ' ἄλλου κατείπηι πρὸς τὸν πατέρα, αἰσχρόν ἐστι μὴ   30
οὐκ ἄλλας πληγὰς ἐμβάλλειν τῶι υἱεῖ. οὕτω πιστεύουσιν ἀλλήλοις
3 μηδὲν αἰσχρὸν προστάττειν τοῖς παισίν. ἐποίησε δὲ καὶ οἰκέταις,
εἴ τις δεηθείη, χρῆσθαι καὶ τοῖς ἀλλοτρίοις. καὶ κυνῶν δὲ θηρευ-
τικῶν συνῆψε κοινωνίαν· ὥστε οἱ μὲν δεόμενοι παρακαλοῦσιν
ἐπὶ θήραν, ὁ δὲ μὴ αὐτὸς σχολάζων ἡδέως ἐκπέμπει. καὶ ἵπποις   35
δὲ ὡσαύτως χρῶνται· ὁ γὰρ ἀσθενήσας ἢ δεηθεὶς ὀχήματος ἢ
ταχύ ποι βουληθεὶς ἀφικέσθαι, ἤν που ἴδηι ἵππον ὄντα, λαβὼν
4 καὶ χρησάμενος καλῶς ἀποκαθίστησιν. οὐ μὴν οὐδ' ἐκεῖνό γε

---

2 post ἀνέμειξε lacunam indicauit c (e.g. <νομίζων>, <τὰς ἡλικίας ὥστε>, <βουλόμε-
νος>)   8 τοῦ c: τὸ D   9 εἰδότες c: εἰδότας D   17–18 μὴ πόνους αὐτοῖς c: μήποτε
αὐτοὶ D   29 τῶν c: τὸν Di   37 ποι c: που D   38 γε c: τὸ D

παρὰ τοῖς ἄλλοις εἰθισμένον ἐποίησεν ἐπιτηδεύεσθαι. ὅπου γὰρ ἂν
ὑπὸ θήρας ὀψισθέντες δεηθῶσι τῶν ἐπιτηδείων, ἢν μὴ συνεσκευασμένοι τύχωσι, καὶ ἐνταῦθα ἔθηκε τοὺς μὲν πεπαμένους καταλείπειν
τὰ πεποιημένα, τοὺς δὲ δεομένους ἀνοίξαντας τὰ σήμαντρα, λαβόν-
5 τας ὅσων ἂν δέωνται σημηναμένους καταλιπεῖν. τοιγαροῦν οὕτως   5
μεταδιδόντες ἀλλήλοις καὶ οἱ τὰ μικρὰ ἔχοντες μετέχουσι πάντων
τῶν ἐν τῆι χώραι, ὁπόταν τινὸς δεηθῶσιν.
  Ἐναντία γε μὴν καὶ τάδε τοῖς ἄλλοις Ἕλλησι κατέστησεν ὁ Λυκοῦρ-   7
γος ἐν τῆι Σπάρτηι νόμιμα. ἐν μὲν γὰρ δήπου ταῖς ἄλλαις πόλεσι
10 πάντες χρηματίζονται ὅσον δύνανται· ὁ μὲν γὰρ γεωργεῖ, ὁ δὲ
ναυκληρεῖ, ὁ δ' ἐμπορεύεται, οἱ δὲ καὶ ἀπὸ τεχνῶν τρέφονται· ἐν   2
δὲ τῆι Σπάρτηι ὁ Λυκοῦργος τοῖς ἐλευθέροις τῶν μὲν ἀμφὶ χρηματισμὸν ἀπεῖπε μηδενὸς ἅπτεσθαι, ὅσα δὲ ἐλευθερίαν ταῖς πόλεσι
παρασκευάζει, ταῦτα ἔταξε μόνα ἔργα αὐτῶν νομίζειν. καὶ γὰρ δὴ   3
15 τί πλοῦτος ἐκεῖ γε σπουδαστέος, ἔνθα ἴσα μὲν φέρειν εἰς τὰ ἐπιτήδεια,
ὁμοίως δὲ διαιτᾶσθαι τάξας ἐποίησε μὴ ἡδυπαθείας ἕνεκα χρημάτων
ὀρέγεσθαι; ἀλλὰ μὴν οὐδ' ἱματίων γε ἕνεκα χρηματιστέον· οὐ γὰρ
ἐσθῆτος πολυτελείαι ἀλλὰ σώματος εὐεξίαι κοσμοῦνται. οὐδὲ μὴν   4
τοῦ γε εἰς τοὺς συσκήνους ἕνεκα ἔχειν δαπανᾶν χρήματα ἀθροιστέον,
20 ἐπεὶ τὸ τῶι σώματι πονοῦντα ὠφελεῖν τοὺς συνόντας εὐδοξότερον
ἐποίησεν ἢ τὸ δαπανῶντα, ἐπιδείξας τὸ μὲν ψυχῆς, τὸ δὲ πλούτου ἔργον. τό γε μὴν ἐξ ἀδίκων χρηματίζεσθαι καὶ ἐν τοῖς τοιού-   5
τοις διεκώλυσε. πρῶτον μὲν γὰρ νόμισμα τοιοῦτον κατεστήσατο, ὃ
δεκάμνων μόνον ἂν εἰς οἰκίαν εἰσελθὸν οὔποτε δεσπότας οὐδὲ οἰκέ-
25 τας λάθοι· καὶ γὰρ χώρας μεγάλης καὶ ἁμάξης ἀγωγῆς δέοιτ' ἄν.   6
χρυσίον γε μὴν καὶ ἀργύριον ἐρευνᾶται, καὶ ἄν τί που φανῆι, ὁ ἔχων
ζημιοῦται. τί οὖν ἂν ἐκεῖ χρηματισμὸς σπουδάζοιτο, ἔνθα ἡ κτῆσις
πλείους λύπας ἢ ἡ χρῆσις εὐφροσύνας παρέχει;
  Ἀλλὰ γὰρ ὅτι μὲν ἐν Σπάρτηι μάλιστα πείθονται ταῖς ἀρχαῖς τε   8
30 καὶ τοῖς νόμοις, ἴσμεν ἅπαντες. ἐγὼ μέντοι οὐδ' ἐγχειρῆσαι οἶμαι
πρότερον τὸν Λυκοῦργον ταύτην τὴν εὐταξίαν καθιστάναι πρὶν
ὁμογνώμονας ἐποιήσατο τοὺς κρατίστους τῶν ἐν τῆι πόλει. τεκμαίρομαι δὲ ταῦτα, ὅτι ἐν μὲν ταῖς ἄλλαις πόλεσιν οἱ δυνατώτεροι   2
οὐδὲ βούλονται δοκεῖν τὰς ἀρχὰς φοβεῖσθαι, ἀλλὰ νομίζουσι τοῦτο
35 ἀνελεύθερον εἶναι· ἐν δὲ τῆι Σπάρτηι οἱ κράτιστοι καὶ ὑπέρχονται
μάλιστα τὰς ἀρχὰς καὶ τῶι ταπεινοὶ εἶναι μεγαλύνονται καὶ τῶι
ὅταν καλῶνται τρέχοντες ἀλλὰ μὴ βαδίζοντες ὑπακούειν,

3 πεπαμένους c: πεπαυμένους D   21 δαπανῶντα c: -τας D   24 οὐδὲ c: οὔτε D
31 εὐταξίαν c: εὐεξίαν D

νομίζοντες, ἢν αὐτοὶ κατάρχωσι τοῦ σφόδρα πείθεσθαι, ἕψεσθαι
3 καὶ τοὺς ἄλλους· ὅπερ καὶ γεγένηται. εἰκὸς δὲ καὶ τὴν τῆς ἐφορείας
δύναμιν τοὺς αὐτοὺς τούτους συγκατασκευάσαι, ἐπείπερ ἔγνωσαν
τὸ πείθεσθαι μέγιστον ἀγαθὸν εἶναι καὶ ἐν πόλει καὶ ἐν στρατιᾶι καὶ
ἐν οἴκωι· ὅσωι γὰρ μείζω δύναμιν ἔχει ἡ ἀρχή, τοσούτωι μᾶλλον   5
ἂν ἡγήσαντο αὐτὴν καὶ καταπλήξειν τοὺς πολίτας τοῦ ὑπακούειν.
4 ἔφοροι οὖν ἱκανοὶ μέν εἰσι ζημιοῦν ὃν ἂν βούλωνται, κύριοι δ᾽ ἐκπράτ-
τειν παραχρῆμα, κύριοι δὲ καὶ ἄρχοντας μεταξὺ καταπαῦσαι καὶ
εἶρξαί γε καὶ περὶ τῆς ψυχῆς εἰς ἀγῶνα καταστῆσαι. τοσαύτην δὲ
ἔχοντες δύναμιν οὐχ ὥσπερ αἱ ἄλλαι πόλεις ἐῶσι τοὺς αἱρεθέντας 10
ἀεὶ ἄρχειν τὸ ἔτος ὅπως ἂν βούλωνται, ἀλλ᾽ ὥσπερ οἱ τύραννοι
καὶ οἱ ἐν τοῖς γυμνικοῖς ἀγῶσιν ἐπιστάται, ἤν τινα αἰσθάνωνται
5 παρανομοῦντά τι, εὐθὺς παραχρῆμα κολάζουσι. πολλῶν δὲ καὶ
ἄλλων ὄντων μηχανημάτων καλῶν τῶι Λυκούργωι εἰς τὸ πείθεσθαι
τοῖς νόμοις ἐθέλειν τοὺς πολίτας, ἐν τοῖς καλλίστοις καὶ τοῦτό μοι 15
δοκεῖ εἶναι, ὅτι οὐ πρότερον ἀπέδωκε τῶι πλήθει τοὺς νόμους πρὶν
ἐλθὼν σὺν τοῖς κρατίστοις εἰς Δελφοὺς ἐπήρετο τὸν θεὸν εἰ λῶιον
καὶ ἄμεινον εἴη τῆι Σπάρτηι πειθομένηι οἷς αὐτὸς ἔθηκε νόμοις. ἐπεὶ
δὲ ἀνεῖλε τῶι παντὶ ἄμεινον εἶναι, τότε ἀπέδωκεν, οὐ μόνον ἄνομον
ἀλλὰ καὶ ἀνόσιον θεὶς τὸ πυθοχρήστοις νόμοις μὴ πείθεσθαι.   20
9 Ἄξιον δὲ τοῦ Λυκούργου καὶ τόδε ἀγασθῆναι, τὸ κατεργάσασθαι
ἐν τῆι πόλει αἱρετώτερον εἶναι τὸν καλὸν θάνατον ἀντὶ τοῦ αἰσχροῦ
2 βίου· καὶ γὰρ δὴ ἐπισκοπῶν τις ἂν εὕροι μείους ἀποθνήισκοντας
τούτων ἢ τῶν ἐκ τοῦ φοβεροῦ ἀποχωρεῖν αἱρουμένων. ὡς τἀληθὲς
εἰπεῖν καὶ ἕπεται τῆι ἀρετῆι τὸ σώιζεσθαι εἰς τὸν πλείω χρόνον 25
μᾶλλον ἢ τῆι κακίαι· καὶ γὰρ ῥάιων καὶ ἡδίων καὶ εὐπορωτέρα καὶ
ἰσχυροτέρα. δῆλον δὲ ὅτι καὶ εὔκλεια μάλιστα ἕπεται τῆι ἀρετῆι· καὶ
3 γὰρ συμμαχεῖν πως πάντες τοῖς ἀγαθοῖς βούλονται. ἧι μέντοι ὥστε
ταῦτα γίγνεσθαι ἐμηχανήσατο, καὶ τοῦτο καλὸν μὴ παραλιπεῖν.
ἐκεῖνος τοίνυν σαφῶς παρεσκεύασε τοῖς μὲν ἀγαθοῖς εὐδαιμονίαν, τοῖς 30
4 δὲ κακοῖς κακοδαιμονίαν. ἐν μὲν γὰρ ταῖς ἄλλαις πόλεσιν, ὁπόταν
τις κακὸς γένηται, ἐπίκλησιν μόνον ἔχει κακὸς εἶναι, ἀγοράζει δὲ ἐν
τῶι αὐτῶι ὁ κακὸς τἀγαθῶι καὶ κάθηται καὶ γυμνάζεται, ἐὰν βού-
ληται· ἐν δὲ τῆι Λακεδαίμονι πᾶς μὲν ἄν τις αἰσχυνθείη τὸν κακὸν
σύσκηνον παραλαβεῖν, πᾶς δ᾽ ἂν ἐν παλαίσματι συγγυμναστήν.   35
5 πολλάκις δ᾽ ὁ τοιοῦτος καὶ διαιρουμένων τοὺς ἀντισφαιροῦντας
ἀχώριστος περιγίγνεται, καὶ ἐν χοροῖς δ᾽ εἰς τὰς ἐπονειδίστους χώρας
ἀπελαύνεται, καὶ μὴν ἐν ὁδοῖς παραχωρητέον αὐτῶι καὶ ἐν θάκοις

καὶ τοῖς νεωτέροις ὑπαναστατέον, καὶ τὰς μὲν προσηκούσας κόρας
οἴκοι θρεπτέον, καὶ ταύταις τῆς ἀνανδρίας αἰτίαν ὑφεκτέον, γυναικὸς
δὲ κενὴν ἑστίαν περιοπτέον καὶ ἅμα τούτου ζημίαν ἀποτειστέον,
λιπαρὸν δὲ οὐ πλανητέον οὐδὲ μιμητέον τοὺς ἀνεγκλήτους, ἢ
5 πληγὰς ὑπὸ τῶν ἀμεινόνων ληπτέον. ἐγὼ μὲν δὴ τοιαύτης τοῖς   6
κακοῖς ἀτιμίας ἐπικειμένης οὐδὲν θαυμάζω τὸ προαιρεῖσθαι ἐκεῖ θάνατον ἀντὶ τοῦ οὕτως ἀτίμου τε καὶ ἐπονειδίστου βίου.
        Καλῶς δέ μοι δοκεῖ ὁ Λυκοῦργος νομοθετῆσαι καὶ ἧι μέχρι γήρως   10
ἀσκοῖτ᾽ ἂν ἀρετή. ἐπὶ γὰρ τῶι τέρματι τοῦ βίου τὴν κρίσιν τῆς γερον-
10 τίας προσθεὶς ἐποίησε μηδὲ ἐν τῶι γήραι ἀμελεῖσθαι τὴν καλοκά-
γαθίαν. ἀξιάγαστον δ᾽ αὐτοῦ καὶ τὸ ἐπικουρῆσαι τῶι τῶν ἀγαθῶν   2
γήραι· θεὶς γὰρ τοὺς γέροντας κυρίους τοῦ περὶ τῆς ψυχῆς ἀγῶνος
διέπραξεν ἐντιμότερον εἶναι τὸ γῆρας τῆς τῶν ἀκμαζόντων ῥώμης.
εἰκότως δέ τοι καὶ σπουδάζεται οὗτος ὁ ἀγὼν μάλιστα τῶν ἀνθ-   3
15 ρωπίνων. καλοὶ μὲν γὰρ καὶ οἱ γυμνικοί· ἀλλ᾽ οὗτοι μὲν σωμάτων
εἰσίν· ὁ δὲ περὶ τῆς γεροντίας ἀγὼν ψυχῶν ἀγαθῶν κρίσιν παρέχει.
ὅσωι οὖν κρείττων ψυχὴ σώματος, τοσούτωι καὶ οἱ ἀγῶνες οἱ τῶν
ψυχῶν ἢ οἱ τῶν σωμάτων ἀξιοσπουδαστότεροι.
        Τόδε γε μὴν τοῦ Λυκούργου πῶς οὐ μεγάλως ἄξιον ἀγασθῆναι; ὃς   4
20 ἐπειδὴ κατέμαθεν ὅτι ὅπου οἱ βουλόμενοι ἐπιμελοῦνται τῆς ἀρετῆς
οὐχ ἱκανοί εἰσι τὰς πατρίδας αὔξειν, ἐν τῆι Σπάρτηι ἠνάγκασε
δημοσίαι πάντας πάσας ἀσκεῖν τὰς ἀρετάς. ὥσπερ οὖν οἱ ἰδιῶται τῶν ἰδιωτῶν διαφέρουσιν ἀρετῆι οἱ ἀσκοῦντες τῶν ἀμελούν-
των, οὕτω καὶ ἡ Σπάρτη εἰκότως πασῶν τῶν πόλεων ἀρετῆι δια-
25 φέρει, μόνη δημοσίαι ἐπιτηδεύουσα τὴν καλοκαγαθίαν. οὐ γὰρ   5
κἀκεῖνο καλόν, τὸ τῶν ἄλλων πόλεων κολαζουσῶν ἤν τίς τι ἕτερος
ἕτερον ἀδικῆι, ἐκεῖνον ζημίας μὴ ἐλάττους ἐπιθεῖναι εἴ τις φανερὸς εἴη
ἀμελῶν τοῦ ὡς βέλτιστος εἶναι; ἐνόμιζε γάρ, ὡς ἔοικεν, ὑπὸ μὲν τῶν   6
ἀνδραποδιζομένων τινὰς ἢ ἀποστερούντων τι ἢ κλεπτόντων τοὺς
30 βλαπτομένους μόνον ἀδικεῖσθαι, ὑπὸ δὲ τῶν κακῶν καὶ ἀνάνδρων
ὅλας τὰς πόλεις προδίδοσθαι. ὥστε εἰκότως ἔμοιγε δοκεῖ τούτοις
μεγίστας ζημίας ἐπιθεῖναι. ἐπέθηκε δὲ καὶ τὴν ἀνυπόστατον ἀνάγκην   7
ἀσκεῖν ἅπασαν πολιτικὴν ἀρετήν. τοῖς μὲν γὰρ τὰ νόμιμα ἐκτελοῦσιν
ὁμοίως ἅπασι τὴν πόλιν οἰκείαν ἐποίησε, καὶ οὐδὲν ὑπελογίσατο
35 οὔτε σωμάτων οὔτε χρημάτων ἀσθένειαν· εἰ δέ τις ἀποδειλιάσειε τοῦ
τὰ νόμιμα διαπονεῖσθαι, τοῦτον ἐκεῖνος ἀπέδειξε μηδὲ νομίζεσθαι ἔτι
τῶν ὁμοίων εἶναι. ἀλλὰ γὰρ ὅτι μὲν παλαιότατοι οὗτοι οἱ νόμοι εἰσί,   8

1 τοῖς c: ἐν τοῖς D   2 ἀνανδρίας d: ἀνδρείας d   3 περιοπτέον c: οὐ περιοπτέον D
20 ἐπιμελοῦνται c: ἐπιμελεῖσθαι D   36 ἐκεῖνος c: ἐκεῖ D   36 μηδὲ c: μήτε D

σαφές· ὁ γὰρ Λυκοῦργος κατὰ τοὺς Ἡρακλείδας λέγεται γενέσθαι·
οὕτω δὲ παλαιοὶ ὄντες ἔτι καὶ νῦν τοῖς ἄλλοις καινότατοί εἰσι· καὶ
γὰρ τὸ πάντων θαυμαστότατον ἐπαινοῦσι μὲν πάντες τὰ τοιαῦτα
ἐπιτηδεύματα, μιμεῖσθαι δὲ αὐτὰ οὐδεμία πόλις ἐθέλει.

11 Καὶ ταῦτα μὲν δὴ κοινὰ ἀγαθὰ καὶ ἐν εἰρήνηι καὶ ἐν πολέμωι· εἰ 5
δέ τις βούλεται καταμαθεῖν ὅ τι καὶ εἰς τὰς στρατείας βέλτιον τῶν
2 ἄλλων ἐμηχανήσατο, ἔξεστι καὶ τούτων ἀκούειν. πρῶτον μὲν τοίνυν
οἱ ἔφοροι προκηρύττουσι τὰ ἔτη εἰς ἃ δεῖ στρατεύεσθαι καὶ ἱππεῦσι
καὶ ὁπλίταις, ἔπειτα δὲ καὶ τοῖς χειροτέχναις· ὥστε ὅσοισπερ ἐπὶ
πόλεως χρῶνται ἄνθρωποι, πάντων τούτων καὶ ἐπὶ στρατιᾶς οἱ 10
Λακεδαιμόνιοι εὐποροῦσι· καὶ ὅσων δὲ ὀργάνων ἡ στρατιὰ κοινῆι
δεηθείη ἄν, ἅπαντα τὰ μὲν ἁμάξηι προστέτακται παρέχειν, τὰ
3 δὲ ὑποζυγίωι· οὕτω γὰρ ἥκιστ᾽ ἂν τὸ ἐλλεῖπον διαλάθοι. εἴς γε
μὴν τὸν ἐν τοῖς ὅπλοις ἀγῶνα τοιάδ᾽ ἐμηχανήσατο, στολὴν μὲν
ἔχειν φοινικίδα, ταύτην νομίζων ἥκιστα μὲν γυναικείαι κοινωνεῖν, 15
πολεμικωτάτην δ᾽ εἶναι, καὶ χαλκῆν ἀσπίδα· καὶ γὰρ τάχιστα λαμ-
πρύνεται καὶ σχολαιότατα ῥυπαίνεται. ἐφῆκε δὲ καὶ κομᾶν τοῖς ὑπὲρ
τὴν ἡβητικὴν ἡλικίαν, νομίζων οὕτω καὶ μείζους ἂν καὶ ἐλευθερι-
4 ωτέρους καὶ γοργοτέρους φαίνεσθαι. οὕτω γε μὴν κατεσκευασμένων μόρας μὲν διεῖλεν ἓξ καὶ ἱππέων καὶ ὁπλιτῶν. ἑκάστη δὲ 20
τῶν ὁπλιτικῶν μορῶν ἔχει πολέμαρχον ἕνα, λοχαγοὺς τέτταρας,
πεντηκοντῆρας ὀκτώ, ἐνωμοτάρχους ἑκκαίδεκα. ἐκ δὲ τούτων τῶν
μορῶν διὰ παρεγγυήσεως καθίστανται τοτὲ μὲν εἰς ἕνα ἄγοντες τὰς
5 ἐνωμοτίας, τοτὲ δὲ εἰς τρεῖς, τοτὲ δὲ εἰς ἕξ. ὃ δὲ οἱ πλεῖστοι οἴονται, πολυπλοκωτάτην εἶναι τὴν ἐν ὅπλοις Λακωνικὴν τάξιν, τό 25
ἐναντιώτατον ὑπειλήφασι τοῦ ὄντος· εἰσὶ μὲν γὰρ ἐν τῆι Λακωνικῆι
τάξει οἱ πρωτοστάται ἄρχοντες, καὶ ὁ στίχος ἕκαστος πάντ᾽ ἔχων
6 ὅσα δεῖ παρέχεσθαι. οὕτω δὲ ῥάιδιον ταύτην τὴν τάξιν μαθεῖν
ὡς ὅστις τοὺς ἀνθρώπους δύναται γιγνώσκειν οὐδεὶς ἂν ἁμάρ-
τοι· τοῖς μὲν γὰρ ἡγεῖσθαι δέδοται, τοῖς δὲ ἕπεσθαι τέτακται. αἱ 30
δὲ παραγωγαὶ ὥσπερ ὑπὸ κήρυκος ὑπὸ τοῦ ἐνωμοτάρχου λόγωι
δηλοῦνται καὶ ἀραιαί τε καὶ βαθύτεραι αἱ φάλαγγες γίγνονται·
7 ὧν οὐδὲν οὐδ᾽ ὁπωστιοῦν χαλεπὸν μαθεῖν. τὸ μέντοι κἂν ταραχθῶσι μετὰ τοῦ παρατυχόντος ὁμοίως μάχεσθαι, ταύτην τὴν τάξιν
οὐκέτι ῥάιδιόν ἐστι μαθεῖν πλὴν τοῖς ὑπὸ τῶν τοῦ Λυκούργου νόμων 35
8 πεπαιδευμένοις. εὐπορώτατα δὲ καὶ ἐκεῖνα Λακεδαιμόνιοι ποιοῦσι

---

11 ὅσων c: ὅσα D   12 ἅπαντα c: ἁπάντων D   13 ἐλλεῖπον c: ἐκλεῖπον D   15–16
καὶ χαλκῆν ἀσπίδα huc transposuit c: φοινικίδα καὶ χαλκῆν ἀσπίδα D   21 ὁπλιτικῶν
i: πολιτικῶν Di   23–4 ἕνα ἄγοντες τὰς c: om D   32 καὶ c: om D

τὰ τοῖς ὁπλομάχοις πάνυ δοκοῦντα χαλεπὰ εἶναι· ὅταν μὲν γὰρ ἐπὶ
κέρως πορεύωνται, κατ' οὐρὰν δήπου ἐνωμοτία ἕπεται· ἐὰν δ' ἐν τῶι
τοιούτωι ἐκ τοῦ ἐναντίου πολεμία φάλαγξ ἐπιφανῆι, τῶι ἐνωμοτάρχωι παρεγγυᾶται εἰς μέτωπον παρ' ἀσπίδα καθίστασθαι, καὶ διὰ
5 παντὸς οὕτως, ἔστ' ἂν ἡ φάλαγξ ἐναντία καταστῆι. ἤν γε μὴν οὕτως
ἐχόντων ἐκ τοῦ ὄπισθεν οἱ πολέμιοι ἐπιφανῶσιν, ἐξελίττεται ἕκαστος ὁ στίχος, ἵνα οἱ κράτιστοι ἐναντίοι ἀεὶ τοῖς πολεμίοις ὦσιν. ὅτι   9
δὲ ὁ ἄρχων εὐώνυμος γίγνεται, οὐδ' ἐν τούτωι μειονεκτεῖν ἡγοῦνται,
ἀλλ' ἔστιν ὅτε καὶ πλεονεκτεῖν. εἰ γάρ τινες κυκλοῦσθαι ἐπιχειροῖεν,
10 οὐκ ἂν κατὰ τὰ γυμνά, ἀλλὰ κατὰ τὰ ὡπλισμένα περιβάλλοιεν ἄν.
ἢν δέ ποτε ἕνεκά τινος δοκῆι συμφέρειν τὸν ἡγεμόνα δεξιὸν κέρας
ἔχειν, στρέψαντες τὸ ἄγημα ἐπὶ κέράς ἐξελίττουσι τὴν φάλαγγα,
ἔστ' ἂν ὁ μὲν ἡγεμὼν δεξιὸς ἦι, ἡ δὲ οὐρὰ εὐώνυμος γένηται. ἢν δ' αὖ   10
ἐκ τῶν δεξιῶν πολεμίων τάξις ἐπιφαίνηται ἐπὶ κέρως πορευομένων,
15 οὐδὲν ἄλλο πραγματεύονται ἢ τὸν λόχον ἕκαστον ὥσπερ τριήρη
ἀντίπρωιρον τοῖς ἐναντίοις στρέφουσι, καὶ οὕτως αὖ γίγνεται ὁ
κατ' οὐρὰν λόχος παρὰ δόρυ. ἤν γε μὴν κατὰ τὰ εὐώνυμα πολέμιοι
προσίωσιν, οὐδὲ τοῦτ' ἐῶσιν, ἀλλὰ προθέουσιν ἢ ἀντιπάλους τοὺς
λόχους στρέφουσι· καὶ οὕτως αὖ ὁ κατ' οὐρὰν λόχος παρ' ἀσπίδα
20 καθίσταται.
　　Ἐρῶ δὲ καὶ ἧι στρατοπεδεύεσθαι ἐνόμισε χρῆναι Λυκοῦργος. διὰ   12
μὲν γὰρ τὸ τὰς γωνίας τοῦ τετραγώνου ἀχρήστους εἶναι κύκλον
ἐστρατοπεδεύσατο, εἰ μὴ ὄρος ἀσφαλὲς εἴη ἢ τεῖχος ἢ ποταμὸν
ὄπισθεν ἔχοιεν. φυλακάς γε μὴν ἐποίησε μεθημερινὰς τὰς μὲν παρὰ   2
25 τὰ ὅπλα εἴσω βλεπούσας· οὐ γὰρ πολεμίων ἕνεκα ἀλλὰ φίλων
αὗται καθίστανται· τούς γε μὴν πολεμίους ἱππεῖς φυλάττουσιν ἀπὸ
χωρίων ὧν ἂν ἐκ πλείστου προορῶιεν εἴ τις προσίοι. νύκτωρ δὲ   3
ἔξω τῆς φάλαγγος ἐνόμισεν ὑπὸ Σκιριτῶν προφυλάττεσθαι· (νῦν δ'
ἤδη καὶ ὑπὸ ξένων . . . αὐτῶν τινες συμπαρόντες.) τὸ δὲ ἔχοντας   4
30 τὰ δόρατα ἀεὶ περιιέναι, εὖ καὶ τοῦτο δεῖ εἰδέναι, ὅτι τοῦ αὐτοῦ
ἕνεκά ἐστιν οὗπερ καὶ τοὺς δούλους εἴργουσιν ἀπὸ τῶν ὅπλων,
καὶ τοὺς ἐπὶ τὰ ἀναγκαῖα ἀπιόντας οὐ δεῖ θαυμάζειν ὅτι οὔτε
ἀλλήλων οὔτε τῶν ὅπλων πλέον ἢ ὅσον μὴ λυπεῖν ἀλλήλους ἀπέρ-
χονται· καὶ γὰρ ταῦτα ἀσφαλείας ἕνεκα ποιοῦσιν. μεταστρατοπε-   5
35 δεύονταί γε μὴν πυκνὰ καὶ τοῦ σίνεσθαι τοὺς πολεμίους ἕνεκα καὶ
τοῦ ὠφελεῖν τοὺς φίλους. καὶ γυμνάζεσθαι δὲ προαγορεύεται ὑπὸ
τοῦ νόμου ἅπασι Λακεδαιμονίοις, ἕωσπερ ἂν στρατεύωνται· ὥστε

18 ἀλλὰ προθέουσιν d: ἀλλ' ἀποθοῦσιν d: ἀλλ' ἀπωθοῦσιν d   18 ἀντιπάλους c: ἐναντίους
ἀντιπάλους D   27 εἴ τις c: εἰ δέ τις D   27 προσίοι c: προίοι D δὲ c: om. D
28 lacunam indicauit c (e.g. <ἢν τύχωσιν>)

92   ΞΕΝΟΦΩΝΤΟΣ

μεγαλοπρεπεστέρους μὲν αὐτοὺς ἐφ' ἑαυτοῖς γίγνεσθαι, ἐλευθεριωτέρους δὲ τῶν ἄλλων φαίνεσθαι. δεῖ δὲ οὔτε περίπατον οὔτε δρόμον μάσσω ποιεῖσθαι ἢ ὅσον ἂν ἡ μόρα ἐφήκῃ, ὅπως μηδεὶς τῶν
6 αὐτοῦ ὅπλων πόρρω γίγνηται. μετὰ δὲ τὰ γυμνάσια καθίζειν μὲν
ὁ πρῶτος πολέμαρχος κηρύττει· ἔστι δὲ τοῦτο ὥσπερ ἐξέτασις· ἐκ   5
τούτου δὲ ἀριστοποιεῖσθαι καὶ ταχὺ τὸν πρόσκοπον ἀπολύεσθαι·
ἐκ τούτου δ' αὖ διατριβαὶ καὶ ἀναπαύσεις πρὸ τῶν ἑσπερινῶν γυμ-
7 νασίων. μετά γε μὴν ταῦτα δειπνοποιεῖσθαι κηρύττεται, καὶ ἐπειδὰν
ᾄσωσιν εἰς τοὺς θεοὺς οἷς ἂν κεκαλλιερηκότες ὦσιν, ἐπὶ τῶν ὅπλων
ἀναπαύεσθαι. ὅτι δὲ πολλὰ γράφω οὐ δεῖ θαυμάζειν· ἥκιστα γὰρ   10
Λακεδαιμονίοις εὕροι ἄν τις παραλελειμμένα ἐν τοῖς στρατιωτικοῖς
ὅσα δεῖται ἐπιμελείας.
13 Διηγήσομαι δὲ καὶ ἣν ἐπὶ στρατιᾶς ὁ Λυκοῦργος βασιλεῖ
δύναμιν καὶ τιμὴν κατεσκεύασε. πρῶτον μὲν γὰρ ἐπὶ φρουρᾶς τρέ-
φει ἡ πόλις βασιλέα καὶ τοὺς σὺν αὐτῶι· συσκηνοῦσι δὲ αὐτῶι   15
οἱ πολέμαρχοι, ὅπως ἀεὶ συνόντες μᾶλλον καὶ κοινοβουλῶσιν, ἤν
τι δέωνται· συσκηνοῦσι δὲ καὶ ἄλλοι τρεῖς ἄνδρες τῶν ὁμοίων· οὗτοι
τούτοις ἐπιμελοῦνται πάντων τῶν ἐπιτηδείων, ὡς μηδεμία ἀσχολία
2 ἦι αὐτοῖς τῶν πολεμικῶν ἐπιμελεῖσθαι. ἐπαναλήψομαι δὲ ὡς
ἐξορμᾶται σὺν στρατιᾶι ὁ βασιλεύς. θύει μὲν γὰρ πρῶτον οἴκοι   20
ὢν Διὶ Ἀγήτορι καὶ τοῖς σὺν αὐτῶι· ἢν δὲ ἐνταῦθα καλλιερήσῃ,
λαβὼν ὁ πυρφόρος πῦρ ἀπὸ τοῦ βωμοῦ προηγεῖται ἐπὶ τὰ ὅρια
3 τῆς χώρας· ὁ δὲ βασιλεὺς ἐκεῖ αὖ θύεται Διὶ καὶ Ἀθηνᾶι. ὅταν δὲ
ἀμφοῖν τούτοιν τοῖν θεοῖν καλλιερηθῇ, τότε διαβαίνει τὰ ὅρια τῆς
χώρας· καὶ τὸ πῦρ μὲν ἀπὸ τούτων τῶν ἱερῶν προηγεῖται οὔποτε   25
ἀποσβεννύμενον, σφάγια δὲ παντοῖα ἔπεται. ἀεὶ δὲ ὅταν θύηται,
ἄρχεται μὲν τούτου τοῦ ἔργου ἔτι κνεφαῖος, προλαμβάνειν βουλό-
4 μενος τὴν τοῦ θεοῦ εὔνοιαν. πάρεισι δὲ περὶ τὴν θυσίαν πολέμαρχοι, λοχαγοί, πεντηκοντῆρες, ξένων στρατίαρχοι, στρατοῦ σκευο-
φορικοῦ ἄρχοντες, καὶ τῶν ἀπὸ τῶν πόλεων δὲ στρατηγῶν ὁ   30
5 βουλόμενος· πάρεισι δὲ καὶ τῶν ἐφόρων δύο, οἳ πολυπραγμονοῦσι
μὲν οὐδέν, ἢν μὴ ὁ βασιλεὺς προσκαλῆι· ὁρῶντες δὲ ὅ τι ποιεῖ
ἕκαστος πάντας σωφρονίζουσιν, ὡς τὸ εἰκός. ὅταν δὲ τελεσθῆι
τὰ ἱερά, ὁ βασιλεὺς προσκαλέσας πάντας παραγγέλλει τὰ ποιητέα. ὥστε ὁρῶν ταῦτα ἡγήσαιο ἂν τοὺς μὲν ἄλλους αὐτοσχε-   35
διαστὰς εἶναι τῶν στρατιωτικῶν, Λακεδαιμονίους δὲ μόνους τῶι
6 ὄντι τεχνίτας τῶν πολεμικῶν. ἐπειδάν γε μὴν ἡγῆται βασιλεύς,

3 μάσσω c: ἐλάσσω D   4 αὐτοῦ c: αὐτῶν D   6 ἀπολύεσθαι c: ὑπο-D
14 φρουρᾶς c: φρουρᾶ D   21 τοῖς σὺν αὐτῶι D: τοῖν σιοῖν c

ἦν μὲν μηδεὶς ἐναντίος φαίνηται, οὐδεὶς αὐτοῦ πρόσθεν πορεύεται,
πλὴν Σκιρῖται καὶ οἱ προερευνώμενοι ἱππεῖς· ἢν δέ ποτε μάχην
οἴωνται ἔσεσθαι, λαβὼν τὸ ἄγημα τῆς πρώτης μόρας ὁ βασιλεὺς
ἄγει στρέψας ἐπὶ δόρυ, ἔστ’ ἂν γένηται ἐν μέσωι δυοῖν μόραιν καὶ
5 δυοῖν πολεμάρχοιν. οὓς δὲ δεῖ ἐπὶ τούτοις τετάχθαι, ὁ πρεσβύτατος   7
τῶν περὶ δαμοσίαν συντάττει· εἰσὶ δὲ οὗτοι ὅσοι ἂν σύσκηνοι ὦσι
τῶν ὁμοίων, καὶ μάντεις καὶ ἰατροὶ καὶ αὐληταὶ καὶ οἱ τοῦ στρατοῦ ἄρχοντες, καὶ ἐθελούσιοι ἤν τινες παρῶσιν. ὥστε τῶν δεομένων
γίγνεσθαι οὐδὲν ἀπορεῖται· οὐδὲν γὰρ ἀπρόσκεπτόν ἐστι. μάλα δὲ   8
10 καὶ τάδε ὠφέλιμα, ὡς ἐμοὶ δοκεῖ, ἐμηχανήσατο Λυκοῦργος εἰς τὸν
ἐν ὅπλοις ἀγῶνα. ὅταν γὰρ ὁρώντων ἤδη τῶν πολεμίων χίμαιρα
σφαγιάζηται, αὐλεῖν τε πάντας τοὺς παρόντας αὐλητὰς νόμος καὶ
μηδένα Λακεδαιμονίων ἀστεφάνωτον εἶναι· καὶ ὅπλα δὲ λαμπρύ-
νεσθαι προαγορεύεται. ἔξεστι δὲ τῶι νέωι καὶ κεχριμένωι εἰς μάχην   9
15 συνιέναι καὶ φαιδρὸν εἶναι καὶ εὐδόκιμον. καὶ παρακελεύονται δὲ τῶι
ἐνωμοτάρχωι· οὐδ’ ἀκούεται γὰρ εἰς ἑκάστην πᾶσαν τὴν ἐνωμοτίαν
ἀφ’ ἑκάστου ἐνωμοτάρχου ἔξω· ὅπως δὲ καλῶς γίγνηται πολεμάρ-
χωι δεῖ μέλειν. ὅταν γε μὴν καιρὸς δοκῆι εἶναι στρατοπεδεύεσθαι,   10
τούτου μὲν δὴ κύριος βασιλεὺς καὶ τοῦ δεῖξαί γε ὅπου δεῖ· τὸ μέντοι
20 πρεσβείας ἀποπέμπεσθαι καὶ φιλίας καὶ πολεμίας, τοῦτ’ αὖ βασιλέως.
καὶ ἄρχονται μὲν πάντες ἀπὸ βασιλέως, ὅταν βούλωνται πρᾶξαί
τι. ἢν δ’ οὖν δίκης δεόμενός τις ἔλθηι, πρὸς ἑλλανοδίκας τοῦτον ὁ   11
βασιλεὺς ἀποπέμπει, ἢν δὲ χρημάτων, πρὸς ταμίας, ἢν δὲ ληίδα
ἄγων, πρὸς λαφυροπώλας. οὕτω δὲ πραττομένων βασιλεῖ οὐδὲν
25 ἄλλο ἔργον καταλείπεται ἐπὶ φρουρᾶς ἢ ἱερεῖ μὲν τὰ πρὸς τοὺς θεοὺς
εἶναι, στρατηγῶι δὲ τὰ πρὸς τοὺς ἀνθρώπους.
    Εἰ δέ τίς με ἔροιτο εἰ καὶ νῦν ἔτι μοι δοκοῦσιν οἱ Λυκούργου   14
νόμοι ἀκίνητοι διαμένειν, τοῦτο μὰ Δία οὐκ ἂν ἔτι θρασέως εἴποιμι.
οἶδα γὰρ πρότερον μὲν Λακεδαιμονίους αἱρουμένους οἴκοι τὰ μέτρια   2
30 ἔχοντας ἀλλήλοις συνεῖναι μᾶλλον ἢ ἁρμόζοντας ἐν ταῖς πόλεσι
καὶ κολακευομένους διαφθείρεσθαι. καὶ πρόσθεν μὲν οἶδα αὐτοὺς   3
φοβουμένους χρυσίον ἔχοντας φαίνεσθαι· νῦν δ’ ἔστιν οὓς καὶ καλλωπιζομένους ἐπὶ τῶι κεκτῆσθαι. ἐπίσταμαι δὲ καὶ πρόσθεν τούτου   4
ἕνεκα ξενηλασίας γιγνομένας καὶ ἀποδημεῖν οὐκ ἐξόν, ὅπως μὴ ῥαιδι-
35 ουργίας οἱ πολῖται ἀπὸ τῶν ξένων ἐμπίμπλαιντο· νῦν δ’ ἐπίσταμαι
τοὺς δοκοῦντας πρώτους εἶναι ἐσπουδακότας ὡς μηδέποτε παύων-
ται ἁρμόζοντες ἐπὶ ξένης. καὶ ἦν μὲν ὅτε ἐπεμελοῦντο ὅπως ἄξιοι   5

---

7 καὶ οἱ c: οἱ. D   9 μάλα c: καλὰ D   14 κεχριμένωι c: κεκριμένωι D   19 δὴ κύριος
βασιλεύς c: λυκούργος βασιλεὺς d: κύριος βασιλεὺς d   20 αὖ D: οὐ c

εἶεν ἡγεῖσθαι· νῦν δὲ πολὺ μᾶλλον πραγματεύονται ὅπως ἄρξουσιν
6 ἢ ὅπως ἄξιοι τούτων ἔσονται. τοιγαροῦν οἱ Ἕλληνες πρότερον μὲν
ἰόντες εἰς Λακεδαίμονα ἐδέοντο αὐτῶν ἡγεῖσθαι ἐπὶ τοὺς δοκοῦντας ἀδικεῖν· νῦν δὲ πολλοὶ παρακαλοῦσιν ἀλλήλους ἐπὶ τὸ δια-
7 κωλύειν ἄρξαι πάλιν αὐτούς. οὐδὲν μέντοι δεῖ θαυμάζειν τούτων 5
τῶν ἐπιψόγων αὐτοῖς γιγνομένων, ἐπειδὴ φανεροί εἰσιν οὔτε τῶι
θεῶι πειθόμενοι οὔτε τοῖς Λυκούργου νόμοις.

15 Βούλομαι δὲ καὶ ἃς βασιλεῖ πρὸς τὴν πόλιν συνθήκας ὁ Λυκοῦργος ἐποίησε διηγήσασθαι· μόνη γὰρ δὴ αὕτη ἀρχὴ διατελεῖ οἵαπερ
ἐξ ἀρχῆς κατεστάθη· τὰς δὲ ἄλλας πολιτείας εὕροι ἄν τις μετακεκι- 10
2 νημένας καὶ ἔτι καὶ νῦν μετακινουμένας· ἔθηκε γὰρ θύειν μὲν βασιλέα
πρὸ τῆς πόλεως τὰ δημόσια ἅπαντα, ὡς ἀπὸ τοῦ θεοῦ ὄντα, καὶ
3 στρατιὰν ὅποι ἂν ἡ πόλις ἐκπέμπηι ἡγεῖσθαι. ἔδωκε δὲ καὶ γέρα
ἀπὸ τῶν θυομένων λαμβάνειν, καὶ γῆν δὲ ἐν πολλαῖς τῶν περιοίκων πόλεων ἀπέδειξεν ἐξαίρετον τοσαύτην ὥστε μήτ᾽ ἐνδεῖσθαι 15
4 τῶν μετρίων μήτε πλούτωι ὑπερφέρειν· ὅπως δὲ καὶ οἱ βασιλεῖς ἔξω
σκηνοῖεν, σκηνὴν αὐτοῖς δημοσίαν ἀπέδειξε, καὶ διμοιρίαι γε ἐπὶ τῶι
δείπνωι ἐτίμησεν, οὐχ ἵνα διπλάσια καταφάγοιεν, ἀλλ᾽ ἵνα καὶ ἀπὸ
5 τοῦδε τιμῆσαι ἔχοιεν εἴ τινα βούλοιντο. ἔδωκε δ᾽ αὖ καὶ συσκήνους
δύο ἑκατέρωι προσελέσθαι, οἳ δὴ καὶ Πύθιοι καλοῦνται. ἔδωκε δὲ 20
6 καὶ πασῶν τῶν συῶν ἀπὸ τόκου χοῖρον λαμβάνειν, ὡς μήποτε
ἀπορήσαι βασιλεὺς ἱερῶν, ἤν τι δεηθῆι θεοῖς συμβουλεύσασθαι. καὶ
πρὸς τῆι οἰκίαι δὲ λίμνη ὕδατος ἀφθονίαν παρέχει. ὅτι δὲ καὶ τοῦτο
πρὸς πολλὰ χρήσιμον, οἱ μὴ ἔχοντες αὐτὸ μᾶλλον γιγνώσκουσι.
καὶ ἕδρας δὲ πάντες ὑπανίστανται βασιλεῖ, πλὴν οὐκ ἔφοροι ἀπὸ 25
7 τῶν ἐφορικῶν δίφρων. καὶ ὅρκους δὲ ἀλλήλοις κατὰ μῆνα ποιοῦνται, ἔφοροι μὲν ὑπὲρ τῆς πόλεως, βασιλεὺς δὲ ὑπὲρ ἑαυτοῦ. ὁ δὲ
ὅρκος ἐστὶ τῶι μὲν βασιλεῖ κατὰ τοὺς τῆς πόλεως κειμένους νόμους
βασιλεύσειν, τῆι δὲ πόλει ἐμπεδορκοῦντος ἐκείνου ἀστυφέλικτον τὴν
8 βασιλείαν παρέξειν. αὗται μὲν οὖν αἱ τιμαὶ οἴκοι ζῶντι βασιλεῖ δέδον- 30
ται, οὐδέν τι πολὺ ὑπερφέρουσαι τῶν ἰδιωτικῶν· οὐ γὰρ ἐβουλήθη
οὔτε τοῖς βασιλεῦσι τυραννικὸν φρόνημα παραστῆσαι οὔτε τοῖς
9 πολίταις φθόνον ἐμποιῆσαι τῆς δυνάμεως. αἱ δὲ τελευτήσαντι τιμαὶ
βασιλεῖ δέδονται, τῆιδε βούλονται δηλοῦν οἱ Λυκούργου νόμοι ὅτι
οὐχ ὡς ἀνθρώπους ἀλλ᾽ ὡς ἥρωας τοὺς Λακεδαιμονίων βασιλεῖς προ- 35
τετιμήκασι.

11 τοῦ D: om. c   13 δὲ c: τε D   14 μήτ᾽ ἐνδεῖσθαι c: μήτε δεῖσθαι D   23 ἀφθονίαν d:
om. d

RESPUBLICA ATHENIENSIUM

ΑΘΗΝΑΙΩΝ ΠΟΛΙΤΕΙΑ

Περὶ δὲ τῆς Ἀθηναίων πολιτείας, ὅτι μὲν εἵλοντο τοῦτον τὸν τρόπον 1
τῆς πολιτείας οὐκ ἐπαινῶ διὰ τόδε, ὅτι ταῦθ᾽ ἑλόμενοι εἵλοντο τοὺς
πονηροὺς ἄμεινον πράττειν ἢ τοὺς χρηστούς· διὰ μὲν οὖν τοῦτο οὐκ
ἐπαινῶ. ἐπεὶ δὲ ταῦτα ἔδοξεν οὕτως αὐτοῖς, ὡς εὖ διασώιζονται τὴν
5 πολιτείαν καὶ τἆλλα διαπράττονται ἃ δοκοῦσιν ἁμαρτάνειν τοῖς
ἄλλοις Ἕλλησι, τοῦτ᾽ ἀποδείξω.

Πρῶτον μὲν οὖν τοῦτο ἐρῶ, ὅτι δικαίως δοκοῦσιν αὐτόθι καὶ οἱ 2
πένητες καὶ ὁ δῆμος πλέον ἔχειν τῶν γενναίων καὶ τῶν πλουσίων
διὰ τόδε, ὅτι ὁ δῆμός ἐστιν ὁ ἐλαύνων τὰς ναῦς καὶ ὁ τὴν δύναμιν
10 περιτιθεὶς τῆι πόλει, καὶ οἱ κυβερνῆται καὶ οἱ κελευσταὶ καὶ οἱ
πεντηκόνταρχοι καὶ οἱ πρωιρᾶται καὶ οἱ ναυπηγοί, οὗτοί εἰσιν
οἱ τὴν δύναμιν περιτιθέντες τῆι πόλει πολὺ μᾶλλον ἢ οἱ ὁπλῖται
καὶ οἱ γενναῖοι καὶ οἱ χρηστοί. ἐπειδὴ οὖν ταῦτα οὕτως ἔχει, δοκεῖ
δίκαιον εἶναι πᾶσι τῶν ἀρχῶν μετεῖναι ἔν τε τῶι κλήρωι καὶ ἐν
15 τῆι χειροτονίαι, καὶ λέγειν ἐξεῖναι τῶι βουλομένωι τῶν πολιτῶν. 3
ἔπειτα ὁπόσαι μὲν σωτηρίαν φέρουσι τῶν ἀρχῶν χρησταὶ οὖσαι
καὶ μὴ χρησταὶ κίνδυνον τῶι δήμωι ἅπαντι, τούτων μὲν τῶν ἀρχῶν
οὐδὲν δεῖται ὁ δῆμος μετεῖναι· οὔτε τῶν στρατηγιῶν κλήρωι οἴονταί
σφισι χρῆναι μετεῖναι οὔτε τῶν ἱππαρχιῶν· γιγνώσκει γὰρ ὁ δῆμος
20 ὅτι πλείω ὠφελεῖται ἐν τῶι μὴ αὐτὸς ἄρχειν ταύτας τὰς ἀρχάς,
ἀλλ᾽ ἐᾶν τοὺς δυνατωτάτους ἄρχειν· ὁπόσαι δ᾽ εἰσὶν ἀρχαὶ μισθοφορίας ἕνεκα καὶ ὠφελείας εἰς τὸν οἶκον, ταύτας ζητεῖ ὁ δῆμος
ἄρχειν. ἔπειτα δὲ ὃ ἔνιοι θαυμάζουσιν ὅτι πανταχοῦ πλέον νέμουσι 4
τοῖς πονηροῖς καὶ πένησι καὶ δημοτικοῖς ἢ τοῖς χρηστοῖς, ἐν αὐτῶι
25 τούτωι φανοῦνται τὴν δημοκρατίαν διασώιζοντες. οἱ μὲν γὰρ πένητες καὶ οἱ δημόται καὶ οἱ χείρους εὖ πράττοντες καὶ πολλοὶ οἱ
τοιοῦτοι γιγνόμενοι τὴν δημοκρατίαν αὔξουσιν· ἐὰν δὲ εὖ πράτ-
τωσιν οἱ πλούσιοι καὶ οἱ χρηστοί, ἰσχυρὸν τὸ ἐναντίον σφίσιν αὐτοῖς
καθιστᾶσιν οἱ δημοτικοί. ἔστι δὲ πάσηι γῆι τὸ βέλτιστον ἐναντίον 5
30 τῆι δημοκρατίαι· ἐν γὰρ τοῖς βελτίστοις ἔνι ἀκολασία τε ὀλιγίστη
καὶ ἀδικία, ἀκρίβεια δὲ πλείστη εἰς τὰ χρηστά, ἐν δὲ τῶι δήμωι
ἀμαθία τε πλείστη καὶ ἀταξία καὶ πονηρία· ἥ τε γὰρ πενία αὐτοὺς
μᾶλλον ἄγει ἐπὶ τὰ αἰσχρὰ καὶ ἡ ἀπαιδευσία καὶ ἀμαθία ἡ δι᾽ ἔνδειαν
χρημάτων ἐνίοις τῶν ἀνθρώπων. εἴποι δ᾽ ἄν τις ὡς ἐχρῆν αὐτοὺς 6

---

7 δικαίως δοκοῦσιν c: δικαίως D: δίκαιοι c: δικαιοῦσ᾽ c   12 ὁπλῖται c: πολῖται D
18 κλήρωι c: κλήρων d: om. d   33 ἀμαθία ἡ c: ἡ ἀμαθία D

μὴ ἐᾶν λέγειν πάντας ἑξῆς μηδὲ βουλεύειν, ἀλλὰ τοὺς δεξιωτάτους
καὶ ἄνδρας ἀρίστους. οἱ δὲ καὶ ἐν τούτωι ἄριστα βουλεύονται ἐῶν-
τες καὶ τοὺς πονηροὺς λέγειν. εἰ μὲν γὰρ οἱ χρηστοὶ ἔλεγον καὶ
ἐβουλεύοντο, τοῖς ὁμοίοις σφίσιν αὐτοῖς ἦν ἀγαθά, τοῖς δὲ δημοτικοῖς
οὐκ ἀγαθά· νῦν δὲ λέγων ὁ βουλόμενος ἀναστάς, ἄνθρωπος πονηρός,   5
7 ἐξευρίσκει τὸ ἀγαθὸν αὑτῶι τε καὶ τοῖς ὁμοίοις αὑτῶι. εἴποι τις ἄν, Τί
ἂν οὖν γνοίη ἀγαθὸν αὑτῶι ἢ τῶι δήμωι τοιοῦτος ἄνθρωπος; οἱ δὲ
γιγνώσκουσιν ὅτι ἡ τούτου ἀμαθία καὶ πονηρία καὶ εὔνοια μᾶλλον
8 λυσιτελεῖ ἢ ἡ τοῦ χρηστοῦ ἀρετὴ καὶ σοφία καὶ κακόνοια. εἴη μὲν
οὖν ἂν πόλις οὐκ ἀπὸ τοιούτων διαιτημάτων ἡ βελτίστη, ἀλλ' ἡ   10
δημοκρατία μάλιστ' ἂν σώιζοιτο οὕτως. ὁ γὰρ δῆμος βούλεται οὐκ
εὐνομουμένης τῆς πόλεως αὐτὸς δουλεύειν, ἀλλ' ἐλεύθερος εἶναι καὶ
ἄρχειν, τῆς δὲ κακονομίας αὑτῶι ὀλίγον μέλει· ὃ γὰρ σὺ νομίζεις οὐκ
εὐνομεῖσθαι, αὐτὸς ἀπὸ τούτου ἰσχύει ὁ δῆμος καὶ ἐλεύθερός ἐστιν.
9 εἰ δ' εὐνομίαν ζητεῖς, πρῶτα μὲν ὄψει τοὺς δεξιωτάτους αὐτοῖς τοὺς   15
νόμους τιθέντας· ἔπειτα κολάσουσιν οἱ χρηστοὶ τοὺς πονηροὺς καὶ
βουλεύσουσιν οἱ χρηστοὶ περὶ τῆς πόλεως καὶ οὐκ ἐάσουσι μαινομένους ἀνθρώπους βουλεύειν οὐδὲ λέγειν οὐδὲ ἐκκλησιάζειν. ἀπὸ
τούτων τοίνυν τῶν ἀγαθῶν τάχιστ' ἂν ὁ δῆμος εἰς δουλείαν κατ-
απέσοι.   20
10 Τῶν δούλων δ' αὖ καὶ τῶν μετοίκων πλείστη ἐστὶν Ἀθήνησιν
ἀκολασία, καὶ οὔτε πατάξαι ἔξεστιν αὐτόθι οὔτε ὑπεκστήσεταί σοι
ὁ δοῦλος. οὗ δ' ἕνεκέν ἐστι τοῦτο ἐπιχώριον ἐγὼ φράσω. εἰ νόμος
ἦν τὸν δοῦλον ὑπὸ τοῦ ἐλευθέρου τύπτεσθαι ἢ τὸν μέτοικον ἢ τὸν
ἀπελεύθερον, πολλάκις ἂν οἰηθεὶς εἶναι τὸν Ἀθηναῖον δοῦλον ἐπά-   25
ταξεν ἄν· ἐσθῆτά τε γὰρ οὐδὲν βελτίων ὁ δῆμος αὐτόθι ἢ οἱ δοῦλοι
11 καὶ οἱ μέτοικοι καὶ τὰ εἴδη οὐδὲν βελτίους εἰσίν. εἰ δέ τις καὶ τοῦτο
θαυμάζει, ὅτι ἐῶσι τοὺς δούλους τρυφᾶν αὐτόθι καὶ μεγαλοπρεπῶς
διαιτᾶσθαι ἐνίους, καὶ τοῦτο γνώμηι φανεῖεν ἂν ποιοῦντες. ὅπου
γὰρ ναυτικὴ δύναμίς ἐστιν, ἀπὸ χρημάτων ἀνάγκη τοῖς ἀνδραπό-   30
δοις δουλεύειν, ἵνα λαμβάνωμεν ὧν πράττηι τὰς ἀποφοράς, καὶ
ἐλευθέρους ἀφιέναι. ὅπου δ' εἰσὶ πλούσιοι δοῦλοι, οὐκέτι ἐνταῦθα
λυσιτελεῖ τὸν ἐμὸν δοῦλον σὲ δεδιέναι· ἐν δὲ τῆι Λακεδαίμονι ὁ ἐμὸς
δοῦλος σ' ἐδεδοίκει· ἐὰν δὲ δεδίηι ὁ σὸς δοῦλος ἐμέ, κινδυνεύσει καὶ
τὰ χρήματα διδόναι τὰ ἑαυτοῦ ὥστε μὴ κινδυνεύειν περὶ ἑαυτοῦ.   35
12 διὰ τοῦτ' οὖν ἰσηγορίαν καὶ τοῖς δούλοις πρὸς τοὺς ἐλευθέρους
ἐποιήσαμεν—καὶ τοῖς μετοίκοις πρὸς τοὺς ἀστούς, διότι δεῖται ἡ

πόλις μετοίκων διά τε τὸ πλῆθος τῶν τεχνῶν καὶ διὰ τὸ ναυτικόν· διὰ τοῦτο οὖν καὶ τοῖς μετοίκοις εἰκότως τὴν ἰσηγορίαν ἐποιήσαμεν.

Τοὺς δὲ γυμναζομένους αὐτόθι καὶ τὴν μουσικὴν ἐπιτηδεύοντας   13
καταλέλυκεν ὁ δῆμος, νομίζων τοῦτο οὐ καλὸν εἶναι, γνοὺς ὅτι οὐ
5 δυνατὸς ταῦτά ἐστιν ἐπιτηδεύειν. ἐν ταῖς χορηγίαις αὖ καὶ γυμνασιαρχίαις καὶ τριηραρχίαις γιγνώσκουσιν ὅτι χορηγοῦσι μὲν οἱ
πλούσιοι, χορηγεῖται δὲ ὁ δῆμος, καὶ γυμνασιαρχοῦσιν οἱ πλούσιοι
καὶ τριηραρχοῦσιν, ὁ δὲ δῆμος τριηραρχεῖται καὶ γυμνασιαρχεῖται.
ἀξιοῖ γοῦν ἀργύριον λαμβάνειν ὁ δῆμος καὶ ᾄδων καὶ τρέχων καὶ
10 ὀρχούμενος καὶ πλέων ἐν ταῖς ναυσίν, ἵνα αὐτός τε ἔχῃ καὶ οἱ πλούσιοι πενέστεροι γίγνωνται. ἔν τε τοῖς δικαστηρίοις οὐ τοῦ δικαίου
αὐτοῖς μᾶλλον μέλει ἢ τοῦ αὑτοῖς συμφόρου.

Περὶ δὲ τῶν συμμάχων, ὅτι ἐκπλέοντες συκοφαντοῦσιν ὡς δοκοῦσι   14
καὶ μισοῦσι τοὺς χρηστούς, γιγνώσκοντες ὅτι μισεῖσθαι μὲν ἀνάγκη
15 τὸν ἄρχοντα ὑπὸ τοῦ ἀρχομένου, εἰ δὲ ἰσχύσουσιν οἱ πλούσιοι καὶ
οἱ χρηστοὶ ἐν ταῖς πόλεσιν, ὀλίγιστον χρόνον ἡ ἀρχὴ ἔσται τοῦ
δήμου τοῦ Ἀθήνησι, διὰ ταῦτα οὖν τοὺς μὲν χρηστοὺς ἀτιμοῦσι
καὶ χρήματα ἀφαιροῦνται καὶ ἐξελαύνονται καὶ ἀποκτείνουσι, τοὺς
δὲ πονηροὺς αὔξουσιν. οἱ δὲ χρηστοὶ Ἀθηναίων τοὺς χρηστοὺς ἐν
20 ταῖς συμμαχίσι πόλεσι σώζουσι, γιγνώσκοντες ὅτι σφίσιν ἀγαθόν
ἐστι τοὺς βελτίστους σώζειν ἀεὶ ἐν ταῖς πόλεσιν. εἴποι δέ τις ἂν ὅτι   15
ἰσχύς ἐστιν αὕτη Ἀθηναίων, ἐὰν οἱ σύμμαχοι δυνατοὶ ὦσι χρήματα
εἰσφέρειν. τοῖς δὲ δημοτικοῖς δοκεῖ μεῖζον ἀγαθὸν εἶναι τὰ τῶν συμμάχων χρήματα ἕνα ἕκαστον Ἀθηναίων ἔχειν, ἐκείνους δὲ ὅσον ζῆν,
25 καὶ ἐργάζεσθαι ἀδυνάτους ὄντας ἐπιβουλεύειν.

Δοκεῖ δὲ ὁ δῆμος ὁ Ἀθηναίων καὶ ἐν τῷδε κακῶς βουλεύεσθαι,   16
ὅτι τοὺς συμμάχους ἀναγκάζουσι πλεῖν ἐπὶ δίκας Ἀθήναζε. οἱ δὲ
ἀντιλογίζονται ὅσα ἐν τούτῳ ἔνι ἀγαθὰ τῷ δήμῳ τῷ Ἀθηναίων·
πρῶτον μὲν ἀπὸ τῶν πρυτανείων τὸν μισθὸν δι' ἐνιαυτοῦ λαμ-
30 βάνειν· εἶτ' οἴκοι καθήμενοι ἄνευ νεῶν ἔκπλου διοικοῦσι τὰς πόλεις
τὰς συμμαχίδας, καὶ τοὺς μὲν τοῦ δήμου σώζουσι, τοὺς δ' ἐναντίους
ἀπολλύουσιν ἐν τοῖς δικαστηρίοις· εἰ δὲ οἴκοι εἶχον ἕκαστοι τὰς δίκας,
ἅτε ἀχθόμενοι Ἀθηναίοις τούτους ἂν σφῶν αὐτῶν ἀπώλλυσαν
οἵτινες φίλοι μάλιστα ἦσαν Ἀθηναίων τῷ δήμῳ. πρὸς δὲ τούτοις   17
35 ὁ δῆμος τῶν Ἀθηναίων τάδε κερδαίνει τῶν δικῶν Ἀθήνησιν οὐσῶν
τοῖς συμμάχοις. πρῶτον μὲν γὰρ ἡ ἑκατοστὴ τῇ πόλει πλείων ἢ ἐν
Πειραιεῖ· ἔπειτα εἴ τῳ συνοικία ἐστίν, ἄμεινον πράττει· ἔπειτα εἴ τῳ   18
ζεῦγός ἐστιν ἢ ἀνδράποδον μισθοφοροῦν· ἔπειτα οἱ κήρυκες ἄμεινον

16 χρηστοὶ c: ἰσχυροὶ Di   37 πράττει c: πράττειν D

πράττουσι διὰ τὰς ἐπιδημίας τὰς τῶν συμμάχων. πρὸς δὲ τούτοις, εἰ μὲν μὴ ἐπὶ δίκας ἥιεσαν οἱ σύμμαχοι, τοὺς ἐκπλέοντας Ἀθηναίων ἐτίμων ἂν μόνους, τούς τε στρατηγοὺς καὶ τοὺς τριηράρχους
καὶ πρέσβεις· νῦν δ᾽ ἠνάγκασται τὸν δῆμον κολακεύειν τὸν Ἀθηναίων εἷς ἕκαστος τῶν συμμάχων, γιγνώσκων ὅτι δεῖ ἀφικόμενον   5
Ἀθήναζε δίκην δοῦναι καὶ λαβεῖν οὐκ ἐν ἄλλοις τισὶν ἀλλ᾽ ἐν τῶι
δήμωι, ὅς ἐστι δὴ νόμος Ἀθήνησι· καὶ ἀντιβολῆσαι ἀναγκάζεται ἐν
τοῖς δικαστηρίοις καὶ εἰσιόντος του ἐπιλαμβάνεσθαι τῆς χειρός. διὰ
τοῦτο οὖν οἱ σύμμαχοι δοῦλοι τοῦ δήμου τῶν Ἀθηναίων καθεστᾶσι
μᾶλλον.   10

19   Πρὸς δὲ τούτοις διὰ τὴν κτῆσιν τὴν ἐν τοῖς ὑπερορίοις καὶ διὰ
τὰς ἀρχὰς τὰς εἰς τὴν ὑπερορίαν λελήθασι μανθάνοντες ἐλαύνειν
τῆι κώπηι αὐτοί τε καὶ οἱ ἀκόλουθοι· ἀνάγκη γὰρ ἄνθρωπον πολλάκις πλέοντα κώπην λαβεῖν καὶ αὐτὸν καὶ τὸν οἰκέτην, καὶ ὀνόματα
20   μαθεῖν τὰ ἐν τῆι ναυτικῆι· καὶ κυβερνῆται ἀγαθοὶ γίγνονται δι᾽   15
ἐμπειρίαν τε τῶν πλόων καὶ διὰ μελέτην· ἐμελέτησαν δὲ οἱ μὲν πλοῖον
κυβερνῶντες, οἱ δὲ ὁλκάδα, οἱ δ᾽ ἐντεῦθεν ἐπὶ τριήρεσι κατέστησαν·
οἱ δὲ πολλοὶ ἐλαύνειν εὐθὺς ὡς οἷοί τε εἰσβάντες εἰς ναῦς, ἅτε ἐν παντὶ
τῶι βίωι προμεμελετηκότες.

2   Τὸ δὲ ὁπλιτικὸν αὐτοῖς, ὃ ἥκιστα δοκεῖ εὖ ἔχειν Ἀθήνησιν, οὕτω 20
καθέστηκεν, καὶ τῶν μὲν πολεμίων ἥττους τε σφᾶς αὐτοὺς ἡγοῦνται
εἶναι καὶ ὀλείζους, τῶν δὲ συμμάχων, οἳ φέρουσι τὸν φόρον, καὶ
κατὰ γῆν κρατιστεύουσι, καὶ νομίζουσι τὸ ὁπλιτικὸν ἀρκεῖν, εἰ τῶν
2   συμμάχων κρείττονές εἰσι. πρὸς δὲ καὶ κατὰ τύχην τι αὐτοῖς τοιοῦτον καθέστηκε· τοῖς μὲν κατὰ γῆν ἀρχομένοις οἷόν τ᾽ ἐστὶν ἐκ μικρῶν 25
πόλεων συνοικισθέντας ἀθρόους μάχεσθαι, τοῖς δὲ κατὰ θάλατταν
ἀρχομένοις, ὅσοι νησιῶταί εἰσιν, οὐχ οἷόν τε συνάρασθαι εἰς τὸ
αὐτὸ τὰς πόλεις· ἡ γὰρ θάλαττα ἐν τῶι μέσωι, οἱ δὲ κρατοῦντες
θαλασσοκράτορές εἰσιν· εἰ δ᾽ οἷόν τε καὶ λαθεῖν συνελθοῦσιν εἰς ταὐτὸ
3   τοῖς νησιώταις εἰς μίαν νῆσον, ἀπολοῦνται λιμῶι· ὁπόσαι δ᾽ ἐν τῆι 30
ἠπείρωι εἰσὶ πόλεις ὑπὸ τῶν Ἀθηναίων ἀρχόμεναι, αἱ μὲν μεγάλαι
διὰ δέος ἄρχονται, αἱ δὲ μικραὶ πάνυ διὰ χρείαν· οὐ γὰρ ἔστι πόλις
οὐδεμία ἥτις οὐ δεῖται εἰσάγεσθαί τι ἢ ἐξάγεσθαι. ταῦτα τοίνυν
οὐκ ἔσται αὐτῆι, ἐὰν μὴ ὑπήκοος ἦι τῶν ἀρχόντων τῆς θαλάττης.
4   ἔπειτα δὲ τοῖς ἄρχουσι τῆς θαλάττης οἷόν τ᾽ ἐστὶ ποιεῖν ἅπερ   35
τοῖς τῆς γῆς ἐνίοτε, τέμνειν τὴν γῆν τῶν κρειττόνων· παραπλεῖν
γὰρ ἔξεστιν ὅπου ἂν μηδεὶς ἦι πολέμιος ἢ ὅπου ἂν ὀλίγοι, ἐὰν δὲ

---

5 δεῖ c: δεῖ μὲν D   18 εὐθὺς ὡς D: εὐθέως c   22 ὀλείζους c: μείζους D: μὴ μείζους c
23 κρατιστεύουσι c: κράτιστοί εἰσι D   23 ἀρκεῖν c: ἀρχειν D

προσίωσιν, ἀναβάντα ἀποπλεῖν· καὶ τοῦτο ποιῶν ἧττον ἀπορεῖ ἢ
ὁ πεζῆι παραβοηθῶν. ἔπειτα δὲ τοῖς μὲν κατὰ θάλατταν ἄρχουσιν   5
οἷόν τ' ἀποπλεῦσαι ἀπὸ τῆς σφετέρας αὐτῶν ὁπόσον βούλει πλοῦν,
τοῖς δὲ κατὰ γῆν οὐχ οἷόν τε ἀπὸ τῆς σφετέρας αὐτῶν ἀπελθεῖν
5 πολλῶν ἡμερῶν ὁδόν· βραδεῖαί τε γὰρ αἱ πορεῖαι καὶ σῖτον οὐχ
οἷόν τε ἔχειν πολλοῦ χρόνου πεζῆι ἰόντα· καὶ τὸν μὲν πεζῆι ἰόντα
δεῖ διὰ φιλίας ἰέναι ἢ νικᾶν μαχόμενον, τὸν δὲ πλέοντα, οὗ μὲν ἂν ἧι
κρείττων, ἔξεστιν ἀποβῆναι, οὗ δ' ἂν μὴ ἧι, μὴ ἀποβῆναι ταύτηι τῆς
γῆς, ἀλλὰ παραπλεῦσαι, ἕως ἂν ἐπὶ φιλίαν χώραν ἀφίκηται ἢ ἐπὶ
10 ἥττους αὐτοῦ. ἔπειτα νόσους τῶν καρπῶν αἳ ἐκ Διός εἰσιν οἱ μὲν κατὰ   6
γῆν κράτιστοι χαλεπῶς φέρουσιν, οἱ δὲ κατὰ θάλατταν ῥαιδίως. οὐ
γὰρ ἅμα πᾶσα γῆ νοσεῖ· ὥστε ἐκ τῆς εὐθενούσης ἀφικνεῖται τοῖς τῆς
θαλάττης ἄρχουσιν.
   Εἰ δὲ δεῖ καὶ σμικροτέρων μνησθῆναι, διὰ τὴν ἀρχὴν τῆς θαλάττης   7
15 πρῶτον μὲν τρόπους εὐωχιῶν ἐξηῦρον ἐπιμισγόμενοι ἄλληι ἄλλοις·
ὅ τι τ' ἐν Σικελίαι ἡδὺ ἢ ἐν Ἰταλίαι ἢ ἐν Κύπρωι ἢ ἐν Αἰγύπτωι ἢ ἐν
Λυδίαι ἢ ἐν τῶι Πόντωι ἢ ἐν Πελοποννήσωι ἢ ἄλλοθί που, ταῦτα
πάντα εἰς ἓν ἤθροισται διὰ τὴν ἀρχὴν τῆς θαλάττης. ἔπειτα φωνὴν   8
πᾶσαν ἀκούοντες ἐξελέξαντο τοῦτο μὲν ἐκ τῆς, τοῦτο δὲ ἐκ τῆς· καὶ οἱ
20 μὲν Ἕλληνες ἰδίαι μᾶλλον καὶ φωνῆι καὶ διαίτηι καὶ σχήματι χρῶνται,
Ἀθηναῖοι δὲ κεκραμένηι ἐξ ἁπάντων τῶν Ἑλλήνων καὶ βαρβάρων.
   Θυσίας δὲ καὶ ἱερὰ καὶ ἑορτὰς καὶ τεμένη γνοὺς ὁ δῆμος ὅτι οὐχ   9
οἷόν τέ ἐστιν ἑκάστωι τῶν πενήτων θύειν καὶ εὐωχεῖσθαι καὶ κτᾶσθαι
ἱερὰ καὶ πόλιν οἰκεῖν καλὴν καὶ μεγάλην, ἐξηῦρεν ὅτωι τρόπωι ἔσται
25 ταῦτα. θύουσιν οὖν δημοσίαι μὲν ἡ πόλις ἱερεῖα πολλά· ἔστι δὲ ὁ
δῆμος ὁ εὐωχούμενος καὶ διαλαγχάνων τὰ ἱερεῖα. καὶ γυμνάσια καὶ   10
λουτρὰ καὶ ἀποδυτήρια τοῖς μὲν πλουσίοις ἔστιν ἰδίαι ἐνίοις, ὁ δὲ
δῆμος αὐτὸς αὑτῶι οἰκοδομεῖται ἰδίαι παλαίστρας πολλάς, ἀποδυτήρια, λουτρῶνας· καὶ πλείω τούτων ἀπολαύει ὁ ὄχλος ἢ οἱ
30 ὀλίγοι καὶ οἱ εὐδαίμονες.
   Τὸν δὲ πλοῦτον μόνοι οἷοί τ' εἰσὶν ἔχειν τῶν Ἑλλήνων καὶ τῶν βαρ-   11
βάρων. εἰ γάρ τις πόλις πλουτεῖ ξύλοις ναυπηγησίμοις, ποῖ διαθήσεται, ἐὰν μὴ πείσηι τὸν ἄρχοντα τῆς θαλάττης; τί δ' εἴ τις σιδήρωι
ἢ χαλκῶι ἢ λίνωι πλουτεῖ πόλις, ποῖ διαθήσεται, ἐὰν μὴ πείσηι
35 τὸν ἄρχοντα τῆς θαλάττης; ἐξ αὐτῶν μέντοι τούτων καὶ δὴ νῆές μοί
εἰσι, παρὰ μὲν τοῦ ξύλα, παρὰ δὲ τοῦ σίδηρος, παρὰ δὲ τοῦ χαλκός,
παρὰ δὲ τοῦ λίνου, παρὰ δὲ τοῦ κηρός. πρὸς δὲ τούτοις ἄλλοσε   12

8 οὗ . . . ἀποβῆναι huc transp. c: post γῆς d: om. d   15 ἄλληι ἄλλοις c: ἀλλήλοις D
16 ὅ τι τ' c: ὅ τι D   18 ἤθροισται c: ἠθροῖσθαι D   23 κτᾶσθαι D: ἵστασθαι c

ἄγειν οὐκ ἐάσουσιν οἵτινες ἀντίπαλοι ἡμῖν εἰσιν ἢ οὐ χρήσονται τῆι
θαλάττηι. καὶ ἐγὼ μὲν οὐδὲν ποιῶν ἐκ τῆς γῆς πάντα ταῦτα ἔχω διὰ
τὴν θάλατταν, ἄλλη δ' οὐδεμία πόλις δύο τούτων ἔχει, οὐδ' ἔστι τῆι
αὐτῆι ξύλα καὶ λίνον, ἀλλ' ὅπου λίνον ἐστὶ πλεῖστον, λεία χώρα καὶ
ἄξυλος· οὐδὲ χαλκὸς καὶ σίδηρος ἐκ τῆς αὐτῆς πόλεως οὐδὲ τἆλλα   5
δύο ἢ τρία μιᾶι πόλει, ἀλλὰ τὸ μὲν τῆι, τὸ δὲ τῆι.

13   Ἔτι δὲ πρὸς τούτοις παρὰ πᾶσαν ἤπειρόν ἐστιν ἢ ἀκτὴ προύχουσα ἢ νῆσος προκειμένη ἢ στενόπορόν τι· ὥστε ἔξεστιν ἐνταῦθα
ἐφορμοῦσι τοῖς τῆς θαλάττης ἄρχουσι λωβᾶσθαι τοὺς τὴν ἤπει-
14   ρον οἰκοῦντας. ἑνὸς δὲ ἐνδεεῖς εἰσιν· εἰ γὰρ νῆσον οἰκοῦντες θαλασ-   10
σοκράτορες ἦσαν Ἀθηναῖοι, ὑπῆρχεν ἂν αὐτοῖς ποιεῖν μὲν κακῶς, εἰ
ἐβούλοντο, πάσχειν δὲ μηδέν, ἕως τῆς θαλάττης ἦρχον, μηδὲ τμηθῆναι τὴν ἑαυτῶν γῆν μηδὲ προσδέχεσθαι τοὺς πολεμίους· νῦν δὲ οἱ
γεωργοῦντες καὶ οἱ πλούσιοι Ἀθηναίων ὑπέρχονται τοὺς πολεμίους
μᾶλλον, ὁ δὲ δῆμος, ἅτε εὖ εἰδὼς ὅτι οὐδὲν τῶν σφῶν ἐμπρήσουσιν   15
15   οὐδὲ τεμοῦσιν, ἀδεῶς ζῆι καὶ οὐχ ὑπερχόμενος αὐτούς. πρὸς δὲ
τούτοις καὶ ἑτέρου δέους ἀπηλλαγμένοι ἂν ἦσαν, εἰ νῆσον ὤικουν,
μηδέποτε προδοθῆναι τὴν πόλιν ὑπ' ὀλίγων μηδὲ πύλας ἀνοιχθῆ-
ναι μηδὲ πολεμίους ἐπεισπεσεῖν· πῶς γὰρ νῆσον οἰκούντων ταῦτ'
ἂν ἐγίγνετο; μηδ' αὖ στασιάσαι τῶι δήμωι μηδέν, εἰ νῆσον ὤικουν·   20
νῦν μὲν γὰρ εἰ στασιάσαιεν, ἐλπίδα ἂν ἔχοντες ἐν τοῖς πολεμίοις
στασιάσειαν, ὡς κατὰ γῆν ἐπαξόμενοι· εἰ δὲ νῆσον ὤικουν, καὶ ταῦτ'
16   ἂν ἀδεῶς εἶχεν αὐτοῖς· ἐπειδὴ οὖν ἐξ ἀρχῆς οὐκ ἔτυχον οἰκήσαντες
νῆσον, νῦν τάδε ποιοῦσι· τὴν μὲν οὐσίαν ταῖς νήσοις παρατίθεν-
ται, πιστεύοντες τῆι ἀρχῆι τῆι κατὰ θάλατταν, τὴν δὲ Ἀττικὴν   25
γῆν περιορῶσι τεμνομένην, γιγνώσκοντες ὅτι εἰ αὐτὴν ἐλεήσουσιν,
ἑτέρων ἀγαθῶν μειζόνων στερήσονται.

17   Ἔτι δὲ συμμαχίας καὶ τοὺς ὅρκους ταῖς μὲν ὀλιγαρχουμέναις
πόλεσιν ἀνάγκη ἐμπεδοῦν· ἢν δὲ μὴ ἐμμένωσι ταῖς συνθήκαις, †ἢ
ὑφ' ὅτου ἀδικεῖ† ὀνόματα ἀπὸ τῶν ὀλίγων οἳ συνέθεντο· ἅσσα δ'   30
ἂν ὁ δῆμος σύνθηται, ἔξεστιν αὐτῶι ἑνὶ ἀνατιθέντι τὴν αἰτίαν τῶι
λέγοντι καὶ τῶι ἐπιψηφίσαντι ἀρνεῖσθαι τοῖς ἄλλοις ὅτι Οὐ παρῆν
οὐδὲ ἀρέσκει ἔμοιγε, ἃ συγκείμενα πυνθάνονται ἐν πλήρει τῶι δήμωι,
καὶ εἰ μὴ δόξαι εἶναι ταῦτα, προφάσεις μυρίας ἐξηύρηκε τοῦ μὴ ποιεῖν
ὅσα ἂν μὴ βούλωνται. καὶ ἂν μέν τι κακὸν ἀναβαίνηι ἀπὸ ὧν ὁ   35
δῆμος ἐβούλευσεν, αἰτιᾶται ὁ δῆμος ὡς ὀλίγοι ἄνθρωποι αὐτῶι
ἀντιπράττοντες διέφθειραν, ἐὰν δέ τι ἀγαθὸν σφίσιν αὐτοῖς τὴν
αἰτίαν ἀνατιθέασι.

ι οἵτινες d: εἴ τινες d: οἳ τινες c   33 ἔμοιγε c: οἵ γε d: εἴ γ' d: εἴ γε μὴν d   33 ἅ c: τὰ D

Κωμωιδεῖν δ' αὖ καὶ κακῶς λέγειν τὸν μὲν δῆμον οὐκ ἐῶσιν, ἵνα μὴ   18
αὐτοὶ ἀκούωσι κακῶς, ἰδίαι δὲ κελεύουσιν, εἴ τίς τινα βούλεται, εὖ
εἰδότες ὅτι οὐχὶ τοῦ δήμου ἐστὶν οὐδὲ τοῦ πλήθους ὁ κωμωιδούμενος
ὡς ἐπὶ τὸ πολύ, ἀλλ' ἢ πλούσιος ἢ γενναῖος ἢ δυνάμενος, ὀλίγοι δέ
5 τινες τῶν πενήτων καὶ τῶν δημοτικῶν κωμωιδοῦνται, καὶ οὐδ' οὗτοι
ἐὰν μὴ διὰ πολυπραγμοσύνην καὶ διὰ τὸ ζητεῖν πλέον τι ἔχειν τοῦ
δήμου· ὥστε οὐδὲ τοὺς τοιούτους ἄχθονται κωμωιδουμένους. φημὶ   19
οὖν ἔγωγε τὸν δῆμον τὸν Ἀθήνησι γιγνώσκειν οἵτινες χρηστοί εἰσι
τῶν πολιτῶν καὶ οἵτινες πονηροί· γιγνώσκοντες δὲ τοὺς μὲν σφίσιν
10 αὐτοῖς ἐπιτηδείους καὶ συμφόρους φιλοῦσι, κἂν πονηροὶ ὦσι, τοὺς δὲ
χρηστοὺς μισοῦσι μᾶλλον· οὐ γὰρ νομίζουσι τὴν ἀρετὴν αὐτοῖς πρὸς
τῶι σφετέρωι ἀγαθῶι πεφυκέναι, ἀλλ' ἐπὶ τῶι κακῶι. καὶ τοὐναντίον
γε τούτου ἔνιοι, ὄντες ὡς ἀληθῶς τοῦ δήμου, τὴν φύσιν οὐ δημοτικοί
εἰσι. δημοκρατίαν δ' ἐγὼ μὲν αὐτῶι τῶι δήμωι συγγιγνώσκω· αὐτὸν   20
15 μὲν γὰρ εὖ ποιεῖν παντὶ συγγνώμη ἐστίν· ὅστις δὲ μὴ ὢν τοῦ δήμου
εἵλετο ἐν δημοκρατουμένηι πόλει οἰκεῖν μᾶλλον ἢ ἐν ὀλιγαρχουμένηι,
ἀδικεῖν παρεσκευάσατο καὶ ἔγνω ὅτι μᾶλλον οἷόν τε διαλαθεῖν κακῶι
ὄντι ἐν δημοκρατουμένηι πόλει μᾶλλον ἢ ἐν ὀλιγαρχουμένηι. καὶ   3
περὶ τῆς Ἀθηναίων πολιτείας, τὸν μὲν τρόπον οὐκ ἐπαινῶ· ἐπει-
20 δήπερ δ' ἔδοξεν αὐτοῖς δημοκρατεῖσθαι, εὖ μοι δοκοῦσι διασώιζεσθαι
τὴν δημοκρατίαν τούτωι τῶι τρόπωι χρώμενοι ὧι ἐγὼ
ἐπέδειξα.
    Ἔτι δὲ καὶ τάδε τινὰς ὁρῶ μεμφομένους Ἀθηναίους, ὅτι ἐνίοτε
οὐκ ἔστιν αὐτόθι χρηματίσαι τῆι βουλῆι οὐδὲ τῶι δήμωι ἐνιαυτὸν
25 καθημένωι ἀνθρώπωι. καὶ τοῦτο Ἀθήνησι γίγνεται οὐδὲν δι' ἄλλο   2
ἢ διὰ τὸ πλῆθος τῶν πραγμάτων οὐχ οἷοί τε πάντας ἀποπέμπειν
εἰσὶ χρηματίσαντες. πῶς γὰρ ἂν καὶ οἷοί τε εἶεν, οὕστινας πρῶτον
μὲν δεῖ ἑορτάσαι ἑορτὰς ὅσας οὐδεμία τῶν Ἑλληνίδων πόλεων (ἐν δὲ
ταύταις ἧττόν τινα δυνατόν ἐστι διαπράττεσθαι τῶν τῆς πόλεως),
30 ἔπειτα δὲ δίκας καὶ γραφὰς καὶ εὐθύνας ἐκδικάζειν ὅσας οὐδ' οἱ σύμπαντες ἄνθρωποι ἐκδικάζουσι, τὴν δὲ βουλὴν βουλεύεσθαι πολλὰ
μὲν περὶ τοῦ πολέμου, πολλὰ δὲ περὶ πόρου χρημάτων, πολλὰ δὲ
περὶ νόμων θέσεως, πολλὰ δὲ περὶ τῶν κατὰ πόλιν ἀεὶ γιγνομένων,
πολλὰ δὲ καὶ περὶ τῶν ἐν τοῖς συμμάχοις, καὶ φόρον δέξασθαι καὶ
35 νεωρίων ἐπιμεληθῆναι καὶ ἱερῶν· ἆρα δή τι θαυμαστόν ἐστιν, εἰ
τοσούτων ὑπαρχόντων πραγμάτων μὴ οἷοί τ' εἰσὶ πᾶσιν ἀνθρώποις
χρηματίσαι; λέγουσι δέ τινες, Ἤν τις ἀργύριον ἔχων προσίηι πρὸς   3
βουλὴν ἢ δῆμον, χρηματιεῖται. ἐγὼ δὲ τούτοις ὁμολογήσαιμ' ἂν

34 περὶ τῶν ἐν c: om. D

ἀπὸ χρημάτων πολλὰ διαπράττεσθαι Ἀθήνησι, καὶ ἔτι ἂν πλείω
διαπράττεσθαι, εἰ πλείους ἔτι ἐδίδοσαν ἀργύριον· τοῦτο μέντοι εὖ
οἶδα, διότι πᾶσι διαπρᾶξαι ἡ πόλις τῶν δεομένων οὐχ ἱκανή, οὐδ'

4 εἰ ὁποσονοῦν χρυσίον καὶ ἀργύριον διδοίη τις αὐτοῖς. δεῖ δὲ καὶ
τάδε διαδικάζειν, εἴ τις τὴν ναῦν μὴ ἐπισκευάζει ἢ κατοικοδομεῖ   5
τι δημόσιον· πρὸς δὲ τούτοις χορηγοῖς διαδικάσαι εἰς Διονύσια
καὶ Θαργήλια καὶ Παναθήναια καὶ Προμήθια καὶ Ἡφαίστια ὅσα
ἔτη· καὶ τριήραρχοι καθίστανται τετρακόσιοι ἑκάστου ἐνιαυτοῦ,
καὶ τούτων τοῖς βουλομένοις δεῖ διαδικάσαι ὅσα ἔτη· πρὸς δὲ τούτοις ἀρχὰς δοκιμάσαι καὶ διαδικάσαι καὶ ὀρφανοὺς δοκιμάσαι καὶ   10

5 φύλακας δεσμωτῶν καταστῆσαι. ταῦτα μὲν οὖν ὅσα ἔτη· διὰ χρόνου δὲ δικάσαι δεῖ στρατηγικὰς καὶ ἐάν τι ἄλλο ἐξαπιναῖον ἀδίκημα
γίγνηται, ἐάν τε ὑβρίζωσί τινες ἄηθες ὕβρισμα ἐάν τε ἀσεβήσωσι.
πολλὰ ἔτι πάνυ παραλείπω· τὸ δὲ μέγιστον εἴρηται πλὴν αἱ τάξεις τοῦ φόρου· τοῦτο δὲ γίγνεται ὡς τὰ πολλὰ δι' ἔτους πέμπτου.   15
φέρε δὴ τοίνυν, ταῦτα οὐκ οἴεσθαι χρὴ χρῆναι διαδικάζειν ἅπαντα;

6 εἰπάτω γάρ τις ὅ τι οὐ χρῆν αὐτόθι διαδικάζεσθαι. εἰ δ' αὖ ὁμολογεῖν
δεῖ ἅπαντα χρῆναι διαδικάζειν, ἀνάγκη δι' ἐνιαυτοῦ· ὡς οὐδὲ νῦν
δι' ἐνιαυτοῦ δικάζοντες ὑπάρχουσιν ὥστε παύειν τοὺς ἀδικοῦντας

7 ὑπὸ τοῦ πλήθους τῶν ἀνθρώπων. φέρε δή, ἀλλὰ φήσει τις χρῆναι   20
δικάζειν μέν, ἐλάττους δὲ δικάζειν. ἀνάγκηι τοίνυν, ἐὰν μὴ ὀλίγα
ποιῶνται δικαστήρια, ὀλίγοι ἐν ἑκάστωι ἔσονται τῶι δικαστηρίωι·
ὥστε καὶ διασκευάσασθαι ῥάιδιον ἔσται πρὸς ὀλίγους δικαστὰς καὶ

8 συνδεκάσαι πολὺ ἧττον δικαίως δικάζειν. πρὸς δὲ τούτοις οἴεσθαι
χρὴ καὶ ἑορτὰς ἄγειν χρῆναι Ἀθηναίους, ἐν αἷς οὐχ οἷόν τε δικάζειν.   25
καὶ ἄγουσι μὲν ἑορτὰς διπλασίους ἢ οἱ ἄλλοι· ἀλλ' ἐγὼ μὲν τίθημι
ἴσας τῆι ὀλιγίστας ἀγούσηι πόλει.

Τούτων τοίνυν τοιούτων ὄντων οὔ φημι οἷόν τ' εἶναι ἄλλως ἔχειν
τὰ πράγματα Ἀθήνησιν ἢ ὥσπερ νῦν ἔχει, πλὴν ἢ κατὰ μικρόν
τι οἷόν τε τὸ μὲν ἀφελεῖν τὸ δὲ προσθεῖναι· πολὺ δ' οὐχ οἷόν τε   30

9 μετακινεῖν, ὥστε μὴ οὐχὶ τῆς δημοκρατίας ἀφαιρεῖν τι. ὥστε μὲν
γὰρ βέλτιον ἔχειν τὴν πολιτείαν, οἷόν τε πολλὰ ἐξευρεῖν, ὥστε μέντοι
ὑπάρχειν μὲν δημοκρατίαν εἶναι, ἀρκούντως δὲ τοῦτο ἐξευρεῖν, ὅπως
βέλτιον πολιτεύσονται, οὐ ῥάιδιον, πλήν, ὅπερ ἄρτι εἶπον, κατὰ
μικρόν τι προσθέντα ἢ ἀφελόντα.   35

2 ἔτι ἐδίδοσαν c: ἐπεδίδοσαν D   3 lacunam post πόλις indicauit c   9 δεῖ c: om. D
12 δὲ δικάσαι c: διαδικάσαι D στρατηγικὰς c: στρατιᾶς d: στρατιὰς d:
ἀστρατείας c   16 χρὴ c: om. D   17 ὁμολογεῖν δεῖ c: ὁμολογεῖ δεῖν D   24 συνδεκάσαι c: συνδικάσαι D   29 πλὴν ἢ c: πλὴν εἰ D

Δοκοῦσι δὲ Ἀθηναῖοι καὶ τοῦτό μοι οὐκ ὀρθῶς βουλεύεσθαι, ὅτι 10
τοὺς χείρους αἱροῦνται ἐν ταῖς πόλεσι ταῖς στασιαζούσαις. οἱ δὲ
τοῦτο γνώμηι ποιοῦσιν. εἰ μὲν γὰρ ἡιροῦντο τοὺς βελτίους, ἡιροῦντ᾽
ἂν οὐχὶ τοὺς ταὐτὰ γιγνώσκοντας σφίσιν αὐτοῖς· ἐν οὐδεμιᾶι γὰρ
5 πόλει τὸ βέλτιστον εὔνουν ἐστὶ τῶι δήμωι, ἀλλὰ τὸ κάκιστον ἐν
ἑκάστηι ἐστὶ πόλει εὔνουν τῶι δήμωι· οἱ γὰρ ὅμοιοι τοῖς ὁμοίοις
εὖνοί εἰσι. διὰ ταῦτα οὖν Ἀθηναῖοι τὰ σφίσιν αὐτοῖς προσήκοντα
αἱροῦνται. ὁποσάκις δ᾽ ἐπεχείρησαν αἱρεῖσθαι τοὺς βελτίστους, οὐ 11
συνήνεγκεν αὐτοῖς, ἀλλ᾽ ἐντὸς ὀλίγου χρόνου ὁ δῆμος ἐδούλευσεν
10 ὁ ἐν Βοιωτοῖς· τοῦτο δὲ ὅτε Μιλησίων εἵλοντο τοὺς βελτίστους,
ἐντὸς ὀλίγου χρόνου ἀποστάντες τὸν δῆμον κατέκοψαν· τοῦτο δὲ
ὅτε εἵλοντο Λακεδαιμονίους ἀντὶ Μεσσηνίων, ἐντὸς ὀλίγου χρόνου
Λακεδαιμόνιοι καταστρεψάμενοι Μεσσηνίους ἐπολέμουν Ἀθηναίοις.
Ὑπολάβοι δέ τις ἂν ὡς οὐδεὶς ἄρα ἀδίκως ἠτίμωται Ἀθήνησιν. 12
15 ἐγὼ δέ φημί τινας εἶναι οἳ ἀδίκως ἠτίμωνται. ὀλίγοι μέντοι τινές· ἀλλ᾽
οὐκ ὀλίγων δεῖ τῶν ἐπιθησομένων τῆι δημοκρατίαι τῆι Ἀθήνησιν,
ἐπεί τοι καὶ οὕτως ἔχει, οὐδὲν ἐνθυμεῖσθαι ἀνθρώπους οἵτινες δικαίως
ἠτίμωνται, ἀλλ᾽ εἴ τινες ἀδίκως. πῶς ἂν οὖν ἀδίκως οἴοιτό τις ἂν 13
τοὺς πολλοὺς ἠτιμῶσθαι Ἀθήνησιν, ὅπου ὁ δῆμός ἐστιν ὁ ἄρχων
20 τὰς ἀρχάς; ἐκ δὲ τοῦ μὴ δικαίως ἄρχειν μηδὲ λέγειν τὰ δίκαια μηδὲ
πράττειν, ἐκ τοιούτων ἄτιμοί εἰσιν Ἀθήνησι. ταῦτα χρὴ λογιζό-
μενον μὴ νομίζειν εἶναί τι δεινὸν ἀπὸ τῶν ἀτίμων Ἀθήνησιν.

17 οὐδὲν D: οὐ δεῖ c   18 ἠτίμωνται c: τιμῶνται D

COMMENTARY ON *HIERO*

Title: The name of the character under instruction gives the title of *Hiero*, as it does in many Platonic dialogues. The alternative ὁ τυραννικός sc. λόγος follows the pattern of *Oeconomicus*, *Cynegeticus*, *Hipparchicus*. Some manuscripts describe the author as Ξενοφῶντος ῥήτορος, presumably to distinguish our Xenophon from others. This does not mean he is a public speaker, but a prose-writer and historian: Lapini (1997) 16, in reference to the authorship of *Ath*.

1.1–10. Simonides the poet comes to Hiero the tyrant and, on the grounds that he has experienced both conditions, asks him whether the ruler or the non-ruler has more or less of the pleasures and pains that constitute happiness and unhappiness. Hiero asks to be reminded of the experiences of the non-ruler in his private life. Simonides catalogues the experiences of the senses, and declares that the tyrant has more pleasure and less pain through these. Hiero responds with hot denial. The central theme is marked throughout the work: 'how the tyrannical life differs from the private in respect of pleasure and pain for mankind' (1.2), 'if in any respect the tyrannical life differs from the private life' (1.7), 'the tyrannical life gets much more joy . . . and far fewer pains', 'tyrants have far less joy than those who live moderate lives as private individuals, but many more and greater pains' (1.8), 'tyrants have the least share of the greatest goods and the largest share of the greatest pains' (2.6). The vocabulary of pleasure and pain is also repeated throughout: ἡδομένους τε καὶ ἀχθομένους 1.4, ἥδεσθαί τε καὶ λυπεῖσθαι 1.5, εὐφραίνεται . . . τὰ λυπηρὰ ἔχει, εὐφραίνονται . . . λυποῦνται 1.8 etc.

1.1. Xenophon's introduction displays his artful simplicity: pp. 22–3. **ὁ ποιητής:** the poet was the traditional wise man of early Greece; see p. 33 on the characterization of Simonides as a wise man. **τὸν τύραννον:** Xenophon elsewhere uses this term for the imperfect ruler, who rules unwilling subjects, in contrast with the better type, who is often called ἄρχων (*Oec.* 21.5.12; *Mem.* 3.9.10–11, cf. 12–13); but in this dialogue Simonides and Hiero define the word neutrally by its opposition to 'non-ruler' ἰδιώτης (see comment below on 1.2) since although Simonides uses ἄρχων and cognates in his vision of reform (8.2, 3, 5; 9.3), and Hiero responds (10.1), both also persist with their earlier uses of τύραννος (8.10, 11.1, 11.6). **σχολῆς δὲ γενομένης ἀμφοῖν** 'when there was leisure for both (of them)'; the dual represents their close partnership: *GG* 155. There is a special point to leisure in Socratic philosophizing. *Symp.* 4.44 has Antisthenes say: 'And you see that the most luxurious thing, leisure, is always at my disposal so that I can see things worth seeing and hear things worth hearing and . . . spend the day in leisure (σχολάζων) with Socrates.' Socrates also engages Ischomachus in conversation when he finds him at leisure (*Oec.* 7.1). **Ἆρ' ἄν μοι ἐθελήσαις:** the polite potential optative conveys his deference toward a man of power, which is a *topos* of meetings of the wise and powerful. Xenophon subverts the *topos* when he has the ruler Cyrus deferentially ask the wise Croesus for his advice (*Cyr.* 7.2.10: ἆρ' ἄν τί μοι ἐθελήσαις συμβουλεῦσαι;).

Herodotean wise men also regularly ask whether they should speak out or be silent (Hdt. 1.88.2, 7.101.3, 104.1), and Xenophon subverts this too when Hystaspes asks whether Cyrus would be annoyed if he were to ask him something (*Cyr.* 8.4.9: Ἄρ᾽ ἄν, ἔφη, ὦ Κῦρε, ἀχθεσθείης μοι εἴ σε ἐροίμην), and Cyrus says he will be annoyed if he does *not* ask. ἃ εἰκὸς (sc. ἐστιν) εἰδέναι σε βέλτιον ἐμοῦ: Simonides disclaims wisdom in the ironic manner of Socrates because he desires to hear the tyrant confess his unhappiness: pp. 36–7. ὁποῖα δή: no suspicion of Simonides' motives need be implied in the particle. Ischomachus' wife uses a similar question to express her disbelief that she can help her husband in his work (*Oec.* 7.16: καὶ τί δή and 32: καὶ ποῖα δή). ἐγώ: the nominative first person pronoun is omitted except (a) for emphasis or (b) for contrast with another person, here σοῦ to underline the opposition of tyrant/wise man: *GG* 896. ἔφη: the early part of the dialogue is punctuated with reminders that this is a conversation. Sometimes they are mere introductions: 'said Simonides', 'said Hiero', but in other instances they interrupt the words spoken and even repeat such introductions, as in 'And Simonides said, "But in these areas", he said, "there is a difference"' (1.8). These recapitulations often create pauses around words of special significance for emphasis, as in this statement of difference and again at 1.6, to enhance Simonides' confession of ignorance; Strauss (1947/1963) 123 n. 41 (= Strauss 2000 116 n. 41) recognizes the device. οὕτως ὄντος σοφοῦ ἀνδρός: 'being a man so wise'; cf. the arrangement of words at *Hell.* 4.8.31: μάλα δοκῶν ἀνὴρ ἀγαθὸς εἶναι; cf. also the emphatic description of Lycurgus as εἰς τὰ ἔσχατα σοφόν (*Lac.* 1.2).

1.2 καὶ ἰδιώτην γεγενημένον καὶ νῦν τύραννον ὄντα: Hiero was the second of three brothers who held the tyranny, and had therefore once been a non-ruler: pp. 34–5. The meaning of ἰδιώτης depends on its context, which is here the opposition with τύραννος. Xenophon uses it of: non-military personnel as opposed to one of military rank (*An.* 1.3.11), an ordinary citizen as opposed to a professional athlete (*Mem.* 3.7.7, 3.12.1; *Hipp.* 8.1, *Hiero* 4.6), a layman as opposed to a sophist (*Cyn.* 13.4), cities that lack honour as opposed to those that have it (*Cyr.* 8.7.7). ἀμφοτέρων πεπειραμένον 'since you have had experience of both conditions'. Hiero endorses Simonides' appeal to his experience when he says that ignorance about tyranny comes from lack of experience (1.10), but Simonides' eventual expression of his own greater theoretical knowledge (8–11) proves his greater inborn wisdom. εἰς εὐφροσύνας τε καὶ λύπας ἀνθρώποις 'with respect to mankind's pleasures and pains'; cf. *An.* 2.6.30: οὔτ᾽ εἰς φιλίαν αὐτοὺς ἐμέμφετο and *Lac.* 2.14: εἰς ἀφροδίσια.

1.3 Τί οὖν . . . οὐχὶ . . . ὑπέμνησάς με: the particle conveys progression, and the aorist is used like an imperative (*M&T* 62; compare τί οὖν οὐ διηγήσω ἡμῖν τὴν συνουσίαν: Plat. *Prot.* 310a: 'so, why don't you relate the gathering for us'); sometimes a sense of urgency is conveyed by an additional reference to speed, as at Ar. *Lys.* 181–2 ('as quickly as possible'). Hiero has not entirely forgotten the experiences of private life, since he later recalls with passion the happiness he had as a private man (6.1–2) and even tells Simonides what he should remember about private life (6.7: εἰ δὲ καὶ σὺ πολεμικῶν ἔμπειρος εἶ . . . ἀναμνήσθητι). He may have buried his pleasant memories because of their painful contrast with his current misery as he buried his cares in drinking when he was a private man (6.1–2) or be deliberately trying to conceal his unhappiness as the reluctant patient or the Straussian dissembler, but it is likeliest that he is merely asking Simonides to provide a list to prompt discussion because, as he says, νῦν γε ἔτι 'still now at least' Simonides is enjoying the experience (unlike Hiero). οὕτως γάρ 'for thus' i.e. 'because if you do this . . .'

1.4 οὕτω δή picks up the previous οὕτως: 'and on this agreed basis then'. Simonides proceeds to the Socratic philosopher's primary task: definition through classification (compare Socrates' description of the process of dialectic in *Mem.* 4.5.11– 12, 4.6: διαλέγοντας κατὰ γένη). The senses are marshalled into those that affect (i) parts of the body, (ii) the whole body, (iii) the soul, (iv) the body and soul together; Aristotle notes similar classes of goods (*NE* 1098b12–16). These foreshadow all the topics discussed in the course of the dialogue. Peace and war, for example, which are the first matters that Hiero raises independently (2.8–18), affect the body and the soul together. The first sentence exhibits the order of words called *anaphora*, in which the first words in particular are repeated in a sequence of *cola* (διὰ μέν . . . διὰ δέ . . . διὰ δέ). The second sentence is a sequence of words joined by καί (1.5 below). The third sentence reverts to *anaphora* (1.5 below: ἔστι μὲν ὅτε . . . ὁτὲ δ' αὖ . . . ἔστι δ' ὅτε). This artfulness and variation give definition and interest to Simonides' list. The phrases that come first in each sentence secure the greatest emphasis. τοὺς μὲν δὴ ἰδιώτας: μὲν δή regularly sums up one section in preparation for the next: 'so', not always followed by δέ. Simonides refers to non-rulers in the third person even though he is himself a non-ruler because it suits a generalized discussion, but cf. note on 1.11. δοκῶ μοι καταμεμαθηκέναι: an expression of philosophical reflection rather than real doubt, which stresses the process of thought that has produced the conclusion, and thus affirms it (as at *Oec.* 11.8, 12.19 and Hdt. 2.93.6: ἐγώ μοι δοκέω κατανοεῖν τοῦτο). Simonides 'knows' (οἶδα) the fact that Hiero has been both ruler and non-ruler (1.2), but expresses his opinions tentatively: e.g. 1.5: μοι δοκοῦμεν, 1.6: δοκῶ μοι αἰσθάνεσθαι, δοκῶ μοι ἀγνοεῖν, 8.1 ἔχειν μοι δοκῶ διδάξαι. Hiero also expresses himself in this tentative way: δοκῶ μεμνῆσθαι 1.10, even when he has strong emotional conviction about his deprivations, as at 1.33: μοι δοκῶ ἐπιθυμεῖν. διὰ μέν . . . διὰ δέ . . . διὰ δέ . . . διὰ δέ: *anaphora* (with expansion of the final item) orders the different physical sensations; for a more emotional example of *anaphora*, see 1.35. τὰ δ' ἀφροδίσια: the accusative of respect breaks the sequence of datives and brings special attention to sexual sensation; δι' ὧν δή: the reference to the sexual organs is oblique because Simonides is bashful about them, perhaps particularly in front of such a man as the tyrant: 'through the things which of course we all know about'. This is typical of polite discourse. Hiero's description of his desire for his boyfriend is equally delicate: 1.32.

1.5 τὰ δὲ ψύχη καὶ θάλπη 'episodes of cold and heat'. ἐπ' αὐτοῖς refers back to the previously mentioned sensations that were dependent on κρίνοντες, but using a phrase that depends on ἥδεσθαι; cf. 1.16, 6.1, 6.15. ἀγαθοῖς δὲ καὶ κακοῖς: these 'good and bad things' turn out to be experiences such as peace and war (2.7). ἔστι μὲν ὅτε . . . ὁτὲ δ' αὖ . . . ἔστι δ' ὅτε 'sometimes (lit. 'there are (occasions) when': *GG* 1029) (we seem to feel pleasure) and at other times (to feel pain) . . . and sometimes (we seem)'; *anaphora* brings attention to the different sources of the sensations; note the difference between ὅτε and ὀτέ. κοινῆι 'in both ways', i.e. through body and soul.

1.6 τῶι δὲ ὕπνωι; this introduces a category of sensation which Simonides says he does not understand. ταῦτα: Xenophon regularly places the demonstrative after the phrase it recapitulates, in a kind of apposition; here it recapitulates the previous sequence of nominal clauses (cf. τὸν . . . ἡδόμενον . . . τοῦτον 1.21, ὁ δὲ σπανίσας . . . οὗτός 1.25, ὃς γὰρ ἂν φιλῆται . . . τοῦτον 3.2, and 2.5, 4.5 with articular infinitives; it is also regular in *Lac.* e.g. 1.7; and *Ath.* e.g. 1.3). The prior placement of the demonstrative occurs less regularly, e.g. τοῦτο . . . εἰ in the following sentence and 1.16: τοῦτο . . . πάνυ συγχωρῶ, τοὺς ἐπαίνους παρὰ τῶν ἐλευθερωτάτων ἡδίστους εἶναι, but the demonstrative in both cases emphasizes what is in the nominal phrase. The pleasures experienced during sleep are dreams. Plato, *Rep.* 571b–572d says that the consuming soul experiences crude pleasures, such as sleeping with one's mother (Hdt. 6.107.1 credits such a dream to the tyrant Hippias), whereas the philosophic soul experiences the pleasure of 'investigating' and 'searching' and acquiring knowledge, it 'fixes upon truth' and the 'sights it sees in sleep' are lawful. *Cyr.* 8.7.20–1 agrees that the soul in sleep is most free and has clearest perceptions of the future. The pains experienced would presumably include nightmares. There seems to be no reference to sleep as a pleasure in its own right as a period of rest and freedom from cares; that is separately addressed in *Hiero* 6.2–3 and 7; *Mem.* 1.5.1; *Symp.* 4.31. σαφεστέρας '(provide perceptions) that are clearer to us'; the adjective is predicative: *GG* 971–2.

1.7 τοίνυν continues what has been announced; Hiero continues by saying that he has nothing to add to what has been said because everyone has such sense organs, so that the ruler seems no different from non-rulers; compare 1.28, where τοίνυν continues his own argument about marriage. οὐδ᾽ . . . ἔχοιμ᾽ ἂν εἰπεῖν 'I would not have the means to say'. μέχρι γε τούτου 'up to this point in the discussion'.

1.8 Ἀλλ᾽ ἐν τοῖσδε, ἔφη, διαφέρει: Simonides objects to Hiero's thesis that there is no difference between the two lives: 'but that's wrong'; the intrusion of 'he said' gives force to the areas of difference. δι᾽ ἑκάστου τούτων 'through each of these' i.e. the sense organs categorized above. μείω . . . μείω . . . πλείω καὶ μείζω: Xenophon uses contracted forms of these types of comparatives in the neuter, and uncontracted forms for other genders: 1.12; 2.10,16; 11.4; but both are used side by side at 4.6. εὖ ἴσθ᾽: Hiero begins to assert the knowledge he has because of his experience; this continues at 1.10 πειράσομαί σε διδάσκειν, 1.17 οἶδά γε, 1.19 εὖ οἶδ᾽, 1.27 σάφ᾽ ἴσθι, 2.6 ἐγὼ δὲ πεπειραμένος σαφῶς οἶδα. τῶν μετρίως διαγόντων ἰδιωτῶν 'than modest-living private individuals'; see 1.19 τῶν μετρίως διαιτωμένων.

1.9 πῶς ἂν πολλοὶ μὲν ἐπεθύμουν τυραννεῖν: Herodotus credits this positive desire for tyranny to the tyrants Pisistratus and Deioces: 1.59.3 and 1.96.2. καὶ ταῦτα takes up a preceding idea and adds to it 'many men *and at that* from among those who seem to be men most capable'; for another example: 1.13 ὀλίγα γε τῶν πολλῶν καὶ ταῦτα τοιαῦτα ὄντα οὕτω τίμια πωλεῖται 'few out of many and *at that*, as well as being such (so few), they are sold at such a high price'; cf. 1.22 καὶ . . . ταῦτα, 2.2 καὶ ταύτας, 7.8 καὶ ταῦτα. There is a compliment to Hiero in the idea that only the most capable aspire to tyranny.

1.10 Ὅτι ναὶ μὰ τὸν Δί, ἔφη ὁ Ἱέρων: the oath and the intrusion of 'he said' indicate that Hiero has taken the bait on Simonides' hook that experience matters; 'both activities' are τὸ τυραννεῖν and τὸ ἰδιωτεύειν. Hiero credits aspirants to tyranny with inquiry, but no experience.

1.11–38: Hiero takes over the conversation and systematically refutes the idea that tyrants have more physical pleasures in the areas that Simonides mentioned: sights 1.11–13, sounds 1.14–16, tastes 1.16–25, the delights of Aphrodite 1.26–38. He anticipates objections from Simonides at 1.13, and Simonides raises objections himself and also reminds Hiero in turn of each of the categories mentioned (1.14, 15, 20, 21, 24). Variation is provided by Simonides' involvement and the range of ideas Hiero presents about his deprivation. Simonides does not press the philosophical ideal that rulers should resist these pleasures (*Mem.* 2.1.1–8, 1.3.5–15) because Hiero is a normal human being who wants them. Simonides will remedy the disadvantages that the tyrant identifies here, but only in the second part of the dialogue when he is sure of his patient's receptivity.

1.11 τοὺς τυράννους: Hiero refers to 'rulers' in the third person most of the time, just as Simonides refers to 'non-rulers' in the third person (1.4), but his first-person plural at 1.27 and singular at 1.31 reflect his special engagement in the discussion of sexual relations (cf. 8.6). Simonides also uses the second person plural (e.g. 1.14) and the second person singular (e.g. 1.31) to refer more personally to Hiero's tyrannical condition. ἐν τοῖς διὰ τῆς ὄψεως θεάμασι 'in the sights that the eyes see' seems an odd expression, but looks forward to the contrast between deceptive appearances and those genuine visions of the truth that are perceived through the intellect at 2.4–5; the contrast between sensation and intellect, and between lies and truth, is common in philosophic thought; the great variety of θεα- compound words in this section reinforces the theme. μειονεκτοῦντας 'having a lesser share'; the dative with preposition (ἔν τινι as here and 1.14 and 1.29) or without (1.18), and the genitive of separation (1.29) convey the area of deprivation; often this is accompanied by the genitive of comparison to indicate the people who have the greater share (1.18). ἄλλα . . . ἐν ἄλληι χώραι 'different (sights) in (every) different land'; cf. *Ath.* 2.7 'mixing with different people in different lands' ἄλληι ἄλλοις. ἐπὶ δὲ τούτων ἕκαστα: Hiero insists on the variety of sights that non-rulers can enjoy: 'for each of these (kinds of) sights'. καὶ εἰς πόλεις ἃς ἂν βούλωνται: he underlines for the first time the essential *freedom* of movement for private individuals, who go to 'whichever cities they like and to common festivals'; it is a commonplace that the tyrant lacks this freedom and is compelled against his desires to stay at home: Appendix 2. Simonides enjoys this freedom as a non-ruler, as does the man freed of the burden of wealth in *Symp.* 4.30–1. *Lac.* 14.2 considers spending time abroad to be a transgression of the community spirit of the Spartans precisely because of the freedom that it implies. The festivals are such as those at Olympia and Delphi. The sights in the cities may include the tyrant's treasures, the buildings to which Simonides refers at 11.2, or even performances, such as those that are an object of 'the gaze' in *Lac.* 4.2, χορούς ἀξιακροατοτάτους . . . ἀγῶνας ἀξιοθεατοτάτους. ἃ . . . δοκεῖ εἶναι 'such (sights) as seem to be'; this reading emphasizes the illusory appearance of worth.

1.12 οὐ μάλα ἀμφὶ θεωρίας ἔχουσιν 'do not have much inclination for sight-seeing'; they might have no inclination, either, toward 'theory' about their unhappiness: pp. 32–3. ἀσφαλὲς . . . φοβερόν: the first reference to the characteristic fear for his life and security that the tyrant experiences, a major cause of his unhappiness; this is developed at 6.4. κρείττονες τῶν παρόντων 'stronger than those present'. There was a threat of assassination on any such public occasion; Jason was assassinated during his review of his cavalry: *Hell.* 6.4.31. Exiles were a special source of danger to the tyrant abroad; those who had been exiled by Euphron the tyrant of Sicyon were able to assassinate him in Thebes: *Hell.* 7.3.4–5. The tyrant's bodyguard could not be trusted to protect him and might even kill him for greater payment (6.10–11). D.S. 14.109 describes how Dionysius I sent his brother-in-law to the Olympic festival of 388 BC, not attending in person perhaps for the reasons that Hiero goes on to describe. παρακαταθεμένους: Herodotus 6.86 tells how property was routinely 'deposited' for safe-keeping in the hands of another party, with pledges exchanged and the gods involved. *Mem.* 4.4.17 says that it is a sign of trust to give a deposit (of money or even of minor-age sons and daughters); the tyrant does not have this trust in others. ἅμα τε . . . καί 'at the same time . . . as', closely connects the two fears; the tyrant who loses his power will have no resources to get back at those who wronged him in taking what he had deposited with them.

1.13 εἴποις οὖν ἂν ἴσως σύ: Hiero anticipates, and then answers, a possible objection from Simonides; narrators engage their audiences with such addresses even in narrative works: *Lac.* 2.8 and *Ath.* 3.1, 6–7. ἀλλ᾽ ἄρα conveys opposition and lively apprehension or inference. καὶ οἴκοι μένουσι: the separation from αὐτοῖς gives force to the substance of the objection, that such sights come to (tyrants) even though they stay at home. καὶ ταῦτα . . . : '(a few out of the many available) and *at that*, though (or as well as) being of such a sort (i.e. so few), they are sold at such a high price'. Hiero agrees that shows do come to town, but he objects to the rarity and high costs. Travelling spectacles would include mime and acrobatics (*Symp.* 1.11–16, 2.2, 9). οἱ ἐπιδεικνύμενοι καὶ ὁτιοῦν 'those who display anything at all' i.e. of little worth; the comparison that follows has many points: the amount of profit they get, the time in which it is acquired, the numbers of spectators from whom it is acquired. παρὰ τοῦ τυράννου: the singular for the tyrant (when the experience of 'tyrants' in the plural has been described) reinforces the idea that he alone pays more than all others put together; the singular is also used effectively for the one-to-one confrontation of the man who is reluctant to criticize a tyrant to his face (1.15); cf. 2.7–18 for further uses of the singular that isolate the tyrant from others, but also 5.3–4, where statements about 'the tyrant' alternate with statements about 'tyrants', apparently in order to distinguish stages in the argument.

1.14 Simonides' reforms will eventually make Hiero so loved that many will want to visit and please him with their shows and his court will become a festival site in its own right (11.10). For the moment, however, Simonides admits defeat and raises the second category, the pleasure of sounds, and the special 'good thing', praise. This is another *topos*: see Appendix 2. γέ τοι: the particle combination restricts the point to a certainty: 'you certainly have the advantage in what you hear (even if not in what you see)'; cf. 6.6, where fear certainly (γέ τοι) destroys the pleasures of the soul. Simonides now groups Hiero along with other tyrants in the second person plural rather than in the third person. τοῦ μὲν ἡδίστου ἀκροάματος . . . οὔποτε σπανίζετε . . . τοῦ δ' αὖ χαλεπωτάτου ἀκροάματος . . . ἀνήκοοί ἐστε: *Mem.* 2.1.31 also has Virtue taunt Vice: τοῦ δὲ πάντων ἡδίστου ἀκούσματος, ἐπαίνου ἑαυτῆς, ἀνήκοος εἶ καὶ τοῦ πάντων ἡδίστου θεάματος ἀθέατος. Because Xenophon's theory of government informs all his works, details are often repeated in different contexts to different effects. καὶ ὅσα ἂν λέγητε καὶ ὅσα ἂν ποιῆτε 'all the things that you say and do'; parallel indefinite relative clauses emphasize the complete lack of discrimination in his eulogists. οὐδεὶς γὰρ ἐθέλει τυράννου κατ' ὀφθαλμοὺς κατηγορεῖν: Simonides notes the lack of freedom to criticize the tyrant in his enslaved community; the pithy wisdom and the rhythm make this sound like a proverb. Isocrates *To Nic.* 2.2–4 counts criticism as one of the many avenues of education open to the private individual, but denied to tyrants since: 'Most men do not go near them and those who do keep their company do so for favour.' Wise men are also subject to this fear and favour.

1.15 τί is either adverbial 'how?' (*GG* 1060–1) or an internal accusative on εὐφραίνειν: 'what joy do they give?' ὕποπτοι marks the tyrant's suspicion of those around him: at 2.17 and 4.1 his lack of trust is a cause of unhappiness. ἕνεκα τοῦ κολακεύειν 'for the purpose of flattering'; *Lac.* 14.2 and *Ath.* 1.18 also recognize this as a corrupt form of praise, designed to secure reward or avoid punishment. For an extended and almost comic development of the *topos* of praise and blame of tyrants from the point of view of the wise, and an illustration of the manoeuvres that the wise adopted to tread the middle path between insincere praise and outright condemnation, see D.S. 15.6–7 for how Philoxenus found a way of both flattering and criticizing Dionysius' poetry, and how Plato was punished for his frank and open comments on his tyranny; this led to the view that 'the wise man should keep company with tyrants as little as possible or as pleasingly as possible'.

1.16 τοῦτο μὲν δὴ ναὶ μὰ τὸν Δία ἔγωγέ σοι . . . πάνυ συγχωρῶ: Simonides agrees with Hiero in the strongest terms in order to draw out his own suggestion that he needs to allow his people freedom of speech if he wants the finest pleasure of praise. ἀλλ', ὁρᾶις: he moves on rapidly to the next point perhaps because he feels that the tyrant would be offended by more talk of freedom, as the stories show above, also because, as in Socratic dialogue, he is more interested in hearing from his interlocutor than delivering lectures himself. Yet the tyrant's lack of pleasure in what he hears will in the end be rectified only through the liberation of his people, who will praise him 'freely' only when he makes them free (11.8). See the Appendix 1 for criticism of the idea in Strauss that Simonides does not envisage the freedom of the citizens as a condition of their happiness. δι' ὧν τρεφόμεθα: in emphatic position in its clause, this announces the topic of the pleasures of food and drink: 'the things through which we feed ourselves'. ἐν αὐτοῖς: recapitulates the relative clause; cf. 1.5, 6.1, 6.15 and *Cyr.* 8.8.16 ὅσα . . . οὐδὲν αὐτῶν.

1.17 καὶ οἶδά γ᾽: Hiero strongly agrees with Simonides that the many do have this view; the combination is found again at καὶ δῶρά γε (7.8). τούτωι looks forward in apposition to the subsequent ὅτι clause. τοῦτο: the demonstrative emphasizes the important idea: 'the thing that surpasses customary things, this thing . . .'; similar abstract expressions describe relative measurements at 4.8.

1.18 ἔκπλεωι is removed from the noun it describes (αἱ τράπεζαι) and placed in this early position in the sentence to emphasize the amount of food and drink available. ταύτηι . . . τῆι εὐφροσύνηι τῆς ἐλπίδος 'in this pleasure that consists of anticipation'; the dative with μειονεκτοῦσι (cf. on 1.11 above) and with a genitive of material; hope is a pleasant experience.

1.19 ἐκεῖνο εὖ οἶδ᾽ ὅτι καὶ σὺ ἔμπειρος εἶ ὅτι 'I know well that (ὅτι) you are also experienced in that (ἐκεῖνο) namely the fact that (ὅτι)'; cf. for the accusative: ἐπιστήμονες δ᾽ ἦσαν τὰ προσήκοντα (*Cyr.* 3.3.9). ὅσωι ἂν πλείω . . . τοσούτωι καὶ θᾶττον: correlative clauses, 'the more abundantly a man is served with goods that exceed sufficiency, the more swiftly does surfeit of consumption intervene'. καὶ τῶι χρόνωι τῆς ἡδονῆς 'also in respect of the duration of the pleasure'; Hiero complained about the brief duration of his entertainments as well; they pass in a flash.

1.20 Ἀλλά: Simonides tries to retrieve his argument from collapse with the objection that there is more pleasure during the consumption, however brief; the pause created by the oath and the insertion of 'he said' emphasizes his objection. ὅσον ἂν χρόνον . . . τοῦτον 'for as much time as . . . for this length of time' picks up the reference to the duration of the pleasure. τῶν . . . παρατιθεμένων: genitive of comparison.

1.21 Οὐκοῦν: the particle announces the next stage of an argument. τὸν ἑκάστωι ἡδόμενον μάλιστα, τοῦτον οἴει καὶ ἐρωτικώτατα ἔχειν: the demonstrative ('the one who takes most pleasure in each (activity) . . . this one') emphasizes the connection between maximum pleasure and maximum desire on which the argument depends; the tyrant has no pleasure in food and drink because he is satiated and does not desire to eat. ἔρως implies a passionate desire, but is not restricted to sex. πάνυ μὲν οὖν: the classic indicator of agreement to the previous statement also in Platonic dialogue; see Xenophon's parody in *Symp.* 4.56–60. Ἦ οὖν ὁρᾶις τι τοὺς τυράννους ἥδιον . . . ἰόντας: the next stage in the argument; τι is an adverbial accusative of respect (*GG* 1060), or qualifies the comparative adverb: LSJ II.11c ('any more pleasantly'); enclitics such as τι regularly move to second place in the clause by 'Wackernagel's rule'. Οὐ μὰ τὸν Δί᾽, ἔφη, οὐ μὲν οὖν: very strong denial. ὡς πολλοῖς ἂν δόξειεν: 'as they would seem to do in the eyes of many'; on the principle that Simonides does not want to criticize a tyrant to his face, his reference to the view of 'many' seems to soften ἀγλευκέστερον, which might be thought too strong a word to use to a tyrant in condemning his pleasures, by crediting it to others; it is also non-Attic. A parallel for the softening effect might be the way Xenophon uses 'he said' to create emphasis (cf. the note on 1.1), or even the problematic reference 'as they seem to' in *Ath.* 1.14, which seems to soften another strong term: 'blackmail'.

1.22 τί γάρ strongly confirms the impression that many have (above); the thought may be translated 'How could I say otherwise?' τὰ τούτων ἀδελφά 'brothers of these', i.e. belonging to the same group as the many sharp and pungent and sour contrivances. καὶ πάνυ γέ μοι δοκοῦντα παρὰ φύσιν εἶναι: this continues the description of the contrivances. The tastes of the dishes are 'unnatural' because they are confected (a reference to the sophistication of Syracusan gastronomy), but also because they artificially stimulate an appetite that has become jaded through excess. Cyrus the Great recommends them as stimulants for men going on an arduous march; they will have no wine, only water, no beds, and these tastes as their stimulus to dry bread (*Cyr.* 6.2.31: ὄψα . . . ὅσα ἐστὶν ὀξέα καὶ δριμέα καὶ ἁλμυρά. ταῦτα γὰρ ἐπὶ σῖτόν τε ἄγει . . .). Hiero's subsequent indication that they are desires of a 'weak and ailing soul' confirms that he has no appetite because he suffers from the sickness of tyranny. The implication is that the tastes described are nasty. R. Jackson (1988) 32–85 describes the connection between cuisine and medicine, where bad-tasting foods were thought to be particularly curative. Bitter absinthe is a good example, which was used to flavour wine and produce a forerunner of vermouth, but whose repellent taste had to be disguised with honey when it was used for medicinal purposes, as Lucretius indicates so well (*De Rerum Natura* 1.936–42). The highly expensive and highly pungent silphium might also be a candidate, with unpleasant medicinal effects too; Aristophanes *Knights* 892–90 has it produce mighty amounts of wind and diarrhoea. See on cuisine: Dalby (1996). Xenophon knew how to produce maximum health by controlling diet and exercise (*Lac.* 1.3, 2.5, 5.8–9) and medicine was a standard branch of the learning that philosophers acquired (*Mem.* 4.2.10, 31). Strauss (1947/1963) 119 n. 18 = 2000 113 n. 18 seems to misread the passage.

1.23 Ἄλλο τι . . . ἢ μαλακῆς καὶ ἀσθενούσης ψυχῆς ἐπιθυμήματα 'anything other than the desires of a weak and ailing soul'. Hiero lacks appetite, both as an overloaded tyrant and because he has the sickness of tyranny in his soul. *Symp.* 4.37 uses the same metaphor to a different effect, of the tyrant as the sick man who has the disease of consumption, who eats constantly but never feels full. που 'I imagine' is like δήπου (1.27), which marks an assumption that the speaker thinks others will share with him; see 1.29 and also 10.4, where γίγνονται δέ που, ὡς πάντες ἐπιστάμεθα spells this out.

1.24 Ἀλλὰ μέντοι: the particle combination introduces a new topic without the idea of opposition; cf. 4.8. Simonides himself confirms and continues the argument against tyranny by denying happiness in the area of smells as well. τῶν γε πολυτελῶν ὀσμῶν τούτων with ἀπολαύειν: smells are related to food and drink because of their use at banquets; they had medicinal effects (as in modern aromatherapy); Faure (1987) discusses the manufacture and use of perfumes in the ancient world. αἷς χρίεσθε 'with which you anoint yourselves'; perfumes came in the form of perfumed liquids such as oil or wine. ὥσπερ γε 'just as' introduces the analogous case, where the one who eats strong-smelling foods does not smell them himself afterwards, but offends others around him. D.L. 6.39 tells the story of Diogenes who anointed his feet so that he could enjoy his expensive myrrh; he noted that when he anointed his head (as was usual), the smell went off into the air. Simonides does not condemn the use of perfumes, though it might be assumed that his later reference to the natural charisma of the ruler (8.5) means that he needs no artificial enhancement. Socrates argues in *Symp.* 2.3–4 that the smell of olive oil and exercise distinguishes the free man from the slave, whereas perfume makes a man unfree because it conceals the difference between them. βεβρωκώς from βιβρώσκω.

1.25 Οὕτω μέντοι indicates agreement; cf. ἀλλὰ μέντοι at 1.24. καὶ τῶν σίτων depends on παντοδαπά. οὗτός ἐστιν ὁ μετὰ χαρᾶς πιμπλάμενος: the article with participle and εἶναι instead of a finite verb shifts the focus from the action onto the property of the action: Willi (2003b) 45–6 on the phenomenon in Aristophanes; cf. *Ath.* 1.2.

1.26 Κινδυνεύουσιν: Simonides takes his chance on the last area of sensual pleasure: sexual relations; see *Mem.* 4.2.34, 39 for the use of this phrase in dialogue. αἱ τῶν ἀφροδισίων . . . ἀπολαύσεις 'the benefits of Aphrodite' include sexual intercourse, but Hiero in his response includes under this heading also the joys of marrying well. ὅ τι ἂν κάλλιστον ἴδητε τούτωι συνεῖναι 'whatever most beautiful thing you see, to keep company with this'; the neuter avoids specifying whether the union is with male or female (later it proves to cover both). συνεῖναι is also used of asexual 'associations': 2.14, 6.2 and *Lac.* 14.2.

1.27 Νῦν δή, ἔφη ὁ Ἱέρων, εἴρηκας ἐν ὧι γε, σάφ' ἴσθι, μειονεκτοῦμεν: Hiero is strongly assertive, as the particles, the intrusion of 'he said', the parenthetic 'know it well' and the use of the first person show; δή emphasizes what is truly the case 'indeed', whereas γε focuses on one idea. His use of the first person to refer to the tyrannical experience marks his growing engagement with the discussion. Hiero's main complaint is that he cannot get pleasure from women or boys because they are his subjects, neither equal to him nor free. He deals first with marriage as one of the accepted categories of ἀφροδίσια. The pleasure lies in having a wife of the highest rank, who brings with her an attachment to another family of wealth and power. Yet there is no other man in a tyrant's enslaved *polis* who is even of equal status, let alone superior; this leaves him with the possibility only of an alliance with the daughter of an inferior family, or with a foreigner, which he finds repellent because he is a patriot (see 5.3–4). It is only by making his citizens free and equal that he will be able to find a wife who fits his criteria. γάμος ὁ μὲν ἐκ μειζόνων δήπου καὶ πλούτωι καὶ δυνάμει κάλλιστος δοκεῖ εἶναι 'the marriage that comes from men who are greater in respect of wealth and power seems to be finest'; Simonides seemed to use 'finest' of physical beauty, but Hiero refers it to the rank of the wife. He sees the men as the source of the marriage because they determine the status of their women and bestow their women on others; with ὁ μὲν ἐκ μειζόνων, compare ὁ ἐκ τῶν ὁμοίων and ὁ δ' ἐκ τῶν φαυλοτέρων. δήπου marks the shared assumption, as at 1.23, 2.15; 3.7; 6.11 etc. τινὰ . . . φιλοτιμίαν: the indefinite adjective could limit the ambition, or make it 'considerable' (LSJ II.8); here the latter, in view of the previous superlative. δεύτερος 'second-best'.

1.28 τοίνυν develops the argument, as at 1.7. ξένην 'a foreign woman'. Historical tyrants regularly married outside their *poleis*, presumably to increase their power through political alliances. Herodotus indicates that Periander of Corinth married the daughter of the tyrant of Epidaurus, and Cleisthenes of Sicyon married his daughter to the Alcmaeonid Megacles of Athens (3.50–2, 6.126–31). Dionysius I took a wife from his own aristocracy, but another from Locris (D.S. 14.44). But Hiero loves his own *polis*: 5.3–4. He laments that he has to use foreigners in preference to citizens, and his preference for a local wife can be explained in these terms. καὶ αἱ θεραπεῖαι αἱ ἀπὸ τῶν μέγιστον φρονουσῶν γυναικῶν: these 'services' include grooming and washing and nursing during sickness. Hiero contrasts services from women 'with the highest thoughts' i.e. from the great houses, with those of slaves. Cf. Dem. 59.122 on the 'services' that *pallakai* give. Women of high thoughts give most pleasure because their pride implies freedom and their service does greatest honour because it is freely given. There is a parallel with the earlier idea that praise is sweetest that comes from those most free, and with the later idea that attentions from the tyrant – such as caring for the sick – carry more pleasure than those from non-rulers (8.2–5). αἱ δ' ὑπὸ δούλων: the contrast between ἀπό for the services of free-born women and ὑπό for the slaves may indicate that the free-born women's service is not subordinate; compare αἱ ἀπὸ τῶν δυνατωτάτων θεραπεῖαι 8.4; however ἀπό is also used of the service that comes from mercenaries (10.3) and the contrast at 7.6 between services ἐξ those who do not love you and ὑπό those who fear you is the product merely of a desire for variety of expression. By 'slaves' Hiero may mean not just his private slave women, but the slaves he has made of his entire population as tyrant. The message is again that the ruled must become free before they can give the ruler the pleasure he desires. δεινὰς ὀργὰς καὶ λύπας: the anger against slaves who fail to please may explain why Hiero thinks that slaves are generally hostile to their masters, at 4.3.

1.29–38: Hiero is most concerned about his lack of pleasure in boys, which Simonides makes a special focus of his reform (8.6–7, 11.11). He shows this in the space he gives the topic, his colourful language and his use of the first person – features that recur when he compares his previous happiness as a non-ruler with his current unhappiness (6.1–3). The emphasis on boyfriends arises from the special intimacy that they could give a man, rather than sexual appetite, since he wants their friendship rather than their bodies. Hiero restates his view about the pleasures of food and drink (1.21) that there is no pleasure without desire, that desire is for what is anticipated rather than what is available, that his boy's body is always available and therefore elicits no desire, but what he does desire is his friendship, without which his body gives no pleasure, and that this is unavailable because he rules over enslaved subjects who hate him. His unhappiness comes again, as in his marriage alliances, from his subjects' lack of freedom.

1.29 ἐν δὲ τοῖς παιδικοῖς ἀφροδισίοις: the relationship is the friendship between *erastes* and *eromenos*, the man and boy. See further Hindley (1999) and the commentary on *Lac.* 2.12–14, which gives the friendship a role in the moral improvement of Spartan youth. The philosophers drew sharp distinctions between physical and spiritual relationships of this kind, endorsing only the latter. *Symp.* 8.9–43 contrasts the 'vulgar' and the 'heavenly' Aphrodite and endorses only a willing friendship between *erastes* and *eromenos* which improves them both. Simonides does not rule out a carnal possibility, however. The view that Hiero espouses is expressed in *Mem.* 2.6.22: that men of virtue delight in τὰ ἀφροδίσια, but make it a point of honour not to harm others in the process. τὰ μετ' ἔρωτος ἀφροδίσια: the connection between 'desire' and 'pleasure' is the main focus of the argument.

1.30 ὁ δὲ ἔρως πολὺ αὖ ἐθέλει ἥκιστα τῶι τυράννωι ἐγγίγνεσθαι 'desire is quite to the contrary least willing to live within a tyrant' because desire would be too readily satiated, and extinguished by the abundance of pleasure available. πολύ frequently intensifies adjectives and adverbs; cf. πολὺ διαφερόντως in the previous sentence. ὥσπερ οὖν . . . οὕτω . . . : for the construction cf. *Lac.* 10.4 ὥσπερ οὖν . . . οὕτω, and compare the construction of *Symp.* 4.37: ὅμοια . . . ὥσπερ εἴ τις. The chiastic word order of the sentence and the repetition of ἄπειρος bring out the point of the argument that there is no pleasure when there is no desire, and the indicative verb in the main sentence, as opposed to the potential optative in the analogy, gives the sexual deprivation more force.

1.31 ἐπιγελάσας: laughter indicates disbelief, because Simonides is well aware that traditional tyrants were most of all prey to lust: Hdt. 9.108. Δαϊλόχου τοῦ καλλίστου ἐπικαλουμένου: the boy is the only third party named in the entire dialogue; the superlative picks up the point that tyrants are able to keep company with whatever is 'most beautiful': 1.26. This recalls inscriptions on pottery designed for use in the symposium which often name a boy and describe him as καλός: Lissarrague in Goldhill and Osborne (1999) 361ff.; these are a mainly Athenian phenomenon, but are here transferred to a Syracusan setting.

1.32 τούτου: the demonstrative emphasizes Hiero's lack of desire for what 'seems to be easy to get'; cf. τοῦ ἥκιστα τυράννωι προσήκοντος κατεργάσασθαι: the boy's willing affection is 'least likely for a tyrant to achieve' because the boy is a slave under tyranny.

1.33 ἐρῶ μὲν Δαϊλόχου (τούτων ἅπερ =) ὧνπερ . . . : 'I desire from Dailochus the things which (relative attraction/suppression of antecedent) . . . ' ἐμαυτὸν κακόν τι ποιεῖν 'to do some harm to myself'.

1.34 παρὰ μὲν γὰρ πολεμίων ἀκόντων . . . παρὰ δὲ παιδικῶν βουλομένων: the comparison between love and war begins a military metaphor for Hiero's unhappiness: that he is at war with those he loves because he has to force them to his will. Alexander of Pherae's relations with his boyfriend show how violence could be used against an *eromenos*: *Hell.* 6.4.37. πάντων ἥδιστον ἔγωγε νομίζω εἶναι: the emphatic pronoun strengthens the previous reference to 'sweetest'. οἶμαι is parenthetic, and has the effect of also strengthening the preceding superlative 'sweetest'. αἱ χάριτες: another word for pleasures freely given; see 9.1–2.

1.35 εὐθύς is adverbial and marks the first point in an argument: 'to start with', as at 1.37, 2.8 and αὐτίκα 2.7. ἡδεῖαι μὲν . . . ἡδεῖαι δὲ . . . ἡδεῖαι δὲ . . . ἥδισται δὲ καὶ ἐπαφροδιτόταται: quadruple *anaphora* with assonance and alliteration and *isocolon* captures the charming progress of a love affair, with the glances leading to questions, the questions to answers, and then to later lovers' quarrels. The final unit carries the greatest weight both linguistically and semantically, with two synonymous superlative adjectives and two synonymous nouns of increasing syllabic length. The battles and strife as a metaphor for the lovers' quarrels are a pleasant foil for the tyrant's more unpleasant war with his political community. See *Symp.* 3.12–13 and *Lac.* 3.5, for the delightful and hesitant answers of boy-loves.

1.36 λεηλασίαι, ἔφη, ἔμοιγε δοκεῖ ἐοικέναι 'seems to me, he said, to resemble robbery'; 'he said' creates a significant pause after the strong reference to robbery; the comparison of the tyrant with the robber is also used of Alexander of Pherae (*Hell.* 6.4.35). καίτοι introduces an objection to the speaker's own case, 'Yet, I would have you know.' τινὰς ὅμως ἡδονάς: for the word order, cf. 1.27. τό τε κέρδος καὶ τὸ ἀνιᾶν τὸν ἐχθρόν: subjects of παρέχει, 'profit (to himself) and distress to his enemy'; at 1.6 too, Xenophon partners a noun and an articular infinitive, in a way that might be considered more typical of the style of Thucydides. τὸ δὲ οὗ ἂν ἐρᾶι τις τούτωι ἥδεσθαι ἀνιωμένωι καὶ φιλοῦντα μισεῖσθαι καὶ ἅπτεσθαι ἀχθομένου 'to take pleasure in this person whom one loves while he is being injured, and to be hated while loving, and to lay hands on him to his displeasure'; the word order and the vivid series of images contrast by juxtaposition the feelings of the boy and his lover and show how the boy's hurt destroys all the lover's pleasure. πῶς οὐχὶ τοῦτο ἤδη: the rhetorical question: 'how is this condition not in fact . . .', with the demonstrative, emphasizes the pain of their conflict.

1.37 καὶ γὰρ δή: a new point, emphatically introduced; the explanatory force of γάρ is not always apparent in such combinations. ὑπουργῆι: the normal sign of friendship between free men is to serve each other. ὡς φιλῶν 'on the grounds that he loves him as a friend'; ὡς conveys the cause as seen by the recipient: *GG* 1574. οὐδεμιᾶς ἀνάγκης οὔσης 'when there is no compulsion on him' emphasizes the role of freedom in successful relationships. ἔστι 'it is possible'.

1.38 τοὺς διὰ φόβον ὑπηρετοῦντας is placed as the object of a main verb rather than the subject of a dependent clause; cf. the archaic English: 'I know thee who thou art'; the proleptic position gives their fearful service more prominence. ἐξεικάζουσιν αὐτοὺς ταῖς τῶν φιλούντων ὑπουργίαις '(as much as possible) they make themselves resemble the services of those who love'; an instance of brachylogy, where the real point of comparison is supplied by the context, i.e. 'make their services resemble the services of those who love'; compare *Cyr.* 5.1.4 ὁμοίαν ταῖς δούλαις εἶχε τὴν ἐσθῆτα. ἐξ οὐδένων πλέονες 'from none in greater number'.

2.1–6 Simonides accepts Hiero's proofs that the ruler has less happiness than the non-ruler in the pleasures of the flesh, but now (infuriatingly? consolingly?) dismisses them as μικρά and points to the greatness of the achievements of the tyrant, the speed of their accomplishment, the abundance of his possessions, his ability to help his friends and harm his enemies. Hiero will refute these alleged pleasures too in a long sequence of arguments, first that true happiness resides in the soul, not in the material world, and that he lacks this true happiness (2.2–4.5), and then that, in any case, his greater power and possessions do not give him any security or material satisfaction (4.6–7); those he must rely on as friends are worthless, and harming his enemies would empty the *polis* of good men (5–6).

2.1 Ἀλλά: Simonides' objection is that they have been talking about the wrong kind of deprivation. ἑκόντας μειονεκτοῦντας καὶ σίτων καὶ ποτῶν καὶ ὄψων καὶ ἀφροδισίων γε ἀπεχομένους 'voluntarily taking a lesser share of food and delicacies, and from sex indeed refraining'; Simonides credits Hiero with the attitude of the ideal ruler who 'willingly' suppresses his appetites in the pursuit of a higher goal: *Mem.* 2.1.17–18; *Ages.* 5.1–5. Cf. 7.1 where he does this again. *Chiasmus* surrounds the pleasures with the participles of deprivation and the particle highlights the special importance of the renunciation of sexual pleasure.

2.2 μεγάλα μὲν . . . ταχὺ δὲ . . . πλεῖστα δὲ . . . διαφέροντας μὲν . . . διαφέροντα δὲ . . . ὑπερέχοντα δὲ: *anaphora* with variation reinforces the quantity and quality of the tyrant's ambitions and possessions. διαφέροντας μὲν ἀρετῆι ἵππους: Strauss (1947/63) 72–3 = (2000) 71 finds it disturbing that the first application of 'virtue' in this dialogue is to horses, but Simonides knows that their virtue is not happiness since he will advise Hiero to transfer the ownership of such horses to his citizens as part of his service to the common good (11.5–7). Cf. Xenophon's comment that Agesilaus thought chariot victories brought him no fame, but that this came from ruling well (making the *polis* friendly, winning friends abroad, defeating them only in serving their interests): *Ages.* 9.7. Both Hiero and Simonides later define the much more important 'virtue' of the good ruler in these terms as service to the common good (7.9, 11.1–8). The reference to horses might be thought to be historical, since Pindar called Hiero 'horse-loving' (*O.* 1.23), and his brother Gelon had risen to power as commander of cavalry, but horses are a regular indication of wealth. ὅπλα: Hiero will also show (2.8, 6.4) that he needs his supremely beautiful armour not to give himself delight, but to ensure his survival (2.8); and Simonides will urge him to arm his citizens rather than himself, when his reform dispels that insecurity (11.3). καὶ ταύτας: the houses are magnificent and equipped *as well* with items of very high value; but the tyrant will show that his house, however magnificent, does not provide him with the security he needs against his citizens (2.10), and Simonides will encourage him to beautify the *polis* as a whole rather than his own house in his final reform (11.2). D.S. 13.112.4, 14.7 mentions the private house of Dionysius I being full of gold and silver and other apparel; contrast the modesty of the house of Agesilaus of Sparta, with its archaic gateway; proof of his virtue: *Ages.* 8.7. Very little is known about ancient palaces, but Nevett (1999) describes more modest houses. πλήθει καὶ ἐπιστήμαις θεράποντας ἀρίστους 'servants excellent in number and skills' – like the *diakonoi* of 4.2. Hiero will show that these servants are in fact a source of pain to him, since they cannot be trusted with his food and drink (4.2). The servants could be skilled slaves and reflect historical circumstances; D.S. 11.25 indicates that the defeat of the Carthaginians at Himera made slaves particularly abundant in Hiero's time; but servants are also a general measure of wealth.

2.3–6: Hiero responds that outer appearances are deceptive; happiness lies in the soul; he expresses amazement that Simonides should side with the ignorant majority and judge on the basis of his eyes rather than with his intellect. See above pp. 36–7 on the significance of this passage. Hiero begins to address that large category of pleasures that affect the soul, or the body and the soul together (see 1.5). Philosophers generally challenged the reliability of sense perception as a method of discovering reality. Parmenides argued that the world of the senses was an illusion and that intellect alone could uncover the realities. Plato's world of ideal forms, of which the world of the senses was a poor reproduction, was also perceptible only through the intellect. His wise judge also enters the heart of the tyrant to find the misery behind the outer appearance (*Rep.* 577a–b). Xenophon, *Symp.* 4.34–6 has Antisthenes confirm the illusory happiness of tyrants.

2.3 τὸ μὲν τὸ πλῆθος . . . ἐξαπατᾶσθαι 'the fact that the masses are completely deceived'; this is repeated at 2.5: τὸ μὲν οὖν τὸ πλῆθος περὶ τούτου λεληθέναι 'the fact that this has escaped the masses'. δοξάζειν ὁρῶν 'to form an opinion by using their eyes'.

2.4 τὰ μὲν δοκοῦντα . . . εἶναι 'the things that *seem* to be' continues to challenge sense perception. ἀνεπτυγμένα θεᾶσθαι φανερὰ πᾶσι 'uncovered visible for all to gaze on', cf. κέκτηται ἀποκεκρυμμένα. The tyrant's possessions are a legitimate extension of the gaze in 'performance culture'. Goldhill in Goldhill and Osborne (1999) 5–6 defines *theoria* as both intellectual 'theory' and physical 'gaze' and mentions *Hiero* 1.10–13 (7–8); to that reference should be added this passage and 7.9, 11.9. Hiero is aware that his possessions are the focus of the public gaze, but he places no value on it; what he wants to attract is the gaze that is given to the man who serves the common good (7.2, 9). He will attract such a gaze when he is reformed (11.9), and his subjects' willing service to him will be a spectacle in turn that will give him pleasure to gaze on (11.12). καὶ τὸ εὐδαιμονεῖν καὶ τὸ κακοδαιμονεῖν 'happiness and unhappiness'. Socrates connects κακοδαιμονία with 'ignorance' and the harming of those who might otherwise help you: *Mem.* 2.3.19. This is indeed the tyrant's condition.

2.5 τὸ δὲ καὶ ὑμᾶς ταῦτ' ἀγνοεῖν: the plural denotes 'tyrants' and 'wise men' as groups; cf. 1.14, 27 etc. τοῦτο: the demonstrative picks up everything that has gone before. The 'sights' that are perceived through the intellect are entirely different from the sights that are seen with the eyes (1.11).

2.6 ἐγὼ δὲ πεπειραμένος σαφῶς οἶδα: Hiero has again (see 1.10) taken the bait that Simonides has offered about the importance of experience and will now reveal his unhappiness over the wide range of the things that Simonides has mentioned.

2.7–18: Hiero demonstrates that tyrants have the least share of the greatest goods and the greatest share of the greatest pains that affect the soul as well as the body. He begins with peace and war. He argues that peace gives more pleasure than war, but he has no peace, and that community wars offer joys and pains, but he has no share of the joys even though he has a full share of the pains; while his own war against his citizens is entirely without pleasure. The argument is organized (i) Peace (2.8). (ii) Campaigns against others (2.9). (iii) Defence against others (2.10). (iv) Truces and peace-treaties

(2.11). (v) Community wars (2.12–16). (vi) The tyrant's own war against his citizens (2.17–18). *Poroi* 5.2 confirms that the happiest *poleis* are those that spend the longest time in peace, when the economy flourishes. Xenophon again varies the singular and plural for tyrants for deliberate effect, reserving the singular for the tyrant isolated within his own house (2.10) and suffering as an individual all the ills of community wars (2.12), as well as those of his own (2.17–18); cf. notes on 1.13; 5.3–4.

2.8 κοινὸν πόλεμον: a war in which the entire community is involved, distinguished from the private war of the tyrant against his citizens. ὅποι ἂν βούλωνται again refers to the freedom of non-rulers, as at 1.11–12. ὡς διὰ πολεμίας (sc. χώρας) 'as if through hostile land', i.e. in a constant state of apprehension and preparedness. γοῦν, 'at least', limits the proof to one strong point; cf. 3.3. Thuc. 1.6.1 also presents the carrying of arms within the *polis* as evidence of personal insecurity. ἄλλους ὁπλοφόρους 'others as spear-bearers', the mark of the stereotyped tyrant.

2.9 εἰς πολεμίαν (sc. χώραν). ἀλλ᾽ οὖν ἐπειδάν γε 'nevertheless at least when' combines objection, progression and restriction. ἐν πλείστοις πολεμίοις ἴσασιν ὄντες: compare the knowledge of the Spartans that they were 'in the midst of their very enemies' when at home and had to take greatest precautions there: *Hell.* 3.3.4.

2.10 ἐὰν δὲ δὴ καὶ ἄλλοι . . . : the opposite situation to the invasion of others' lands, in which others campaign against them in greater numbers. εἴσω τοῦ ἐρύματος . . . εἴσω τῆς οἰκίας: a fortified wall around most cities gave citizens security: *Mem.* 2.1.14, but the tyrant does not feel safe even within his own house. The seriousness of this threat is demonstrated in the Athenians' imposition of the death penalty for 'house invasion': *Mem.* 1.2.62. ἐνταῦθα δὴ καὶ μάλιστα φυλακτέον οἴεται εἶναι 'he is of the opinion that in that very place there is most of all a need to be on his guard'; the verbal adjective indicates another one of the ways in which the tyrant is not free to do as he wishes.

2.11 καὶ διὰ σπονδῶν καὶ δι᾽ εἰρήνης 'truces' are periods of peace during a war; 'peace' ends the war and persists until the declaration of another. οὔτε σπονδαῖς ἂν ποτε πιστεύσας ὁ τύραννος θαρρήσειε: because of his constant war against the citizens the tyrant lacks the psychological pleasures of 'trust' and 'confidence' in truces. Hiero makes a later feature of his lack of πίστις: 4.1; Simonides diagnoses his depression (ἀθυμία 8.1), but exhorts him to 'confidence' in his reform: θαρρῶν πλούτιζε (11.13–14).

2.12 τούτων . . . τῶν πολέμων: possessive on χαλεπά. ὅσα . . . ταῦτα: the tyrant shares 'all the distresses' of the community war; cf. 2.14 ἃ δὲ ἔχουσιν ἡδέα . . . ταῦτα. ὁ σὺν ταῖς πόλεσι: the non-ruler, the man who belongs to the communities as opposed to the tyrant who is by himself; see note on σύν below.

2.13 καὶ γάρ: the lively explanation 'indeed so, because'.

2.14 οἱ συνόντες ταῖς πόλεσι πρὸς τὰς πόλεις 'those who are with cities against the cities', another expression (cf. 2.12 above ὁ σὺν ταῖς πόλεσι) for the citizens in their community wars, as opposed to the tyrant in his private war, alone and without a community. Editors suspect corruption, but συνόντες effectively underlines the collective enterprise of citizens (cf. 4.3). ὁ συνών is used of any συνουσία (4.1, 6.2), sexual (1.26), educational (*Mem. passim*) or political (*Lac.* 5.5, 7.4, 13.1, 14.2). *Hiero* 6.2 has Hiero keep his own company: συνῆν δὲ ἐμαυτῶι. *Lac.* 14.2 uses ἀλλήλοις συνεῖναι to describe the *homonoia* of citizens. *Hell.* 1.7.8 describes the community ties of a festival: οἵ τε πατέρες καὶ οἱ συγγενεῖς σύνεισι σφίσιν αὐτοῖς. A possible emendation συνίοντες might convey their collective military enterprise; cf. *Poroi* 4.32: ἀλλ’ ὥσπερ σύμμαχοι, ὅσωι ἂν πλείους συνιῶσιν ἰσχυροτέρους ἀλλήλους ποιοῦσιν.

2.15 ὅσην μὲν . . . ὅσην δ’ . . . ὅσην δ’ . . . ὡς δὲ . . . ὡς δὲ . . . ὡς δ’: two sets of triple *anaphora* describe the pleasures of the citizens’ war, capturing phases in the action described: ‘Turning, chasing and killing’ are sequential phases during battle. ‘Rejoicing, taking credit and increasing the *polis*’ are a further sequence after battle – reflected in the change to ὡς clauses. τὴν πόλιν νομίζοντες ηὐξηκέναι: the ‘increase of the *polis*’ is of course the aim of ideal government: see Introduction p. 5.

2.16 τῆς βουλῆς μετεσχηκέναι: each man claims to have had a hand in formulating the successful battle plan. χαλεπὸν δὲ εὑρεῖν ὅπου ‘it is difficult to find any case where’. οὐχί: Homeric and in tragedy, but seldom in prose; it is an emphatic negative. πλέονας . . . ἢ ὅσοι ἂν τῶι ὄντι ἀποθάνωσιν ‘more than the total number that die in truth’; their exaggeration looks forward to the contrast with the tyrant, who in his war against the citizens has to conceal the numbers he has killed: 2.17. καλόν τι ‘some very fine thing’; contrast the tyrant, who considers his killing of citizens no ‘fine thing’ even to himself: 2.17. τὸ πολὺ νικᾶν ‘to win a great victory’, the subject of δοκεῖ.

2.17 Hiero’s account of his war against the citizens systematically denies the tyrant-ruler the pleasures of ‘increasing’ his *polis*. He has no joy in killing his enemy, takes no pride or credit from it, tries to diminish the numbers killed rather than exaggerate them, and finds nothing noble in his ‘victory’. ὑποπτεύσηι reveals his distrust of his community. τῶι ὄντι replaces mere suspicion with the unpleasant reality of true perception. οἶδεν ὅτι οὐκ αὔξει ὅλην τὴν πόλιν, ἐπίσταταί τε ὅτι μειόνων ἄρξει: the two main verbs stress his consciousness of what he does and the pun stresses the contrast; his murders of citizens do not increase the *polis*, in contrast to the increase of power that his citizens secure in killing the enemy in their war (2.15), and they deny him the further pleasure of ruling a large population, so that he must ask at 6.14 ‘whom will he then rule’ τίνων γὰρ ἔτι ἄρξει. Simonides will encourage Hiero αὖξε . . . τὴν πόλιν once he is reformed and there is nothing more to fear from his community: 11.13. φαιδρός τε οὐ δύναται εἶναι: the pleasure of appearing ‘bright’ is important enough to be subject to the control of the government in Sparta: *Lac.* 13.9, *Hell.* 6.4.16. ἀλλὰ καὶ μειοῖ . . . καὶ ἀπολογεῖται: in contrast to the boasting of the citizens in their war, he diminishes the numbers he has killed and is virtually on trial for his injustice, as he says again at 7.10 and 12.

2.18 When those whom he feared are dead, the tyrant is even more on his guard than before because of the possibility of repercussions. οὐδέν τι μᾶλλον τοῦτο θαρρεῖ ‘he feels not much more confidence for this reason’; cf. *GG* 1060 for τοῦτο used as an adverb.

3.1–9: Hiero identifies the next great 'good thing' as friendship, calling it a 'possession' (3.6), giving it equal status with those material possessions that Simonides described (2.2), and addressing for the first time the role of law in securing good things for the community. For paradigms of the rule of law: pp. 9–10, 11–13. *Poleis* show how they value friendship in the laws that they pass about *moicheia*. Tyrants do not have friendships like these or the protections that go with them. At 11.11–12, Simonides' reform will provide the solution to his lack of friendship by making the citizens want to extend their friendship and protection to him. See the importance of friendship to the ruler, pp. 7–8.

3.1 καταθέασαι: imperative. ἐπισκεψώμεθα: the traditional dialectical invitation 'let us consider'.

3.2 ὃς γὰρ ἂν φιλῆται . . . τοῦτον: the demonstrative focuses on the definition of the friend. ἡδέως μὲν . . . ἡδέως δ᾽ . . . ποθοῦσι δέ . . . ἥδιστα δὲ . . . συνήδονται δ᾽ . . . συνεπικουροῦσι δέ: *anaphora* and restatement with variation represent a sequence of stages in friendship, first greeting the friend when he appears, then doing him some service, then missing him when he is away and feeling pleasure in receiving him back, then rejoicing in his success and commiserating in his failure. *Symp.* 8.13 declares that there can be no συνουσία without φιλία.

3.3 μόνους γοῦν τοὺς μοιχοὺς νομίζουσι πολλαὶ τῶν πόλεων νηποινεὶ ἀποκτείνειν: the strong proof of the value that citizens place on friendship is the death penalty they impose on seducers for stealing the friendship of their wives: 'many of the cities think it right to kill without penalty seducers alone'. See Harrison (1968) 32–8, Carey (1995) 407–17, Edwards (1999) 56–62. Hiero stresses the death penalty because it shows the importance placed on friendship and friendship is his major concern. In fact there were other lesser penalties for seduction such as physical abuse. Yet Athenian law did allow citizens to kill seducers without penalty if they were found *in flagrante delicto* with a married woman and confessed to the deed, and the law was not restricted to the seduction of married women; it could also apply to daughters; *Cyr.* 3.1.39, in an Armenian context (!), suggests that it might even apply to sons. The reason for the death penalty is controversial. Lysias 1.32–3 agrees that it protected the friendship of husband and wife, but also ensured that the seducer did not gain control of the household through the woman, and that the woman did not introduce his children into the house. Carey (1995) rates these last two motives above the loss of affection as the main intention of the law, but they are the direct consequences of the loss of friendship. Xenophon shows that the loss of friendship could even have fatal consequences, when Hiero goes on to assert that the wives of tyrants, because of their lack of friendship, have often killed their husbands: 3.8, and that the wife and other members of the intimate household are a special threat to the husband if untrustworthy, since they are in a convenient position to put poison in his food or drink: 4.1–2. This fear would explain why Lysias extends the crime to the alienation of the friendship of the *pallake*; she was also in a position of intimacy she could take advantage of. Antiphon, *Or.* 1 describes a case where family members poisoned the head of the household. Xenophon does allow Hiero to overstate his case when he argues that citizens could kill seducers 'alone' without penalty, since Hiero himself later says that they could also kill tyrants without penalty (4.5) – but this exaggeration is the natural product of his emotion. He may also exaggerate the extent of the law among 'many' *poleis*, but cf. on the communality of Greek law: Osborne in Mitchell and Rhodes (1997) 74–82. δῆλον ὅτι 'obviously'. νηποινεί: an archaic and legal term. λυμαντῆρας: poetic (λυμαντήριος only in Aeschylus, *Pr.* 991, *Agam.* 438, *Ch.* 764) and may also be archaic/legal. On Xenophon's vocabulary: pp. 22, 25.

3.4 ὅταν γε ἀφροδισιασθῆι κατὰ συμφοράν τινα γυνή: a euphemistic reference to rape, where the passive indicates that the woman is an unwilling party. *Mem.* 1.3.14 uses the active voice for men. ἐάνπερ ἡ φιλία δοκῆι αὐταῖς ἀκήρατος διαμένειν: adultery implied the alienation of the wife's affection, whereas rape amounted to the alienation only of her body (Lysias 1.32–3 and *Cyr.* 3.1.39). Therefore, in contrast to the victim of rape, the seduced woman could no longer live with her husband without him forfeiting his rights, and she was formally dishonoured herself, being barred from religious rites: Harrison (1968) 35–6. The argument is similar to that of *Hell.* 7.3.9, which makes one who is forced to injustice less culpable than one who is bribed. ἀκήρατος is found in the poets and Herodotus 2.86, 4.152, 7.10, and Plato, but is still sufficiently unusual in prose to give special status to the friendship.

3.5 τοσοῦτον δέ τι ἀγαθόν 'a good thing of such great value'. τὸ φιλεῖσθαι 'being loved/treated as a friend' becomes a theme song of the programme of Simonides' reform: 8.1, 11.8. αὐτόματα 'of their own accord' i.e. not enforced in the laws. καὶ παρὰ θεῶν καὶ παρὰ ἀνθρώπων: Hiero evidently believes in gods as a source of good things, in accordance with Xenophon's Socrates' characterization of them as supremely philanthropic in their care for men, providing what men need in return for honour (*Mem.* 1.4 and 4.3). However, his need for security clashes with the honour he knows is their due (4.2, 4.11). Xenophon usually gives the gods a special place in his instruction of rulers, as can be judged by the conclusions to *Hipparchicus* and *Poroi*. Simonides' failure to raise the topic is the result of Hiero's preoccupation with his relations with men.

3.6 ἐπίσκεψαι: an imperative invitation to dialectic, as at 3.1.

3.8 πολλοὺς . . . πολλοὺς . . . : quadruple *anaphora* emphasizes the great number of murders within the personal associations of tyrants, such as families and comradeships.

3.9 τῶν φύσει πεφυκότων μάλιστα φιλεῖν καὶ νόμωι συνηναγκασμένων: alliteration binds this striking phrase: 'by those born by nature and compelled by custom most of all to love', because it is natural to love members of your kinship group and because of the laws against murder. Examples to support the threat to tyrants are not far to seek in myth or history. Clytaemnestra murdered her husband. Orestes killed his mother, with the assistance of Electra, her daughter. Oedipus was left to die in the mountains on his father's orders, but survived to slay him; Polyneices and his brother killed one another. Medea murdered her children. In Herodotus Candaules is killed by his wife, with the assistance of Gyges. Polycrates does away with his brothers. Xenophon presents the contemporary murder of Alexander of Pherae by his wife, with the assistance of his brothers-in-law (*Hell.* 6.4.35–7) and the murder of Mania by her son-in-law (*Hell.* 3.1.14) as the result of a lack of friendship in their houses.

4.1–5: Hiero addresses 'trust' πίστις, another 'great good' – and cause of pleasure to the body and soul, not only because it is pleasant to be able to trust others, but because lack of trust means a threat to the tyrant's person. Household associations with wives and servants pose a particular danger, since they are subject to poison in the food and drink. Citizens can trust in protection from their fellow citizens, but there is no such protection for the tyrant. The law protects citizens against violent death, whereas it actually encourages the bloody murder of the tyrant.

4.1 ἀλλὰ μήν: the transition to the new argument, as at 4.3, 5.4. ποία μὲν . . . ἡδεῖα ἄνευ πίστεως . . . ποία δ᾽ . . . τερπνὴ ἄνευ πίστεως . . . ποῖος δὲ . . . ἡδὺς ἀπιστούμενος: rhetorical questions in *anaphora* with interesting variation capture the lack of trust to be found in the tyrant's most intimate associations; the variation in the last element is deliberate, in a jarring juxtaposition of 'pleasant' and 'distrusted'.

4.2 καὶ τούτου τοίνυν τοῦ πιστοῦ πρός τινας ἔχειν 'of this condition furthermore of trusting people'. ὁπότε γε: an illustrative example: 'in a situation where'. τούτων with ἀπογεύεσθαι. πρὶν ἀπάρχεσθαι τοῖς θεοῖς 'before beginning with the gods'; his insistence on having his food and drink tasted even before the prayer that customarily preceded the meal emphasizes the tyrant's obsession with security. *Cyr.* 1.3.8–12 has the young Cyrus interpret this tasting as the sheer greed of the waiter. τοὺς διακόνους 'waiters', a specialized class of servants.

4.3 ἀλλὰ μὴν καὶ αἱ πατρίδες: a new topic. Citizens enjoy security as a result of their trust in each other through their 'homelands'. Socrates lists personal sources of security as laws, friends, allies, walls, weapons in a context where he emphasizes the vulnerability of the man without a 'homeland' (*Mem.* 2.1.14–15). δορυφοροῦσι μὲν ἀλλήλους ἄνευ μισθοῦ ἐπὶ τοὺς δούλους, δορυφοροῦσι δ᾽ ἐπὶ τοὺς κακούργους: *anaphora* emphasizes the metaphor in which citizens 'bear spears' for one another as the tyrant's bodyguard are 'spear-bearers' for him. Their service 'without pay', which is based on mutual trust, contrasts with the service of the 'spear-bearers' of the tyrant, who work only for pay and cannot be trusted because they could get more pay for killing the tyrant than protecting him: 6.11. Fisher (1993) 70–7 offers evidence for and against the idea that slaves were natural enemies of their masters. Xenophon thinks that the ideal master can win the willing support of slaves (*Oec.* 12–15), and that slaves were normally hostile only when subject to their masters' irrational anger (*Hell.* 5.3.7), but he refers to their hostility again at 10.4. Aeschines 1.91 includes murderers and highwaymen among those who were subject to the law against κακουργία; these wrongdoers are mentioned again at 10.4. ὑπὲρ τοῦ μηδένα τῶν πολιτῶν βιαίωι θανάτωι ἀποθνήισκειν 'to prevent any of the citizens dying by a violent death'; the preposition with articular infinitive conveys purpose: *GG* 1548. βιαίωι θανάτωι seems to refer to intentional homicide by violent means; cf. Gagarin (1981) 141–3, who refers it to unintentional homicide as well.

4.4 οὕτω δὲ πόρρω προεληλύθασι φυλακῆς 'they have come to such an extent of watchfulness'. Law is seen as a deterrent. τῶι μιαιφόνωι: a brutal intentional homicide; it is used of tyranny by Herodotus 5.92.αι, is the regular epithet for Ares in the *Iliad*, and is widespread through Euripides (*Med.* 266, 1346; *Andr.* 335; *Tr.* 881); see also Dem. 25.84. μηδὲ τὸν συνόντα καθαρεύειν 'that not even the one who associates (with a killer) should be clean'. The lawgiver Dracon excluded killers from religious activities and the agora (Dem. 20.157–9). Lysias 13.79 extends the exclusion to tent, table, tribe, talk. This was because the killer was impure; MacDowell (1963) 3: 'Killers . . . had incurred pollution . . . which affected all with whom they came into contact and the whole of the state in which the crime was committed.' Hiero here extends the pollution to the killer's associates and subjects them to the penalty of the law. Parker (1983) 116: pollution is a kind of 'shadowy spiritual *Doppelgänger* of the law', and 'Xenophon offers a purely secular version of the belief' about the pollution of the associate (129).

4.5 ἔμπαλιν ἀνέστραπται 'is reversed'; the law of Demophantus confirms that the killer of one seeking to establish a tyranny among the Athenians was pure and free from penalty and would acquire half his goods; even those who failed in the attempt were honoured: Andocides 1.96–8. Dem. 20.157–9 includes the murder of tyrants among the categories in which homicide could be justified. Those who assassinated Euphron of Sicyon also relied on the universal agreement that tyrants could be killed without penalty: *Hell.* 7.3.7. αὐτοῖς: a dative of interest or disadvantage (cf. ἡ φιλία . . . αὐταῖς at 3.4), echoing τοῖς . . . τυράννοις of the previous sentence and comparable to the possessive genitive in the subsequent αἱ πόλεις τῶν τοιοῦτόν τι ποιησάντων. If dependent on τιμωρεῖν, it should be transposed. *Hell.* 6.4.32 indicates that the assassins of Jason of Pherae were honoured in 'most of the cities' they went through, but Hiero suggests that this happens in the tyrant's own *polis*. ἀντὶ τούτου: apposition with ἀντί γε τοῦ εἴργειν emphasizes the contrast between the consequences for the murderer of the tyrant and the murderer of the citizen. καὶ εἰκόνας ἐν τοῖς ἱεροῖς ἱστᾶσιν: Lycurgus *Ag. Leocrates* 51 notes that in the sacred agora of Athens there are statues of good generals and 'those who killed the tyrant' i.e. Harmodius and Aristogeiton, who killed Hipparchus, son of Pisistratus. Xenophon found it paradoxical that the Sicyonians buried Euphron of Sicyon in their agora and honoured him as a founder because of his benefits to them (*Hell.* 7.3.12); they honoured him as others honoured the tyrant-slayers.

4.6–11: Hiero moves back to the pleasures of possessions (2.1–2) and develops a metaphor of the games to prove that the tyrant gets no pleasure when he has more than his own ordinary citizens, who are his inferiors, but feels pain when he has less than other tyrants. He was in the same dilemma (either no pleasure or actual pain) in his unhappiness about the attentions of slaves (1.28). In his reform, Simonides will advise him to transfer his competition to other rulers and by securing the prosperity of his city, gain the pleasure of a victory over equals (11.1–8). Hiero also denies the speed with which Simonides said the tyrant accomplishes his desires on the ground that they are so great. He redefines the wealth he is said to possess in relation to needs and finds himself the poorest of the poor since he does not have the means to live according to justice. This is the first mention of justice in the work, and it is presented as a self-evident 'good'.

4.6 ἰδιωτῶν 'than amateurs' as opposed to 'professional athletes': see the note on the meaning at 1.2. οὐχ ὅταν . . . ἀλλ᾽ ὅταν . . . οὕτω . . . οὐχ ὅταν . . . ἀλλ᾽ ὅταν: *anaphora* gives order to a significant comparison between athletes and tyrants, clearly marking the times when victory does and does not bring pleasure. ἀνταγωνιστὰς . . . τοῦ πλούτου 'equal competitors in wealth'; *Mem.* 2.6.26, also in the context of the metaphor of the games, opposes such 'competitors' to 'partners and associates' in the association of friends in government; for the genitive: ἔρωτος ἀνταγωνιστὰς (Eur. *Tr.* 1006).

4.7 οὐδέ γε θᾶττον: the next deprivation. ὧν ἐπιθυμεῖ 'what he desires', a relative clause containing its own antecedent: *GG* 1026, subject of γίγνεται; compare ἐγὼ καὶ ὧν ἐγὼ κρατῶ as subject of μενοῦμεν (*Cyr.* 5.1.26). The tyrant's desire for whole *poleis*, extensive land, harbours and strong fortresses would appropriately account for the possessions of Dionysius the Elder and Younger, with their control of Sicily, their harbours in Syracuse and their palace on the fortified island of Ortygia.

4.8 ἀλλὰ μέντοι: the particle combination makes a fresh point without implying opposition, as at 1.24. οὕτως ὀλίγους τῶν ἰδιωτῶν ὡς πολλοὺς τῶν τυράννων 'as few among private citizens as they are numerous among tyrants'; the thought is found also in *Mem.* 4.2.38–9. οὐ γὰρ τῶι ἀριθμῶι . . . ἀλλὰ πρὸς τὰς χρήσεις 'not by (mere) counting . . . but in relation to uses'. This is the definition to be expected from a philosopher, since Socrates describes even a dung-basket as beautiful in relation to the use to which it is put (*Mem.* 3.8.2–7). Xenophon in character voices the same sentiment about the relativity of measure at *An.* 7.7.36. τὰ μὲν ὑπερβάλλοντα τὰ ἱκανά 'things which surpass sufficiency'; cf. τὰ δὲ τῶν ἱκανῶν ἐλλείποντα 'things which fall short of sufficiency'.

4.9 ὅπηι βούλονται 'as they wish' contrasts the freedom and trivial needs of non-rulers with the more serious concern of the tyrant with his day-to-day survival, which is entirely compelling. οὐκ ἐνδέχεται 'it is not possible'. αἱ γὰρ μέγισται αὐτοῖς δαπάναι καὶ ἀναγκαιόταται: the superlatives press the idea that the tyrant is a complete slave to the great compulsions of his great expenditures on his security.

4.10 ὅσοι μὲν δύνανται . . . ὅσοι δ᾽ ἀναγκάζονται 'as many as have the power', implying freedom, is contrasted with 'as many as are subject to (slavish) compulsion'. The general view was that poverty compelled men to injustice: *Ath.* 1.5. Hiero is poor by this definition because he does not have the means to preserve himself through justice, but must kill, rob and imprison to achieve it: 7.7, 10. For the same thought: *Mem.* 4.2.38. *Symp.* 4.36 cites stealing, burglary, enslaving, destroying entire households, enslaving whole *poleis* as the crimes to which tyrants were driven – this is summed up as the pitiable disease of consumption. ἀπὸ τοῦ δικαίου: cf. *Ath.* 1.11 and 3.3 ἀπὸ χρημάτων.

4.11 ἀναγκάζονται . . . ἀναγκαίας . . . ἀναγκάζονται: continued emphasis on his lack of freedom. πλεῖστα συλᾶν ἀδίκως καὶ ἱερὰ καὶ ἀνθρώπους 'to plunder unjustly in very great number the possessions of the gods and people'. Plundering temples was a stereotyped tyrannical action; Jason of Pherae was suspected of having designs on the sacred treasures of Delphi: *Hell.* 6.4.30. ὥσπερ γὰρ πολέμου ὄντος: 'as if there were a state of war' continues the central metaphor of the tyrant's war against his citizens, which began at 2.8.

5.1–2: Hiero introduces other 'good things' of which he is compelled to deprive himself if he is to be secure. He knows the brave, the wise, the just, but he must eliminate them because their love of freedom threatens his security, and he must then use inferior men in his administration. This pain is both introduced and summed up as χαλεπόν (5.1 and 5.2). Simonides will improve the tyrant's relations with the brave and wise and just when he encourages him to establish competitions in valour and in justice and in devising new ways to benefit the *polis* (9.6–10). They are the men whom Hiero considers valuable in administration (6.14–16), whom Socrates thinks should be partners in government (*Mem.* 2.6.21–7), and whom Cyrus is concerned to befriend (*Cyr.* 8.1.47–8.2.28). Once he is reformed, people who must include the brave and wise and just will bring Hiero whatever is 'wise or fine or good' for his benefit (11.10).

5.1 οὐδὲν ἧττον τῶν ἰδιωτῶν 'no less than private men *do*'. ἀλκίμους: κοσμίους (*codd.*) does not capture the subsequent emphasis on courage. μή τι μηχανήσωνται: Strauss (1947/1963) 41–3 = (2000) 41–3 interprets the 'contrivances' of the wise as a possible reference to the pursuit of tyranny, but their desire to produce a liberal and free constitution is easily supplied from the preceding clause (the tyrant fears that the brave will act 'for the sake of *freedom*)'; and the subsequent clause (that the just will be 'champions of the masses', which implies their *freedom*). The next sentence also confirms that, after his elimination of the brave and wise and just, the tyrant will be left with their opposites, who are the 'unjust and uncontrolled and slavish', the unjust being trusted by him because *freedom* threatens their licence as much as it threatens the tyrant's, the uncontrolled because they like the *licence* available under tyranny, which they would not enjoy in a *free* state, and the slavish because they are not designed for *freedom*. The contrivances of the wise regularly secure the common good, as when Simonides describes his improvements in agriculture as 'contrivances' (μεμηχανημένος 11.4), Socrates has friends 'contrive' good for each other (*Mem.* 2.6.35), and Lycurgus 'contrives' ways to secure obedience to his excellent laws (*Lac.* 8.5 μηχανημάτων καλῶν; see also 11.1 and 13.8). Where contrivances are shameful, they are said to be so: κακόν τι καὶ αἰσχρὸν μηχανώμενοι ζῆν 4.10. The three types of virtuous men in 5.1 indeed constitute a sort of 'liberation movement' and show again (cf. 2.15) how Xenophon uses *anaphora* to describe sequential phases in a single action. The brave begin the movement against the tyrant in armed struggle or assassination. The wise devise ideal government (as Simonides will do for Hiero: 9–11) and the just implement it for the masses. The omission of the reason for which the wise 'contrive' is an instance of the regular truncation of the middle colon in Xenophon's arrangements of *tricola* in *anaphora*. The rule is that if the other two elements contain a leading idea, it will be the point of the third as well even when not explicit. Cf. 2.15 where τοὺς πολεμίους is omitted from the middle colon but present in the first and third, and 5.2, where the motives of the uncontrolled in the middle colon are reduced from the status of a clause to a compressed prepositional phrase: τῆς εἰς τὸ παρὸν ἐξουσίας ἕνεκα. μὴ ἐπιθυμήσηι τὸ πλῆθος ὑπ' αὐτῶν προστατεῖσθαι: cf. the democratic προστάται τοῦ πλήθους in *Poroi* 1.1. Simonides envisages that Hiero will become such a champion of the *polis* at 11.5: πόλεως ἧς προστατεύεις.

5.2 τίνες ἄλλοι . . . ἀλλ' ἤ 'which others . . . apart from . . . ?' φοβοῦνται . . . τὰς πόλεις μήποτε 'they fear the cities lest they'; the proleptic position makes the object of the fear more prominent. τῆς εἰς τὸ παρὸν ἐξουσίας ἕνεκα 'because of the licence (they enjoy) in regard to the present state of affairs (i.e. tyranny)'; ἐξουσία is opposed to ἐλευθερία, as 'licence' is opposed to true 'freedom'. Isocrates, *Areop.* 7.20 has the radical democracy wrongly equate παρανομία with ἐλευθερία and ἐξουσία with εὐδαιμονία. οὐδ' αὐτοί 'not even themselves' are inclined to want freedom, let alone produce it for others. τὸ ἄλλους μὲν ἡγεῖσθαι ἀγαθοὺς ἄνδρας, ἄλλοις δὲ χρῆσθαι ἀναγκάζεσθαι: the first reference to the tyrant's dilemmas, a series of conflicting options which he cannot resolve. See also 6.4, 6.14–16 and 7.11–13, where he is unable either to endure the consequences of being tyrant or of stepping aside from his tyranny. *Ath.* 2.19 shows that the *demos* has no such concern as Hiero: though it can distinguish the men of virtue, it makes a positive choice to make friends of the bad.

5.3–4: An associated dilemma is that the tyrant must want to be a 'friend of his *polis*' because no man can survive without the protective support of community (as Socrates argues in *Mem.* 2.1.14–15). To be such a friend, he must treat his fellow citizens well, even those who oppose him (*Ages.* 7.1–3 offers this definition). But the tyrant, because his citizens are hostile and their prosperity threatens his security, is compelled through fear to disarm them and arm foreigners against them, fostering their poverty rather than their prosperity. The alternation between the singular and plural number for tyrants in this section marks the development of the argument by introducing a fresh point; cf. the comment on 1.13, 2.5, 2.7–18.

5.3 ἀνάγκη . . . ἀναγκάζει: compulsion continues to produce a conflict of emotions in the tyrant. οὔτ' . . . σώιζεσθαι . . . οὔτ' εὐδαιμονεῖν closely identifies security with happiness. ἐνοχλεῖν (Marchant) 'cause trouble to'; cf. ἐνοχλοῦντα ἀεὶ τῆι ὑμετέραι εὐδαιμονίαι (*An.* 2.5.13). ἐγκαλεῖν in the manuscripts seems a less appropriate description of the troubles that Hiero inflicts on his community here, since they involve his bodyguard rather than any legal process. τοὺς ξένους: 'foreigners' form the tyrant's bodyguard; Aristotle said that the tyrant generally preferred foreigners to citizens because they posed no threat to his status: *Pol.* 1314a10–14, but here the tyrant focuses firmly on the lack of freedom he has in the matter. δορυφόροις 'as spear-bearers'; cf. 4.3, where the citizens bore spears in defence of one another. In his reform, Simonides will reveal how to use the mercenaries for the benefit of the citizens (10.2–8) and how to arm citizens without fear (11.2–3).

5.4 οὐδ' ἂν εὐετηριῶν γενομένων ἀφθονία . . . γίγνηται 'not even if, as the result of good harvests, an abundance occurs'. συγχαίρει ὁ τύραννος: the model ruler shows 'sympathy with' the ruled in good times and bad: *Ages.* 7.3; the ideal friend also shares the other's pleasure (3.2): pp. 7–8. ἐνδεεστέροις . . . ταπεινοτέροις 'they think that they have ('use') them more humble if they are more in want of resources'. This was the reason why Croesus after his rebirth as a wise man advised Cyrus not to let his Persians acquire the booty of Sardis (Hdt. 1.88–9). *Ath.* 1.14–15 says that the *demos* fleeces the rich among the allies for the same reason. In his reform, Simonides will show how Hiero can promote prosperity without fear and at the same time make his citizens rejoice in his own pleasure (11.12).

6.1–6: Hiero for the first time directly contrasts the happiness he had as a private citizen with his present unhappiness, firmly focusing on friendship and community; he uses the first person and his lament culminates in a powerful image of his isolation, deep insecurity and contradictory desires.

6.1 ὅσαις: the case of the relative depends on the participle χρώμενος rather than the main verb, in a construction not uncommon in English: e.g. 'to whom donations would be appreciated'. αὐτῶν: (i.e. εὐφροσύνων) refers back to the relative clause: see 1.5.

6.2 ξυνῆν μὲν . . . συνῆν δὲ . . . διῆγον δ᾽ . . . πολλάκις μὲν μέχρι . . . πολλάκις δὲ μέχρι . . . πολλάκις δὲ μέχρι . . . : two sets of triple *anaphora* emphasize the company he once enjoyed as a private man and the extent of the delights that this so often gave him: pleasure with his companions, pleasure in his own peaceful company, companionship in the symposium, then in that setting: forgetting the pains of life, saturating his soul in celebration, and going to sleep. ἡλικιώταις ἡδόμενος ἡδομένοις ἐμοί: the arrangement produces a word picture of Hiero taking pleasure side by side with his companions; the assonance and dactylic rhythm bring attention to the idea. ἡσυχίας 'peace', genitive singular. πάντων εἴ τι χαλεπὸν . . . ἦν 'of every single sorrow in human life'. μέχρι τοῦ . . . τὴν ψυχὴν συγκαταμιγνύναι 'up to the point of saturating my soul', a poetic expression; Pindar *O.* 1.22 also says of Hiero's horse κράτει δὲ προσέμειξε δεσπόταν 'he mingled his master with victory'. μέχρι κοίτης ἐπιθυμίας ἐμῆς τε καὶ τῶν παρόντων 'to the point of the desire of myself and my colleagues for sleep' looks forward to Hiero's contrasting lack of pleasure as a tyrant, where he positively avoids not only the inebriation that gave him such pleasure as a private individual, but also the sleep that he once was able to desire (6.3).

6.3 ἀπεστέρημαι μὲν . . . ἀπεστέρημαι δ᾽ αὖ: *anaphora* now emphasizes his isolation; the first deprivation is of those who take pleasure in him, the second of the pleasure he takes in them. διὰ τὸ δούλους ἀντὶ φίλων ἔχειν τοὺς ἑταίρους 'through having comrades who are slaves instead of friends', the consequence of his elimination of the free: cf. 5.1–2. The reversal of the status of the slaves and the free is a commonplace of tyranny: *Hell.* 7.3.8. ὁμοίως ἐνέδραι 'in the same manner as an ambush' continues the metaphor of the tyrant at war from 2.8. The tyrant is 'on guard' even against the pleasures he once enjoyed.

6.4 φοβεῖσθαι . . . φοβεῖσθαι . . . φοβεῖσθαι . . . φοβεῖσθαι . . . πῶς οὐκ ἀργαλέον ἐστὶ πρᾶγμα: quadruple *anaphora* and a rhetorical question sum up the unhappiness of the tyrannical life in a sequence of conflicting fears that reflect the confusion in his soul: fear both of crowds and of isolation; both of lack of guards and the guards themselves, and the conflicting desire not to want to be without armed men but not to be pleased in seeing them armed. Plato, *Rep.* 579 characterizes the tyrant as one whose soul is abuzz with multiple desires; Xenophon here makes the condition an internal struggle in which the desires and fears fight each other for supremacy.

6.5 ἔτι δὲ . . . οὐ πάντα σοι ταῦτα δοκεῖ: another rhetorical question and the demonstrative bring attention to the unnatural desires expressed in the previous infinitives.

6.6 οὐ μόνον αὐτὸς ἐνὼν . . . ἀλλὰ καὶ πάντων τῶν ἡδέων συμπαρακολουθῶν: fear's occupation of the soul in its own right is distinguished from the corrupting effect that it has on the pleasures that the soul might otherwise enjoy, 'accompanying' these pleasures like a courtier, never absent, an old familiar of the tyrant. λυμεών: this poetic word, used also by Isocrates 4.80, 8.141, but only twice and only in the grand phrase σωτῆρας ἀλλὰ μὴ λυμεῶνας, gives solemnity to the image; cf. λυμαντῆρας 'spoilers' of the friendship of a wife (3.3).

6.7–11: Hiero returns to the terrors of war, to make Simonides fully appreciate the fear and isolation of the tyrant. Simonides enters the conversation again. They discuss the security provided to the ruler and the non-ruler by their guards, the non-ruler in his community war, the tyrant in his war against the citizens. For the second time (cf. 3.3), the tyrant envies the citizens their protection in law.

6.7 ἀντετάξω 'you were disposed against (an enemy line)'. ποῖον μέν τινα σῖτον ἤροῦ . . . ποῖον δέ τινα ὕπνον ἐκοιμῶ: anaphora emphasizes the poor quality of the experience in the sequence of sleeping and eating. *Cyr.* 3.1.24 shows how fear destroys pleasure in sleep and food.

6.8 μέντοι: progressive; contrast 8.1 and 9.1. ἐξ ἐναντίας . . . πάντοθεν: whereas the citizens had the enemy only in front of them (ἀντετάξω), the tyrant is completely surrounded.

6.9 ἡμεῖς γε . . . λαγχάνομεν 'we (private men) at least get our share of', the language of the sharing, democratic community; compare the use of the word for communal sharing at *Ath.* 2.9.

6.10 ὥστε περὶ ἑαυτῶν φοβοῦνται καὶ ὑπὲρ ὑμῶν: the laws stand guard over the human guards, providing a double line of defence; so that the guards fear 'about themselves', apparently because they fear the penalty if they do not do their duty according to the law, and 'on your behalf' because the citizens asleep or eating inside the camp have transferred their fear of the enemy to the guards. ὥσπερ θεριστάς 'like seasonal workers' is another apt image, since the tyrants' men are not part of the regular community and work only for short seasons for pay – like 'fair-weather friends'.

6.11 μηδὲν οὕτω ποιεῖν δύνασθαι ὡς πιστοὺς εἶναι 'to have the capacity to do nothing so much as to be trustworthy'. ἐργάτας ὁποίου βούλει ἔργου 'workers of whatever kind of work you like', which includes, as it turns out, the 'work' of murdering the tyrant. ἄλλως τε καὶ ὁπόταν 'especially when'. ἐν ὀλίγωι χρόνωι πολὺ πλείω λαβεῖν . . . ἢ ὅσα: the comparison of what the showmen expect to get is developed in similar terms: 1.13.

6.12–16: Hiero addresses the last item mentioned by Simonides: helping friends and harming enemies (2.2). The tyrant has no friends; those he treats well do not consider the benefit secure until they are out of his reach. His enemies are too numerous to harm without reducing his *polis* to nothing. They are like horses with an unpredictable temper; he has to use them in running his administration because of their good qualities but he has also to guard against their wild streaks. This contradicts 5.1–2, where he killed men of talent, but reveals Hiero's emotional state of mind, in which he exaggerates his miseries and then contradicts them (as in 3.3 and 4.4). The good ruler was supposed to have the knowledge to use his possessions, including horses and friends and enemies, for his own benefit (*Oec.* 1.6 and 15: enemies, 1.8: horses) but Hiero admits that he has no such knowledge.

6.12 ὃ δ' ἐζήλωσας ἡμᾶς: double accusative 'the thing you envied us'. οὐδὲ ταῦθ' οὕτως ἔχει 'this is not correct either'.

6.13 φίλους μὲν γὰρ πῶς: rhetorical questions about friends and enemies organize this section; 6.14 begins ἐχθροὺς δ' αὖ πῶς. ἐξ ὀφθαλμῶν σου 'out of your sight', contrast 3.2 where the one who loves you will be pleased to see you. ἑαυτοῦ: possessive genitive 'belonging to himself'.

6.14 τίνων γὰρ ἔτι ἄρξει 'whom will he then rule?'; the direct question breaks into Hiero's sequence of temporal clauses, marking his awareness of the dilemma of tyranny, that it cannot free itself from fear without murdering its subjects and ending up with a desert to rule, since all those it rules are its enemies. Cf. how it murders the better classes in the interests of preserving its rule but must then rule over a community that exists of the worse classes and the slaves (2.17, 5.1–2).

6.15 εἰδότα: this word comes first because it is the tyrant's knowledge of their enmity that makes his need to use them so galling; cf. the knowledge of his crimes that he emphasizes at 2.17. τούτους ἅμα μὲν φυλάττεσθαι δέῃ, καὶ χρῆσθαι δ' αὐτοῖς ἀναγκάζηται; the subjunctive continues in the ὅταν clause from 6.14; the connective καὶ . . . δέ is characteristic of Xenophon; he uses it to add a final item in a sequence, repeating words from the previous item, here the idea of compulsion and the reference to his enemies; cf. *Lac.* 2.7. χαλεπῶς: quadruple *anaphora* underlines the dilemma, that the tyrant cannot even harm his enemies without harming himself. ὥσπερ γε . . . 'Just as, if there were a horse of good quality, but giving cause to fear that he would do some irreparable harm, a man would be hard put to kill him because of his good quality, but hard put to make use of him while alive, (because one would be) watching constantly to see that he did not do some irreparable harm in the midst of battle, so other possessions too, as many as cause difficulty, but are useful, all alike cause pain to those who possess them and to those who get rid of them.' The comparison (cf. 4.6, 6.10) pays the tyrant's enemies the compliment of being horses of excellent breeding but bad temperament; it turns out that the person responsible for their bad temper is the tyrant himself, who does not know how to use them until Simonides tells him to set up competitions in excellence to tap their talents. The equine interests of Hiero make the metaphor particularly appropriate. φοβερός . . . μή 'a source of fear that'; cf. 7.10: φροντιζόμενον μή.

6.16 λυπεῖ μέν . . . λυπεῖ δέ: the dilemma in the tyrant's soul is that there is pain no matter what course he takes.

7.1–4: Simonides moves on to the final area in which he thinks that tyranny has the greater share of good things: φιλοτιμία. He accepts that the pleasures of power and possessions are illusory, as he accepted the argument about the pleasures of owning fine horses. He describes instead as the outward manifestations of honour unswerving obedience, admiring gazes, physical deference, and argues that tyrants have a special advantage in this; it is closest to the pleasure that the gods have.

7.1 μέγα τι 'a very great thing'. πάντα μὲν πόνον ὑποδύονται, πάντα δὲ κίνδυνον ὑπομένουσι: Simonides credits tyrants with the attitudes of the ideal ruler, as he did also at 2.1. Socrates had taught Xenophon that the ruler must endure toil and danger: *Mem.* 2.1.17–18. *Symp.* 4.35 says also of those who work for wealth: πάντα μὲν πόνον, πάντα δὲ κίνδυνον ὑποδύονται.

7.2 ὑπηρετῶσι . . . περιβλέπωσι . . . ὑπανιστῶνται . . . παραχωρῶσι, γεραίρωσι: *anaphora* captures a sequence of actions that express honour: 'do service, turn their heads to look at him, get to their feet, move aside, honour'. The image of the honoured man begins with Homer, who describes the first public appearance of Telemachus in *Od.* 2.12–14: 'Athena poured her divine delight on his head; all the folk gazed at him as he went on; he sat in his father's seat; the old men gave way to him'. Hiero will also become περίβλεπτος for his benefactions once he is reformed (11.9). Socrates sees the same advantage (ironically) for the witless Glaucon (*Mem.* 3.6.2). Rising and moving aside for elders is found as a mark of honour in Hdt. 2.80 and *Mem.* 2.3.16, and *Lac.* 9.5 has the coward defer in this way to the younger men, while *Lac.* 15.6 makes the ephors the exception to the deference shown to the Spartan king. *Symp.* 4.31 also has Charmides claim that his poverty makes the rich stand up and make way for him in the streets and honour him 'like a tyrant' where he was once a slave. ποιοῦσι first takes a dative of advantage τοῖς τυράννοις, with accusative τοιαῦτα, then another accusative in place of the dative: ἄλλον (*GG* 1073) – probably because it is antecedent to the accusative ὄντιν'.

7.3 Simonides distinguishes non-human creatures (ζῶια), ordinary people (ἄνθρωποι) and 'real men' such as tyrants (ἄνδρες) in respect of φιλοτιμία. οὗτοί εἰσιν . . . οἱ . . . διαφέροντες: see note on 1.25 for the participial construction; it focuses further attention on the difference of the real men. *Oec.* 13.6–12 uses φιλοτιμία as a measure of worth to different effect, agreeing that creatures have none, nor all human beings either, but that it does occur among some slaves.

7.4 ἐπείπερ: strong cause, 'since indeed'. τοῦ θείου ἐγγυτέρω 'nearer to the divine' because of the pleasure the gods take in being honoured. *Mem.* 1.4.10, 18 and 4.3.15–17 indicate that men honour gods for the benefits they bestow on them. The reformed tyrant will also be like the god in this respect (7.9).

7.5–10 As in his previous denial of the sensual pleasure of the tyrant, Hiero replies that the honour is as insincere as the praise he hears, that nothing gives pleasure which is forced, that honours from tyrannized people are no better than those from slaves, and are given only to avoid suffering at his hands. He is enlightened enough to recognize that the ruler who is truly honoured is honoured for pursuing the proper aim of government, which is to benefit those he rules and secure the 'common good'.

7.5 ὅμοιαι ... οἷάπερ 'exactly similar to those which'. αὐτῶν means 'of tyrants'.

7.6 ἐξ ἀντιφιλούντων ... ὑπὸ τῶν φοβουμένων: the different prepositions are probably just for stylistic variation; see note on 1.28.

7.7 τοὺς βίαι ἐξανισταμένους θάκων ... τοὺς ὁδῶν παραχωροῦντας τοῖς κρείττοσι: the earlier definition of the marks of honour (7.2) is varied by introducing the element of force and the power of the stronger into the equation, thus invalidating it. τοὺς ἀδικοῦντας: the tyrants do wrong because they use force against their subjects.

7.8 καὶ δῶρά γε: Hiero's claim that people give gifts to those they fear recalls his own argument about false praise (1.14–16), but also the 'gift-devouring kings' of Hesiod, W&D 38–40, who gave crooked judgements in return. Thersites suggests that the gifts given to Agamemnon were similarly motivated: *Iliad* 2.225–34. καὶ ταῦτα ὅταν 'and when at that' i.e. 'especially when'. ἀλλὰ ταῦτα μὲν οἶμαι δουλείας ἔργα εἰκότως ἂν νομίζοιτο: the intrusive parenthetical 'I think' and the potential 'would be rightly thought' emphasize Hiero's continuing characterization of those who honour him as slaves. ἐκ τῶν ἐναντίων τούτοις 'from activities opposite to these'.

7.9 ὅταν γάρ: the beginning of a periodic sentence of ten *cola*. ἄνθρωποι is recapitulated at the end in οἱ αὐτοὶ οὗτοι 'these same men'. The verbs capture a chronological sequence of actions that greet the progress of the honoured man. θεῶνταί τ' αὐτὸν ὡς οἰκεῖον ἕκαστος ἀγαθόν: the word order may convey a picture of the benefit surrounding each single individual. See 2.4 and 7.2 for the importance of the 'gaze', which is here becoming more educated, since the masses have moved their eyes from the ruler's possessions (2.4) to his virtuous person. κοινῆς ἀρετῆς καὶ εὐεργεσίας ἕνεκα 'both for his virtue and his benefit in which all have a share'; κοινός means 'shared', as well as describing 'his virtue and his benefit together'. This first reference to human virtue is solidly focused on the virtue of the ruler. *Hiero* contains no abstract discussion of the nature of virtue, or even of the need for it. Rather, as here, it exemplifies virtue and makes the need self-evident. In a similar fashion, *Hiero* gives concrete examples of the specific laws that secure friendship among citizens rather than an abstract discussion of the benefits of law in general (3). ἐθέλωσιν: the free will of the citizens is again an important part of the happiness of the ruler, as at 1.16. ὁ τούτων ἀξιούμενος 'the man thought worthy of these (honours)'.

7.10 φροντιζόμενον μή τι πάθηι 'being an object of concern that he suffer any harm'; Simonides tells Hiero that his fear for his own security will be transferred from himself to his citizens when he secures their common good at 11.11: φόβον δ' οὐκ ἂν ἔχοις ἀλλ' ἄλλοις παρέχοις μή τι πάθηις. καὶ ἀφόβως καὶ ἀνεπιφθόνως καὶ ἀκινδύνως καὶ εὐδαιμόνως: four adverbs, three of them alpha-privatives, capture Hiero's envy of the security of the honoured man; *Rep.* 580a has a similar sequence, of adjectives, describing the moral failings of the tyrant: 'envious, faithless, unjust, friendless, unholy'. ὡς ... κατακεκριμένος δι' ἀδικίαν ἀποθνήισκειν 'like one condemned to die for injustice'; Hiero recognizes his injustice toward his citizens, as at 4.11, 7.7.

7.11–13: Simonides provokes the final denunciation: if tyranny is so utterly miserable, why is there no recorded case of any tyrant willingly laying aside his power? The good things and bad things are no longer the pleasures and pains of tyranny, but the tyranny *in toto*. Hiero says that he is hanged if he does and hanged if he does not. In a kind of *topos* of tyranny, Maeandrius of Samos tried to lay aside his tyranny of Samos, but when prominent men called him to account for his actions as a tyrant, he decided that he would continue as tyrant and used force against them (Hdt. 3.142–3). Hiero rejects both options in favour of suicide. The contrast of his suicidal disposition with the previous vision of the truly honoured man could not be greater.

7.11 διήκουσεν 'heard it through completely'; this signals the end of Hiero's lead part in the conversation; cf. *Oec.* 11.1: διακούσας καὶ καταμαθών. οὔτε ἄλλος μὲν δὴ οὐδείς: the particle combination marks a progression involving a negative expression: *GP* 293. ἑκὼν εἶναι 'willingly'. In this stereotyped phrase, the infinitive seems redundant; cf. τὸ νῦν εἶναι 'at present' and *GG* 1535 for other examples. Simonides' suggestion that the tyrant has the freedom to lay down his tyranny runs completely counter to Hiero's argument so far, that the tyrant has no freedom. ὅσπερ ἂν ἅπαξ κτήσαιτο: for the optative plus ἂν in a relative clause: *M&T* 557; cf. *Lac.* 1.8, 2.10, where the text however, is also uncertain.

7.12 πῶς γὰρ ἂν τίς ποτε ἐξαρκέσειε τύραννος 'how would a single tyrant suffice . . . ?'; ἢ . . . ἐκτίνων . . . ἢ . . . ἀντιπάσχων: the participles express the leading ideas: *GG* 1580, 1586. ὅσους . . . ὅσους: the relative clauses contain their own antecedent: cf. *GG* 1026, 'pay back money to all those he has taken it from' etc. See Lysias 12.82–3 for the thought. ἀποθανουμένας 'expecting to die', is a future participle denoting intention or expectation: cf. *M&T* 71, the equivalent of μέλλειν with the future; the tyrant has only one life, which could compensate only one of those he killed.

7.13 ἀλλ' εἴπερ τωι ἄλλωι, ὦ Σιμωνίδη, λυσιτελεῖ ἀπάγξασθαι, ἴσθι, ἔφη: hanging was a normal type of suicide for men who could not endure their dishonour: Hdt. 7.232. Simonides' name and the intrusion of 'he said' produce strong pauses before and after the bold idea of 'profit' in 'hanging' and Hiero's sure knowledge of this. Hiero has diagnosed an impossible dilemma, in the manner of the Socratic ἀπορία.

8.1–4: The first movement of the dialogue has ended. Simonides, armed with Hiero's diagnosis of his misery, now shows that the ruler can secure more friendship than the non-ruler by doing service to his subjects. He acknowledges Hiero's concern about expenditures by postponing more expensive favours and beginning with 'the very smallest examples'. In other paradigms of rule too, small gestures always counted for more than greater gifts when rulers were winning friendship. *An.* 1.9.24 says of the Younger Cyrus: 'The fact that he had great victories over his friends in doing them services is no wonder, since he had more resources; but the fact that he surpassed them in his care and his enthusiastic desire to give them pleasure, these things seem to me to be more wonderful.' Exactly the same judgement is made of the Elder Cyrus in *Cyr.* 8.2.13. Simonides asks Hiero to take the initiative in reciprocal relations with his citizens even though he is their superior, just as Socrates, when two brothers quarrelled, urged the younger brother to open negotiations with the elder:

Mem. 2.3.14–16. This acknowledges the need for equality in friendships between rulers and subjects, but in fact, the ruler's natural charisma adds to the pleasantness of his attentions (8.5).

8.1 ἀθύμως: the tyrant's depression comes from his ἀπορία and makes him receptive to instruction, as was the case with Euthydemus: *Mem.* 4.2.39–40. ἐμποδών σοι τούτου 'in the way of you (achieving) this'; the adjective is indeclinable and agrees with αὐτὴν i.e. tyranny. καὶ πλεονεκτεῖ γε 'and (ruling) actually has a greater share'; Simonides restates the case for the greater happiness of the ruler.

8.2 αὐτὸ picks up the assertion of the previous sentence, that the ruler can win more love. ἐκεῖνο looks forward to the following clause. ὁ ἄρχων: Simonides uses a new word for the ruler (also 8.3, 5, 6), but does not abandon 'tyrant' (11.1). ἐννόει: a second person imperative; Simonides begins to tell Hiero what to think.

8.3–4 προσειπάτω . . . ἐπαινεσάντων . . . τιμησάτω . . . θεραπευσάτωσαν . . . δότωσαν: Simonides issues a series of third person imperatives followed by rhetorical questions, inviting Hiero to accept that the ruler has greater power to win friends by giving others the pleasure and delight (εὐφροσύνη, χάρις) that he wanted for himself; so that whereas he wanted praise from his citizens (1.14–16), now the citizens may hear praise from him and respond with love. The singular and the plural for the rulers and non-rulers alternate for variation. The third person continues the wise man's use of distancing language in telling the ruler what to do (as opposed to what to think – above); the 'hypothetical case' will not offend the tyrant as much as the second person; cf. the use of the second person imperative in the final part of the dialogue, when Simonides is supremely confident: 11.13–15. ἴθι δή: parenthetical. ἐξικνεῖσθαι μᾶλλον εἰς εὐφροσύνην 'come to give more joy'. θύσας δὲ τιμησάτω: *Mem.* 2.3.11, 2.9.4 and 8, *Cyr.* 8.4.1 show that sharing sacrifice with another recognizes his worth and does him honour.

8.4 κάμνοντα 'a sick man'; the ideal ruler cared for the sick in all kinds of associations e.g. *Cyr.* 1.6.15–17, *Oec.* 7.37. αἱ ἀπὸ τῶν δυνατωτάτων θεραπεῖαι: the idea that attentions from the most powerful bring the most pleasure to others echoes Hiero's remark about the attentions of the proudest ladies giving most pleasure to him (1.28); but the tyrant is now to give these attentions to his citizens. δότωσαν: another reversal; previously the citizens gave gifts to the tyrant under the compulsion of fear: 7.8, but now the tyrant gives gifts to them and wins their love; *Cyr.* 8.2.7 notes the πολυδωρία of Cyrus. αἱ ἀπὸ τῶν δυνατωτάτων ἡμίσειαι χάριτες πλέον ἢ ὅλον τὸ παρὰ τοῦ ἰδιώτου δώρημα δύνανται 'half the favours from the most powerful have more power than the entire stock of gifts that the private citizen can give'; this is an echo of the proverbial πλέον ἥμισυ παντός (Hesiod *W&D* 40); the distinction measures the greater impact of the ruler's favour on his citizens. Xenophon knows his Hesiod elsewhere too: *Mem.* 2.1.20. Plato *Laws* 690e uses the proverb to other effect.

8.5–7: the god-given 'charisma' of the ruler gives these small attentions special value, so that he can appear more attractive even to those favourites whose love he wants. Homer *Od.* 2.12 has Athena pour 'charm' on the head of Telemachus as he goes out in public too: θεσπεσίην δ' ἄρα τῶι γε χάριν κατέχευεν Ἀθήνη. Pindar at the end of *Pythian* 1 endorsed the greater importance of what the tyrant does: 'Forge your tongue on a truthful anvil. Even if a small spark flies, it flies big, because it is from you.'

8.5 καὶ ἐκ θεῶν: see the note on 3.5 on the role of the gods. τιμή τις καὶ χάρις: the combination of honour and delight is like the pleasure Hiero wanted from his marriage: τινὰ . . . φιλοτιμίαν μεθ' ἡδονῆς (1.27). Now he gives this delight to others. μὴ . . . ὅτι: 'not to mention that' effectively means 'not only': cf. *GG* 1504. ἥδιον θεώμεθά τε . . . διαλεγόμενοί τε ἀγαλλόμεθα: Simonides, who is even now in conversation with the tyrant and gazing upon him, is experiencing the pleasure he describes. τοῖς ἐκ τοῦ ἴσου ἡμῖν οὖσι 'with those who are on equal terms with us'.

8.6 ἐν οἷς δὴ καὶ σὺ μάλιστα κατεμέμψω τὴν τυραννίδα: cf. the tyrant's lament at 1.29–38; the particles mark an item of special importance. ἥκιστα . . . ὑπολογίζεται 'least does old age annoy, least is any ugliness of this man (the ruler) put to his account (as a debt) in the eyes of whomsoever he happens to associate with'. Socrates says that the inevitable ugliness of old age makes the carnal lover disgusting to his partner, whereas the spiritual lover never loses his appeal because it comes from his character: *Symp.* 8.13–15. Here the ruler has the everlasting appeal of the spiritual lover. λαμπρότερα ἀναφαίνειν: the adjective is predicative 'to make . . . more visible'.

8.7 γε μήν moves on to a fresh area of argument, as at 10.5, 8. How much more pleasure will the leader give and get if he deploys his *greater* power and resources in the game of giving delight?

8.8–10: Hiero makes an objection to the rosy vision that he is being offered: not that it is invalid, but that Simonides is ignoring part of Simonides' tyrant's role: he needs to do things that make people hate him, more or less all those things that involve coercion of the citizens. He needs also to keep a bodyguard.

8.8 Ὅτι: Hiero directly answers Simonides' rhetorical question, putting the most essential thoughts first: '"Because, by the god", he said, "Simonides, in matters from which men earn hatred as well, we rulers, much more than non-rulers, must conduct business."'

8.9 πρακτέον . . . ἀναγκαστέον . . . κολαστέον . . . κωλυτέον . . . οὐκ ἐπιτρεπτέον: verbal adjectives (*GG* 1594–8) show the compulsion that Hiero thinks he is under to do unpopular business, which denies him the freedom to be loved; cf. *Lac.* 9.5. ἕξειν δαπανᾶν εἰς τὰ δέοντα 'to have the means to spend on necessities'. ἐξορμᾶσθαι specifies the application of τάχους καιρός 'a time for speed in setting out': cf. *GG* 1530.

8.10 οὐ γὰρ τυράννοις ἰσοτιμίας, ἀλλὰ πλεονεξίας ἕνεκα: 'equal honour' (= 'equality') is opposed to 'having more' (= 'inequality'). The dative is one of advantage. The citizens think that the bodyguard gives tyrants the advantage over them, but the tyrant needs it to preserve his life, which he thinks merely puts him on equal terms with them. D.S. 14.65.3 expresses the same opposition to the tyranny of Dionysius II: 'The mass of his bodyguards has been assembled for the enslavement of Syracuse, and the tyrant controls the *polis*, not acting as referee for justice on equal terms (ἐπ' ἴσης), but as a monarch judging that he do everything for his own advantage (πλεονεξίαι)'.

9.1–11: Simonides divides the tasks of government into those that win hatred and those that win love. He suggests that Hiero delegate the former while keeping the latter for himself, on the model of the production of a dramatic chorus, in which the archon awards the prizes, but delegates the training. He extends the competitive model to encourage the brave and wise and just to compete for honour in securing the military and economic prosperity of the *polis*, and to make citizens more just in their dealings with one another. This section points to another reversal: that if Hiero wants his share of honour, he must arrange for others to secure theirs. For arguments against Strauss' contention that Simonides produces only a limited kind of virtue in the citizens, and that financial justice is an inferior kind of justice, see Appendix 1.

9.1 πρὸς ἔχθραν ἄγειν **. . .** διὰ χαρίτων εἶναι 'to lead to enmity . . . to produce pleasure'; compare διὰ χαρίτων γίγνεται . . . δι' ἀπεχθείας . . . γίγνεσθαι below (9.2).

9.2 αὕτη μὲν ἡ ἐπιμέλεια: 'this care' is in apposition to the first preceding group of articular infinitives describing popular actions. ταῦτα δέ: in apposition to the second group, describing unpopular actions.

9.3 τὸν μὲν ἀνάγκης δεόμενον ἄλλοις προστακτέον εἶναι κολάζειν 'orders must be given (by the ruler) to others to punish the one who needs compulsion' (taking the verbal adjective as impersonal: cf. *GG* 1597). δι' αὐτοῦ ποιητέον: Simonides produces a new set of verbal adjectives conveying pleasant obligations; these replace those unpleasant obligations described by Hiero.

9.4 χορούς **. . .** ἀγωνίζεσθαι 'to conduct choral competitions'; our knowledge of choral production comes mainly from Athens: Wilson (2000) 50–103, but Simonides may be right to speak as though the practices he describes were in force throughout Greece ('we'); see Wilson (2000) 279–302 on *choregoi* and choral productions outside Attica, including for example in Aegina (Hdt. 5.83.3). ὁ ἄρχων: the comparison of the tyrant to the main official of Athenian choral competitions suits the poet in Simonides. He emphasizes the role of the archon in awarding prizes, since that is the point most relevant to his comparison of the ruler; cf. the panel of judges that makes the decision in classical Athens: Wilson (2000) 98–102. ἀθροίζειν **. . .** ποιοῦσιν 'the gathering of the performers stands delegated to *choregoi* and to others the instruction and discipline of those who perform anything inadequately'. Wilson (2000) 81–4 indicates that the instruction involved the physical and vocal training of the performers, and the discipline covered these aspects and even their diet and sexual activity. Simonides says that the archon's delegation of these duties secured his popularity, but *Mem.* 3.4.3–6 indicates that the *choregos* delegated to secure the technical skills required; and the archon would delegate for the same reason. However, Xenophon allows Simonides to be as adept at providing explanations of practices that suit his purposes as Hiero is in explaining the intention of the laws he mentions: 3.3. Simonides' *choregoi* resemble those Athenian 'liturgists' who were chosen because of their wealth to produce a festival chorus (*choregia*), athletic events (*gymnasiarchia*), or feasts (*hestiasis*), maintain a trireme for the navy (*trierarchia*), or finance a delegation to religious festivals (*architheoria*).

9.5 καὶ τἆλλα τὰ πολιτικά 'other matters to do with the *polis* also' include warfare, honesty in financial dealings, farming, trade. κατὰ φυλάς . . . κατὰ μόρας . . . κατὰ λόχους: the various military divisions of the *polis*; the tribe was an important division in Athens; the *mora* and the *lochos* were military divisions in Sparta (*Lac.* 11.4; *Hell.* 6.4.13, 7.2.4); see also Arist. *Pol.* 1309a12 for *lochoi* at Thebes and Argos.

9.6 ἆθλα . . . καὶ εὐοπλίας καὶ εὐταξίας καὶ ἱππικῆς καὶ ἀλκῆς τῆς ἐν πολέμωι καὶ δικαιοσύνης τῆς ἐν συμβολαῖοις: Agesilaus set up competitions for the best physical condition, best arms and the best horsemanship to produce the best fighting forces to take with him back to Greece from Asia: *Hell.* 3.4.16, 4.2.5–7. The prizes go to the leaders of the units as well as to the individuals in them. Cf. also *Cyr.* 2.1.22–4. *Poroi* 3.3 recommends competitions for 'whosoever resolves disputes with the greatest justice and the greatest speed' when seeking to improve the economy of the Athenians and make their empire more just, and financial justice is in fact the most prominent sign of justice in Agesilaus (*Ages.* 4). 'Contracts' cover a variety of legal agreements between two parties, from betrothals to loans. διὰ φιλονικίαν: love of honour is the quality of the best men: 7.3; Simonides recommends that Hiero encourage them to compete for honour at his hands, in order to produce an all-round improvement of the prosperity of the *polis*. There are four other strong references in 9.6–10 to their desire for this honour: τιμῆς ὀρεγόμενοι, τιμώμενος, τιμήσεται, οὐκ ἀτίμητος.

9.7 ὁρμῷντό γ' ἂν θᾶττον ὅποι δέοι: the solution to Hiero's previous concern for speedy implementation (8.9), which was also one of Simonides' suggested areas of tyrannical strength (2.2: ταχὺ δὲ κατεργάζεσθε). τὸ πάντων γε χρησιμώτατον . . . ἡ γεωργία αὐτὴ ἂν πολὺ ἐπιδοίη: the apposition emphasizes the supreme usefulness of farming. Hiero is to be like the successful estate manager who naturally inspires a competition based on φιλονικία and φιλοτιμία among the farm workers (*Oec.* 21.10). Cyrus also used rewards and punishment to encourage agricultural productivity throughout his dominions (*Oec.* 4.8). κάλλιστα 'most productively', though the sight of crops flourishing might also be 'most beautiful' to some. τοῖς . . . τῶν πολιτῶν 'for those among the citizens (who)'.

9.8 καὶ γὰρ αἱ πρόσοδοι αὔξοιντ' ἄν, καὶ ἡ σωφροσύνη πολὺ μᾶλλον σὺν τῆι ἀσχολίαι συμπαρομαρτεῖ: the increase in revenues and 'moderation' among the citizens that comes from their engagement in agriculture could benefit the tyrant, who is much concerned to reduce his expenditures and the insolence of his citizens (5.4, 10.2), but these effects are presented first and foremost as an explanation (καὶ γάρ) of the benefits that will come to citizens in the preceding sentence. The revenues do improve the citizens' prosperity, since they later become capable of sending expensive chariot teams to the games (11.7). The moderation had an additional benefit to the citizens, in that it discouraged those doers of evil from whom the citizens themselves had most to fear (4.3, 10.4 and 10.8). Perhaps there are benefits all round. Cf. Strauss (1947/1963) 71–2 = (2000) 70, who believed that the purpose of Hiero's agricultural competitions was to keep his citizens poor in order to make them attend to their own business, and be too busy to plot against him. καὶ μὴν κακουργίαι γε ἧττον τοῖς ἐνεργοῖς ἐμφύονται: at 4.3, 10.4, 10.8 it is the citizens who need to be protected against 'wrongdoers', which may confirm the implication above that these are benefits to citizens. The subsequent sentence implies also that the benefits come to the *polis* as a whole: 'if trade *also* helps the *polis* . . .'

9.9 τιμώμενος 'if he were honoured' is in an emphatic position in the sentence and stresses again the reversal of the distribution of honour in the *polis*, from the ruler to the ruled. πρόσοδόν τινα ἄλυπον 'some harmless revenue' i.e. that produces none of the 'pain' of unhappiness for others; *Mem.* 2.6.22–3 sees this lack of pain as a special feature of the pursuit of the common good in friendship; cf. *Lac.* 6.1 ὡς ἂν μηδὲν βλάπτοντες ἀπολαύοιέν τι οἱ πολῖται ἀλλήλων ἀγαθόν and also *Cyr.* 8.7.11: εὐδαιμονίαν δὲ σοὶ ἀλυποτέραν. τιμήσεται: the future tense (with 9.10 οὐκ ἀτίμητος ἔσται) conveys a stronger promise of honour than the optatives that surround it. οὐδ' αὕτη ἂν ἡ σκέψις ἀργοῖτο 'this inquiry would not be left unworked'.

9.10 ὡς δὲ συνελόντι εἰπεῖν 'to summarize in brief'; cf. phrases like ὡς ἔπος εἰπεῖν 'so to speak': *GG* 1534. ἔργον ποιεῖσθαι τὸ σκοπεῖν τι ἀγαθόν: the indication that this competition would encourage many 'to make it their business to find some good thing' means that the ruler harnesses the talents of a large number in the pursuit of 'the good'. καὶ ὅταν γε πολλοῖς περὶ τῶν ὠφελίμων μέλῃ: the concern of 'many' in the pursuit of the 'useful', like the pursuit of the 'good', can be interpreted in a concrete sense (new ideas for trade etc.) but is also philosophical shorthand for the pursuit of virtue. *Mem.* 4.6.8 gives a dialectical definition of the 'good' as the 'useful' and *Mem.* 4.1.1 describes Socrates himself as supremely ὠφέλιμος. Hiero would thus be encouraging his citizens to pursue virtue.

9.11 πολλοὺς . . . πολλά: *anaphora* soothes Hiero's fears about expenses by stressing the amount of effort he will secure from the citizens for relatively small prizes – because the competitions appeal to their love of honour rather than wealth. The same point is made in *Hipp.* 1.26: that choruses, which were Simonides' original analogy for the *polis*, produce huge efforts μικρῶν ἄθλων ἕνεκεν. The expenditures on choral productions certainly did not match their sometimes merely symbolic prizes (ivy crowns, animals, bronze tripods): Wilson (2000) 147, 89–95. *Hell.* 4.2.7 has Agesilaus offer armour and crowns worth no less than four talents to secure worthy fighting forces, but he was rich with the booty of Asia. *Poroi* 3.6 makes a similar point about the way to develop trade, that it could be done at no cost, merely by passing laws to encourage it.

10.1–8: Hiero praises this advice, but mentions the area not yet addressed in which he incurs hatred: the bodyguards (8.10). Simonides divides men into rogues who cannot be managed without fear and 'gentlemen' of virtue who respond to positive incentives; see the paradigms of Proxenus and Socrates on the challenges of rogue elements: pp. 8, 15. He recommends that Hiero use the bodyguards against rogues, but gives a long list of uses to which they could be put for the benefit of those who are capable of being won over: relieving them of their previous service as 'bodyguards' for one another against slaves and wrongdoers (cf. 4.3), securing their property, freeing them to pursue their own business, defending their land, fighting in the army and frightening neighbours into making peace ('a very great good thing': 2.7). Moreover, the citizens will pay for them if they protect the *polis*, as they pay already for private guards of their own households.

10.1 ὡς μὴ μισεῖσθαι: Xenophon uses ὡς to introduce clauses of result; cf. *GG* 1456, *M&T* 608. The result can also be 'aimed at as a purpose': *M&T* 587.3; here the avoidance of hatred is indeed both result and purpose.

10.2 δεήσεται μὲν οὖν: strong assent, like πάνυ μὲν οὖν. ὥσπερ ἐν ἵπποις . . . : the horse image continues for the enemies of the tyrant (6.15–16), accepting that some of them will continue to threaten his rule.

10.3 τοῖς δὲ καλοῖς κἀγαθοῖς: the 'gentlemen' who are by definition not inclined to become insolent must include the brave, the wise and the just, whom the tyrant previously oppressed (5.1–2); such men have successful relations in the associations of households, friends and *polis*: *Mem.* 1.2.48, so that the proposed use of the bodyguards for the protection and promotion of their households and *polis* will have great appeal for them. *Oec.* 6.14–17 refers to Socrates' search for such a gentleman in Ischomachus. ἄν μοι δοκεῖς . . . παρασχεῖν 'it seems that you would provide'; this shows the preference for the personal over the impersonal δοκεῖν.

10.4 σαυτῶι φύλακας '*as* guards for yourself'. δεσπόται 'masters of private households'. ὡς πάντων ὄντας δορυφόρους τῶν πολιτῶν: the first instruction to the bodyguards is to help all citizens 'on the grounds that they are the bodyguards of all citizens'. τι τοιοῦτον: i.e. any incident such as a citizen being attacked by his slaves. γίγνονται δέ που: their second use is against wrongdoers. καὶ τοῦτ' . . . ὠφελούμενοι 'helped in this way as well'.

10.5 πρὸς δὲ τούτοις: their third function. καὶ θάρρος καὶ ἀσφάλειαν: here in another reversal, the tyrant provides the 'goods' of confidence and security to his citizens, whereas before he wanted these goods only for himself. ἱκανοί γε μήν: their fourth benefit is to give the citizens leisure to pursue their own business. Hdt. 5.78 says that the tyrant makes the citizens work for him as slaves, but here he releases them to pursue their own work. τὰ ἐπίκαιρα 'appropriate positions'.

10.6 πρὸς δὲ τούτοις: their fifth function is to act as a standing military force in case of emergency. ἀλλὰ μήν: their sixth use is as a fighting force, one that because of its professionalism is able to take the brunt of attacks and protect the citizens in the front ranks. προπονεῖν καὶ προκινδυνεύειν καὶ προφυλάττειν: the prefixes indicate that the mercenaries will work 'on behalf of' and 'in front of' the citizens so as to preserve their property and their lives.

10.7 Their seventh use is to scare neighbouring *poleis* into wanting peace, which is one of the very best things that can be secured (cf. 2.7). Their ability to help friends and harm enemies constitutes an essential happiness that Hiero said he lacked himself (2.2; 6.12–16).

10.8 ὅταν γε μήν: the final benefit, that the citizens will willingly pay for such a source of benefit as the bodyguards will prove to be. ἐπὶ μείοσι τούτων 'for lesser purposes than these': *GG* 1210.2c, i.e. those which have been summarized.

11.1–7: Simonides turns the tyrant's attention away from getting the citizens to pay for their own security toward spending his own great resources for their advantage. Pindar gave similar economic advice to Hiero at the end of *Pythian* 1.88–92: 'You are the guardian of much wealth. Many are the trusty witnesses on both sides. Remaining in the flower of your pride, if you wish to hear a constant sweet report, *do not labour too much about expenditures*. Let out the sail to the wind like a helmsman.' Hiero is directly urged to compare the benefits to himself of spending his money on his *oikos* or their *polis*, his weapons or their armaments, his lands under cultivation or all the citizens', his private chariot victories or the chariot victories of the prospering citizenry, in a competition which is not that of tyrant against citizens but against other tyrants. Multi-syllabic words give a poetic flavour to the vision.

11.1 εἰς τὸ κοινὸν ἀγαθόν: the focus is transferred from his private good to the common good, which is of course the aim of ideal government (pp. 4–5). εἰς τὸ δέον: 'necessities' are redefined as expenditures on the *polis* rather than exactions from it; cf. 8.9. καθ' ἓν δ' ἕκαστον 'in each detail separately'.

11.2 οἰκίαν πρῶτον: Simonides had included magnificent houses among the advantages of tyranny (2.2), but Hiero proved them to be an illusory good, which did not even give him security (2.10); now Simonides dismisses the value of even the most magnificent house when compared with the magnificence of the *polis* as a whole. ἄν σοι παρέχειν: the participles have conditional force, and so ἄν is retained when the apodosis ('it would bring you greater credit') is placed in indirect speech. τείχεσί τε καὶ ναοῖς . . . : buildings designed to promote the security of the citizens (fortification walls), the beauty of their surroundings and their religious life (temples), and their commercial facilities (porticoes and market-places and harbours); *Ath.* 2.9–10 establishes the importance of buildings as a constituent of the happiness of the Athenians.

11.3 ὅπλοις . . . τοῖς ἐκπαγλοτάτοις αὐτὸς κατακεκοσμημένος 'you alone completely resplendent in the most amazing armour'; a second category of good thing. Simonides had included beautiful arms among the tyrant's happy possessions (2.2), but these could not protect him against the threats of his citizens (2.8–9). He is now encouraged to arm them instead, since they will be no longer a threat to himself, but to his enemies. The adjective is poetic, used by Homer of that which is frightening (Achilles is πάντων ἐκπαγλότατ' ἀνδρῶν). The point is that even with the superlative splendour of a Homeric warrior, he would not be more frightening in warfare than an entire *polis* in arms. Simonides seems to move Hiero's focus from aristocratic to democratic values. ἢ τῆς πόλεως ὅλης εὐόπλου σοι οὔσης 'or with the whole city well armed for you': genitive absolute.

11.4 προσόδους δέ: the third category of good thing. εἰ . . . μεμηχανημένος εἴης 'if you were to have contrived'; the word that has been used of the activities of the wise (5.1) here refers to the improvements that Simonides suggested in agriculture and trade (9.7–9). The perfect potential optative is used again at 11.8: κατειργασμένος ἂν εἴης to convey the perfect vision of the happiness that Hiero will enjoy if he employs these 'contrivances'.

11.5 τὸ δὲ πάντων κάλλιστον καὶ μεγαλοπρεπέστατον νομιζόμενον εἶναι ἐπιτήδευμα ἁρματοτροφίαν 'that which is thought to be the finest and most magnificent practice', and in apposition, 'maintaining a chariot team', is the subject of the infinitive ἂν . . . κοσμεῖν. The qualification 'thought to be' challenges the traditional aristocratic definition of excellence. Pindar and Bacchylides celebrate Hiero's chariot victories, but Agesilaus considered them to be nothing in comparison with successful rule (*Ages*. 9.6–7). Evidently 'the most worthy practice of a man' is to rule others and make them happy, as Simonides goes on to say. πλεῖστοι μὲν . . . πλεῖστοι δ' 'the greatest number' would rear horses and compete because their private revenues will have increased as a result of Hiero's good management of agriculture and trade. ἅρματος ἀρετῆι ἢ πόλεως . . . εὐδαιμονίαι: a metaphor of the games for the rule of the *polis* presents the tyrant as a winner, but suggests that the success of the *polis* is a more worthy arena for his competition than the excellence of his chariot team. The comparison suggests an equation between the 'virtue' of his horses and the 'success' of his *polis*.

11.6 νικῶν μὲν γὰρ . . . νικώμενος δ': the idea that Hiero found no pleasure in competition with his citizens because he was like a professional athlete competing against amateurs (4.6) is developed, and new negative outcomes of such competition are discovered: if conquering, no admiration but envy, if conquered, the most humiliating laughter; the participles have conditional force. ὡς . . . ποιούμενος 'because (in their eyes) you make': cf. *GG* 1574.

11.7 ὧν: partitive with εὐδαιμονεστάτην 'among whom, if you make the city which you champion the happiest'. κηρυχθήσηι νικῶν 'you will be announced as winner'. For κηρυχθήσηι, cf. Xen. *Symp*. 8.37. The announcement was the climax of the games; Miltiades won the favour of the tyrant Pisistratus when he had him 'announced' as victor instead of himself: Hdt. 6.103.2. The echo of the previous description of chariot racing (11.5) creates ring-composition around this section, replacing chariot racing with good government.

11.8–15: Simonides paints a vision of friendship with his citizens that will meet Hiero's desire to hear true praise, see the best sights, win the affection of his beloved, become an object of public honour, longed for and loved, cared about and trusted, free from fear, to achieve the personal *eudaimonia* that comes from the assent of his people to his rule, to help his friends and harm his enemies; to replace his suicidal depression with confidence. Sometimes Simonides envisages an even greater share of happiness than Hiero desired; at all points, there are reversals of his previous unhappy condition.

11.8 τὸ φιλεῖσθαι ὑπὸ τῶν ἀρχομένων: Simonides offers the cure for the main unhappiness of tyranny, its lack of love, which he diagnosed from Hiero's account of his condition: 8.1. οὐκ ἂν εἶς εἴη ὁ ἀνακηρύττων . . . : the voice of the single herald of the games is replaced by the voices of all mankind, and the mere announcement with hymns; *Mem*. 2.1.33 also speaks of 'men who are hymned' for their virtue. The final lines of Pindar *Pythian* 1 contrast the songs that immortalize the goodness of Croesus with the infamy of Phalaris, who burned his enemies alive in the bull of bronze.

11.9 περίβλεπτος δὲ ὤν . . . : he will secure the admiring gaze that he wanted (7.2), from entire communities rather than just his own, not just from individuals in private life, but in public among all mankind.

11.10 ἐξείη μὲν . . . ἐξείη δ': *anaphora* emphasizes the freedom he will have to see the sights that he previously said were available only to non-rulers, both overseas and at home (1.11–12). ἀεὶ γὰρ ἂν παρὰ σοὶ πανήγυρις εἴη: the festival will come to him at his home on a permanent basis. τῶν βουλομένων . . . τῶν δὲ καὶ ἐπιθυμούντων: this emphasizes how the citizens are willingly engaged in his pleasure. εἴ τίς τι σοφὸν ἢ καλὸν ἢ ἀγαθὸν ἔχοι: the exhibits will be feasts not just for the eyes, but for the soul as well – perhaps the products of the activities of the wise and brave and just that his competitions seek to secure.

11.11 The language of friendship and war continues; where Hiero was in a constant state of war against his citizens (2.7–18), every person will now be his 'ally', and where he had said that men wished to be out of his sight (6.13), now anyone out of his sight will long to see him, as the ideal friend does (3.2). ὥστε οὐ μόνον φιλοῖο ἂν, ἀλλὰ καὶ ἐρῷο: 'desire' for the tyrant will accompany 'friendship', transferring to his citizens the pleasure of desire that Hiero was previously denied in his relations with his boyfriend (1.30). οὐ πειρᾶν, ἀλλὰ πειρώμενον ὑπ' αὐτῶν ἀνέχεσθαι: his relations with the fair are also reversed, so that now they want and truly desire him (cf. 1.29 and 8.6–7). A goddess gave Sappho the same reversal in her relations with the object of her desire, but Hiero is encouraged to secure it Xenophontically through his own good management: *GL* I: Sappho 1.21–4. φόβον δ' οὐκ ἂν ἔχοις . . . ἀλλ' ἄλλοις παρέχοις μή τι πάθῃς: the tyrant's previous fear of his citizens is replaced by their fear for his well-being.

11.12 ἑκόντας δὲ τοὺς πειθομένους: those who were previously compelled to obey now do it willingly. θεῷο ἄν: their voluntary concern for his welfare is a spectacle upon which the ruler himself might gaze, reversing even the ideal in which they gazed upon him as the source of their welfare (7.9). πολλῶν μὲν δωρεῶν ἀξιούμενος: his worth now replaces the fear that previously drove his citizens to give him gifts (7.8). εὐμενεῖ: predicative: not at a loss (to find a person) to whom you will give a share of these gifts 'as to one well disposed'; he was previously at a loss because he had no friends of goodwill (6.13). πάντας μὲν συγχαίροντας . . . ἐπὶ τοῖς σοῖς ἀγαθοῖς: in another reversal, whereas previously the tyrant said he was unable to rejoice in the successes of his citizens (5.4), here the citizens rejoice in his own successes, like ideal friends (3.2: συνήδονται δ'ἐπὶ τοῖς αὐτοῦ ἀγαθοῖς). πρὸ τῶν σῶν ὥσπερ τῶν ἰδίων: the ultimate reversal and expression of friendship: whereas the tyrant once took the citizens' goods as his own, but was then encouraged to use his own goods for their benefit (11.1), they now reciprocate by defending his goods as if they were their own, looking upon him as their own private source of benefit as they looked upon the truly honoured man (7.9).

11.13 Simonides shows his confidence in his reform; he abandons his deference in favour of the direct approach and summarizes his advice in a series of second-person imperatives accompanied by brief rationale. This didactic style of wise advice to rulers is found in Pindar *P.* 1.88–92 and also, for example, in Isocrates' address *To Nicocles* 2.13–14. θησαυρούς: cf. *Cyr.* 8.2.14–23 for the same thought, where Croesus suggests that Cyrus should amass treasure chests (such as those he once possessed), but

Cyrus shows that he has moveable treasure chests in the form of his living friends and can command their wealth whenever he wants it because of their friendship. ἀλλὰ θαρρῶν . . . πλούτιζε μὲν τοὺς φίλους: the ἀθυμία that he previously felt (8.1) and his fear that enrichment encouraged insurrection (5.4) are dispelled, as he identifies his own good with the good of his citizen friends. αὖξε δὲ τὴν πόλιν: the diminishing effect of Hiero's elimination of opponents is reversed (2.17–18, 5.1–2, 6.14) in his new adoption of good government; previously only citizens increased the *polis* (2.15).

11.14 κτῶ δὲ αὐτῆι συμμάχους . . . : the lacuna requires some statement of the results for Hiero, as in the previous instructions. τὴν σὴν ψυχήν: the qualification ὅ τιπερ suggests that this means 'soul'; cf. 'life' at 7.12. The vexed question of the nature of the soul, which perhaps might have been settled in a more abstract dialogue, is left open. καὶ τούτους πάντας πειρῶ νικᾶν εὖ ποιῶν: the supreme expression of friendship; compare below ἐὰν . . . τοὺς φίλους κρατῆις εὖ ποιῶν. *Mem.* 2.6.35 agrees that it is the virtue of a real man to conquer his friends in doing them good and his enemies in doing them harm (νικᾶν τοὺς μὲν φίλους εὖ ποιοῦντα, τοὺς δ' ἐχθροὺς κακῶς). For comments on the interpretation of this passage by Strauss: Appendix 1.

11.15 οὐ μή σοι δύνωνται: the negatives with subjunctive (more usually with the aorist) convey a strong future negative (*GG* 1360; cf. *An.* 2.2.12 with the present tense). Hiero's acquisition of friends reverses the situation in which the tyrant had no friends and no power either to harm his enemies (6.12–16). εὖ ἴσθι: parenthetic, produces a pause in the sentence between the description of the finest possession and the condition on which Hiero will acquire it. κεκτήσει: the tense conveys the sense of the perfected future acquisition of this finest and most blessed possession. εὐδαιμονῶν γὰρ οὐ φθονηθήσηι: the conclusion subverts the idea that it was better to be hated as a ruler than pitied as a subject (e.g. Pindar *Pythian* 1.85) by introducing a new option of the beloved ruler. *Lac.* 15.8 also protects the Spartan kingship against φθόνος by moderating its privileges.

This climax gives the sense of a conclusion to the work. The identification of the tyrant's interests with his community's is such a reversal of the usual definition of tyranny that the tyrant remains in name only a tyrant. The winning paradox is that in merging his interests with those of the community, he gets their support for his own. We do not find out whether Hiero implemented the wisdom he was given, but he has a strong motivation in the unhappiness he currently experiences, and there is the automatic penalty of continuing unhappiness if he ignores the advice (*Mem.* 3.9.12). Modern parallels prove the power of the ideas that Xenophon develops. The ordinary person singled out of the crowd for the politician's (or the monarch's) kind word, the well-publicized visit to the hospital, the gaze of the television camera, these remain central to the display of good government. Delegation of unpopular tasks away from senior management still secures a large degree of support in businesses and universities. The incentive schemes of modern governments endorse competition as a way of rousing the citizens to greater efforts in their own cause, which contributes to the common good. The distribution of goods still remains the central concern of government.

COMMENTARY ON *RESPUBLICA LACEDAEMONIORUM*

Politeia (Latin *Respublica*) may not be the original title (*Lac.* uses it only once, and in reference to the constitutions of other *poleis*: 15.1), but *Cyr.* 1.2.15 sums up the laws of the Persians as their *politeia*, making this an obvious title for a description of the laws of a *polis*.

1.1–2 Introduction

The writer explains the reflection that led him to praise the laws of Lycurgus (just as in *Cyropaedia* he explains how he came to praise Cyrus the Great). This reflection is subsequently shown in his use of rhetorical arguments (for instance, the argument from probability) in passages of special importance, such as how Lycurgus secured obedience (8.1–3), and why he imposed such severe penalties for not pursuing virtue (10.6). It persuades the reader of the authority behind his praise.

1.1 Ἀλλ' 'inceptive' can be assentient, adversative or just introduce a new topic (*GP* 20–1); here it may object to, or substantiate, an imagined preceding premise that a *polis* requires a large population for success. τῶν ὀλιγανθρωποτάτων πόλεων οὖσα 'although being among the states with lowest populations'; this means the free citizen population, not the more numerous slaves and *perioikoi*. The view that the Spartans were successful in spite of their small population runs counter to Aristotle *Pol.* 1270a 33–4, who says their ὀλιγανθρωπία partly caused them to lose their success. We cannot know the size of the population in earlier times, but Herodotus says that Lycurgus' reforms made improvements in a flourishing population (1.66.1) and that Sparta had 8,000 hoplites in the Persian Wars (7.234.2, and 5,000 'youth': 9.10.1, 9.12.2). Xenophon is likely to be exaggerating in order to make Lycurgus' achievement the more admirable, but could also be (a) taking the low population of his own times as indicative of earlier times (the 700 at Leuctra represent two-thirds of the total force in seven age groups: *Hell.* 6.4.15, with 6.1.1 and 6.4.17) or (b) in view of the comparisons he regularly makes with other *poleis*, judging Sparta relative to other *poleis* such as Athens, which had a large population even in earliest times (Thuc. 1.2.6). A large population was normally considered necessary for success (*Oec.* 4.8 for farming, *Poroi* 4.49–50 for the silver mines, *Hell.* 5.2.16; Thuc. 1.11.1), but the quality of the citizens was of equal importance, and this is the focus of Xenophon's argument in *Lac.* This is also why Hiero complains that his elimination of citizens leaves him with fewer and worse ones to use (*Hiero* 2.17–18, 5.1–2, 6.14–16), and why Socrates chastises Critias and Charicles for making the citizens fewer and worse by massacring the good (*Mem.* 1.2.32). Quality could indeed outweigh quantity. Hdt. 7.102.2–3,104.3–5 and Isocrates, *Archid.* 6.81 share the view that the Spartans relied on the quality of their citizens for success rather than their numbers. Plato, *Rep.* 423a agrees that quality is more important. There were disadvantages in large populations.

Critias says that the Athenian *demos* was hostile to good order because it was very numerous and most used to freedom (*Hell.* 2.3.24). Aristotle, *Pol.* 1326a8–1326b25 agrees that too large a population could not achieve *eunomia* even though a small population might not have the numbers to flourish. ἐφάνη 'emerged'; Xenophon dates this emergence to the time of the Heraclids in order to make a rhetorical point (10.8); a modern historian would date it after the successes over Arcadia and Argos in the mid-sixth century, as Herodotus does: 1.65–8. ἐθαύμασα: *Mem.* 1.1.1 also begins ἐθαύμασα τίσι ποτὲ λόγοις; 'wonder' is the philosophic impulse for inquiry; here the initial wonder at the success of the small *polis* is replaced by the greater wonder at Lycurgus as the instrument of success. μέντοι: in 1.1 and 1.2 this is adversative and progressive. τὰ ἐπιτηδεύματα τῶν Σπαρτιατῶν: the focus of the entire work. 'Spartiate' is one term for a Spartan citizen (5.2, 9), but *Lac.* prefers Λακεδαιμόνιοι: 11.2, 11.8, 12.7, 13.5,8, 14.2, 15.9; these can include non-citizens in other contexts, but not in *Lac.*, which is concerned only with full citizens. *Lac.* uses Σπάρτη for the place (1.1, 1.10, 5.5, 7.1, 8.1–2, 8.5, 10.4) and Λακεδαίμων (9.4, 14.6), with Λακωνική (2.14, 11.5).

1.2 τὸν θέντα αὐτοῖς τοὺς νόμους: see pp. 44–5 on Lycurgus. *Lac.* uses a variety of words for 'making' the laws, with a variety of constructions, expressing law as a command, praise, contrivance or a bestowal of privilege: ἔταξε (1.4), ἔθηκε (1.5), ἐποίησεν (1.7), ἔδωκε (2.2), ἐνόμιζεν (2.4), ἐπήινει (2.13), ἐμηχανήσατο (3.2), ἐνομοθέτησεν (5.1), ἐπέταξε (5.8); in some cases the law is the agent of impersonal passives (12.5: προαγορεύεται ὑπὸ τοῦ νόμου). οἷς πειθόμενοι ηὐδαιμόνησαν 'in obedience to which they achieved success'; the pairing of obedience and success is characteristic of Xenophon's political thought: pp. 7–8. εἰς τὰ ἔσχατα σοφόν 'supremely wise'; the main manuscripts have μάλα σοφόν but this is not found in the *deteriores*; Strauss (1939) 512 n. 4 gives this an ironic twist: 'very wise with regard to the extremes', but εἰς τὰ ἔσχατα = 'supremely' is standard in Xenophon's vocabulary: *Hell.* 5.4.33. οὐ μιμησάμενος τὰς ἄλλας πόλεις ἀλλὰ καὶ ἐναντία γνοὺς ταῖς πλείσταις sc. πόλεσι: see p. 11 for the claim to originality as a *topos* of constitutional literature. ἐπέδειξεν 'displayed' as a model to other Greeks; Pericles also made Athens a παράδειγμα (Thuc. 2.37.1).

1.3–4 The education of girls for child-bearing

Xenophon praises the ἐπιτηδεύματα of girls of free birth as eugenic (*Lac.* 1.6: εὐγονία) i.e. designed to enable them to produce infants of the best quality who would serve the *polis* as future mothers or soldiers. Plutarch adopts the same interpretation of Spartan legislation for women (*Lyc.* 14.3, 14.8) and confirms the importance of the physical excellence of women and their infants in his story of how the ephors warned Agesilaus' father against marrying a small wife on the grounds that she would produce only 'kinglets' (*Ages.* 2.6). Xenophon takes it for granted that Lycurgus also made men healthy and strong for their part in procreation (2.1–5, 5.8–9). Selective breeding for best results was a feature of animal husbandry from an early period (see Varro, *De*

Re Rustica, and Columella, *De Re Rustica*). Theognis 183–92, West, *IEG*, extends this to humans in his comment about the 'confusion of the race' through the mating of noble lineage with mere wealth. Stobaeus 4.29c.53 comments: 'It seemed good to (Theognis) to use other animals as a parallel, such as are not randomly bred but cultivated with skill (τέχνης) so that they become best-born (γενναιότατα)'. Medical science had an interest in human procreation from the fifth century BC [Hippocrates] wrote on human reproduction (*Nature of the Child*), Plato *Laws* 775b–d on the perils of drink to the quality of the embryo, and Aristotle gave his own account of good breeding practice (*Pol.* 1334b29–1336a2), recommending that parents-to-be study 'the writings of physicians and natural philosophers about generation' (1335a39–1335b2). His main eugenic point is that procreation by those too young or old will produce 'imperfect' and 'weak' issue. Foucault (1986) 125 captures the thinking: 'An entirely traditional theme said that noble offspring – *euteknia* – could not be engendered unless one took a certain number of precautions. The disorders of conception would be reflected in one's progeny. Not only because the descendants would resemble their parents, but because they would bear the characteristics of the act that brought them into existence': The sexual act itself required: 'a prudent and calm behaviour, one that avoids all the disturbances, all the intoxications that might be reflected in the embryo, since the latter would be a kind of mirror and witness of these excesses': Foucault (1986) 127.

See Pomeroy (2002) for a full account of Spartan women's lives. Aristophanes makes Lampito a marvellous muscular product of their system: *Lysistrata* 77–84.

1.3 Lycurgus legislates for a good diet and rigorous exercise for those destined to be mothers, to make them strong and healthy and pass on such characteristics to their children. Presumably the arrangements were supervised in a communal system by the female equivalent of the *paidonomos* for boys (2.2); cf. the *gynaikonomos* in inscriptions of the second century AD from other *poleis*: Wehrli (1962) 33–8. [Hippocrates] *Regimen* 1.2.18–23 confirms the importance of diet and exercise for general health and how different foods and exercises produce different physiologies (1.2.39–56, 61–5). A poor diet and lack of exercise for such girls in other *poleis* is confirmed in *Oeconomicus*, where Ischomachus' Athenian wife, not yet fifteen, had learned only the sedentary task of making wool and controlling her appetite (*Oec.* 7.6). Ischomachus leans toward Spartan arrangements, however, when he encourages his wife not to remain seated like a slave at her loom (μὴ δουλικῶς ἀεὶ καθῆσθαι – since sedentary crafts also ruin men's bodies: *Oec.* 4.2–3) but to stand and direct her slaves like a ruler and 'take exercise' by a 'walk' around the house: περίπατος (*Oec.* 10.10–13; an exercise for Spartan men at *Lac.* 12.5–6). He also suggests that the γυμνάσιον of kneading bread and shaking out heavy cloth will improve her appetite. Plato, *Laws* 789e and Aristotle *Politics* 1335b12–19 recommend that even pregnant women take exercise for eugenic ends. Plato, *Laws* 804d–806c describes the Spartan woman's regime as mid-way between the indoor life of weaving and house-keeping and the martial life of the Sauromatides.

Αὐτίκα γὰρ . . . ἵνα ἐξ ἀρχῆς ἄρξωμαι: the production of excellent children was the standard beginning for idealized legislation: Aristotle, *Pol.* 1334b29–1336a2; and

Critias, DK, fr. 32. Critias also emphasizes the importance of diet and exercise for expectant parents: 'I shall begin with the birth of a person, how he should be excellent in body and very strong: if the father exercises and eats heartily and works his body and the mother of the child-to-be strengthens her body and takes exercise.' Stobaeus 4.29c.53 comments on Theognis' poem about good breeding (183–92, West, *IEG*): 'the beginning is correct; for he begins with good breeding' ἀπὸ τοῦ εὖ γενέσθαι. τὰς μελλούσας τίκτειν καὶ καλῶς δοκούσας κόρας παιδεύεσθαι 'those destined to be mothers and who *seem to be* well brought up girls' stresses the illusory appearance of their excellence. 2.1 offers the male parallel in 'those who *claim* that they educate their sons best' (οἱ φάσκοντες κάλλιστα τοὺς υἱεῖς παιδεύειν). Cf. for the position of κόρας: τὰ . . . δοκοῦντα πολλοῦ ἄξια κτήματα εἶναι (*Hiero* 2.4). καὶ σίτωι . . . καὶ ὄψωι: the customary dietary partners 'bread, and food to go with the bread (either protein or vegetable)' (*Mem.* 3.14). The balanced phrases emphasize the meagreness of both. ἧι ἀνυστόν/ἧι δυνατόν means 'as little as possible', like ὡς with the superlative. γε μήν introduces the new topic; having no wine or only watered wine kept them sober, but the main point is that the girls had fewer of the other benefits of wine. ὑδαρεῖ: regularly used in scientific contexts. διάγουσιν: related to the later use of the *agoge* for the Spartan education system: Kennell (1995) 113–16. ἠρεμιζούσας ἐριουργεῖν 'to make woollen cloth while sitting still'. This was the traditional occupation of women in Homer, and remained so for Ischomachus' wife (*Oec.* 7–10), and those who made profit from their wool-work in *Mem.* 2.7.7–10; cf. Pomeroy (2002) 30–2. However, 'sitting' applies more to spinning than to weaving, since weaving involved movement: Homer, *Od.* 5.62, 10.222, 10.226. *Oec.* 10.10 indeed contrasts 'sitting like a slave' with 'standing at the loom like a mistress' and *Oec.* 7.6 indicates that spinning is for slaves even in Athens. Evidence for the decline of weaving in Sparta after 580 BC may reflect Lycurgus' reforms: Hodkinson (2000) ch. 9. μεγαλεῖον . . . τι: the size of the infant was thought to indicate the quality of the future adult; see Plutarch's story of the mother of 'kinglets' above, as well as, for example, the large size of the baby Cyrus, which proved so attractive to his foster parents (Hdt. 1.112.1 μέγα τε καὶ εὐειδὲς ἐόν).

1.4 καὶ δούλας: the measure of freedom was its difference from slavery; δοῦλος marks the contrast between the free and the unfree here, and at 2.2; οἰκέτης is an alternative in contexts where the focus is rather on the slave as belonging to a particular household: 6.3, 7.5. Xenophon does not use the term 'helot', which was the characteristic Spartan 'serf'. MacDowell (1986) 37–9 thinks there were slaves other than helots; cf. Pomeroy (2002) 100. Fisher (1993) 6–7, 22–32 discusses terminology for the Laconian underclasses. μέγιστον νομίσας εἶναι τὴν τεκνοποιίαν: not a popular modern view of the major work of free women, but one in keeping with woman's very special contribution to the 'increase of the *polis*' through providing future men and women: p. 5. πρῶτον μὲν σωμασκεῖν ἔταξεν . . . ἔπειτα δὲ δρόμου καὶ ἰσχύος . . . ἀγῶνας . . . ἐποίησε: girls pursue the habits of boys in order to produce parents who are both strong; cf. *Lac.* 3.4–5 for more gender blurring, where boys develop the modesty appropriate to girls. The passage differentiates exercises that strengthened the body from the proving of this strength in running and trials of strength such as wrestling and throwing. Foot races for women are attested elsewhere: Calame (1977), Arrigoni in Arrigoni (1985) 95–104; but trials of strength are peculiar to the Spartans. *Laws* 833c–834a recommends foot races for girls and fighting in armour. ἐξ ἀμφοτέρων ἰσχυρῶν 'from (parents who were) both strong'.

1.5–10 Marriage customs

Lycurgus limited intercourse between newly married couples for eugenic purposes, and ensured that parents represented the best breeding stock. To this end he permitted marriages in which the older husband allows a man in his prime to have children by his younger wife, and the husband with existing children allows the bachelor unwilling to live with a wife, but wanting good-quality children of his own, to use for this purpose a wife who has already proven her breeding ability as one εὔτεκνον καὶ γενναίαν. Xenophon's eugenic interpretation of these measures is overlaid in modern scholarship with economic and demographic interpretations (cf. e.g. Hodkinson (2000)), but see Gray in Millender (ed.) forthcoming.

There is a debate also about the effects for women. See: Cartledge (2001) 106–26, Kunstler (1983) 423–95, Pomeroy (2002) 33–49.

Xenophon may omit arrangements for women mentioned in later sources because he has a greater focus on eugenics or because they were not current in his time or are a product of those later sources: (1) bridal 'capture' (Plutarch, *Lyc.* 15.5) has nothing to do with eugenics and contradicts *Lac.*'s more normal description of marriage as 'when a woman went to a man' (1.5); (2) exposure of defective infants at birth (Plut. *Lyc.* 16.1–2) was unnecessary if Lycurgus prevented the conception of such infants in the first place; (3) penalties on bachelors for not breeding lacked a eugenic focus (Plut. *Lyc.*15.1–3) and could lead to the breeding of children of poor quality from the wrong kind of parents; and (4) 'the law about child-making', which honoured men who had many children (Aristotle *Pol.*1270a40), again did not secure a necessarily eugenic outcome.

1.5 Lycurgus restricts the sexual activity of newly married couples. This is a recognizable eugenic measure. The physician Andreas (3rd century BC) explains in his 'Preparation for conception' (*CMR Lib. Incert.* 23.2) that abstinence allows the sperm to reach maturity, whereas frequent intercourse produces immature sperm: 'let (the parents) live an orderly life then (εὐτακτείτωσαν δή) even in the days immediately preceding conception, in order that the sperm created be ready and mature (ὅπως ἱκανόν τε καὶ πεπεμμένον ὑπάρχηι τὸ συνηγμένον σπέρμα) . . . for those who have frequent unions produce raw and unripe sperm (οἱ γὰρ συνεχῶς πλησιάζοντες ὠμὰ καὶ ἄωρα τρυγῶσι τὰ σπέρματα)'. Such abstinence also produced better issue in the animal world. Columella (*De Re Rustica* 6.37.2) indicates that a stallion must be excited before being put to the mare 'so that the seed by some invisible force be fashioned of more active elements'. The human 'longing' that Lycurgus takes to be the result of such abstinence would produce an equivalent excitement. ἐπεί γε μὴν γυνὴ πρὸς ἄνδρα ἔλθοι: the allusion to normal marriage rules out the interpretation of the arrangement as a 'trial marriage' in which the partners did not live together until they produced children: Cartledge (2001) 123. τὸν πρῶτον τοῦ χρόνου: see Hdt. 1.36.3, *Cyr.* 3.1.36 for the sexual indulgence of the νεόγαμος. The first part of marriage is the time up to the birth of the first child, when sexual desire might naturally diminish. Plut. *Lyc.* 15.3–9 indicates that this was the extreme limit of the period involved. *Cyr.* 1.2.4 indicates that the newly married Persian ephebe could spend nights with his wife, but not too often. αἰδεῖσθαι μὲν εἰσιόντα ὀφθῆναι, αἰδεῖσθαι δ' ἐξιόντα: whether this applies to the house or the bedroom, the shame in being seen entering would restrict sexual activity at least to the night-time and possibly to only occasional visits. The *anaphora* emphasizes the αἰδώς that Lycurgus had developed in young men by the time of their marriage; this receives detailed treatment at 3.4, 5.5. See Richer in Hodkinson and Powell (1999) 91–115. ποθεινοτέρως μὲν ἀνάγκη σφῶν αὐτῶν ἔχειν 'they must be more desirous of each other'; the reflexive pronoun is occasionally used for the reciprocal: *GG* 996, as at *Hell.* 1.7.8 οἵ τε πατέρες καὶ οἱ συγγενεῖς σύνεισι σφίσιν αὐτοῖς. The courtesan Theodote uses abstinence to provoke a stronger desire for her own commercial services when she guards against satiating her customers (*Mem.* 3.11.14). ἐρρωμενέστερα sc. ἔκγονα.

1.6 Lycurgus legislates for a prime-time eugenic marriage age. ἀποπαύσας τοῦ ὁπότε βούλοιντο ἕκαστοι γυναῖκα ἄγεσθαι 'stopping them from taking a wife whenever individuals wanted' (just as he stopped newly-weds having sex whenever they wanted). ἐν ἀκμαῖς τῶν σωμάτων: Aristotle in his account of procreative measures (*Pol.* 1334b29–1336a2) notes the poor issue that comes of those too young or too old, because children take on their parents' immature or aged features. Aristotle says there that women should be married at 18 and men at 37, but *HA* 582a28–9 says that females are ready πρὸς τὰς τεκνοποιίας at 21. Plato, *Rep.* 460e suggests 20 for women, 30 for men (see also Plato, *Laws* 721b, 772d for an ideal age for men of between 25 and 35). On the marriage age of women in other *poleis*, note the fourteen-year-old bride of Ischomachus (*Oec.* 7.5, with Pomeroy (1975) 64). Hesiod *W&D* 695–8 told men to marry at 30 a woman who is four years from puberty.

1.7 In the first of two laws about wife-sharing for eugenic purposes (cf. 1.8), Lycurgus requires that an older husband get children for his younger wife-sharing by importing a younger man of better quality. εἰ γε μέντοι συμβαίη γεραιῷ νέαν ἔχειν 'if ever it *did* happen to an old man to have a young wife'. Enforcement of the marriage age should have prevented this; but it could have arisen from the marriage of the Spartan equivalent of the Athenian *epikleros* to an older relative: the *patrouchos* who held her father's wealth, and whose future was important enough to be determined by the kings: Hdt. 6.57.4; Pomeroy (2002) 84–6. The older man is not good for breeding because of his age; cf. *Mem.* 4.4.22–3, which has the older man 'make children badly' with his younger daughter in the law against intergenerational incest. φυλάττοντας 'guarding' young wives was normal even for younger husbands up to the birth of the first child (Lysias, *On the Killing of Eratosthenes* 1.6), but the elder had more reason, since though not necessarily incapable of sexual function, he may have been unattractive to his younger wife or not have been able to give the child she wanted. Herodotus

6.68–9 tells the story about the Spartan King who, though perfectly capable of sex, as the story shows, was said to have had no 'child-making seed'; the rumour spread that his wife had resorted to a slave in order to get the child she wanted. ἐποίησεν 'made a law'; cf. καὶ τοῦτο νόμιμον ἐποίησεν below (1.8). ὁποίου ἀνδρὸς σῶμά τε καὶ ψυχὴν ἀγασθείη 'the man of the kind whose body and spirit he admired'; for the shape of the relative clause: χαριζόμενον οἵωι σοὶ ἀνδρί (*Mem.* 2.9.3). τοῦτον: the demonstrative in apposition emphasizes the quality of the imported male. The older man's desire for children of excellence makes him look for qualities in the imported male which he will pass on to the child. The arrangement perhaps exploited the woman, but, as well as controlling two households (below), she might prefer a youthful partner of physical and moral excellence to her older husband; cf. *Hiero* 8.6; *Oec.* 10.1–8.

1.8 εἰ δέ τις αὖ γυναικὶ μὲν συνοικεῖν μὴ βούλοιτο, τέκνων δὲ ἀξιολόγων ἐπιθυμοίη: the bachelor's positive 'desire for *worthy* children' indicates that he is not just meeting the cold requirements of the law, but wanting to make a eugenic contribution; cf. Cartledge (2001) 124f. who sees this as a reference to the penalty for not producing children: Plut. *Lyc.* 15.1–3. ἥντινα ἂν εὔτεκνον καὶ γενναίαν ὁρώιη 'whatever woman he might see as a good breeder and of good productivity'. εὔτεκνος (cf. ὑδαρής 1.3) is another rare word dictated by the semi-scientific content. *Cyr.* 8.3.38 links the word with the generous production of the earth. See the note on *Hiero* 7.12 for the potential optative in a relative clause. τὸν ἔχοντα: the one who had charge of her (her husband, her *kurios*)'.

1.9 καὶ πολλὰ μὲν τοιαῦτα συνεχώρει 'and there were many such agreements'; this seems to refer only to the arrangements for bachelors, since the benefit that came to the woman of controlling two estates limits it to bachelors; cf. Cartledge (2001) 124. αἵ τε γὰρ γυναῖκες . . . οἵ τε ἄνδρες: the mutual benefits of both wives and husbands in these unusual relationships are spelled out in the present tense. κατέχειν 'to control'; the role of the wife even in an Athenian household was managerial (*Oec.* 7–10). ἀδελφοὺς τοῖς παισί: the 'increase' of the clan through providing brothers for existing children is an obvious source of happiness. *Mem.* 2.3.4, *Cyr.* 8.7.14–17 describe the benefits of brothers. τῶν δὲ χρημάτων οὐκ ἀντιποιοῦνται: the boys inherit from their biological fathers, so that there is no undue splitting of the inheritance. The avoidance of such division is sometimes said to be the entire aim of the arrangement, but *Lac.* presents it only as a motive that made the arrangement acceptable.

1.10 μὲν δή sums up the previous thought and moves on, as at 2.14, 13.10. ὁ βουλόμενος ἐπισκοπείτω 'let anyone who wishes investigate', a device for closure of a section; cf. 2.14. The proof is the Spartan record of success.

2–4 *The education of young males*

Lycurgus divides the young males into three age-groups: παῖδες, παιδίσκοι and ἡβῶντες and legislates separately for each group because they had different characteristics that needed different kinds of supervision. MacDowell (1986) 159–67 discusses the ages in question. Lycurgus produced warrior qualities: endurance, obedience, reverence and resourcefulness in boys, self-control in striplings and love of victory in ephebes. There is a similar organization and focus in the training of Athenian ephebes (aged 18–20) in Aristotle *Ath. Pol.* 42, and of the 'boys and young men' up to the age of thirty in the Law of the Gymnasiarch from Beroia in Macedonia: Gauthier and Hatzopoulos (1993). The *sophronistes* of the ephebes at Athens was for example responsible for the supervision of the food consumed in their common messes, and the expenditure on it (Arist. *Ath. Pol.* 42.3): ἀγοράζει τὰ ἐπιτήδεια πᾶσιν εἰς τὸ κοινόν (συσσιτοῦσι γὰρ κατὰ φυλάς). See Cartledge (2001) 79–90 and 91–105 on Spartan education.

2 The education of the first age group (παῖδες)

Other Greeks leave the supervision of their boys in the hands of slaves as soon as they understand what is being said to them, but this makes them slavish in their habits (Plato, *Prot.* 325c–d confirms the supervision by slaves and parents). Lycurgus had them supervised instead by a *paidonomos*, a free Spartan adult of high status, who taught them the ways of free people. Lycurgus dictated what they should wear, what they should eat and drink, and how they should behave. They learned to endure deprivation and physical pain and to obey those in charge of them. On the positive side, he encouraged friendships in which the men could improve the boys through their association with them.

2.1 ἑκατέρων: each of the *poleis*, Sparta and the others. τοίνυν: the particle announces the next stage in an argument, often developing a topic already mentioned: cf. *Hiero* 1.7; *Lac.* 2.12; 4.3; 5.2; 9.3; 11.2. ἐπειδὰν τάχιστα . . . εὐθὺς μὲν . . . εὐθὺς δέ: *anaphora* stresses the speed with which boys' supervision is transferred to slave attendants in other *poleis* and to low-ranking teachers. αὐτοῖς: dative of advantage or interest, to be translated as a possessive: 'their boys' (Smyth *GG* 1481); cf. *Hiero* 4.5. εἰς διδασκάλων sc. οἴκους. καὶ γράμματα καὶ μουσικὴν καὶ τὰ ἐν παλαίστραι: reading and writing, the performing arts and the activities of the wrestling-ground reflect the traditional divisions of Attic education: Beck (1964) 80–1. Spartan education in contrast emphasized the virtues of physical education that produced military success. Lycurgus' focus on these qualities means that he does not pursue others, but Plut. *Lyc.* 19–21 mentions their speech-making, music and poetry. Physical education was a focus of the Athenian *palaistra*, but the exercises were not as demanding as at Sparta: Beck (1964) 134. ἱματίων μεταβολαῖς 'changes of cloaks' to suit different seasons, rather than having just one for all seasons. The lack of need for clothing helps explain the lower status of weaving at 1.4.

2.2 ἀντὶ μὲν τοῦ ἰδίαι ἕκαστον παιδαγωγοὺς δούλους ἐφιστάναι, ἄνδρα ἐπέστησε κρατεῖν αὐτῶν: this contrasts (a) the public control of the boys' education with the private control in other *poleis* and (b) the control by a free man of high status rather than the supervision of a slave. In recapitulating 2.1 ἐπ' αὐτοῖς παιδαγωγοὺς θεράποντας ἐφιστᾶσιν it replaces 'servants' with 'slaves' to emphasize that the rejected education is slavish, and replaces 'supervision' with more forceful 'control'. ἐξ ὧνπερ αἱ μέγισται ἀρχαὶ καθίστανται: this makes the quality of the control very high indeed; cf. 4.7. Isocrates uses the same term of the highest Spartan offices (*Panath.* 12.212). παιδονόμος: the name of the important office, that of the 'supervisor of the boys' laws', the equivalent for the boys of the Athenian *sophronistes*, who supervised the Athenian ephebes (Arist. *Ath. Pol.* 42.2). καὶ ἀθροίζειν τοὺς παῖδας καὶ ἐπισκοποῦντα, εἴ τις ῥαιδιουργοίη, ἰσχυρῶς κολάζειν: the *choregos* and others had these same powers over members of choruses in Athens (*Hiero* 9.4). ῥαιδιουργεῖν is common in Xenophon (Richards [1897] 134–5). μαστιγοφόρους: the whip is the final symbol of the complete power of the *paidonomos* over the boys; the gymnasiarch too in the decree from Beroia carries the whip (Gauthier and Hatzopoulos (1993) B 8–10 in the decree, pp. 65–8 in the commentary), as do those who drive away Lichas from the Olympic Games (*Hell.* 3.2.21). πολλὴν μὲν . . . πολλὴν δὲ: *anaphora* highlights the abundance of an important pair of qualities in the education of the young boys.

2.3 ἀντί γε μὴν τοῦ ἀπαλύνειν τοὺς πόδας ὑποδήμασιν ἔταξεν ἀνυποδησίαι κρατύνειν: *chiasmus* ('softening' v. 'hardening' and 'shoes' v. 'shoelessness') strengthens the contrast with others. The boys were peculiarly deprived if, as Critias says, Spartan adults wore shoes (Critias DK fr. 34). ἀνυπόδητον . . . ὑποδεδεμένον: Stobaeus omits, but Xenophon does repeat key ideas when he wants to recapitulate a long sentence, particularly when he uses καὶ . . . δέ as here (*GP* 202). Compare 2.5 καὶ ὑγιεινοτέρως δ' ἂν διάγειν, and 2.7 καὶ κατασκόπους δὲ ἐτοιμάζειν τὸν μέλλοντά τι λήψεσθαι which repeats the earlier τὸν μέλλοντα κλωπεύειν.

2.4 ἐνόμιζεν: 'laid it down as a *nomos*'. δι' ἔτους 'through (all seasons of) the year'.

2.5 συμβολεύειν: *Symp.* 1.16 has Philippus pun on συμβολαί as 'encounters' as well as 'dinner contributions'. τὸν εἴρενα is a Laconian variant of the word for 'male' ἄρσην/ἄρρην: *Lac.* 1.4, 2.11. He may be the young boy himself, but 2.11 uses *eiren* for an older boy, as does Plut. *Lyc.* 17.2. ὡς introduces a clause of result in which the result is also aimed at as a purpose (*M&T* 587.3 and 608; see the note on *Hiero* 10.1). τοῦ δὲ ἐνδεεστέρως διάγειν μὴ ἀπείρως ἔχειν 'not to be inexperienced in living in need'. The model for these arrangements for the boys is the men's *syssition* (*Lac.* 5.1–7), where, for the adults also, καὶ σῖτόν γε ἔταξεν αὐτοῖς ὡς μήτε ὑπερπληροῦσθαι μήτε ἐνδεεῖς γίγνεσθαι. μᾶλλον μὲν ἂν . . . μᾶλλον δ' ἂν . . . ἧττον δ' ἂν . . . δὲ . . . καὶ . . . δ' ἂν: a list of the military benefits of practising starvation. τὴν αὐξάνεσθαι ῥαδινὰ τὰ σώματα ποιοῦσαν τροφήν 'the food that made bodies grow up slender'; cf. τὴν διαπλατύνουσαν τῶι σίτωι 'the (food) that filled them out sideways with its feeding'. τῶι σίτωι seems to be pleonastic for τροφή; cf. the recapitulating ἐπ' αὐτοῖς at *Hiero* 1.5. Xenophon's theory distinguishes food and exercise that create height from those that create bulk; Plut. *Lyc.*17.6–7 expresses the same sentiment. [Hippocrates] is already discussing how different foods and exercises develop different physiologies (*Regimen* 29–57; 61–5). The first five books of *CMR* 1 are about the properties of different foods (e.g. 3.1–4 on foods that fatten and foods that thin). ῥαδινά is found in poetry rather than prose; the semi-scientific content here suggests that it is also used in technical literature; cf. ὑδαρεῖ, 1.3.

2.6–9 Lycurgus permitted the boys to alleviate the hunger that came of his dietary laws by allowing them to steal food, which trained them to find provisions in war, and he beat those who were caught for stealing badly. Xenophon engages his readers in the first person in his praise of this custom because it was controversial; Isocrates still finds the theft to be uniquely unjust (*Panath.* 12.211–14). However, the aim was to secure food and provisions that were of vital importance in warfare, as the paradigm of Agamemnon shows (*Mem.* 3.2). *An.* 4.6.14–16 has Xenophon cite this custom as qualification for 'stealing' a position on a mountain slope, and hoping that they will not be caught for fear of the beating prescribed in law. Lycurgus' restriction of the theft to only 'some items' ἔστιν ἅ, is expressed at *An.* 4.6.14 as ὅσα μὴ κωλύει νόμος, 'what the law does not prevent'. This may refer to the property of friends. *Cyr.* 1.6.31–4 says that the Persians taught their boys to steal from enemies, but restricted this to older youths when boys used their skills against friends. The 'teacher' who instructed them to steal and not to steal, depending on whether their targets were friends or enemies, is a Socratic figure. Xenophon's Socrates also teaches Euthydemus that it is right and wrong to steal, depending on the target (*Mem.* 4.2.14–19).

2.6 ὡς: regularly used by Xenophon to introduce purpose clauses (*M&T* Appendix IV); compare 2.11. οὐκ ἔδωκε λαμβάνειν . . . κλέπτειν δ᾽ ἐφῆκεν: *chiasmus* reinforces the careful contrast; that he did not *give them permission* to *take* whatever they wanted without effort but *laid the responsibility* on them *to steal* some things to assist their hunger'.

2.7 αὐτοῖς γε: the emphasis falls on the boys' own resourcefulness. καὶ . . . δὲ: see the note on 2.3. οὐδένα οἶμαι τοῦτο ἀγνοεῖν: the assumption of universal knowledge rhetorically counters any idea in the audience that Lycurgus did not have the resources to feed the boys, because it would make his government entirely unsuccessful. ταῦτα . . . πάντα are objects of ἐπαίδευσεν. μηχανικωτέρους τῶν ἐπιτηδείων 'more resourceful in (acquiring) provisions'; objective genitive (*GG* 1139–40).

2.8 εἴποι δ᾽ ἂν οὖν τις: the previous section defends Lycurgus' motives for endorsing theft; this section has the reader object to the very idea that he endorsed it by questioning his punishment of those who were caught. δ᾽ . . . οὖν is here the equivalent of ἀλλά: *GP* 460. τί δῆτα is common in dialogue, here between author and audience: 'Why then indeed . . . ?' φημὶ ἐγώ: the author answers the challenge in the first person. τἄλλα may be an accusative of specification 'with respect to other matters' (*GG* 1058), or the object of ὑπηρετοῦντα.

2.9 ἁρπάσαι τυροὺς . . . καλὸν θείς sc. Lycurgus. The reference to the beating of boys who steal cheeses from the altar of Artemis Orthia in the ritual in her sanctuary near the Eurotas River again meets the objection at 2.8; it is another case of beating boys who fail to steal effectively because those boys who are slowest in seizing the cheeses get the biggest beating. Suspicion of the text is aroused because there is no mention of cheese-rituals in later sources: Kennell (1995) 78–82. In particular, the Spartan Megillus in Plato, *Laws* 633b–c says that Spartans developed courage 'in fist-fights against one another and in certain thefts accompanied in each case by many blows', but with no mention of cheese. ἁρπάσαι τυρούς may be corrupt then, but deletion of the passage (Marchant) would mean that the lesson about 'the need for speed' had to be drawn from the first kind of theft, yet that is described more in terms of stealth than speed, whereas speed is a feature of this second kind of theft since the boys had to run through the blows as quickly as possible ('bearing pain for a short time'). Plut. *Lyc*.18.2 says that 'we' had seen ephebes in his own time die as a result of such beatings. ἔστιν 'it is possible'.

2.10–11 The boys are never without the supervision of free citizens. When the *paidonomos* is not there, any other adult citizen has power over them, and in the absence of an adult, one of the older boys. The constant presence of adults engenders αἰδώς both here and at 5.5.

2.10 ἔρημοι . . . ἄρχοντος: repeated at 2.11, and in ring-composition, since it is the key idea. τὸν ἀεὶ παρόντα τῶν πολιτῶν 'whoever of the citizens was present at any time'; the Law of the Gymnasiarch required 'those present' to assist the gymnasiarch if he was insulted or attacked (Gauthier and Hatzopoulos (1993) B 39–45 and pp. 94–5). ὅ τι ἂν ἀγαθὸν δοκοίη: see note on *Hiero* 7.12.

2.11 μηδ' ὡς (οὕτως) sums up the preceding conditional clause 'not even in this circumstance'. τῆς ἴλης ἑκάστης 'in each company': Kennell (1995) 107–8 indicates that little is known about this 'company'. *An*. 1.2.16 uses it for a cavalry brigade in the army of Cyrus.

2.12–14 describes the relationship of the *erastes* and *eromenos*, the homosexual partnership of man and boy. Xenophon distinguishes lust for the body from love of the moral and physical excellence of a boy, and sees the latter as a force for education in Sparta. There are examples of such relationships in his other works. *Hell*. 5.4.25–33 describes the partnership of Archidamus, the son of King Agesilaus, and Cleonymus, the son of Sphodrias, who is described as ἡλικίαν τε ἔχων τὴν ἄρτι ἐκ παίδων and κάλλιστός τε καὶ εὐδοκιμώτατος τῶν ἡλίκων; their partnership encourages moral excellence in Cleonymus, who died fighting bravely at Leuctra because of the kindness he had received from Archidamus. Agesilaus had his own favourite, but he stoutly resisted his kisses: *Ages*. 5.4–5. *Symposium* presents the Athenian partnership of Callias and Autolycus, which conforms to the Spartan ideal. The boy is athletic (1.2: victor in the *pankration*), modest, and has his father at his side, approving the relationship (3.12–13). Socrates encourages them to pursue a spiritual relationship to improve each other for future service to the *polis* (8.37–43). *Symp*. 8.32–5 refers to the idea that bands of lovers made the best soldiers (these bands could even be made up of boys: *An*. 7.4.7–10), but *Lac*. sees friendship between all citizens as a wider basis for military success. For views on the other purposes of such relationships (a natural activity, a bond between families like marriage, a power game, the passing on of power through anal penetration, a sexual release that does not produce children, a ritual abandonment of masculinity): Dover (1978) 185–96, Buffière (1980) 49–106, Cartledge (2001) 91–105. Ephorus, *FGH* 70 F. 149 = Strabo 10.4.21, describes a ritual from Crete: how with the approval of his family, the boy is taken to his lover's *andreion*, how the pair hunt in the countryside for two months, until the boy returns to his family, with gifts that suggest a rite of initiation into manhood: battledress, an ox to sacrifice and a cup. See further Hindley (1999) 74–99 on male relationships in Xenophon.

2.12 Λεκτέον: the verbal adjective (*GG* 1597) conveys a sense of obligation, which is purely rhetorical, in that it gives the impression of a wish to preserve a decent silence about anything to do with sex; cf. the reticence of Simonides at *Hiero* 1.4. ἔστι γάρ τι καὶ τοῦτο πρὸς παιδείαν 'this *also* has some bearing on education'. τοίνυν: see note on 2.1. ὥσπερ Βοιωτοὶ . . . ὥσπερ Ἠλεῖοι: Boeotians and Eleans are standard examples of different types of homosexual practices (*Symp.* 8.34, Plato, *Symp.*182a–b). The Boeotians have something like a marriage partnership. Eleans engage more in courtship, which involves favours freely given. τοῦ διαλέγεσθαι τοὺς ἐραστὰς εἴργουσιν ἀπὸ τῶν παίδων 'keep the lovers from the boys [and] from conversing with them'. The Platonic Socrates indicates that Athenians put boys with lovers in the charge of tutors and 'do not permit them to speak to their lovers' in order to test their lovers' motives (Plato, *Symp.* 183c–184e).

2.13 οἷον δεῖ: the elder partner is already 'as he should be' as a result of training (shorthand in Xenophon for 'perfect': *Cyr.* 1.6.7). ἄμεμπτον φίλον ἀποτελέσασθαι καὶ συνεῖναι 'to make him a friend without blame and keep his company' is the aim of non-sexual friendship: *Mem.* 1.2.7–8; 1.6.14. γονεῖς παίδων . . . ἀδελφοὶ ἀδελφῶν: Xenophon is thinking here of respect among family members as the deterrent rather than the poor breeding of partners of different ages (*Mem.* 4.4.20–3); both he and Plato, *Laws* 838a-d agree that incest is also against the unwritten law of the gods. εἰς ἀφροδίσια: 'in respect of sexual relations'; cf. *Hiero* 1.4.

2.14 τὸ μέντοι ταῦτα ἀπιστεῖσθαι ὑπό τινων: again addresses the imagined opposition to the argument. ὧν δεῖ ἐγκρατέστεροι 'having more control over what it is necessary (to control)'.

3 *The education of the* παιδίσκοι

The education of the 'striplings' focuses entirely on repressing the insolence that is characteristic of their age group (*Mem.* 1.2.5, Aristotle, *Rhet.* 1389a5–9). The other cities release them from controls at this age, but Lycurgus controlled even their body language. The Spartans had considerable awareness of body language, controlling also the appearance of the coward (9.5), and the young man going into battle (13.9). *Hell.* 6.4.16 confirms that those who had lost relatives at Leuctra strode about in public exhibiting positive body language: λιπαροὺς καὶ φαιδροὺς ἐν τῶι φανερῶι ἀναστρεφομένους, whereas those who had not remained unseen, and looked downcast when they did venture out in public: σκυθρωποὺς καὶ ταπεινοὺς περιόντας.

This is the first passage in which Xenophon's present-tense description of the effects of the laws for this age group may seem to contradict the abandonment of the laws in 14, on which see Appendix 3.

3.1 τὸ μειρακιοῦσθαι: another way of referring to the age of παιδίσκοι; cf. 3.5. παύουσι μέν . . . παύουσι δέ . . . ἄρχουσι δὲ οὐδένες . . . ἀλλ' αὐτονόμους ἀφιᾶσιν: *anaphora* and restatement with variation emphasize the progressive liberation of boys in other *poleis* from control to complete autonomy, representing sequential phases; cf. *Hiero* 1.35.

3.2 μέγιστον μὲν . . . μάλιστα δὲ . . . ἰσχυροτάτας δέ: the phases of adolescent insolence are set out: pride breeding inside them, insolence coming to the surface, desires for pleasures stepping out and standing alongside them; *anaphora* indicates the severity of the onset. **πλείστους μὲν πόνους . . . πλείστην δὲ ἀσχολίαν:** *anaphora* emphasizes also the intensity of the instruments of repression that counter the emerging insolence.

3.3 μηδενὸς ἔτι τῶν καλῶν τυγχάνειν 'to obtain no longer any of the fine things'. τὰ καλά come from meeting the requirements of the laws. See 2.9, 13; 4.4: where 'the fine things' include the honour of being one of the ἱππεῖς. In *Hell.* 5.4.32 Sphodrias completes τὰ καλά in all the age groups, and his son completes them too (5.4.33). Cf. *Hell.* 5.3.9 of non-citizens: μάλα εὐειδεῖς τε καὶ τῶν ἐν τῆι πόλει καλῶν οὐκ ἄπειροι. *Cyr.* 1.2.15 also uses the same term for the *cursus honorum* of the Persian age groups. **μὴ μόνον τοὺς ἐκ δημοσίου ἀλλὰ καὶ τοὺς κηδομένους ἑκάστων:** the magistrates who represent the community work with 'the relatives of each of the youths'; this counters the usual impression that in Sparta the state suppressed the family; rather, here, it harnesses them. **ἀποδειλιάσαντες** 'playing the coward' means shrinking from the hard work required by the laws; cf. ῥαιδιουργεῖν (2.2, 4.4).

3.4 καὶ ἐν ταῖς ὁδοῖς 'even in the streets' (let alone when they were under direct control in some toil or task); the boys proceed modestly along the streets to the adult messes, where they will learn still more modesty (5.1–7). Plato, *Charm.* 159b defines σωφροσύνη as ἡσυχιότης τις, which exactly describes the boys' decorum here: the stillness of their hands, voices, heads, eyes. See David in Hodkinson and Powell (eds.) (1999) 117–46. **ἐντὸς μὲν τοῦ ἱματίου τὼ χεῖρε ἔχειν . . . :** 'To keep *both* hands inside their cloaks' is what Aeschines 1.25 attributed to the older generation of Athenians public speakers, including Solon; Cleon in contrast threw back his cloak, thumping his thigh and running about while speaking (Plut. *Nicias* 8.6). *Hell.* 2.1.8 shows that the habit was a mark of deference in Persia, but also a way of preventing assault. The novelty is that the Spartans transfer the requirement even to youths at their most boisterous.

3.5 αἰδημονεστέρους δ' ἂν αὐτοὺς ἡγήσαιο καὶ αὐτῶν τῶν ἐν τοῖς ὀφθαλμοῖς παρθένων: the focused proof (γοῦν) of the statement that the boys are more modest than girls comes in the form of three comparisons. The first two comparisons (to stone and bronze statues) capture their previously mentioned stillness, silence, and downcast eyes; stone statues are silent and the eyes of bronze statues do not wander. The third makes them 'more modest than the very maidens in their eyes'. The manuscripts read 'more modest than the very maidens in their bridal chambers' καὶ αὐτῶν τῶν ἐν τοῖς θαλάμοις παρθένων, but Stobaeus and [Longinus] *On the Sublime* 4.4–6 read ὀφθαλμοῖς and took παρθένων as a synonym for κορῶν, which means pupils of the eye as well as maidens. This is preferred because it is the *lectio difficilior*, and because of the parallel that [Longinus] cites (loc. cit.) from Timaeus: ἐν ὀφθαλμοῖς κόρας, μὴ πόρνας ἔχων, 'if he did not have harlots rather than maidens in his eyes'. The image captures their habit of keeping their eyes downcast on the ground. Prodicus' 'Vice' in contrast has wide-open eyes and looks around for her admirers (*Mem.* 2.1.22). The boy παρθένιον βλέπων in Anacreon 15 (*PMG*) gives the comparison a poetic pedigree and a clear erotic quality. Longinus considered the image frigid, but the evident need for a climax in the series of images explains any impression of strain. Xenophon indeed then softens the impression with a comment on the complete loveliness of hearing the voices of the boys when they do speak, in answer to questions put to them in the *syssition*. Xenophon's special emphasis on the decorum of the youth can be seen in his use of the second person three times in the course of the comparisons (ἀκούσαις . . . στρέψαις . . . ἡγήσαιο), with *anaphora* of ἧττον. There is of course also something to be said for the reading of the main manuscripts. The parallel of the mime of the meeting of Dionysus and Ariadne in her bridal chamber (*Symp* 9.2–4) would support θαλάμοις, where the maiden's modesty is a central idea, and the girls' behaviour in the bedroom makes an effective comparison with the boys' behaviour in the public streets (3.4: ἐν ταῖς ὁδοῖς). εἰς τὸ φιλίτιον: a Spartan word for the *syssition*, used also at *Hell.* 5.4.28. Plut. *Lyc.* 12.1–2 discusses its variant *phidition* and how by changes and losses of various consonants it could be derived from 'friendship', 'parsimony' or even 'food'. καὶ τὸ ἐρωτηθέν 'even the question that has been asked'. *Hiero* 1.35 finds delight in the questions and answers from the beloved. *Symp.* 3.12–13 has the male company delighted because Autolycus responded when questioned (the only word he spoke at the entire banquet): ἡσθέντες ὅτι ἤκουσαν αὐτοῦ φωνήσαντος. μὲν αὖ sums up what has preceded in order to move on, from the *paidiskoi* to the ephebes.

4 The education of the ἡβῶντες

The characteristic of boys of this age is their aggression. The laws cannot repress this, but they use it to promote virtue by dividing the ephebes into two competing 'gangs' who compete for selection as *hippeis* by the officials called the *hippagretai*. Lycurgus thus taps their natural competitiveness. Their 'competition' is like the competition in virtue that the old men face for entry to the *Gerousia* (10.1–3).

4.1 οἵους δεῖ: see on 2.13. ἐπὶ τὸ ἀγαθὸν τῆι πόλει 'to (what is) good for the *polis*', the common good, the aim of government.

4.2 οἷς . . . τούτων . . . : the demonstrative in apposition (cf. *Hiero* 1.6) and the subsequent multisyllabic superlatives bring attention to the effects of the natural inner 'love of fighting'. εἰς ἔριν περὶ ἀρετῆς 'into a competition about excellence'. Hesiod *W&D* 11–26 defined two kinds of strife, good and bad; this strife is the good one since it aims at virtue. *Hiero* 9.4–11 recommends similar competitions based on φιλονικία. ἐπὶ πλεῖστον . . . ἀνδραγαθίας 'to the highest point of manhood'.

4.3 αἱροῦνται . . . αὐτῶν . . . ἐκ τῶν ἀκμαζόντων: *Hipp.* 2.2 describes a similar process in similar language: τούτων . . . δεκαδάρχους . . . καταστῆσαι ἐκ τῶν ἀκμαζόντων, identifying οἱ ἀκμάζοντες with those 'most ambitious' for honour. The ephors have a role to play in the supervision of the competitions even though the *paidonomos* remains in general charge: cf. 4.6. The present tense 'they choose' describes customs contemporary with the past introduction of the laws. ἱππαγρέται 'gatherers of the *hippeis*' conduct in effect a *dokimasia* of the ephebes in selecting their teams. The *hippeis* perform various state missions in other authors: Hdt. 1.67.5 on the role of those who graduate from the *hippeis* as 'benefactors'; Hdt. 8.124.3 on 'those who are called *hippeis*', the escort for Themistocles numbering 300; Thuc. 5.72.4 on 'the so-called 300 *hippeis*' who fight with the King; *Hell.* 3.3.9 has the ephors send them to arrest Cinadon.

4.4 τοῖς τε ἀποστείλασιν αὐτοὺς καὶ τοῖς αἱρεθεῖσιν ἀνθ' αὑτῶν: 'those who dismissed them and those who were chosen in their place' give two focuses for their hostility; see on 3.3 for 'the fine things' (τῶν καλῶν). παραφυλάττουσιν ἀλλήλους: the policing of each group by the other is an informal way in which lapses from the laws would come to the attention of the authorities. Plut. *Lyc.* 25.6 tells the story of Paidaretus however, who was delighted to have missed out on selection because the *polis* evidently had 300 youths who were better than he was.

4.5 ἡ θεοφιλεστάτη τε καὶ πολιτικωτάτη ἔρις 'most beloved to the gods' because it produces excellence and 'most political' because it benefits the political community in the highest degree. ἀποδέδεικται . . . ἃ δεῖ ποιεῖν τὸν ἀγαθόν the perfect tense implies a present condition: the *hippagretai* had made it clear in making their selection, so that it is clear 'what the good man must do'. χωρὶς δ' ἑκάτεροι 'each group separately' i.e. the *hippeis* and those who did not make the grade; this contrasts with καθ' ἕνα 'as one body'; for this latter meaning: *Hell.* 5.2.16, Hdt. 7.104.4.

4.6 καὶ εὐεξίας ἐπιμελεῖσθαι: the care of physical condition was one of the areas for which prizes were offered in the Law of the Gymnasiarch (Gauthier and Hatzopoulos (1993) B 46–7 on εὐεξία, εὐταξία and φιλοπονία; pp. 98–9, 102–5); but here no prize is needed since competition leads naturally to fist fights, for which such condition is essential. καὶ γὰρ πυκτεύουσι: for boxing contests as a special Spartan pursuit: Plato, *Prot.* 342b–e, where Socrates tells his audience that the Spartans are actually philosophers; their cauliflower ears and the thongs on their knuckles are just a front. Plato, *Gorgias* 515e describes cauliflower ears as typical of Spartan sympathizers in Athens. πᾶς ὁ παραγενόμενος κύριος 'every single man who is present has the authority' to separate the youths before they go too far; see the note on 2.10 for the authority of 'those present'. εἰς τὸ μήποτε ὀργὴν τοῦ μὴ πείθεσθαι τοῖς νόμοις κρατῆσαι: wishing to produce in them a disposition where 'anger never prevails over obeying the laws'; two articular infinitives: ὀργήν is the subject of τὸ κρατῆσαι, τοῦ μὴ πείθεσθαι is dependent on κρατῆσαι; verbs containing a negative idea can take the negative μή to strengthen the negation: *GG* 1615. Socrates' ideal friends limit their natural aggression in a more self-controlled way, but they are adults (*Mem.* 2.6.23).

4.7 Τοῖς . . . τὴν ἡβητικὴν ἡλικίαν πεπερακόσιν: the dative is in a loose connection with the rest of the sentence (of advantage?); the group is referred to again in the recapitulating genitive αὐτῶν, αὐτοῖς; cf. note on *Hiero* 1.5. Ephebes at Athens were aged 18 to 20, but the Law of the Gymnasiarch rules males up to 30 years of age

(Gauthier and Hatzopoulos (1993) A 24 and B 1, pp. 47, 56–7) and it is likely that Spartans were not fully adult until that age too (MacDowell (1986) 166–7). ἐξ ὧν ἤδη καὶ αἱ μέγισται ἀρχαὶ καθίστανται: cf. 2.2; public office was the expectation for this age group. τὸ θηρᾶν: Xenophon, *Cyn*. describes the athletic pursuit of hunting on foot and the qualities it produces in the practitioners. Plato, *Laws* 633b confirms that Lycurgus sponsored hunting. εἰ μή τι δημόσιον κωλύοι 'unless some public duty prevented them'; i.e. the conduct of the highest offices above; in Beroia, the Law of the Gymnasiarch excuses the *paidotribes* from attendance at the gymnasium 'if he is sick or some other necessity occurs' (B 17–18), but only a public duty has precedence over hunting for the Spartans.

5 The regime prescribed for adults

Lycurgus established public dining in *syssitia* for all adult citizens, so that their food and drink and behaviour continued to be subject to the same kind of public scrutiny as that of the boys and younger men (who indeed attended the *syssition* and learned from their elders). The customs of the *syssitia* are given in rapid succession. Plato, *Rep.* 548a acknowledges the danger when men retire into private houses and do what they like, unseen. Nafissi (1991) 173–226 traces the historical development of the *syssition*, which finds a private parallel in the men's *symposion* at Athens.

5.1 Ἃ μὲν οὖν . . . οἷαν δέ: the change from the younger age groups to the whole population. δίαιταν: the consumption of food and drink and sex: *Mem.* 1.3.5–8.

5.2 σκηνοῦντας lit. 'camping', but the word is used of various forms of accommodation and is not restricted to military life. πλεῖστα ῥαιδιουργεῖσθαι 'that there was a great deal of easy living', passive, in parallel with the subsequent παραβαίνεσθαι but elsewhere in the active voice (2.2, 4.4). εἰς τὸ φανερόν: his behaviour out of doors is also a major proof of Socrates' virtue: *Mem.* 1.1 *passim*.

5.3 καὶ σῖτόν γε ἔταξεν αὐτοῖς: cf. 2.5 for similar arrangements for the boys. Lycurgus made the law, but it is unclear who implemented it; perhaps the eldest, since 5.8 says that the lead in exercise be taken by 'the eldest in each exercise'. ὡς for ὥστε: see the note on 2.5, and see 5.8. παράλογα 'food that is extra to the basic rations'. ἄρτον: bread made from wheat, costlier to produce. ἔστιν ὅτε: the rich contribute bread only 'sometimes', whereas 'many' courses come from hunting, indicating that there was no reliance on the rich. Xenophon recognizes the existence of wealth among Spartans, as does Hdt. 7.134.2, but the equal life-style prevented them from flaunting it: cf. Thuc.1.6.4. *Mem.* 1.2.61 mentions Lichas' expenditures on entertaining visitors to Spartan festivals, but adds that it was to the glory of the entire *polis*, which presumably made it acceptable. ἔστ' ἂν διασκηνῶσιν: the idea that the table is never clear 'until such time as they separate off (to their own quarters)' indicates they had enough food, but there was no waste. The men slept at home, cf. 5.7, and *Hell.* 5.4.28.

5.4 καὶ μὴν moves on to a new topic, as at 5.7, 9.5 (*GP* 351–2). τοῦ πότου ἀποπαύσας τὰς ἀναγκαίας πόσεις 'removing from drinking the (habit of) compulsory drinking', such as is rejected also in Plato, *Symposium* 176; Critias, DK, fr. 6 confirms Spartan avoidance of the habit. σφάλλουσι μὲν σώματα, σφάλλουσι δὲ γνώμας: *anaphora* emphasizes the ruinous effects of such drinking. ὁπότε διψώη ἕκαστος 'whenever each man was thirsty'; this is also the Socratic rule about drinking: *Mem.* 1.3.5. πῶς ἄν τις ... ἢ αὐτὸν ἢ οἶκον διαφθείρειεν: the laws assume private households and private wealth. DK, Critias, fr. 6.14 also refers to οἰκοτριβὴς δαπάνη 'expense that wears down the estate' as the result of such drinking games.

5.5 καὶ γὰρ δή: the particle combination introduces a new point (the mixture of ages in the *syssitia*); cf. 5.6, 7.3. ὡς τὸ πολύ 'generally speaking'; this admits that the comments about other *poleis* are generalizations. οἱ ἥλικες ἀλλήλοις σύνεισι: this produces unruly behaviour because αἰδώς is shown only toward rulers and elders; cf. 2.10 and *Mem.* 3.5.15, not coaevals. ἀνέμειξε παιδεύεσθαι 'he mixed (the age groups) for the purpose of (the younger men) being taught . . .'; there need be no lacuna (cf. Schenkl, Richards) if the infinitive is one of purpose (*M&T* 770): *Hell.* 5.1.14: θύρα ἡ ἐμὴ ἀνέωικτο . . . εἰσιέναι 'my door is opened for the purpose of entering'.

5.6 ἐν τοῖς φιλιτίοις: the technical word for the *syssition* is used. ὅ τι ἂν καλῶς τις ... ποιήσηι: καλῶς in the early position in its clause emphasizes and anticipates the contrast of these 'noble' subjects with the disgraceful topics that follow heavy drinking. Agesilaus and Agesipolis in their συσκήνια (*Hell.* 5.3.20) also tell each other noble stories of ephebes and boys, and deeds of hunting and horses. ἥκιστα μὲν . . . ἥκιστα δὲ . . . ἥκιστα δέ: triple *anaphora* with an expanded final item emphasizes through negative representation the vices that Lycurgus' customs prevent; cf. *Hiero* 1.35. Critias, DK, fr. 6.9–10, 16–17 says that compulsory drinking 'looses tongues for shameful stories', whereas moderate drinking 'leads tongues to kindliness and moderate laughter', but Xenophon attributes the moderation to the αἰδώς shown to elders and to the encouragement of noble topics of discussion as well as avoidance of drink.

5.7 ἡ ἔξω σίτησις 'feeding outdoors', another way of referring to the public dining arrangements. περιπατεῖν: the light exercise prescribed for the wife of Ischomachus (*Oec.* 10.10–11) and for men in military camp (12.5). τοῦ ὑπὸ οἴνου μὴ σφάλλεσθαι ἐπιμελεῖσθαι 'to take care not to fall down as a result of the wine'; the particle combination καὶ μήν occurs more usually at the beginning of a sentence; but cf. 9.5. καὶ τῆι ὀρφνῆι ὅσα ἡμέραι χρηστέον: the quality of the ideal leader: cf. *Ages.* 6.6, where Agesilaus νυκτὶ μὲν ὅσαπερ ἡμέραι ἐχρῆτο, and *Hell.* 6.1.15, where Jason is said: καὶ νυκτὶ ὅσαπερ ἡμέραι χρῆσθαι. ὀρφνη, a poetic word for 'night', seems to have no special poetic effect and might represent Spartan vocabulary. ὑπὸ φανοῦ 'by torchlight'; Plut. *Lyc.* 12.14 repeats Xenophon's description in his own words: πιόντες δὲ μετρίως ἀπίασι δίχα λαμπάδος. οὐ γὰρ ἔξεστι πρὸς φῶς βαδίζειν . . . ὅπως ἐθίζωνται σκότους καὶ νυκτὸς εὐθαρσῶς καὶ ἀδεῶς ὁδεύειν. τὸν ἔτι ἔμφρουρον 'the one still of military age'.

5.8 ἀπὸ τῶν σίτων: i.e. from the same food. εὐχροί τε καὶ εὔσαρκοι καὶ εὔρωστοι . . . πεφυσημένοι τε καὶ αἰσχροὶ καὶ ἀσθενεῖς 'with good skin, good flesh, good muscles . . . with puffy skin, ugly flesh and no strength'; Xenophon shows his familiarity with the vocabulary of physiology. αὐτός τις τῆι ἑαυτοῦ γνώμηι: this emphasizes the voluntary nature of exercise in other *poleis*, which produces a body in 'sufficiently' good condition; Lycurgus makes the voluntary practice compulsory in order to achieve excellence; cf. 10.4. ἐν τῶι γυμνασίωι ἑκάστωι 'in each type of exercise'. Socrates identifies exercises that develop the upper and the lower body separately in *Symp.* 2.16–20; cf. the reference to exercising from the legs and the hands and the neck (5.9 below). ὡς μὴ πόνους αὐτοῖς ἐλάττους τῶν σιτίων γίγνεσθαι 'so that their labours should never be less than the food (they were given)', a clause of result: cf. the note on 2.5. Richards' emendation produces the expected reference to the need to balance intake and output of calories. ὡς μήποτε αὐτοὶ ἐλάττους, the transmitted text, makes no sense. [Hippocrates] *Regimen* frequently describes exercise in these terms as being 'less than' or 'greater than' the food: 3.67.3, ὥστε πρὸς τὸ πλῆθος τοῦ σίτου τὴν ξυμμετρίην ποιεῖσθαι τῶν πόνων; cf. 3.85.1–2, 3.85.4.

5.9 Σπαρτιατῶν: genitive of comparison. [Hippocrates] *Regimen* 2.61–5 identifies the need for this balance in various exercises: περίπατοι 2.62, running (2.63), wrestling (2.64) and strengthening the arms (χειρονομίη). *Mem.* 1.2.4 has Socrates also disapprove of overeating followed by over-exertion: τὸ μὲν οὖν ὑπερεσθίοντα ὑπερπονεῖν ἀπεδοκίμαζε.

6 Private ownership, communal rule

Those who pursue the common good are likely to conclude that they should share in both the production and the enjoyment of good things. Thus, though heads of households in other *poleis* have private 'control' of their children, slaves and property, Lycurgus legislates that citizens share the supervision of children and the enjoyment of slaves, horses, dogs and other property even though they are privately owned. The common supervision of the children in *Lac.* makes their control as effective as possible and improves them. Borrowing of the goods of others means sharing round the wealth. However, the borrowing is subject to need, and to consent. Xenophon uses seven expressions to justify borrowing in terms of need in this section, and the owner of the dogs consents to their use (ἡδέως ἐκπέμπει). Aristotle, *Pol.* 1263a35–7 has read this passage: 'In Sparta too they use each others' slaves as their own, so to speak, and horses and dogs too, and if they need it, the produce in the fields over the countryside.'

6.1 τῶν ἑαυτοῦ ἕκαστος . . . ἄρχουσιν: the change from the singular to the plural is not unexpected since 'each' denotes a collective idea; cf. *Hiero* 7.9. μηδὲν βλάπτοντες 'without doing harm' is Xenophon's customary description of service to the common good; see the note on *Hiero* 9.9. παίδων ἕκαστον ὁμοίως τῶν ἑαυτοῦ καὶ τῶν ἀλλοτρίων ἄρχειν 'that over children each man exercise rule alike, his own (children) and those of others'; the children are the first topic of communal rule.

6.2 'When a man realizes that these (the whole adult population) are fathers of the boys, he must rule the boys he rules himself (as such a father) as he would wish rule to be exercised over his own boys (of whom he is the biological father)'. The Spartan system placed importance on ruling and being ruled in turn: Plut. *Ages.* 20.2. μὴ οὐκ accompanies a negative infinitive when the leading verb is negative: *GG* 1616; αἰσχρόν is not strictly negative, but implies '*dis*honourable'.

6.3 καὶ οἰκέταις, εἴ τις δεηθείη, χρῆσθαι καὶ τοῖς ἀλλοτρίοις: Xenophon uses a word for slaves appropriate to the household context (see the note on 1.4) and recognizes that in these households slaves belong to individuals in the same way as children. MacDowell (1986) 37–9 recognizes various categories of Spartan slaves, but Xenophon would be lessening the strength of his argument if he were excluding helots from the possibility of communal use. Helots were the property of the *polis* in the sense that their master could not dispose of them freely (Fisher (1993) 25–6, Strabo, 8.5.4: the slaves are τρόπον . . . τινα δημοσίους δούλους), but they could be considered to belong to him when they came to be borrowed. *Hell.* 3.3.5 presents helots working for an individual master on an estate. *Hell.* 6.5.28 indicates that the authorities could liberate helots in a very serious military emergency. κοινωνίαν 'common possession'; see above on hunting: 5.7. καὶ ἵπποις δὲ ὡσαύτως χρῶνται: only wealthy Spartans reared horses, so this is also a way of spreading privilege: *Hell.* 6.4.11. Lysias 24.10–12 shows how useful a horse was to a disabled person; the care of the sick regularly marks Xenophon's ideal government. καλῶς ἀποκαθίστησιν 'gives back in good condition'; injury to borrowed animals was a crime for which laws were made in other *poleis*: p. 47.

6.4 οὐ μὴν οὐδ' . . . ἐποίησεν ἐπιτηδεύεσθαι 'nor indeed did he lay it down as a law that (that custom adopted by others) be practised (by them)'; cf. 1.7 for the use of ἐποίησεν and 5.1 for the connection of law and custom: ἐνομοθέτησεν . . . ἐπιτηδεύματα. In other *poleis* there was apparently an arrangement, in which food was jealously guarded. ὅπου γὰρ ἂν ὑπὸ θήρας ὀψισθέντες δεηθῶσι τῶν ἐπιτηδείων: sound effects bind the words; another instance follows: τοὺς μὲν πεπαμένους (πάομαι) καταλείπειν τὰ πεποιημένα. συνεσκευασμένοι 'prepared with food'. τοὺς δὲ δεομένους . . . ὅσων ἂν δέωνται . . . ὁπόταν τινὸς δεηθῶσιν: a continued emphasis on the condition of need that justifies the borrowing. ἀνοίξαντας τὰ σήμαντρα: 'seals' mark ownership (see the seal of the Spartan Pausanias: Thuc. 1.132.5), and that is the required connotation here, but seals also protect the food from animals and keep it uncontaminated.

6.5 τοιγαροῦν emphasizes a logical progression of thought and gives a strong explanation of the results: *GP* 566–8. The statement therefore sums up the significance of the sharing of those goods that have been mentioned.

7 Wealth

Observing that in other *poleis* everyone makes as much money as they can, from 'farming, ship-owning, export/import and the trades', Lycurgus legislated against activities that involved profiteering (χρηματισμός), favouring instead those that promoted the freedom of the *polis*. The passage later defines these as the development of the body, and assistance to friends; cf. the definition of the activities of free men at *Oec.* 4.2–3. Plut. *Ages.* 26.7–9 confirms that the Spartans were left sitting when Agesilaus called on his troops to stand up if they practised trades. Some Spartans held hereditary offices as heralds, cooks and flute-players, but these τέχναι (Hdt. 6.60) were not for profit. Socrates says that the indoor trades were held in no repute by warlike *poleis* because they weakened the body, leaving no strength or leisure for the activities of free men (*Oec.* 4.2–4), but the point here is about profiteering. Lycurgus bans farming as well, which Socrates considered to be good physical and moral training, on the grounds that it can be profiteering. Nevertheless, even Socrates is sceptical about farming when he hears Ischomachus' declaration that his father *profited* from buying unimproved land cheap and selling it dear (*Oec.* 20.22–9).

There were wealthy men among the Spartans in spite of this legislation (5.3), and citizens may have run industries as they undoubtedly ran farms: Cartledge (2001) 182, but the passage shows that wealth was not necessary for success, and so there was no point in profiteering. Xenophon does not say that the helots and *perioikoi* engaged in trade and commerce because he is intent on the development of virtue in the citizens only.

See Cartledge (1976) 115–19 on the trades, and Hodkinson (2000) *passim*.

7.1 δήπου: the 'shared assumption'; cf. *Hiero* 1.27. οἱ δὲ καὶ ἀπὸ τεχνῶν τρέφονται 'some also/even make a living from trades' suggests that this is not a great source of profit-making, certainly not as great as farming, ship-owning and trading.

7.2 τῶν μὲν ἀμφὶ χρηματισμὸν ἀπεῖπε μηδενὸς ἅπτεσθαι 'he forbade (them) to lay hand to any of the things that make money'. ὅσα δὲ ἐλευθερίαν ταῖς πόλεσι παρασκευάζει: as explained at 10.4–7: making a contribution to the welfare of friends and *polis*. ἔταξε . . . νομίζειν 'he laid it down that they should consider', another connection of law and custom; see note on 6.4.

7.3–4 Three reasons follow that remove the obligation to pursue wealth (conveyed by the verbal adjectives σπουδαστέος, χρηματιστέον, ἀθροιστέον): (1) their equal consumption of food and equal lifestyle; (2) the greater value placed on bodily condition than on expensive garments (the cloak is a symbol of wealth and indulgence; cf. 2.4, which restricts the boys to one cloak for all seasons in order to develop endurance); (3) the greater honour in using one's body and soul to assist comrades than one's wealth.

7.4 τὸ δαπανῶντα: ὠφελεῖν τοὺς συνόντας must be supplied. τὸ μὲν ψυχῆς, τὸ δὲ πλούτου ἔργον (sc. εἶναι): for the thought: *Ages.* 9.6.

7.5 τό γε μὴν ἐξ ἀδίκων χρηματίζεσθαι: profit-making is pursued to its obvious conclusion, which is injustice. νόμισμα: Spartan 'money' consisted of heavy iron bars: *obeloi* or *obeliskoi*: Plut. *Lys.* 17.4–5. δεκάμνων μόνον . . . εἰσελθόν 'if it came in only to the value of ten minae'. Coinage was measured in value and weight. Ten minae of silver would not weigh much; the Attic silver mina weighed only 433 g., the Aeginetan mina (the standard that prevailed among the Spartans) weighed 630 g., so that ten minae in silver coin could be easily hidden, but iron to that value would be massive.

The large mass and weight of the currency is confirmed by the need for 'a great space and a waggon to carry it in'. Plut. *Lyc.* 9.1 repeats Xenophon in detail. Hodkinson (2000) 160–5 calculates the weights and values.

7.6 ἐρευνᾶται . . . ζημιοῦται: the present tense describes the searches that were contemporary with the introduction of the law, and perhaps still went on inside Sparta in Xenophon's time.

8 Assent and Obedience

Lycurgus secured assent to his laws from the most powerful individuals, in the negotiation between the legislator and the citizens that is presented as good practice also in Plato's *Laws*. The kings are the powerful individuals mentioned. Their exemplary obedience provided an excellent model for imitation by others because it indicates that obedience actually secures powerful position. Together with Lycurgus, they established the ephors to enforce obedience from other people in power, and secured the obedience of the masses through the religious sanction of Delphi. This neatly combines the two traditions, that either the early kings or Lycurgus authorized the constitution (Strabo, C 366 = 8.5.5). The oracle also reflects the poem called *Eunomia*, written by the Spartan Tyrtaeus, which prescribed obedience from the people to the 'straight sayings' of the kings and elders: Van Wees in Hodkinson and Powell (eds.) (1999). Xenophon engages with his readers in making his points about Lycurgus' arrangements for obedience more cogent by his use of the first person (8.1) and his arguments from inference (8.2) and probability (8.3).

8.1 Ἀλλὰ γὰρ: a fresh point is introduced, as at 10.8. The present-tense description of obedience in Sparta contradicts 14.1–6, unless 'in Sparta' means 'under the system Lycurgus introduced', or describes the local situation as contrasted with the disobedience of the harmosts overseas: cf. Appendix 3. The obedience of the kings (ὑπέρχονται: 8.2) certainly did continue into the time of composition: *Lac.* 15.1, 15.7, *Ages.* 7.2. **ἴσμεν ἅπαντες**: a rhetorical assertion. **ταύτην τὴν εὐταξίαν**: *Mem.* 4.4.1 describes Socrates as εὐτακτῶν in obedience to the laws of Athens and their officers. **τοὺς κρατίστους τῶν ἐν τῆι πόλει**: the kings, since no other offices had yet been introduced; cf. τοὺς δοκοῦντας πρώτους εἶναι at 14.4, which does not mean the kings.

8.2 τεκμαίρομαι δὲ ταῦτα 'I make these inferences', suggestive of formal rhetoric. **ὑπέρχονται** 'approach submissively' in manners and gestures that we can only guess at; cf. *Ath.* 2.14. **τῶι ταπεινοὶ εἶναι μεγαλύνονται** 'they glory in being humble (and in obeying whenever they are called by running and not walking)' – a nice paradox. Prominent men also set an example in obedience in the Persian system (*Cyr.* 1.2.8, 8.1.21–33).

8.3 εἰκὸς δέ: the rhetorical argument from probability. **τὴν τῆς ἐφορείας δύναμιν**: the powers of the ephors are limited here to their enforcement of the laws even though Xenophon knows of others (*Hell.* 2.4.36, 3.1.1, 3.2.6, 3.2.23, 3.3.4–11). They particularly represent the law with eyes that punishes disobedience (cf. Cyrus in *Cyr.* 8.1.22).

Xenophon knew that they also honoured those who obeyed the law (*Hell.* 3.2.6), and that the best paradigms both reward and punish, but he may think the kings delegated the unpleasant task of punishment while they won popularity themselves by being pleasant, in the manner of the ruler in *Hiero* 9–10.1. Agesilaus would be a candidate for this: *Ages.* 8. The name 'ephor' probably implies that he 'over-sees' the citizens to check their obedience to the laws, just as Cyrus 'over-sees' (ἐφορᾶι) his governors (*Oec.* 4.8–11). There is perhaps even an emphasis on the personal nature of their supervision as the 'law with eyes' (cf. pp. 12–13). This function is consistent with the oaths they exchanged with the kings on behalf of the *polis* with a view to preserving the laws (*Lac.* 15.7), their proclamations on entering office that men shave their moustaches and obey the laws, the fear they inspired in the citizens, and their declaration of war on the helots (Plut. *Cl.* 9.1–5, *Lyc.* 28.7). The most recent analysis of the ephorate is Richer (1998). τοῦ ὑπακούειν: the insistence on obedience merits the retention of the manuscripts' unusual genitive; *GG* 1548, *Cyr.* 1.3.9 τοῦ . . . μὴ λυσιτελεῖν αὐτοῖς, Thuc. 1.4: τοῦ τὰς προσόδους μᾶλλον ἰέναι αὐτῶι.

8.4 ἱκανοὶ . . . κύριοι . . . κύριοι: *anaphora* sums up the complete power of the ephors to enforce the laws. καὶ ἄρχοντας μεταξὺ καταπαῦσαι 'to depose even rulers in mid-office', cf. ἀεὶ ἄρχειν τὸ ἔτος 'to rule continuously through the year without interruption'. *Hell.* 3.2.6–7 confirms that they have this power over harmosts abroad. *An.* 2.6.2–4 reveals their powers to depose and condemn Clearchus in mid-office. ὥσπερ οἱ τύραννοι καὶ οἱ ἐν τοῖς γυμνικοῖς ἀγῶσιν ἐπιστάται: the ephors are also compared to tyrants in Plato, *Laws* 712d, Arist., *Pol.* 1270b12–16. *Pol.* 1270b 28–31 calls them αὐτογνώμονας and contrasts their judgements with those κατὰ τὰ γράμματα καὶ τοὺς νόμους, which might suggest that they observed no law; *Pol.* 1272a36–9 makes the same charge against the *Gerousia*. Xenophon appears to say more credibly that their autonomy lay only in their implementation of the law. *Hell.* 3.2.21 shows how supervisors in the games punish in a similar manner. *Hell.* 7.3.6 has the prosecution abuse those who executed Euphron without recognizing the proper authorities as αὐτογνωμονήσαντες.

8.5 πολλῶν δὲ καὶ ἄλλων ὄντων μηχανημάτων καλῶν . . . εἰς τὸ πείθεσθαι τοῖς νόμοις ἐθέλειν τοὺς πολίτας: it is paradoxical that the terrifying ephors should be among 'fair measures' to win 'willing obedience', but the imitation of the obedience of the most prominent men is 'fair' enough, and the positive incentive of honour that the laws offer to the obedient is also 'fair'. *Ages.* 7.2 asks, 'Who would be *willing* to disobey?', seeing the King's own obedience. εἰ λῶιον καὶ ἄμεινον εἴη: a formulaic expression in requests to gods: cf. Homer, *Od.* 1.376, 2.141 (λωίτερον καὶ ἄμεινον); *An.* 3.1.7, *Poroi* 6.2. οἷς αὐτὸς ἔθηκε νόμοις: the form of his request emphasizes Lycurgus' own authorship of the laws, which other traditions said he procured ready-made from Delphi. ἀνεῖλε: formulaic for an oracular response. τῶι παντὶ ἄμεινον εἶναι 'better in every respect' (*Cyr.* 8.8.20 τῶι παντὶ χείρους), perhaps also suggesting 'better for the entire body of citizens', since Lycurgus was about to give his laws τῶι πλήθει (*Mem.* 1.2.45, also in a legal context: τὸ πᾶν πλῆθος, and Tyrtaeus fr. 12.15 West, *IEG*: πολήί τε παντί τε δήμωι). οὐ μόνον ἄνομον ἀλλὰ καὶ ἀνόσιον: 'unlawful' because they were men's laws, 'unholy' because endorsed by the god. See Van Wees in Hodkinson and Powell (1999) 1–41 on the role of oracles in Spartan reforms.

9 A fine death preferable to a disgraced life

The laws made it particularly hard for cowards. They were punished by humiliation in public συνουσίαι: the *syssitia*, wrestling and ball games, choral competitions, and in public arenas such as the agora and the streets. They were also subject to various other marks of ἀτιμία in their private households. Their humiliation and isolation reflected a lack of friendship. Hdt. 7.229–31 illustrates these penalties in the story of the two Spartans suffering from eye disease at Thermopylae. One decided to be led by his slave into battle and died, while the other decided not to fight. When he returned to Sparta and incurred ὄνειδός τε . . . καὶ ἀτιμίην, no one lit a fire for him, no one talked to him and he was called The Runaway (ὁ τρέσας). He tried to acquit himself by deliberately courting death at Plataea, but the Spartans did not honour him in spite of his achievements because he had deliberately sought death and left his station to do so (9.71). Xenophon perhaps presses the distinction from other Greeks too much, since Solon's Athenian laws also included penalties for cowardice; Aeschines 3.175–6 mentions exclusion from sacred sites and rites.

9.1 αἱρετώτερον . . . ἀντί: 'preferable to' continues to credit citizens with positive choice of the better life. Xenophon presents the positive incentives as ones that occur naturally (9.1–2), but legislation punishes the coward (9.3–6). ἐπισκοπῶν τις ἂν εὕροι: the invitation to inquire brings special conviction to the point, perhaps because it is paradoxical; there is the same engagement with the reader about the thieving boys (2.7–8), and their abstinent homosexuality (2.14). The rule that the brave suffer fewer casualties recalls Tyrtaeus (fr. 11.11–13, West, *IEG*): οἳ μὲν γὰρ τολμῶσι παρ'ἀλλήλοισι μένοντες /ἔς τ'αὐτοσχεδίην καὶ προμάχους ἰέναι/παυρότεροι θνήσκουσι 'Those who dare, remaining alongside one another, to go to close quarters among the foremost, die in fewer numbers.' Homer, *Il.* 5.529–32 expresses a similar thought, and Xenophon, *An.* 3.1.43 repeats the sentiment.

9.2 ὡς τἀληθὲς εἰπεῖν 'to speak the truth' (*GG* 1534) brings special attention to a truth that will be unpalatable to some. εἰς τὸν πλείω χρόνον 'for a longer time', distinguishes long-term salvation from temporary survival. ῥᾴων καὶ ἡδίων καὶ εὐπορωτέρα καὶ ἰσχυροτέρα: the sequence of four adjectives in pairs of ascending size multiplies the benefits; compare the four adverbs at *Hiero* 7.10 and two sets of three adjectives at *Lac.* 5.8. καὶ εὔκλεια μάλιστα ἕπεται τῆι ἀρετῆι: cf. Tyrtaeus, fr. 12.37–42, West, *IEG*: 'all honour him, young and old, and he goes to Hades having experienced the greatest joy, and in old age he stands out among citizens, and no one wishes to harm him in respect or justice, and all give way to him from their seats, young men, coevals and elders.'

9.3 ἧι . . . ἐμηχανήσατο 'in what way he devised'. Lycurgus legislated to ensure the preference for bravery by making the coward an outcast from the community.

εὐδαιμονίαν . . . κακοδαιμονίαν: 'success' or 'failure', 'happiness' or 'unhappiness' for individuals; cf. *Hiero* 2.4.

9.4 κακὸς εἶναι 'he is only called a coward'; as though ἐπίκλησιν . . . ἔχει generates the infinitive of reported speech. The Spartans called the coward ὁ τρέσας: Hdt. 7.231 and Tyrtaeus (fr. 11.14, West, *IEG*: τρεσσάντων δ' ἀνδρῶν πᾶσ' ἀπόλωλ' ἀρετή); the word is widespread also in Homer. ἀγοράζει δὲ ἐν τῶι αὐτῶι ὁ κακὸς τἀγαθῶι: the word order places the good and bad in verbal juxtaposition to reflect their juxtaposition in real life in other *poleis* in the activities mentioned. πᾶς . . . πᾶς: *anaphora* emphasizes the coward's total lack of those willing to treat him as a friend.

9.5 πολλάκις . . . περιγίγνεται 'is often left over', an instance of true isolation. Kennell (1995) 59–61 describes the ball games associated with passage of the ephebes to adulthood, but Lycurgus here legislates for adults. Cf. DK, Critias fr. 36. εἰς τὰς ἐπονειδίστους χώρας: presumably the most shameful positions are at the very back of the chorus-line as the audience saw it; such competitions were held at the festival of Gymnopaidia: *Hell.* 6.4.16. παραχωρητέον begins a sequence of nine verbal adjectives that convey the necessity laid on the coward. καὶ ἐν θάκοις καὶ τοῖς νεωτέροις ὑπαναστατέον: his deferential rising up even to younger men in a society that revered elders is particularly galling (*Hiero* 7.2, 7 for this mark of honour). τὰς μὲν προσηκούσας κόρας οἴκοι θρεπτέον 'he must feed at home the unmarried girls that are his kin'; no man will marry a girl from his household (a special case of the central theme of no man wishing to befriend a coward: 9.2–3), and he must also bear the economic burden of supporting her; *Mem.* 2.7.1–2 laments the cost of feeding women, which would be higher for well-nourished Spartan girls. καὶ ταύταις τῆς ἀνανδρίας αἰτίαν ὑφεκτέον 'and the coward must bear the blame for their (the girls') lack of husbands'; the dative is one of disadvantage to the girls (*GG* 1165). Spartan women in general did share in the disgrace of their men (cf. Plutarch, *Moralia* 240c–242d), but Xenophon's thought is about unmarried girls (κόρας). To translate ἀνανδρία (the reading of the *deteriores*) as 'lack of a husband' rather than 'cowardice' (in spite of ἀνάνδρων at 10.6) is therefore attractive; the poets use ἄνανδρος in this sense, as does Plato *Laws* 930c, and Plutarch *Mor.* 2.302. The penalties would fall on his mother and other female relatives as well if it were merely a case of his womenfolk suffering for his cowardice. The unmarried girls would be aggrieved that his cowardice denied them their function not only as wives, but as child-bearers, which was their main honour (cf. 1.4). καὶ ἅμα τούτου ζημίαν ἀποτειστέον: possibly an early reference to a penalty for the crime of remaining unmarried, the ἀγαμίου δίκη (Plut. *Lys.* 30.7, who also mentions trials for late marriage and bad marriage!). The coward would also be barred from fathering children in the arrangement described at 1.8. λιπαρὸν δὲ οὐ πλανητέον: see the note on 3.4–5 for the importance of body-language; the disgrace of the coward is reflected in the behaviour of those whose relatives had dishonourably survived the battle of Leuctra: *Hell.* 6.4.16. ἢ πληγὰς . . . ληπτέον: this may mean that he is reduced to the status of a slave or a child who can be beaten: 6.2, but the central theme of isolation might also mean he is treated like an enemy outcast.

10.1–3 Old age

Lycurgus sets up a competition in the continuing practice of virtue in men beyond the age of military service, 60 years, and makes membership of the *Gerousia* their prize. For the description of the *Gerousia* as a prize of virtue and the honour in which it was held: Dem. 20.107, Aesch., *Tim.* 1.180, Isoc. 12.154, Arist., *Pol.* 1270b 24–5. Xenophon restricts his account of their powers to their jurisdiction of cases carrying the death penalty because this was the most serious measure of their honour. He does not specify the laws they adjudicated because only their penalty, of death, is relevant here. Cartledge (1987) 120–5 describes their other powers. There were only 28 members (apart from the two kings) and they had membership for life, so that very few acquired the honour.

10.1 τὴν κρίσιν τῆς γεροντίας 'the test of the *Gerousia*'; a Laconian word is used for the institution, not attested in other contemporary writing. τὴν καλοκἀγαθίαν: cf. 10.4; *Mem.* 1.2.48 defines καλοκἀγαθία among the Athenians as the ability to care for one's household, friends and *polis*, and this covers the definition of Spartan virtue as well. Agesilaus in old age proves supremely 'useful to his homeland', τελέως ὁ ἀνὴρ τῆι πατρίδι ὠφέλιμος ὢν διεγένετο (*Ages.* 11.14–16); on service to friends: *Lac.* 7.4.

10.2 ἀξιάγαστον δ' αὑτοῦ: 'admirable in him (is)'. κυρίους τοῦ περὶ τῆς ψυχῆς ἀγῶνος: 'soul' and 'contest' are used in two senses in this passage: for the 'contest in court' involving the death penalty as here, where the 'soul' in the sense of 'life' was at stake, and for the 'contest of the soul' as the 'seat of virtue' below, when the elders compete for the *Gerousia*. Respect for the elders is one of the signs of the general Spartan respect for old age (*Mem.* 3.5.15).

10.3 εἰκότως δέ τοι 'rightly, I tell you'; the author intervenes to reinforce the point. The superiority of the activities of the soul over those of the body was an old theme: (Xenophanes fr. 2.11–12, West, *IEG)* ῥώμης γὰρ ἀμείνων ἀνδρῶν ἠδ' ἵππων ἡμετέρη σοφίη. οὗτος ὁ ἀγών: this contest is for membership of the *Gerousia*, as the subsequent ὁ δὲ περὶ τῆς γεροντίας ἀγὼν ψυχῶν ἀγαθῶν κρίσιν παρέχει shows, even though the reference to κυρίους τοῦ περὶ τῆς ψυχῆς ἀγῶνος in the previous sentence is to the cases they determine that carry the death penalty.

10.4–8: Lycurgus assumes that the aim of successful government is to 'increase' one's country (τὰς πατρίδας αὔξειν); see p. 5. He increased the power and fame of Sparta by making compulsory the practice of 'all the virtues' as they have been described throughout *Lac.* Failure to develop them meant the ultimate disgrace of exclusion from citizenship, a greater penalty than for even the most horrific crimes against individuals, because those who were 'cowards and slackers' betrayed the whole community, not just other individuals. The Spartans were criticized for promoting military virtues above others (Arist., *Pol.* 1333b5–1334a10). Here Lycurgus certainly promotes them, but not at the expense of others. *Agesilaus* shows that the King had the more sociable virtues of piety and justice and affability as well.

10.4 ἠνάγκασε δημοσίαι πάντας πάσας ἀσκεῖν τὰς ἀρετάς: Lycurgus compelled everyone to practise all the virtues in public; i.e. he made compulsory what is done voluntarily by 'those who wish' in other *poleis*, in the same way that he made voluntary competitions compulsory for the ephebes (4.2), and voluntary exercise compulsory for the men (5.8); and he brought the practice of virtue into the open just as he did with their dining habits (5.2). ὥσπερ οὖν introduces an analogy from athletics; cf. *Hiero* 4.6. διαφέρει: the use of the present tense to describe the superiority of the Spartans should be understood in the same way as the present tense in 8.1.

10.5 ἀμελῶν τοῦ ὡς βέλτιστος εἶναι 'taking no care about being as good as possible'; *Cyr.* 1.6.7 requires such self-development in the ruler; here the citizen develops himself under the guidance of the laws.

10.6 ὡς ἔοικεν: answered by ὥστε εἰκότως. The argument brings attention to the new idea, that some transgressions harm only individuals, and are less culpable than those that harm the entire community. *Hell.* 5.2.32 indicates that a commander should be judged only on the basis of whether he helped or harmed Sparta.

10.7 τὴν πόλιν οἰκείαν ἐποίησε: to 'own' the *polis* is to have a share in its goods. καὶ οὐδὲν ὑπελογίσατο οὔτε σωμάτων οὔτε χρημάτων ἀσθένειαν 'and he made no *negative* account of weakness of body or of wealth': i.e. did not prevent even the poor or old or lame possessing the *polis* as long as they obeyed the laws; cf. *Hiero* 8.6. An alternative meaning is that he did not take such weaknesses as an excuse for not obeying the laws. What favours the first interpretation is that the μέν sentence to which this sentence is joined emphasizes Lycurgus' rewards for those who obeyed the laws; only the subsequent δέ sentence focuses on the penalties for those who did not. The remark that Agesilaus 'did not avoid toil, shirk dangers, spare expense, or use his physical condition or old age as an excuse' to avoid benefiting his city (*Ages.* 7.1) might be an instance of his meeting the second interpretation, but is not incompatible with the law that these factors did not stand in the way of citizenship. The first meaning need not contradict Aristotle, *Pol.* 1271a26–37 either, who says that according to ancient custom those Spartans who could not make financial contributions to the *syssitia* lost their citizenship; their contributions of food in *Lac.* 5.3–4 appear so meagre and so far from destroying their meagre households, that it is hard to imagine anyone falling short of such a target. μηδὲ νομίζεσθαι ἔτι τῶν ὁμοίων εἶναι 'no longer even to be considered one of the equals', one of the terms for a full citizen (*Hell.* 3.3.5); such demotion explains the existence of 'inferiors' among the Spartans (*Hell.* 3.3.6, 5.3.9).

10.8 ἀλλὰ γάρ: closure is achieved for the first part of the work by the development of a paradox that challenges other Greeks to imitation (pp. 43–4): that though the laws are very ancient and all praise them, none has imitated them (because they demand too much hard work) and so they remain in their eyes entirely novel. The *topos* is found in [Lysias], *Epitaphios* 2.26, that 'though the deeds happened long ago (πάλαι), still in our time their virtue is pursued by all mankind as if they were new (καινῶν)'. The time of the Heraclidae is the time of the first kings of Sparta. Xenophon uses rhetoric to establish the date, saying that it is 'clear' and appealing to an outside authority ('it is said'). He does this to facilitate the paradox. Plutarch *Lyc.* 1.5 calls the early date ἀρχαιότης. ἐπαινοῦσι μὲν πάντες: the exaggeration moves the audience toward rhetorical agreement (cf. 2.8, where not all in his imagined audience did praise them).

11 The army

The preceding chapters are said to have developed qualities for war and peace, but attention now shifts entirely to military campaigns: how the laws dictate the marshalling of the army, its equipment and dress, organization and chain of command and manoeuvres. The content belongs to a literary tradition of handbooks on technical subjects, such as Xenophon's own *De Re Equestri*, *Hipparchicus* and *Cynegeticus*. Of military handbooks, we have Aeneas Tacticus on sieges in the fourth century, and later examples from Asclepiodotus and Onasander. See modern discussions of the Spartan army in Anderson (1970), Lazenby (1985) 3–40 and Pritchett (1971/1985). Xenophon may be describing the fourth-century army he had served with, but he contrasts the arrangements of Lycurgus with one practice in his own time at 12.3. He continues to represent the practices as dictated by the laws (11.7, 12.5).

11.1 εἰ δέ τις βούλεται καταμαθεῖν: the imagined request for information about the army comes naturally after Xenophon's assumption that everyone admires the laws described so far at 10.8.

11.2 οἱ ἔφοροι προκηρύττουσι: the main point of this section is that the announcement of the ephors ensured that the army was fully supplied in every detail with what it needed for the expedition; the special feature of Spartan military preparation is that nothing is left to chance. τὰ ἔτη εἰς ἃ δεῖ στρατεύεσθαι: The army was divided into age groups, as were the youth; the call-up is therefore expressed as 'the years up to which' they serve in five year periods 'from service as an ephebe' and these equate to ages 20–25, 25–30, 30–35, 35–40, 40–45, 45–50, 50–55, 55–60; so, the call-up for the battle of Leuctra was μέχρι τῶν πέντε καὶ τριάκοντα ἀφ' ἥβης, 'up to thirty-five years from service as an ephebe' i.e. the first seven out of the eight age classes: *Hell.* 6.4.17. The division was useful in action, since the younger men were faster; see *Hell.* 4.5.13–16, how τὰ δέκα ἀφ' ἥβης 'ten years from service as an ephebe' were first sent out because of the need for speed, then τὰ πεντεκαίδεκα ἀφ' ἥβης 'fifteen years from service as an ephebe'. ἔπειτα δὲ καὶ τοῖς χειροτέχναις: there seems to be no reason why the craftsmen should be organized in age groups, so perhaps the military age groups are announced 'to the craftsmen as well', who were helots or *perioikoi*, because they need to know how many are going out. See Anderson (1970) 43–66 on commissariat. ὅσοισπερ . . . πάντων τούτων . . . καὶ ὅσων δὲ ὀργάνων . . . ἅπαντα τὰ μὲν . . . τὰ δέ: the ephors ensure the complete satisfaction of all the needs of the army; the pronominal articles are in partitive apposition to ἅπαντα (*GG* 914): 'some are commissioned to a waggon to provide (explanatory infinitive, *GG* 1530), others to a beast of burden'. τὸ ἐλλεῖπον 'omission'.

11.3 Lycurgus also made the army look good. στολὴν μὲν ἔχειν φοινικίδα: Anderson (1970) 13–42 for the 'bright red uniform', and 39–40 on the 'red tunic' that went under the armour (also Lazenby (1985) 30–2). The colour φοῖνιξ is not easily distinguished from other red shades, such as πορφύρεος, but there was a distinction: *Cyr.* 8.3.3. Red dyes could be produced by the expensive murex 'sea snail' (*Rytiphloea tinctoria* πόντιον φῦκος: Theophrastus *HP* 4.6.5), by insect dyes (kermes or cochineal), more cheaply by madder root (*Rubia tinctoria* ἐρυθρόδανον). Cf. Ponting (1980). Wool took colour best, then linen. The clothing would be manufactured by the slaves involved in textile-work, described at 1.4. **καὶ χαλκῆν ἀσπίδα:** The phrase needs to be transposed from its position in the manuscripts to make sense of the following reference to the bright polish it took. Anderson (1970) 14–20, esp. 16 n.13 describes a shield covered with a thin bronze plating, and with bronze handle and trim, but many shields had bronze only for the fittings: Pritchett Part 1 (1971) 146–8. The red uniform and the high polish produce descriptions of the army as ἅπαντα μὲν χαλκόν, ἅπαντα δὲ φοινικᾶ: *Ages.* 2.7. **κομᾶν:** Xenophon says Lycurgus permitted adults to wear their hair long (and groomed) as part of his plan to make the army look good, but Hdt. 1.82.7–8 tells another story; in the competition for the land of Thyrea the Spartans defeated the Argives; the Argives cut their hair though previously ἐπάναγκες κομῶντες 'wearing their hair long by compulsory custom', whereas the Spartans who previously did not wear their hair long adopted this custom: οὐ γὰρ κομῶντες πρὸ τούτου ἀπὸ τούτου κομᾶν. The Argives are here presumably in mourning for their enslaved land; short hair is a sign of slavery or mourning. Whereas the Spartans are showing their acquisition of new land through their flourishing appearance. Hdt. 7.209.3 confirms that the Spartans at Thermopylae 'taking exercise and combing their hair' were observing their νόμος.

11.4 This passage focuses on the chain of command from the largest to the smallest unit, which dictates the organization even of the smallest unit. **οὕτω γε μὴν κατεσκευασμένων:** sc. 'the Spartans'. **μόρας μὲν διεῖλεν ἓξ καὶ ἱππέων καὶ ὁπλιτῶν:** six *morai* of infantry and six separate *morai* of cavalry (*Hell.* 3.3.10–11, 4.5.11–12; though Lipka (2002) has argued that there were six *morai* in total, of mixed infantry and cavalry). There seem to have been 600 men in a *mora* of infantry (*Hell.* 4.5.12) and around 120 in a *mora* of cavalry (based on the figures for the battle of Nemea: *Hell.* 4.2.16). Xenophon calls the main infantry units *morai* up to the battle of Leuctra (*Hell.* 4.3.15, 6.4.17), but thereafter *lochoi* (*Hell.* 7.1.30, 7.4.20, 7.5.10), and it has been argued that the *morai* were abolished in a reform of military structures after Leuctra. However, Thucydides complicates the issue when he calls the main units *lochoi* rather than *morai* even in the Peloponnesian War (5.68.3). **ὁπλιτικῶν:** Stobaeus' reading picks up the previously mentioned division into separate cavalry and infantry *morai*; cf. τῶι ὁπλιτικῶι at *Hell.* 6.5.19. The manuscripts' πολιτικῶν is used to distinguish citizens from allies in *Hell.* 4.4.19, 5.3.25. Ar. *Knights* 1369 plays on the closeness of the two words: ὁπλίτης ὁ πολίτης. Xenophon restricts the rest of his discussion to the hoplite *morai*, probably because cavalry was not a traditional Spartan strength: Thuc. 4.55.2. He mentions the performance of their cavalry in his own times (*Hell.* 4.2.16, 4.4.10, 4.5.16), their disarray at Leuctra (*Hell.* 6.4.10–11) and their improvement only when they enrolled 'foreigners' (*Hipp.* 9.4: a possible reference to the cavalry that came from Dionysius: *Hell.* 7.1.21). **λοχαγοὺς τέτταρας:** the number has been challenged on the grounds that, if there were four *lochoi* to a *mora*, the conversion of the previous six *morai* in the reform after Leuctra would have produced 24 *lochoi*, whereas *Hell.* 7.4.20, 7.5.10 mention only 12: Lazenby (1985) 5–10. Anderson (1970) 225–41 explains that the population had been so reduced that only half the number of original units was needed. Lipka (2002) believes that Xenophon's 12 *lochoi* are only the infantry *lochoi*, that cavalry *morai* made up another 12, and that each *mora* was made up of two cavalry and two infantry *lochoi* and had four *lochagoi*. ἐκ δὲ τούτων τῶν μορῶν διὰ παρεγγυήσεως καθίστανται τοτὲ μὲν εἰς <ἕνα ἄγοντες τὰς> ἐνωμοτίας, τοτὲ δὲ εἰς τρεῖς, τοτὲ δὲ εἰς ἕξ 'out of these *morai* via verbal orders down the chain of command they deploy the *enomotiai* sometimes one abreast, sometimes three abreast, sometimes six'. This text adopts Anderson's supplement (see below). εἰς . . . ἄγοντες is normal language for the internal deployment of the military unit of the *enomotia*: εἰς τρεῖς τὴν ἐνωμοτίαν ἄγειν 'to lead the *enomotia* three abreast' (*Hell.* 6.4.12), εἰς δύο ἄγων (*Hell.* 7.4.22). Lipka (2002) argues that the description is of the deployment of entire *enomotiai*, but *Cyropaedia* 2.3.21 confirms the reference to internal deployment when it describes the deployment of entire units as well as their internal deployment, but reserves the εἰς terminology for the internal deployment. See also *An.* 4.3.26, where the *lochos* is deployed into its *enomotiai* and then into line of battle. The first point about this deployment is that παρρεγγύησις (relayed verbal command described in *Hipp.* 4.9 as παράγγελσις) controlled it, and this was superior to an announcement by a herald or orders advanced before the battle because the enemy could not hear it or find out how the units were marshalled; it also allowed for last-minute changes of plan. Cf. 11.6, the comparison with the herald. The deployment produced 'fronts' of varying breadth in the main line of battle, and therefore also varying depths, and these determined the ability of the line to withstand assault: Pritchett Part 1 (1971) 134–43. Anderson (1970) 74 n. 41 argues that the lacuna requires the numeral one. His reasoning is based on division: 'a unit drawn up in two files cannot be re-formed in three without departing from the principle that the file is a complete unit'. *Cyr.* 2.3.21 describes formations of four, two and one abreast in a *lochos* of 20 men, subdivided into files of five.

11.5 ὃ δὲ οἱ πλεῖστοι οἴονται: Xenophon contradicts common opinion about the difficulty; the point is that ease of learning facilitates willingness to learn, as indicated at *Oec.* 15.10–16.1. πολυπλοκωτάτην 'with many convolutions', a good word for the weaving to and fro of the *enomotiai* and their sub-files in the counter-marching described here. Anderson (1970) 388–97 presents Figures I–V, which are invaluable for clarifying what is happening. οἱ πρωτοστάται ἄρχοντες: the 'file-leaders' within the *enomotia*, under the direct command of the *enomotarch*; Asclepiodotus, *Tactics* 2.3. πάντ' ἔχων ὅσα δεῖ παρέχεσθαι: each sub-file under the command of their file leader has 'all things that need to be provided'. *Cyr.* 2.1.21 confirms that each soldier is provided with everything he needs, in order to avoid being distracted from fighting.

11.6 ὡς ὅστις τοὺς ἀνθρώπους δύναται γιγνώσκειν, οὐδεὶς ἂν ἁμάρτοι 'so that no one could go wrong who is able to recognize men'; this could be a sort of joke, since it is easy to recognize men as distinguished from e.g. logs of wood, but recognizing men is often associated with recognizing their qualities as good or bad (*An.* 1.7.4, *Mem.* 4.8.11) and this would explain the subsequent comment that some must lead and others must follow, since the good were meant to lead and the less good followed; cf. *Mem.* 3.1.9, which uses διαγιγνώσκειν of distinguishing brave soldiers from cowardly ones in putting them in line. τοῖς μὲν . . . τοῖς δὲ . . . : the easy-to-learn division between ruler and ruled is reflected in the balanced phrasing. αἱ δὲ παραγωγαὶ ὥσπερ ὑπὸ κήρυκος ὑπὸ τοῦ ἐνωμοτάρχου λόγωι δηλοῦνται: verbal command at the level of the smallest unit is directly compared with the command of a herald (see comment on 11.4); *enomotiai* were deployed for battle from a column of march through 'passing manoeuvres', by marching files of men from the rear of the *enomotia* to a new position on the left of the leading file, 'passing' the leading file in the process and ending up alongside them to the left. ἀραιαί: Asclepiodotus 4.1 uses this word to contrast an open formation with a densely packed one. ὧν οὐδὲν οὐδ' ὁπωστιοῦν χαλεπὸν μαθεῖν: the negatives protest too much about the lack of difficulty in learning.

11.7 τὸ μέντοι κἂν ταραχθῶσι μετὰ τοῦ παρατυχόντος ὁμοίως μάχεσθαι 'to fight as before even when they become disordered, with the man who is nearby'; this man is not the predictable partner of the file formations. ταύτην τὴν τάξιν: in apposition.

11.8 τὰ τοῖς ὁπλομάχοις πάνυ δοκοῦντα χαλεπὰ εἶναι 'those moves that appear very difficult to teachers of tactics'. Plato, *Laches* 183b says that such teachers avoided going to Sparta to teach their tactics because they would be shown up. *Mem.* 3.1.5 says they falsely claimed to teach leadership as well (cf. *Cyr.* 1.6.12–14). These tactics are then illustrated in four situations in which the column meets the enemy in its march, and in which various technical manoeuvres, as well as the effectiveness of the chain of command, are demonstrated: an attack from the front (ἐκ τοῦ ἐναντίου), from the rear (ἐκ τοῦ ὄπισθεν), from the right (ἐκ τῶν δεξιῶν), from the left (κατὰ τὰ εὐώνυμα). The arrangements for frontal, right and left-hand attack are reasonably straightforward, but the rear attack produces a more complex response: Anderson (1970) 106–10, 394–7, Figures IV–V, Lazenby (1985) 26–8. ἐπὶ κέρως 'in marching column'. δήπου 'I think we all know this'. ἐνωμοτία ἔπεται sc. ἐνωμοτίαι. τῶι ἐνωμοτάρχωι παρεγγυᾶται: the operation of the chain of command; cf. 11.4, διὰ παρεγγυήσεως. εἰς μέτωπον 'to the front' i.e. to produce the broad front line of battle. παρ' ἀσπίδα 'by the left'; Asclepiodotus, *Tactics* 10.2 explains these commands; movement to the left is in the direction of the shield, which was held on the left-hand side of the body (cf. παρὰ δόρυ 'the right-hand': 11.10). καὶ διὰ παντὸς οὕτως 'and in this fashion (the word of command goes) through the whole army'. The παραγωγή is complete and the line of battle is deployed. The men in the rear of each *enomotia* (and the *enomotiai* in the rear of each *lochos*) have marched out from behind and moved into positions to the left of the leading file. οὕτως ἐχόντων: sc. 'the soldiers' or 'their affairs'. ἐξελίττεται ἕκαστος ὁ στίχος each file 'unfolds' in the practice of 'counter-marching'. Anderson (1970) 106 explains that the Laconian counter-march is distinct from others; each soldier first 'about-faces' through 180 degrees, but this left a file-leader within the *enomotia* at the rear of his unit. To restore him to his usual position at the front, the man who had been in the rear of the file (but was now leading it after the turn) stood fast while the leader marched the rest of the file from the rear to re-form in front of him. The advantage of this style of counter-march was that the Spartans appeared to the enemy to be advancing toward them rather than retreating: Asclepiodotus, *Tactics* 10.14. Agesilaus ἐξελίξας turns to attack the enemy to his rear at *Hell.* 4.3.18. οἱ κράτιστοι: the file leaders; the aim of the counter-march is to keep them always in front facing the enemy.

11.9 ὅτι δὲ ὁ ἄρχων εὐώνομος γίγνεται: commanders took up their position on the extreme right-hand 'wing' of their formation, but the counter-march left them on the extreme left of the new formation. κυκλοῦσθαι: to encircle is to outflank and attack from the flank. κατὰ τὰ γυμνά 'on the unarmed side'; the right-hand was unarmed because the soldiers carried their shields on the left; cf. κατὰ τὰ ὡπλισμένα: the protected left-hand side. στρέψαντες τὸ ἄγημα ἐπὶ κέρας 'turning the company toward the (right) wing' (a line of men turned toward the wing is seen as a 'column' heading to the right across the field i.e. through 90 degrees to the right since this is the direction in which the leader wishes to move). They counter-march the line, this time *across* the field (as described in Asclepiodotus, 10.16) 'until the file-leader is on the right-hand wing'.

11.10 ἐπὶ κέρως πορευομένων 'when they (the Spartans) are marching in column' and the attack comes from the right, the focus shifts from the *enomotia* to the larger unit of the *lochos*; the *lochoi* turn to the right through 90 degrees toward the enemy, and the *lochos* which is in the rear of the marching column (ὁ κατ᾽ οὐρὰν λόχος) becomes the right-hand end (παρὰ δόρυ) of the line. Anderson (1970) 107–10 identifies this as the '*lochoi* in column' manoeuvre (*orthioi lochoi*) and indicates that Xenophon is no longer thinking of an enemy phalanx, but of light-armed attackers on the flank. *An.* 4.8.9–13 indicates that the formation could leave gaps between the *lochoi*; it is used on uneven ground when the continuous formation could not be kept. ὥσπερ τριήρη ἀντίπρωιρον τοῖς ἐναντίοις 'like a trireme prow-on to the enemy'; *Hell.* 7.5.23 uses the ship image of a formation in which Epaminondas hoped to use the strongest part of the army line (the 'prow') to cut through the enemy line. προθέουσιν 'they run forward' (as parts of the line ran forward at Coronea: *Hell.* 4.3.17, or Lechaeum: *Hell.* 4.5.14–15); manuscript C alone provides this reading, but the scribe of C has a reputation for solving textual problems inventively. It is difficult to explain this manoeuvre: Anderson (1970) 110. As an alternative to it, they turn the *lochoi* to the left to face the enemy instead, leaving the rear *lochos* on the left-hand side of the new line.

If Xenophon assumes that these manoeuvres have been easy to understand, he must be assuming some basic military experience in his readers.

12 Encampment

Xenophon focuses on the security of the camp and camp routine. He mentions the internal threat of the helots for the first and only time in *Lac.*, emphasizing the special danger of helots with access to arms (see p. 40 for the place of slaves in constitutional literature). The plot of Cinadon dramatically demonstrates the threat that armed helots and other inferiors could pose even within Sparta; the ephors ask their informer whether the conspirators have weapons available and their reaction when this is confirmed is immediate: *Hell.* 3.3.7–8. Thucydides 4.80.3 indicates that Spartan relationships with the helots were arranged entirely with a view to security. Aristotle, *Pol.*1269a36–b12 identifies the relationship as one of its constitutional weaknesses. Anderson (1970) 59–66, Pritchett Part 2 (1974) 133–46, Lazenby (1985) 32–6 discuss Spartan encampment.

12.1 ἀχρήστους: more men were needed to defend right-angles, and corners are of less use than open spaces to those living in a fortified camp; *Hell.* 3.4.24 refers to the circular encampment of Agesilaus.

12.2 οὐ γὰρ πολεμίων ἕνεκα ἀλλὰ φίλων: the 'friends' are the helots inside the camp (cf. 12.4); this is an example of true irony (as opposed to the Straussian kind: cf. Appendix 1). ἀπὸ χωρίων ὧν ἂν ἐκ πλείστου προορῷιεν i.e. elevated positions.

12.3 ἔξω τῆς φάλαγγος: φάλαγξ is an encampment here, an enemy line at 11.8. ὑπὸ Σκιριτῶν: people like the *perioikoi*, who had their main town of Oios on the northern border of Laconia: *Hell.* 5.2.24, 6.5.24–5; 7.4.21. They fought on foot: Anderson (1970) 249–51; Lazenby (1985) 10, even though *Cyr.* 4.2.1 compares them for their robustness with the horse-riding Hyrcanians. *Hell.* 5.4.52–3 shows them working with cavalry and going uphill, which suggests they were light-armed. Thuc. 5.67.1 says that they held the position of danger on the left wing of the army. νῦν δ᾽ ἤδη καὶ ὑπὸ ξένων . . . αὐτῶν τινες συμπαρόντες: the content of the lacuna is unclear. The sentence marks a contrast between Xenophon's own time and past time, but it is not clear when the change occurred.

12.4 τὸ δὲ ἔχοντας τὰ δόρατα ἀεὶ περιιέναι: 'the fact that they always go around carrying their spears' is the subject of the ὅτι clause and comes first in its sentence to emphasize the great concern with security that it represents. Critias, DK, fr. 37 describes the same custom: '(the Spartan) always goes about with his spear on the assumption that in this respect at least he will be stronger than the helot' (τὸ δόρυ ἔχων ἀεὶ περιέρχεται, ὡς κρείττων γε ταύτηι τοῦ εἴλωτος ἐσόμενος). καὶ τοὺς δούλους: the term contrasts helots with free citizens; cf. note on 1.4 and the subsequent description of the Spartans as ἐλευθεριωτέρους (12.5). The claim that helots were kept away from the hoplite weapons suggests that they were unarmed craftsmen or those light-armed helots who attended Spartiates in the Persian Wars: Hdt. 7.229.1, 9.10, 28.2, 29.1, 80. Cf. those helots who fought in arms alongside the Spartans in the Peloponnesian War (Thuc. 5.57.1, 5.64.2) and were armed for hoplite fighting at *Hell.* 6.5.28–9. καὶ τοὺς ἐπὶ τὰ ἀναγκαῖα ἀπιόντας: 'necessary things' means defecation; the phrase describing men doing this is the subject of the subsequent ὅτι clause and comes first in the sentence for emphasis; their proximity to one another and to the weapons even in their private moments constitutes a transgression of normal social behaviour that shows how complete their concern was for security against the helots. Cf. the belief that one ought not to be seen doing the 'necessary things' in *Cyr.* 8.8.11: 'not to eat or drink or be visible doing any of the necessary things that comes from these'. πλέον ἢ ὅσον μὴ λυπεῖν ἀλλήλους: ὅσον is used adverbially with the infinitive like ὥστε. *Mem.* 2.6.24–5 also insists that the limit on activities is not causing pain to friends.

12.5 καὶ τοῦ σίνεσθαι τοὺς πολεμίους ἕνεκα καὶ τοῦ ὠφελεῖν τοὺς φίλους: pillaging and destroying enemy land was normal Spartan policy; *Cyr.* 3.3.23 says that changes of camp secured provisions and damaged the enemy; frequent changes of camp in allied territory would also mean that no one area bore the brunt of occupying forces, which was a major concern of the Spartan authorities (*Hell.* 3.1.10, 3.2.6–7). καὶ γυμνάζεσθαι δὲ προαγορεύεται ὑπὸ τοῦ νόμου: the law requires that the Spartans dominate others in the camp by showing them their concern for physical fitness, a special display of their freedom; 'Lacedaemonians' are the Spartans as distinct from their inferior populations and other Greeks. αὐτοὺς ἐφ᾽ ἑαυτοῖς: 'by themselves in isolation', looking forward to the subsequent contrast with 'the others'. δεῖ δὲ οὔτε περίπατον οὔτε δρόμον μάσσω ποιεῖσθαι ἢ ὅσον ἂν ἡ μόρα ἐφήκηι 'it is permitted neither to walk or run further than the distance a *mora* extends'; for a similar expression of distance, cf. *An.* 6.5.5, 'as many as the column of the army covered'. Even in exercising the Spartans are preoccupied with security. [Hippocrates], *Regimen* 2.62–3 discusses the obvious benefits of running and the less obvious benefits of walking: walking after dinner helps digest food; walking early reduces moisture, which is the enemy of health; walking after exercise purges the flesh melted by exercise; Xenophon himself does the *peripatos* with Proxenus after dinner in camp (*An.* 2.4.15). The poetic comparative of μακρός could be a word actually used by the Spartans in their ordinary speech.

12.6–7 μετὰ δὲ τὰ γυμνάσια . . . ἐκ τούτου δὲ . . . ἐκ τούτου δ᾽ αὖ . . . μετά γε μὴν ταῦτα: subsequent stages in the camp routine from dawn to dusk. ὥσπερ ἐξέτασις: Xerxes also used for his review of troops a confined space known to hold a certain number of men: Hdt. 7.60.2–3. These exercises and the review precede eating to make Spartans toil on an empty stomach, as they had learned in their younger days (2.5). The 'first polemarch' commanded 'the first *mora*': *Hell.* 4.2.22. διατριβαὶ καὶ ἀναπαύσεις 'chores and rest breaks'.

12.7 ἐπὶ τῶν ὅπλων: they even sleep 'in arms' in order to be secure. ὅτι δὲ πολλὰ γράφω: the first-person intrusion justifies the length of the analysis by appealing to the length to which the law has gone in attending to the details; it is this that makes the Spartans 'expert' in the art of war (13.5). Isocrates *Panath.* 12.74–5 justifies a digression in similar terms, and *Hipp.* 9.8 justifies the number of times the work has referred to the need for consultation of the gods. Λακεδαιμονίοις: the dative of the agent with παραλελειμμένα: 'are least of all neglected by the Lacedaemonians'.

13 The power and honour of the King on campaign

Lycurgus legislated so that the King could focus on his role as chief priest and war leader: ἱερεῖ μὲν . . . στρατηγῶι δέ. The account is presented as a sequence of what happens on campaign. Xenophon refers to the kings in the singular and the plural (13.1); it is indeed natural to say: 'the King does this', even when two kings are in mind. *Lac.* 15 also refers to kings in both the singular and plural. In his account of the duties and privileges of kings, Hdt. 6.56–8 speaks of two kings because his account arises out of the establishment of the dual kingship. See Carlier (1984) 249–315 on the King's duties and privileges in war and in peace.

13.1 ἐπὶ φρουρᾶς 'on duty', a technical term used by the Spartans for ἐπὶ στρατιᾶς; cf. Richards (1897) 135; Gautier (1911) 41; *Lac.* 13.11 and the customary phrase φρουρὰν φαίνουσι. συσκηνοῦσι δὲ αὐτῶι οἱ πολέμαρχοι: *Hell.* 1.1.30 shows another way that consultation could be achieved, with morning and evening meetings in the general's tent. καὶ ἄλλοι τρεῖς ἄνδρες τῶν ὁμοίων: the use of 'equals' rather than helots to see to the King's needs points to the high quality of the service.

13.2 ἐπαναλήψομαι: another editorial intrusion (cf. 12.7) orders the description of his duties; the 'return' is to the beginning of the campaign. ἐξορμᾶται 'moves out' of Laconia, at the beginning of an expedition. Διὶ Ἁγήτορι καὶ τοῖς σὺν αὐτῶι 'to Zeus Leader and those with him'; the latter is a reference to Castor and Polydeuces, the Tyndaridae, brothers of Helen. Marchant actually emends to τοῖν σιοῖν (dual, = τοῖν θεοῖν in Laconian dialect). The Dioscuri led the Spartan kings out on campaign: Hdt. 5.75.2. They were also important to the youth: Kennell (1995) 138–42. Zeus the Leader is not attested elsewhere: Burkert (1985) 257, but he may be identified closely with the kings who are descended from him. ὁ πυρφόρος: a subordinate priest; fire was important in ancient ritual: Burkert (1985) 60–4. Διὶ καὶ Ἀθηνᾶι: temples are vowed in the Great Rhetra to Zeus Syllanios and Athena Syllania: Plut. *Lyc.* 6.1.

13.3 διαβαίνει τὰ ὅρια: there were special sacrifices on crossing borders: διαβατήρια; see *Hell.* 3.4.3, 3.5.7, 4.7.2, 5.1.33, 5.4.37, 5.4.47, 6.5.12; Pritchett Part 3 (1979) 67–71. σφάγια: 'sacrificial victims' were vital for the King's function as chief priest: Pritchett Part 3 (1979) 83–90. κνεφαῖος: a poetic word for darkness; cf. note on 5.7; the ritual described in Alcman's *Partheneion* is also probably held just before dawn, presumably for the reason given here, to get the early attention of the god.

13.4 πάρεισι δὲ περὶ τὴν θυσίαν: cf. 11.4 for the ranks of those attending; the *enomotarchoi* are excepted, but the *stratiarchoi* of *xenoi* (presumably the *xenagoi* who mustered troops from the allied cities: *Hell.* 3.5.7, 4.2.19, 4.5.7, 5.1.33, 5.2.7, 7.2.3), commanders of the baggage train (*Hell.* 3.4.22) and volunteer *strategoi* from the allied cities are added. Lipka (2002) points out that the attendance of *enomotarchoi* would have made the numbers impossibly large.

13.5 ὡς τὸ εἰκός: the argument from probability is used again to underline the sobering effect the ephors have on the citizens even when they are abroad on campaign; see note on 8.3. προσκαλέσας πάντας παραγγέλλει τὰ ποιητέα: the alliteration calls attention to this important phrase, in which the King issues orders for the day. ὥστε ὁρῶν ταῦτα ἡγήσαιο ἄν: the reader is engaged in the second person as a witness (cf. 3.5) in order to emphasize the complete professionalism of the ritual. Xenophon is impressed because he credits all success to the gods (*Poroi* 6.2–3, *Hipparchicus* 1.1), but also because each commander had his orders from the King's mouth at the beginning of each day. αὐτοσχεδιαστὰς . . . τῶν στρατιωτικῶν . . . τεχνίτας τῶν πολεμικῶν: 'extemporizers in military matters' leave the commander to use his own initiative, whereas 'experts in warfare' leave nothing to initiative, but dictate details. Agesilaus found an old law that allowed a commander to αὐτοσχεδιάζειν in the best interests of the Spartans when the ephors and the people condemned Phoebidas' initiative in seizing the Cadmea, but this exception just proves the rule against such freedom (*Hell.* 5.2.32). *Mem.* 3.5.21 equates military extemporizing with ignorance.

13.6 Σκιρῖται: see the note on 12.3. τὸ ἄγημα τῆς πρώτης μόρας 'the leading part of the first *mora*' seems to be a 'royal guard', perhaps composed of the ephebic *hippeis*: Anderson (1970) 245–9. τὸ ἄγημα is used of an entire company at 11.9. The nature of the manoeuvre is unclear: cf. Anderson (1970) 248, Lazenby (1985) 28–30. ἐν μέσωι δυοῖν μόραιν καὶ δυοῖν πολεμάρχοιν: the dual emphasizes the close association of the two companies and their commanders around the King; the position protects the King from undue exposure to danger and facilitates consultation. Thuc. 5.66.3 describes how the King gives orders to the polemarchs, and they send them down through the units to the *enomotiai*.

13.7 οὓς δὲ δεῖ ἐπὶ τούτοις τετάχθαι: the equals are positioned near to the King because they see to his personal needs (mentioned at 13.1), the seers because they interpret his sacrifices (*Hell.* 3.3.4), the doctors because they tend his wounds (*Hell.* 5.4.58; compare the attendance of the Greek doctor Ctesias on the Persian King in *An.* 1.8.26–7), the pipers because they determine the pace of battle-march (on the 'Chigi Vase', they march between the ranks of hoplites) and signal the victory (*Hell.* 4.3.21 and 13.8 below); other army leaders and volunteers also have special status, like those who joined Teleutias: *Hell.* 5.3.9. ὁ πρεσβύτατος τῶν περὶ δαμοσίαν: the eldest is in charge because of the authority of age (see on 5.8, 10); the Laconian dialect is used; cf. the Attic σκήνην . . . δημοσίαν at 15.4. ὥστε τῶν δεομένων γίγνεσθαι οὐδὲν ἀπορεῖται 'so that not one of the things that need to happen is wanting'.

13.8 μάλα δὲ καὶ τάδε ὠφέλιμα . . . ἐμηχανήσατο Λυκοῦργος εἰς τὸν ἐν ὅπλοις ἀγῶνα: this digression from the duties of the King nevertheless describes the next phase in his duties: the commencement of battle. The statement recalls 11.3: εἴς γε μὴν τὸν ἐν τοῖς ὅπλοις ἀγῶνα τοιάδ' ἐμηχανήσατο, but the emphasis this time is on morale on the eve of military action, not just how the army looks. The mention of the pipe-players in the King's retinue may provoke the digression, since an early focus is the practice of the pipers in going into battle. ὁρώντων ἤδη τῶν πολεμίων: the sacrifice of the she-goat in view of the enemy is a form of psychological warfare because it indicates a complete lack of panic; the good omens also encouraged their troops: *Hell.* 4.2.20. αὐλεῖν τε πάντας . . . νόμος καὶ μηδένα . . . ἀστεφάνωτον εἶναι: infinitives of what the law commands; to enter battle wearing a garland and playing pipes is a sign of utter confidence; garlands are worn and pipes play only in the wake of victory at *Hell.* 4.3.18, 21. προαγορεύεται: the previous προαγορεύεται ὑπὸ τοῦ νόμου ἅπασι (12.5) suggests that this instruction comes from the law too.

13.9 καὶ κεχριμένωι: the emendation 'anointed with oil' continues the reference to public appearance, as at 3.4–5, 9.5; anointing with oil was regular in the gymnasium; here, by embellishing the appearance of the ephebe, it lifts morale. Plut. *Ages.* 34.7–11 describes the uplifting sight that young Isidas presented, who went into battle without armour after anointing himself with oil. παρακελεύονται: the subject of the verb is unstated; soldiers encourage one another at *An.* 4.2.11, but here the encouragement is given to the *enomotarch*, apparently to pass on to the soldiers. Anderson (1970) 78–9 explains that commanders of the larger units are responsible for seeing that words of encouragement reach the smallest units. Lipka (2002) suggests that the verb means 'pass on instructions', but the emphasis in this passage on the promotion of morale would support Anderson. οὐδ᾽ ἀκούεται γὰρ . . . 'for except from each enomotarch, no voice is heard over the whole of each *enomotia*' i.e. the more senior commanders cannot make their voices heard over the entire army. Pritchett (2002) 52–65 discusses the range of the human voice in battle.

13.10–11 returns to the duties of the King after the battle is over, with mention of encampment, diplomacy, booty. τὸ μέντοι πρεσβείας ἀποπέμπεσθαι . . . τοῦτ᾽ αὖ βασιλέως 'and to dispatch embassies . . . this is also (the duty) of the King'. *Hell.* 5.3.24 bears this out when it presents Agesilaus as angry that the Phliasians seek to make him ἄκυρος in the matter of embassies. Carlier (1984) 264–5 accordingly retains the manuscript reading αὖ. Lipka (2002) argues that the sentence structure begs οὐ (Weiske), citing *Lac.* 2.14 τὸ μέντοι ταῦτα ἀπιστεῖσθαι ὑπό τινων οὐ θαυμάζω and 11.7 τὸ μέντοι . . . μάχεσθαι . . . οὐκέτι ῥάιδιον, but among his other examples, *Hell.* 2.3.48 has a positive statement, 7.5.19 has two negatives and one positive statement. καὶ ἄρχονται μὲν πάντες ἀπὸ βασιλέως 'and everyone makes a beginning from the King (whenever they wish to transact business)'. *Hell.* 3.4.7–10 confirms the principle through a transgression: because Agesilaus was unknown in Asia, people went to Lysander if they wanted anything done by the King (ἀξιοῦντες διαπράττεσθαι αὐτὸν παρ᾽Ἀγησιλάου ὧν ἐδέοντο); but his Spartiate colleagues considered this 'outside the law'. Hdt. 9.76 says also that Pausanias the regent handed over the captive woman from Cos to 'those of the ephors who were present' only after he had heard her business and decided whether it should proceed.

13.11 δ᾽ οὖν marks a contrast involving a more important point: cf. 2.8; people come to the King first with their business, but he *then* sends them on to others; this confirms that he has overall authority, but limits his involvement in the detail in order to keep him free of non-military distractions. ἑλλανοδίκας: little is known of their functions, except that they deal with disputes: Anderson (1970) 69. ταμίας: officials who supervised the military accounts (cf. the *Hellenotamiai* who supervised the revenues of Athenian Empire); again, little is known of their precise functions. λαφυροπώλας: those who were responsible for the disposal of booty: *Hell.* 4.1.26. οὕτω δὲ πραττομένων 'since things are managed in this fashion'.

14 The decline of Sparta

The notes on this chapter should be read in conjunction with the fuller discussion in Appendix 3. *Lac.* 1–13 has argued that the Spartans secured success through obedience to the laws of Lycurgus. This chapter brings the reader up to date and indicates that at the time of writing the Spartans have ceased to obey the laws and have lost their success as a result. Their harmosts have succumbed to corruption overseas and have alienated those who once asked the Spartans for leadership, who now call on each other to prevent them ruling. The connection of their disobedience with their loss of success proves the excellence of the laws, which is the main theme of the work. The decline is represented in a comparison of the present and the past situation that consists of sweeping commonplaces about the detrimental effects of empire abroad. Xenophon's analysis is reproduced in Plutarch, *Lyc.* 30.1–2, who says that while the laws remained in force, the *polis* 'with a single *skytale* and cloak ruled a glad and willing Greece', but Lysander changed this all in the latter part of the Peloponnesian War when the country was filled with the corruption of gold and silver.

14.1 εἰ δέ τίς με ἔροιτο: the audience is not supposed to know whether the laws are still in force. ἀκίνητοι 'unmoved' or 'intact' is appropriately used of laws that had been approved by Delphi (8.5), since it is found mainly in the poets and in Herodotus describes particularly sacred institutions, such as the island of Delos (6.98.3) or the secrets of Demeter (6.134). τοῦτο in apposition along with μὰ Δία strengthens the idea of the laws being no longer unmoved.

14.2 αἱρουμένους οἴκοι τὰ μέτρια ἔχοντας ἀλλήλοις συνεῖναι: 'choosing to live together in moderation at home' is the result of the friendly harmony produced by obedience to the laws; it is contrasted with wanting to acquire wealth through warfare and competition in *Mem.* 2.6.22, where, on account of their virtue, friends αἱροῦνται μὲν ἄνευ πόνου τὰ μέτρια κεκτῆσθαι μᾶλλον ἢ διὰ πολέμου πάντων κυριεύειν. ἁρμόζοντας: the Spartans sent out 'harmosts' to govern the *poleis* that they controlled from the time of the Peloponnesian War down to Xenophon's times (*Hell.* 2.4.28, 4.8.1, 5.2.37, 5.4.20; Parke (1930) 37–79). κολακευομένους διαφθείρεσθαι: they are subject to the same corrupting flattery as the unreformed Hiero: *Hiero* 1.15–16, the Athenian *demos*: *Ath.* 1.18, and Alcibiades, when he escapes Socrates' control (*Mem.* 1.2.24).

14.3 νῦν 'in this generation': pp. 42–3. ἔστιν οὓς καὶ καλλωπιζομένους: merely fearing to be seen in possession of gold is contrasted with 'even flaunting' their possession of it; restricting the flaunting to 'some' indicates the extent of the transgression. The harmosts thus contravene the law of 7.6, but not as a result of those occupations that the law had most particularly banned. Empire found new avenues for profits that Lycurgus had not envisaged.

14.4 γιγνομένας . . . ἐξόν: participles after a verb of knowing. Thuc. 2.39.1 has Pericles imply that the notorious expulsions of foreigners stopped military secrets from getting out, but Xenophon suggests here that they stopped the dangerous foreign habit of 'slacking' from getting in. The ability to spend time abroad was a sign of freedom in *Hiero* 1.11–13, but here leads to corruption. Plato, *Laws*, 949e–953e finds both emigration and immigration a problem for the *polis*, but considers that complete *xenelasia* and a complete ban on visits abroad are undesirable. Aristotle *Pol.* 1272b17–19 sees *xenelasia* as a safeguard for a state that is the equivalent of isolation from its enemies. Xenophon says nothing more of expulsions in this chapter; *xenelasia* has been made entirely superfluous by Spartans going abroad.

14.5 καὶ ἦν μὲν ὅτε 'and there was a time when' = πρόσθεν. ἐπεμελοῦντο ὅπως ἄξιοι εἶεν ἡγεῖσθαι 'they took pains to be worthy of leadership', is contrasted with πραγματεύονται ὅπως ἄρξουσιν 'they make it their business to rule'. Aristotle, *Pol.* 1271b7–10 agrees that they began to esteem the prizes of empire above the virtue that was meant to win it. This attitude can already be seen in Xenophon's view that the Spartans would prevent him taking command of the 10,000 because they alone had the right to rule (*An.* 6.1.25–31).

14.6 τοιγαροῦν: a strong and climactic explanatory connection: cf. 6.5. ἐδέοντο αὐτῶν ἡγεῖσθαι ἐπὶ τοὺς δοκοῦντας ἀδικεῖν: Greeks went to Sparta to ask her to prevent the unjust expansion of the Athenian empire at the outbreak of the Peloponnesian War (Thuc. 1.67). παρακαλοῦσιν ἀλλήλους ἐπὶ τὸ διακωλύειν ἄρξαι πάλιν αὐτούς: πάλιν could mean 'to the contrary', reinforcing the contrast implied in the opening νῦν δέ, or 'again' (since the cities could encourage one another to prevent the Spartans from ruling 'in contradiction of' their previous request to have them rule, or they could prevent them from ruling 'again' after their rejection of their first hegemony at the outbreak of the Corinthian War in 395 BC). In view of the contrasts between 'previously' and 'now' through this section, πάλιν should highlight the reversal, that those whom the allies previously called on to lead them are now the focus of their resistance. The position is unusual, but highlights the contrast between 'ask to lead' and 'prevent from ruling'. Xenophon uses πάλιν to contrast two opposing or inconsistent actions in *Mem.* 2.4.4 οὓς ἐν τοῖς φίλοις ἔθεσαν πάλιν τούτους ἀνατίθεσθαι, and in *Mem.* 4.4.14: πόλεμον . . . πολλάκις ἀράμεναι αἱ πόλεις πάλιν εἰρήνην ποιοῦνται. Cf. Ar., *Ecc.* 797f.: ἐγᾦδα τούτους χειροτονοῦντας μὲν ταχύ, ἅττ' ἂν δὲ δόξῃ, ταῦτα πάλιν ἀρνουμένους.

14.7 οὔτε τῷ θεῷ πειθόμενοι οὔτε τοῖς Λυκούργου νόμοις 'neither obeying the god (Apollo of Delphi, who endorsed the laws) nor the laws of Lycurgus'.

15 The privileges of kings inside Sparta

Section 14 held that Lycurgus' laws are no longer ἀκίνητοι 'unmoved' among the most powerful Spartiates overseas. Section 15 holds that the kingship, which was the prerogative of *the* most powerful Spartiate, remained stable within Sparta, because Lycurgus introduced laws that limited the King's privileges in order to discourage tyrannical pride on his part, and envy on the people's. Thucydides describes the type as 'hereditary kingships with stated privileges', ἐπὶ ῥητοῖς γέρασι πατρικαὶ βασιλεῖαι (1.13.1) and notes the stability (1.18.1). Plato, *Laws* 691e–692b, Arist. *Pol.* 1313a 23–33 agrees that curbing its power ensured its stability. Xenophon's interest in how the laws secured the kingship leads him to focus on royal service to the *polis* and on small privileges such as sacrificial meat, and food and drink, and having attendants. He does not mention the King's supervision of heiresses, thoroughfares and adoptions, or his membership of the *Gerousia* (Hdt. 6.57.4) – perhaps because these would not increase his pride or incur his people's envy in the same way as extra rations would. He does not mention the King's private wealth either (such as Agesilaus' inheritance of Agis' estate: *Ages*. 4.5), presumably because that did not come to him from his public position, which is the focus of this chapter. He does mention the gifts of land from the *perioikoi*, even though he emphasizes their moderate size. He continues to speak of a single King, except at 15.4–5; see the note on *Lac*. 13. No source explains whether the kings acted in concert within Sparta or whether they had separate responsibilities, such as separate priesthoods: Carlier (1984) 256.

15.1 βούλομαι . . . διηγήσασθαι: the authorial intrusion gives the same sense of order to the account as ἐπαναλήψομαι (13.2). **αὕτη ἀρχή . . . οἷαπερ ἐξ ἀρχῆς κατεστάθη** 'this first foundation office . . . as it was from the first foundation': a pun. **τὰς δὲ ἄλλας πολιτείας . . .** : the comparison of the continuity of the Spartan kingship with the discontinuity of 'the other constitutions' recurs at *Ages*. 1.4: 'no other ἀρχή has continued ἀδιάσπαστος, either democracy or oligarchy or tyranny or kingship; this alone continues as a constant kingship.' The comparison of one office in a constitution with other entire constitutions seems strange, but Xenophon is thinking in terms of rulers being overthrown by the ruled, as is shown in the focus of this chapter on the relations between the King and his people; such an overthrow is also the context in the passage from *Agesilaus*. For Xenophon, the ruler is the King and the ruled are his people and this is the point of resemblance to the other cases where oligarchs or others are the rulers over their populations; *Lac*. is making the same point that *Cyropaedia* made in its introduction. Cf. Bordes (1982) 194–203 on this problem.

15.2 θύειν . . . πρὸ τῆς πόλεως: *Hell*. 3.3.4 has Agesilaus θύοντος αὐτοῦ τῶν τεταγμένων τινὰ θυσιῶν ὑπὲρ τῆς πόλεως. Herodotus also refers to sacrifice at public expense: δημοτελής (6.57.1). Burkert (1985) 95–6 notes the similarity of the privileges of priests and kings. **ὡς ἀπὸ τοῦ θεοῦ ὄντα**: the kings were descended from Zeus ('the god') through Heracles: *Ages*. 1.2. **ὅποι ἂν ἡ πόλις ἐκπέμπηι** 'wherever the *polis* sends him out'; this emphasizes his service to the *polis* as chief military commander. Hdt. 6.56.1 says that kings could 'initiate war' πόλεμόν γ' ἐκφέρειν against any land they wished, but Carlier (1984) 257–60 confirms that the city and the ephors initiate wars: *Hell*. 5.4.35, 47, 59.

15.3 γέρα ἀπὸ τῶν θυομένων 'privileges from the sacrificed animals', i.e. the meat and hides: Hdt. 6.56–7. **καὶ γῆν δὲ ἐν πολλαῖς τῶν περιοίκων πόλεων . . . ἐξαίρετον**: the earliest known reference to this royal privilege of owning land: Cartledge (1987) 108, and one of the earliest to the perioecic communities as *poleis*: cf. *Hell*. 6.5.21. The privilege is a survival of the granting of choice land to kings by their people, which is abundantly attested in Homer (*Iliad* 6.194–5, 9.574–80, 12.310–14, 20.184–6). **τοσαύτην ὥστε**: Xenophon takes care to demonstrate that the amount of land is limited to the King's needs, in the same way that the food of other groups was limited (2.5, 5.3): 'so as not to fall short of moderate needs nor exceed the limit in wealth'.

15.4 σκηνὴν . . . δημοσίαν: the kings have a 'public tent' to curb their indulgence inside Sparta, as the citizens have their *syssitia* (5.2): *Hell.* 5.3.20 and *Cyr.* 2.2.1, 2.3.1. **καὶ διμοιρίαι γε**: 'the double portion' of dinner given to kings: Hdt. 6.57.1. **οὐχ ἵνα . . . ἀλλ' ἵνα**: Lycurgus is protected against the charge of allowing the kings to consume more than the rest; *Ages.* 5.1 confirms that the double portion was used to honour others.

15.5 Πύθιοι: these officials are thought to have looked after oracles from Delphi: Hdt. 6.57.2, 4 and Carlier (1984) 267–9. They should therefore have some special role in preserving the laws, which were πυθοχρήστοις (8.5), but Xenophon does not mention their function because he is interested only in the privilege of the kings in being able to appoint them. They go unmentioned elsewhere. When Hdt. 5.90–1 shows how the Spartans used oracles to influence foreign policy, the *Pythioi* are nowhere to be seen. *Hell.* 3.3.1–3 tells the story of the seer who produced the oracle about the lame kingship against Agesilaus, but he is not called a *Pythios*. **πασῶν τῶν συῶν ἀπὸ τόκου χοῖρον** 'one piglet from each litter of all sows'; Hdt.1.56.1 also notes the King's share of προβάτοισι; τόκος also means 'interest' or 'commission'. **ἀπορῆσαι**: third-person aorist optative (*GG* 480.1, 732).

15.6 ἀφθονίαν: an 'abundance' may seem at odds with the frugality of the other arrangements for the King, but the root meaning 'not grudging' plays on the lack of envy that the King enjoys from his people; he also enjoys an ungrudged and ungrudging supply of water. The comment that those who do not have such a pond know best its many uses charmingly justifies such a slight thing as a privilege to those of moderate means. **ὑπανίστανται** 'stand up from their seat', the regular mark of honour: cf. *Hiero* 7.2,7,9. **ἀπὸ τῶν ἐφορικῶν δίφρων**: the seats of the ephors indicate their special standing; *Ages.* 1.36 refers to the building in which they were found.

15.7 καὶ ὅρκους δὲ ἀλλήλοις κατὰ μῆνα ποιοῦνται: Xenophon is the earliest source for a sworn agreement between kings and ephors; the monthly reaffirmation makes it a ritual in the religious calendar. Plato, *Laws* 683d–684a describes a similar oath between King and people that he says was current in Argos and Messene as well as Sparta: '(the rulers swear) not to make their rule harsher . . . and the others (swear) that if the rulers remain by (ἐμπεδούντων) these (undertakings) they will never dissolve the kingships themselves or allow others who try to do so'; Isocrates, *Archidamus* 6.20–2 refers to the perhaps allied compact in which the Heraclids gave the Dorians their land in the Peloponnese, while the Dorians gave the Heraclids the kingship; their King Archidamus tells the Dorians, now represented by the people of Sparta: 'You remain by your compacts and oaths', ἐμμένετε ταῖς συνθήκαις καὶ τοῖς ὅρκοις. *Cyr.* 8.5.24–5 has Cyrus and his Persians swear a similar oath: that if anyone attacks Persia or tries to subvert her laws, he will protect them; and that if anyone tries to depose Cyrus or revolts, the people will come to their own rescue and his. **τῶι μὲν βασιλεῖ . . . τῆι δὲ πόλει**: a sentence of two mirroring parts with almost exactly the same number of syllables captures the reciprocity of the oaths sworn between the two parties. **ἐμπεδορκοῦντος . . . ἀστυφέλικτον**: two unusual words mark the legal solemnity of the oath; ἐμπεδορκεῖν is legal language not only in Herodotus, but in *IG²* 2 111 line 79. ἀστυφέλικτον 'unabused' is rare and poetic.

15.8–9 ζῶντι βασιλεῖ . . . τελευτήσαντι . . . βασιλεῖ: the greater honours given to the King in death are balanced against those he received in life. τυραννικὸν φρόνημα: Herodotus' constitutional debate also represents the King as a figure prone to pride (3.80), and Aristotle, *Pol.* 1313a19–20 indicates that kingships are secured 'by leading kingships toward more moderation' τῶι τὰς μὲν βασιλείας ἄγειν ἐπὶ τὸ μετριώτερον.

15.9 αἱ δε τελευτήσαντι τιμαὶ βασιλεῖ δέδονται, τῇδε βούλονται δηλοῦν οἱ Λυκούργου νόμοι '(by) the honours that are given to the King when he dies, by this means, the laws of Lycurgus seek to show'; the demonstrative is in apposition to the relative clause and the antecedent is attracted (*GG* 1037). ὡς ἥρωας 'like heroes', mortals who were worshipped after their death; there is a need to distinguish actual heroization from treatment 'like' heroes. Xenophon elsewhere suggests special treatment for kings, such as the return of their bodies for burial (*Hell.* 5.3.19: Agesipolis, and *Ages.* 11.16: Agesilaus), but that falls short of heroization. Agis' burial is also merely 'more solemn than befits a man' (*Hell.* 3.3.1). However, the closing description has a sonorous rhythm appropriate to hero status: οὐχ ὡς ἀνθρώπους ἀλλ' ὡς ἥρωας τοὺς Λακεδαιμονίων βασιλεῖς προτετιμήκασι. Hdt. 6.58 gives an account of the dead King's honours so sensational that he finds parallels in the East: 6.58.2, but Xenophon maintains that the Spartans were as disciplined in death as in other matters. Agesilaus mourned Agesipolis only with longing and tears (*Hell.* 5.3.20). The aftermath of Leuctra also reflects discipline in the midst of death: the ephors tell the women not to mourn, but to bear their grief in silence: *Hell.* 6.4.16.

COMMENTARY ON *RESPUBLICA ATHENIENSIUM*

1.1 The author states his anti-democratic *prohairesis* and the paradox of political thought, that though the democracy is not the best constitution since it does not promote the best, yet it survives and prospers.

δέ: the conjunction is most likely 'inceptive', like the ἀλλά that introduces *Lac. GP* 172–3 notes that it occurs at the opening of speeches and oracles in Herodotus (1.115.2, 8.142.1 for speeches, 1.174.5, 7.142.2 for oracles). Caballero López (1997) 107–12 cites other examples. Yet it might indicate that the author has a view opposed to that of others, like the ἀλλά that introduces *LP*, or connect *Ath.* to a previous work (*Lac.* has been proposed). εἵλοντο . . . ἑλόμενοι εἵλοντο: the constitution is the product of deliberate choice rather than accidental evolution, as shown in references to how the *demos* has deliberately worked out every detail: 2.19, 3.10 etc. Their choice of constitution is matched by the author's choosing not to praise the choice; Isocrates *Panath.* 12.200 describes a pupil who 'lived in an oligarchy and chose to praise the Spartans' ἐν ὀλιγ-αρχίαι δὲ πεπολιτευμένον, προηιρημένον δὲ Λακεδαιμονίους ἐπαινεῖν. The emphasis on 'choice', as well as 'errors' becomes a constitutional commonplace: Isocrates *Panath.* 12.115 (οὐδεὶς ἂν δικαίως ἐπιτιμήσειε τοῖς ἑλομένοις αὐτήν. οὐ γὰρ διήμαρτον τῶν ἐλπίδων), 130 (ἄπειροι πολιτειῶν ὄντες, οὐ διήμαρτον αἱρούμενοι). τοὺς πονηροὺς ἄμεινον πράττειν ἢ τοὺς χρηστούς: *Ath.* takes for granted that the many poor who constitute the *demos* are bad and the rich few are good; for further description of the qualities and characteristics of the two groups: cf. 1.4, 7, 9, 14, 2.19; to have the bad do better than the good was not good government. Hiero laments the compulsion he feels to eliminate the good and make the bad prosper (5.1–2). ἐπεὶ δὲ ταῦτα ἔδοξεν οὕτως αὐτοῖς: this recalls the formula that expressed the collective will of the *demos* in their formal decisions and is recorded in inscriptions such as *IG* 1² 63 = *IG* 1³ 71 (Meiggs and Lewis (1988) no. 69: the Tribute Decree) line 3: ἔδοχσεν τῖ βολῖ καὶ τῶι δέμοι . . . διαπράττονται is also used in decrees of conducting the general business of the *polis* (lines 35–7 of the decree above); cf. 3.2. εὖ qualifies both διασώιζονται and διαπράττονται 'preserve the constitution and manage the other things *well* which they seem to the other Greeks to manage *badly*'. Those Greeks who are here described as critics emerge in the analysis as the opposition to the argument, whom the author engages at various points. There is no need to find specific critics, though Kalinka (1913) *loc. cit.* notes that Philostratus, *VS* 1.16 = 502 says that Critias 'criticized all democracy and slandered the Athenians as most mistaken of men' when he was in Thessaly (cf. *Mem.* 1.2.24).

1.2 The greater share that the *demos* gets represents justice in their own eyes (and perhaps in the eyes of others), because they give the city its power by 'hauling' the fleet as rowers. (The rich make no such contribution because they are hoplites and not numerous.)

ἐρῶ: such intrusions stamp the author's presence and views firmly on his text; cf. φράσω (1.10). δικαίως δοκοῦσιν: the transmitted text makes no sense; the concluding δοκεῖ δίκαιον εἶναι (lines 13–14) suggests we supply δοκοῦσιν in view of the author's fondness for repetitions and ring-composition. δικαίως is also emended to δικαιοῦσ' 'they think it their right' (Lapini 1997) or δικαῖοι 'they are right to take' (Münscher). This raises the question whether the *demos* rightly has a greater share or simply claims a greater share as its right. The author could champion the latter view about the rights of the *demos* in an expression of irony. In the same spirit he identifies with the Athenians in the creation of their arrangements below (1.12). αὐτόθι 'at Athens': p. 55. καὶ οἱ πένητες καὶ ὁ δῆμος: the *demos* is defined as the poor in the traditional way (cf. *Mem.* 1.2.58 τοὺς δημότας καὶ πένητας, and 4.2.37), but editors delete καί and change the order of 'the poor and the demos'. Their poverty does not seem relevant at this stage. It would be simpler if the author had said: δικαίως αὐτόθι δοκεῖ ὁ δῆμος . . . ὁ δῆμός ἐστιν ὁ ἐλαύνων τὰς ναῦς: the article and participle plus εἶναι puts the emphasis on the property of the action rather than the action itself; cf. note on *Hiero* 1.25; cf. ὁ δῆμός ἐστιν ὁ ἄρχων (3.13). The idea of 'attaching power to the *polis*' refers to their creation of a naval empire and is repeated below for further emphasis. καὶ οἱ κυβερνῆται καὶ οἱ κελευσταὶ καὶ . . .: Amit (1965) 29–30, Jordan (1975) 138–43, 145–6, describe these as the ὑπηρεσία, 'the officers': trained seamen as distinct from the rowers. The 'helmsmen' steered the ship by operating the oar, but as the trireme evolved they became the operational ship's captains; the 'boatswains' gave instructions about the rhythm to the rowers, and converted the captain's orders into action; the 'pursers' took on administrative roles as paymaster, recruitment officer; 'those on the prow' chart the course and watch for the wind and other obstacles; the 'ship's carpenters' speak for themselves. The author knows the terms for the members of the crew of a trireme like any good member of the *demos*; see 1.19–20, where the *demos* has had to learn ὀνόματα . . . τὰ ἐν τῆι ναυτικῆι, as rowers and then as helmsmen of their own merchant and passenger ships. Ar., *Knights* 541ff. gives the naval *cursus honorum*: to row, take the rudder, act as look-out, then finally guide the ship as captain. πᾶσι τῶν ἀρχῶν μετεῖναι . . . 'that there be a share of the offices to all'. This introduces the great democratic principles: universal access to office through random selection and election, and universal freedom to participate in decision-making through speaking in public. Arist., *Ath. Pol.* 43.1–2, 44.1–2 makes constant references to the ballot and vote, the former making a random selection, the latter relying on the majority vote for a decision. The power to speak is the famous ἰσηγορία on which the herald called when he asked the assembly τίς ἀγορεύειν βούλεται: Dem. 18.170; ἰσηγορία is used of the 'equality' given to the slaves, which lets them behave as they like at 1.12.

1.3 They control the magistracies with a view to security and profit. They leave to the rich those military offices that ensure the preservation of the democracy against enemies if well managed. They reserve for themselves those offices that carry payment or give them expenses.

ὁπόσαι μὲν . . . τῶν ἀρχῶν . . . τούτων μὲν τῶν ἀρχῶν: the offices that secure the preservation of the *demos* are soon to be balanced against the offices that carry payment below: ὁπόσαι δ' εἰσὶν ἀρχαὶ μισθοφορίας ἕνεκα. The repetition of ἀρχ-words emphasizes the topic of political office. On the use of the demonstrative see note on *Hiero* 1.6. σωτηρίαν . . . χρησταὶ οὖσαι καὶ μὴ χρησταὶ κίνδυνον: *chiasmus* binds the contrast; 'if they are well managed' means held by the better classes. The idea that bad government reserved the profits for itself while giving the dangers to others is commonplace: cf. Thuc. 6.39.2 on oligarchy, *Hell.* 3.5.12 on the Spartans. σφισι: this form of the reflexive is found alongside σφίσιν αὐτοῖς (1.4, 1.6) and αὐτῶι (1.6, 1.7): Caballero López (1997) 31–6. γιγνώσκει: the author stresses the deliberate calculation of the *demos* here and again at 1.7, 11, 13, 14,18; 2.9, 16, 19, 20; 3.10. ἀλλ'(sc. ἐν τῶι) ἐᾶν τοὺς δυνατωτάτους ἄρχειν: their 'permission' shows that they are in complete control of the offices and could take them if they wished. τοὺς δυνατωτάτους is another term for the better classes, as at 2.18. μισθοφορίας ἕνεκα καὶ ὠφελείας εἰς τὸν οἶκον 'for the sake of the payment they carry and assistance to the individual household'. Aristotle, *Ath. Pol.* 62.2 refers to many offices that carried payments in the fourth century. This is the first indication that the *demos* has created the democracy with the cash profit of individuals and their households in mind. Isoc. *Areop.* 25 recalls the good old days when the *demos* did not pursue its own profit, but the profit of the commonwealth.

1.4 The argument is extended to their greater share 'in all areas'. They preserve the *demos* by 'increasing' the poor in this general way. By making the rich and good prosper, they would 'increase' their enemies.

ὃ ἔνιοι θαυμάζουσιν: cf. the opinion about the errors of the *demos* at 1.1, 6, 7, 8, 9, 10, 11, 15, 16; 2.17; 3.1, 3, 6, 7, 12; on the restriction of the opinion to 'some people' see notes on 1.5, 1.11. φανοῦνται τὴν δημοκρατίαν διασώιζοντες: the first use of the word 'democracy' implies the constitution itself as well as the power of the people in it. φανοῦνται seems to present the claim as the results of investigation: 'they will appear (after investigation)'; see also φανεῖεν ἄν (1.11). εὖ πράττοντες καὶ πολλοὶ οἱ τοιοῦτοι γιγνόμενοι: the participles are conditional 'if they do well and if (in consequence) people of their sort become many'; the great numbers that characterized the poor are not taken for granted here, but are the result of deliberate cultivation. 'Increasing the democracy' is a pointed subversion of the aim of good government, which was to 'increase' the *polis* (p. 5). *Hiero* 11.13 is told to 'increase the *polis*' rather than his household, whereas this *demos* increases its households and thereby the power of its majority.

1.5 The author explains their suppression of the good men with a sweeping generalization: that the best is in every land opposed to 'the power of the *demos*' (this idea recurs at 1.14, 2.19, 3.10). The qualities of the rich and poor are in actual conflict.

ἔστι δὲ πάσηι γῆι τὸ βέλτιστον ἐναντίον τῆι δημοκρατίαι: Arist., *Pol.* 1310a8–12 confirms the proverbial hostility of the rich to the poor in his quotation of the oath of the oligarchs: 'And I shall be ill-disposed to the *demos* and will devise for them whatever harm I can.' ἔνι (ἔνεστι) 'there is in (them)'. ἀκολασία τε ὀλιγίστη καὶ ἀδικία, ἀκρίβεια δὲ πλείστη εἰς τὰ χρηστά: two balanced phrases, one negating, the other positive, describe the qualities of the men of worth; 'most exactitude with regard to excellence' is a Thucydidean quality: Thuc. 1.22.1 and Caballero López (1997) 55–6. ἀκολασία 'lack of restraint' is a characteristic of the *demos* in the 'politics of dissent': cf. pp. 49–51. ἥ τε γὰρ πενία αὐτοὺς μᾶλλον ἄγει ἐπὶ τὰ αἰσχρά: the connection between crime and poverty was commonplace. *Hiero* 4.10 applies it to the tyrant, whose great needs make him poor in spite of his great wealth and who must then commit the traditional crime of sacking shrines. *Poroi* 1.1 applies it to Athenian politicians, who commit injustices against the allies in order to remedy the poverty of the *demos*. Thucydides' Pericles (2.40.1) controversially finds no cause for shame in poverty, only in not attempting to escape from it – presumably not through crime. καὶ ἀμαθία ἡ δι᾽ ἔνδειαν χρημάτων ἐνίοις τῶν ἀνθρώπων: Kalinka's reading makes sense of the transmitted text; sense might also be made by supplying ἔνι = ἔνεστι to the manuscript reading καὶ ἡ ἀμαθία . . . The phrase 'for some among mankind' may gloss the previous αὐτούς (i.e. the poor) as 'some' of the wider community. Otherwise, the ignorance is extended only to some of the poor. *Ath.* thus also restricts other expressions that appear to have universal application: 1.11, 2.4, 2.10.

1.6 εἴποι δ᾽ ἄν τις: the author imagines that his opposition will object that the *demos* is, precisely because of these flaws in its character, in 'error' in allowing its people to speak. He responds that this licence is contrived also to serve its interests. The poor man speaks to find some good for himself and those of his kind because of their common identity; the rich man speaks in the interests of his class too. μὴ ἐᾶν λέγειν πάντας ἑξῆς μηδὲ βουλεύειν: λέγειν could carry the technical sense 'to propose a motion', and βουλεύειν 'to be a member of the Council'; the adverb means 'without discrimination'; cf. Thuc. 1.125.1: ἑξῆς καὶ μείζονι καὶ ἐλάσσονι πόλει. The idea that commoners had no right to speak was what most took from Odysseus' beating of the commoners (*Il.* 2.188–205), though Xenophon's Socrates drew another conclusion: *Mem.* 1.2.58–9. ἄριστα βουλεύονται plays on βουλεύειν above; they do 'take the best deliberation' in deciding that they are the best at deliberation; the author is not lacking in wit. εἰ μὲν γὰρ οἱ χρηστοὶ ἔλεγον . . . ἦν ἀγαθά: the apodosis lacks ἄν, but is unreal: 'if the good spoke . . . there would be/have constantly been good things'; cf. σ᾽ ἐδεδοίκει at 1.11 below. The particle is normally lacking when the apodosis contains an idea of obligation or propriety, and the usage here may be related: *GG* 1400–2; cf. for another unreal statement without ἄν Andocides 1.58: οὐδεὶς ἄλλος ἀπώλλυεν ἢ ἐγὼ μὴ εἰπών. τοῖς ὁμοίοις σφίσιν αὐτοῖς 'for those like themselves'. Homer, *Od.* 17.218 already makes the proverbial claim ὡς αἰεὶ τὸν ὁμοῖον ἄγει θεὸς ὡς τὸν ὁμοῖον. λέγων ὁ βουλόμενος ἀναστάς, ἄνθρωπος πονηρός: standing up is the sign of being about to speak. The unconnected sequence of participles and adjectives can be found in Thucydides' ἀλλὰ πᾶς τέ τις διαβῆναι αὐτὸς πρῶτος βουλόμενος (7.84.3); there is a similarly unconnected pair of participles at 1.13: νομίζων τοῦτο οὐ καλὸν εἶναι, γνοὺς ὅτι. ἄνθρωπος distinguishes the ordinary man from the ἄνδρας ἀρίστους of 1.6; see also 1.7, 1.9 and perhaps 3.13.

1.7 εἴποι τις ἄν: another objection is that an ignorant man has no knowledge of what is good for himself or others. The response is that the *demos* care about 'good or bad will' rather than wisdom/ignorance, because wisdom with bad will is worse than ignorance, since it will not be exercised in the interests of the *demos*. Better the fool who loves you than the wise man who does not.

ἡ τούτου ἀμαθία καὶ πονηρία καὶ εὔνοια . . . ἡ τοῦ χρηστοῦ ἀρετὴ καὶ σοφία καὶ κακόνοια: this varies the order of the contrasting qualities of ignorance/virtue, vice/wisdom, but stresses the good/ill-will, which comes almost as an element of surprise, by putting it in last place in each sequence. Lysias 25.7–8 begins his speech by proving to the court that none of his actions have ever been κακόνουν to the masses under the democracy or the oligarchy; λυσιτελεῖ is a very bold word of 'profit' for the *demos*.

1.8 The author contrasts the best constitution, which restrains and enslaves the base to the good, with the democracy, which does the opposite, the *eunomia* that the rich would impose and the *kakonomia* that the poor prefer, knowing that the continuance of their power is incompatible with *eunomia*. *Eunomia* was a word of political propaganda. Herodotus defines it as the essentially democratic condition of pursuing one's own interests and not those of a master, and finds it in operation even under enlightened kings in Egypt: 2.124. Solon's *eunomia* also rescued the *demos* from their enslavement to the rich and gave appropriate rights to each group (Solon fr. 4.30ff., West, *IEG*). But the imagined opponents of the democracy see it as the condition in which the *demos* is quite rightly restrained and enslaved to the better men. Dem. 15.19–20 also equates oligarchy with enslavement of the *demos* and democracy with their liberation.

ἀπὸ τοιούτων διαιτημάτων: political arrangements are seen as 'customs', and success depends on them, as in *Lac.* εὐνομουμένης τῆς πόλεως: the placement of the genitive absolute brings 'the *polis* under good government' into effective juxtaposition with 'enslavement of the *demos*'. ἐλεύθερος εἶναι καὶ ἄρχειν: the equation between freedom and rulership is commonplace. ὃ γὰρ σὺ νομίζεις οὐκ εὐνομεῖσθαι 'what you think (to be) not to enjoy *eunomia*'; the second person singular identifies the opposition as one of the best men.

1.9 *Eunomia* means that the clever people make the laws, the best restrain the base, the good take counsel about the city and do not allow raving madmen to serve on the council, propose motions or serve in the assembly. These four consequences are marked: πρῶτα μὲν . . . ἔπειτα . . . καὶ . . . καί.

τοὺς νόμους τιθέντας: cf. the νομοθεσία of the *demos* (3.2). κολάσουσιν οἱ χρηστοὶ τοὺς πονηρούς: cf. their refusal to have their freedom restrained (1.8). μαινομένους ἀνθρώπους: the designation of the *demos* as 'mad fools' is no idle or unexpected abuse, but follows on from their need for restraint; it recalls the image of the *demos* as a river in flood in Herodotus 3.81.2, without a clear direction, rushing at everything and needing to be constrained for the damage it does. *Mem.* 1.2.50 shows the need for physical restraint of the truly mad. βουλεύειν οὐδὲ λέγειν οὐδὲ ἐκκλησιάζειν: the technical ἐκκλησιάζειν is added to the previous references to speaking and advising. τοίνυν: the particle here picks up the mention of the good things that would lead to enslavement of the *demos* under εὐνομία.

1.10 The contrast of the freedom enjoyed by the *demos* under *kakonomia* with their possible enslavement under *eunomia* leads by association to the lack of restraint (ἀκολασία) that they extend to their own slaves (and metics and freedmen). The unreformed tyrant was compelled to 'make slaves free' through fear of the better classes (*Hiero* 6.5 and *Hell.* 7.3.8), but the Athenian *demos* does it just for profit. They not only give their slaves equality, but become slaves of their slaves (contrast their unwillingness to be slaves of their rich fellow citizens under *eunomia*), because naval power needs slaves to run the industries that support it, and slave-owners make a profit by taking a cut of their wages. Slaves are used as a measure of the condition of the free, as also in *Lac.* 1.4 etc. This shows the typical interest of constitutional literature in the free population.

πατάξαι 'to beat (slaves) physically' is the strongest kind of restraint. οὔτε ὑπεκστήσεταί σοι ὁ δοῦλος: a slave who does not 'stand out of the way for you' insults a superior: *Hiero* 7.7; σοι 'you' means 'any rich man such as you, my interlocutor'. τὸν δοῦλον . . . ἢ τὸν μέτοικον ἢ τὸν ἀπελεύθερον: a 'metic' was resident in Athens, free but liable to military service and taxes, a non-Athenian and therefore without political rights; a 'freedman' was one released from slavery; slaves could be freed after the death of their owner as a legacy, or by purchasing their freedom, or as a special reward in their lifetime: Fisher (1993) 67–70. Pasion was freed in the late fifth century as a result of his importance to his owner in the banking business: Fisher (1993) 77–8. οἰηθεὶς εἶναι τὸν Ἀθηναῖον δοῦλον 'thinking that an Athenian was a slave'; the definite article is regular in such expressions: cf. Ar. *Birds* 1035, ἐὰν δ'. . . τὸν Ἀθηναῖον ἀδικῆι. *Mem.* 1.2.58–9 shows that the idea of the biter being bit (the beater being beaten himself) has become a *topos*; it clears Socrates of the charge of encouraging the beating of the poor on the grounds that he would get a beating himself if he did. Athenian law did protect slaves as the property of their masters, but *Ath.* takes their generous treatment to extremes; in comedy by contrast, slaves spend their lives trying to avoid beatings, and Xenophon also assumes that owners can beat their own slaves with impunity: *Mem.* 3.13.4. ἐσθῆτά τε . . . καὶ τὰ εἴδη: a singular dress for the singular *demos*, but a plural when they are referred to in the plural. The fine clothing and appearance of the slaves of the rich courtesan Theodote (*Mem.* 3.11.4), and the superior clothing that Ischomachus gave as a reward to good slaves (*Oec.* 13.10) seem exceptional, but Fisher's (1993) Figures 8–11 suggest that citizens could indeed be confused with slaves, since slaves were marked out in vase painting only by tattoos or nakedness or general ugliness.

1.11 εἰ δέ τις καὶ τοῦτο θαυμάζει: the opposition is imagined to express astonishment at the luxury that slaves enjoy. καὶ μεγαλοπρεπῶς διαιτᾶσθαι ἐνίους: the rest merely 'luxuriate', but 'there are even some that they allow to adopt a magnificent life-style'; cf. *Lac.* 14.3 ἔστιν οὓς καὶ καλλωπιζομένους 'there are even some who flaunt it'. ἀπὸ χρημάτων ἀνάγκη τοῖς ἀνδραπόδοις δουλεύειν 'it is necessary that (Athenians) be slaves to their slaves for money'; even if he is a ruler, a free man is a slave if he depends too much on others or is a slave to money, or his own appetite: *Mem.* 1.5 *passim*. ἀνδράποδον is used rather than δοῦλος to indicate that the citizen bought the slave, to make the indignity of his serving him for money even worse; cf. 1.18, ἀνδράποδον μισθοφοροῦν of the slave who is let out for hire. Fisher (1993) 6–7 discusses the vocabulary for slaves. For ἀπὸ χρημάτων, cf. 3.3 and *Hiero* 4.10: ἀπὸ τοῦ δικαίου. Gargiulo (1999) 63–9 discusses alternative meanings. ἵνα λαμβάνωμεν ὧν πράττηι τὰς ἀποφοράς 'in order that we receive the dues of whatever he (the slave) earns'; λαμβάνων μέν in the manuscripts makes little sense, but Lapini (1997) retains it. The emendation 'we' identifies the author with the Athenians and anticipates the later reference to 'you' and 'I'. The ἀποφορά is the portion of his pay that a slave who was hired out or ran his own business gave as commission to his owner (*Poroi* 4.49). Nicias had 1,000 slaves and leased them out at the rate of an obol each a day; Hipponicus had 600 which brought in a mina per day; Philemonides had 300 in such arrangements (*Poroi* 4.14); it is significant that these are rich men, whose profits *Ath.* does not care to acknowledge. καὶ ἐλευθέρους ἀφιέναι 'to let them go free', enjoying their ἀκολασία, free from the usual constraints of slavery, such as rough clothing, beatings, reporting back to the master, being locked up at night. Thus *Oec.* 14.9 treats slaves 'like free men' by enriching and honouring them, but they remain slaves. 'To set them free from the condition of slavery' by manumission (see Fisher (1993) 67–70) would deny the master any profits at all except from the sale. οὐκέτι ἐνταῦθα λυσιτελεῖ τὸν ἐμὸν δοῦλον σὲ δεδιέναι: profit continues to dictate the arrangements: 'it is no longer in that place (or case, i.e. where slaves are rich) monetarily profitable that my slave fears you'. ἐν δὲ τῆι Λακεδαίμονι ὁ ἐμὸς δοῦλος σ' ἐδεδοίκει . . . 'In Sparta my slave would fear you (but not in Athens)'. Cf. the unreal condition without ἄν at 1.6. The argument is that fear would make the slave part with the money he earns and give it to the man he fears; and this would reduce the profits for his owner. The smooth conduct of Athenian mercantile life requires that slaves be immune to such pressure from free men. In fact, the slave in question is not fearful of his own master, since his master is already a slave to him for profit, nor evidently does he fear others, since he does not defer to them in the streets (above). The whole statement refers to a hypothetical situation 'where there are rich slaves (Athens) . . . where there are not (Sparta)' rather than suggesting that the writer and his slave have met the person he addresses in Sparta. Sparta had no naval power, no cash dependence, and so no elevated slaves. ἐὰν δὲ δεδίηι ὁ σὸς δοῦλος ἐμέ: the change from 'my slave's fear of you' to 'your slave's fear of me' draws the interlocutor into the experience. κινδυνεύσει . . . ὥστε μὴ κινδινεύειν 'he will run the risk . . . so that he does not run the risk' is another play on words, as in βουλεύειν above (1.6).

   1.12 ἰσηγορίαν . . . ἐποιήσαμεν: the author's first-person identification with the *demos* must be ironically rueful, since he evidently does not approve of the arrangement. *Isegoria* is a term of propaganda, like *eunomia*. Hdt. 5.78 understands it as the liberation of citizens from the enslavement of tyranny to pursue their own interests; Dem. 15.18

uses it as a synonym for the general freedoms of democracy: τοῖς μετ᾽ ἰσηγορίας ζῆν ἡιρημένοις. Here, it refers to the equality of appearance, the possession of wealth and the absence of fear and of beatings; Dem. 9.3 also refers to how the citizens give the παρρησία that they value so much for themselves 'even to the foreigners and slaves in the *polis*'. δεῖται ἡ πόλις μετοίκων: for the trading activities of metics: Whitehead (1977) 84–6. *Poroi* 2–3 recognizes their contribution when it sets up a programme to attract them to Athens, to give a boost to revenues; *Hipp.* 9.6 mentions their cavalry service. *Ath.* does not mention the tax on metics, which would have been a respectable source of revenue to the *demos* because it would not involve the kowtowing described in this section. Evidently he wants the *demos* to degrade themselves in their pursuit of profit. To profit from taxes would have them act as superiors. Isocrates *Panath.* 12.116 says that the *demos* performed the τέχναι here attributed to the metics, but *Ath.* regularly presents its case in black and white rather than shades of grey.

1.13 An apparently abrupt change of topic, but the theme of cash profit continues; the *demos* has ended the private practice of athletics and performing arts because they know they are incapable of it; but they endorse mass participation in the liturgies because they get payment: ἀργύριον. Their contrariness, abolishing private practice but encouraging public, is proof of their cultivation of profit. See Fisher in Cartledge, Millett and von Reden (eds.) (1998) 84–104 for the participation of the *demos* in athletics. It is unclear whether such arrangements were secured by the sanction of the public opinion of the *demos* or through laws. The same question arises in their arrangements for comedy: 2.18.

καταλέλυκεν ὁ δῆμος: other evidence suggests that wealthy classes neglected athletic pursuits more than the *demos*, and confirm this as a *topos* of criticism. *Mem.* 3.5.15 says that the hoplites show contempt for physical exercise and mock those who practise it. [And.] *Ag. Alc.* 39 has the arch-aristocrat Alcibiades 'putting an end to' (καταλύων) the gymnasia in contempt of its pursuits. Ar. *Frogs* 1070 refers to 'emptying the palaestra' as an instance of decline. νομίζων ... γνούς the *parataxis* is awkward but effectively emphasizes the calculation of the *demos*, 'thinking this is not noble, knowing that they are incapable of practising these activities' (because they are common and uneducated and lack the resources). ἐν ταῖς χορηγίαις αὖ καὶ γυμνασιαρχίαις καὶ τριηραρχίαις 'in productions of choral performances on the other hand, athletic games and in maintaining ships' i.e. the 'liturgies', which the wealthy were required to finance (*Oec.* 2.6); the trierarchy seems to be the odd man out because it has no evident application to athletics or music, but sailing in ships might be construed as athletic activity. *Ath.* presents the liturgies as a burden on the rich because he is intent on the profit of the *demos*, but liturgists often enjoyed their reputation for φιλοτιμία for service, as at Dem. 18.257. χορηγοῦσι μὲν οἱ πλούσιοι, χορηγεῖται δὲ ὁ δῆμος: the *demos* literally plays the passive part in the productions. γοῦν: the proof that focuses on one essential item: the fact that they demand payment. καὶ ᾄδων καὶ τρέχων καὶ ὀρχούμενος καὶ πλέων ἐν ταῖς ναυσίν: the *demos* practise different athletic and musical activities from those that the rich once practised. ἔν τε τοῖς δικαστηρίοις:

their concern for self-interest rather than justice 'in the courts' seems incongruously connected to the liturgies, but confirms that they look to what they can get for themselves rather than what is right. There may be a specific connection too; liturgies led to court cases when the liturgist challenged his selection: 3.4. A self-interested judicial decision on the part of the *demos* might secure their profit better than justice in this area.

1.14 describes their pursuit of profit in judicial dealings with allied *poleis*. The profits that the *demos* acquire in 'sailing out' to allied territory (1.14) are balanced against those of obliging the allies to 'sail in' to Athens (1.16); they would rather control them ἄνευ νεῶν ἔκπλου because a fleet costs money, but both secure profit, one through blackmail and extortion, the other through paid services and bribes. The criticism of them for profiting by sailing out, as well as forcing the allies to sail in, is in keeping with the ingenious argument of the 'Old Oligarch'.

Περὶ δὲ τῶν συμμάχων ὅτι ἐκπλέοντες συκοφαντοῦσιν 'concerning the allies, that by sailing out they blackmail them . . . ' For the structure of this sentence, cf. 1.1 and Hippocr. *Aer.* 19: περὶ δὲ τῶν ὡρέων καὶ τῆς μορφῆς, ὅτι πολὺ ἀπήλλακται τῶν λοιπῶν ἀνθρώπων τὸ Σκυθικὸν γένος . . . and other examples in Gargiulo (1999) 70. Strictly speaking, 'blackmail' is the judicial practice whereby false charges are threatened against rich people in order to make them settle out of court: cf. *Mem.* 2.9. Themistocles practised a public version of it when he sailed out against the islands in order to procure money, threatening to use the fleet against them if they did not pay: Hdt. 8.111–12. συκοφαντεῖν is also used of extorting money from allies in Ar., *Birds* 1410–69 and Isoc., *Panath.* 142. ὡς δοκοῦσι 'as they seem to' softens the harshness of the charge of blackmail while also drawing attention to it: cf. Gargiulo (1999) 74 and the use of 'as would seem to the many' at *Hiero* 1.21, to soften an unusually strong word. μισεῖσθαι μὲν ἀνάγκη: the belief that the ruler is necessarily hated by the ruled (Thuc. 2.64.4, *Hell.* 3.5.10 and *Hiero* 1–7) is here restricted to rich allies, whom the Athenians exploit as their natural enemies; in contrast, they assist the allied poor because they are natural friends: Thuc. 3.47.2, 82.1, *Hell.* 4.8.20, 7.1.44. διὰ ταῦτα οὖν: the connective in mid-sentence resumes the original shape of the sentence and develops the idea in μισοῦσι τοὺς χρηστούς: *GP* 427–8. The actions are those of the tyrant: Hdt. 5.92e2, making this a tyrant *demos* toward the allies.

1.15 εἴποι δέ τις ἄν: the opposition argues that to destroy wealthy allies destroys the tax base (Thuc. 3.46 has Diodotus use a similar argument), but the *demos* is intent on securing what cash it can for each individual member of their group, and keeping the rich in harmless poverty working the land for their benefit. χρήματα εἰσφέρειν 'to make enforced payments', as at *Hiero* 9.7, *Oec.* 2.6, *Poroi* 3.7–11; these were often required in time of war. ἐκείνους δὲ (sc. ἔχειν) ὅσον (sc. δεῖ) ζῆν, καὶ ἐργάζεσθαι ἀδυνάτους ὄντας ἐπιβουλεύειν 'that they (the allies) have (only) as much as is required (for them) to survive on, and that they work the land, being unable to plot'. The arrangement may refer to the cleruchies in which local owners worked the land, but paid rent to Athenians as 'landlords' (Thuc. 3.50.2). *Mem.* 2.8.1, *Symp.*

4.31 show that people could live off their overseas possessions. The desire to prevent plots by keeping subjects busy conforms to the tyrannical stereotype: Aristotle, *Pol.* 1313b20–1.

1.16–20 Another area in which the Athenians seem to be in error is in making the allies come to Athens for judicial trials. Presumably their 'error' is in creating so much judicial business for the democracy. See their arrangements with Phaselis (Meiggs and Lewis (1988) no. 31, lines 6–11): 'whenever there is a contract at Athens with a citizen of Phaselis, judicial claims should be processed in front of the polemarch, as in the case of the Chians, and nowhere else.' The author allows the *demos* itself to begin to 'reason out in response' the many advantages of this arrangement, some of them public, others private. These are listed very clearly: πρῶτον μὲν . . . εἶτ' . . . πρῶτον . . . ἔπειτα . . . ἔπειτα . . . πρὸς δὲ τούτοις . . . καὶ . . . πρὸς δὲ τούτοις.

1.16 οἱ δὲ ἀντιλογίζονται: the reasoning of the Athenians is first expressed in reported speech, but soon the author continues their arguments as his own, showing again (as at 1.11) that he understands their point of view. ἔνι (= ἔνεστι). ἀπὸ τῶν πρυτανείων: the first profit is the public acquisition of money 'from the deposits' made when two parties went to law; the loser's deposit was forfeit to the *demos* as payment. ἄνευ νεῶν ἔκπλου: the second general profit is that they manage the allies 'without sending out ships', avoiding the expense and discomfort of an expedition. ἕκαστοι 'each group (of the allies)'. σώιζουσι . . . ἀπολλύουσιν: the third profit is that they 'save' the friends of the Athenians and 'destroy' their enemies in the courts.

1.17 ἡ ἑκατοστὴ (sc. μοῖρα) . . . πλείων (sc. ἐστι): Ar. *Wasps* 658–9 lists a host of 1 per cent taxes; Andoc. 1.133–4 emphasises the profit to be made from the 2 per cent tax on cargoes; Eupolis in Kassel-Austin *PCG* 5 fr. 55 mentions a passenger tax (ἐλλιμένιον), paid as soon as you embarked on a ship.

1.18 εἴ τωι (= τινι) συνοικία ἐστίν, ἄμεινον πράττει: a boarding house holds many paying customers; the author seems blind to the idea that profits would also accrue to the rich, if they also run boarding houses, but there is an assumption that they are farmers rather than landlords (2.14). ζεῦγος: an ox offers transport of goods around the city. ἀνδράποδον μισθοφοροῦν: a slave for hire is also useful for a visiting ally. οἱ κήρυκες: such people were paid and were numerous, as shown by the frequent references in Arist. *Ath. Pol.* (heralds of archons and *dikasteria*). ἐτίμων ἄν: the profit of being honoured by the allies is transferred from rich individuals (generals, trierarchs and ambassadors: 1.3, 1.13) to members of the *demos*. The settlement between the Athenians and the Selymbrians *IG* I² 116 = *IG* I³ 118 (Meiggs and Lewis (1988), no. 87, lines 28–31) confirms that honour went to the rich when it names 'the generals and [the trierarchs] and the hoplites and any other Athenian present'. κολακεύειν: the author shows his prejudice by saying that the allies are obliged to 'flatter' members of the *demos* whereas they would genuinely 'honour' the rich. *Hiero* 1.14 finds flattery to be an insincere form of honour. *Lac.* 14.2 criticizes Spartan harmosts for enjoying its corrupting pleasures. δίκην δοῦναι καὶ λαβεῖν οὐκ ἐν ἄλλοις τισὶν ἀλλ' ἐν τῶι δήμωι, ὅς ἐστι δὴ νόμος Ἀθήνησι 'to undergo judicial processes among no others but the *demos*, which is the custom at Athens'; the relative takes the entire sentence as its antecedent and has been attracted to the case of its complement. The context of having to court the *demos*, as well as other references to what is the 'custom' at Athens (cf. the use of νόμος at 1.10), make this meaning preferable to the startling idea that the *demos* 'is the law', in the sense that it makes law as it likes at Athens. εἰσιόντος του (= τινος) ἐπιλαμβάνεσθαι τῆς χειρός: 'to grab the hand of anyone who enters the court'. The gesture conveys humility: Eur. *IA* 339 ὡς ταπεινὸς ἦσθα, πάσης δεξιᾶς προσθιγγάνων. This gave the jurors a sense of pleasurable importance; Socrates refused to give his jurors this pleasure in Plato's *Apology* and *Mem.* 4.4.4, but it is what the jurors want in Aristophanes' *Wasps* 548–75. δοῦλοι τοῦ δήμου: a graphic description in keeping with their fearful flattery.

1.19–20 The argument proceeds to this further advantage, that they have learned to manage ships while indulging their love of profit in overseas offices and property, without the pain of school learning or hard training. *Oec.* 15.10–16.1, *Lac.* 11.5 also emphasize the pleasures of easy learning. διὰ τὴν κτῆσιν τὴν ἐν τοῖς ὑπερορίοις καὶ διὰ τὰς ἀρχὰς τὰς εἰς τὴν ὑπερορίαν 'on account of the possession of overseas properties and on account of overseas offices': see 1.15 for the properties; Aristotle: *Ath. Pol.* 24.3 tots up the number of paid offices in his time, including those overseas; a textual problem prevents us accepting the figure of 700 in the text, but the other offices certainly number in the hundreds. λελήθασι μανθάνοντες 'they have unconsciously learned' (in spite of their characteristic ἀμαθία: 1.5). The effort that went into making the Athenians a nation of naval experts is variously represented. A speaker who argues for their natural leadership on sea agrees that they became naval experts in the course of their daily lives because they lived surrounded by sea (*Hell.* 7.1.3–5), but in the context of his theory of power, Thucydides' Pericles attributes their expertise to their continual practice of naval warfare since the Persian Wars, which, contrary to *Ath.* here, required huge effort (Thuc. 1.142.7–9). αὐτοί τε καὶ οἱ ἀκόλουθοι . . . καὶ αὐτὸν καὶ τὸν οἰκέτην: the terms for slaves capture their inferior status as mere followers or household members. The insistence that they acquired the same skill as their masters then reduces the status of the citizen-rower; there may be a similarly negative connotation in the use of ἄνθρωπον for the master. Homer (*Il.* 13.330f.) and Herodotus use the grouping of free men and slaves to indicate completeness (5.21.1: the complete destruction of the embassy, 9.76.1: the complete wealth of the fugitive woman). οἱ μὲν πλοῖον . . . οἱ δὲ ὁλκάδα, οἱ δ᾽ ἐντεῦθεν ἐπὶ τριήρεσι κατέστησαν: the passenger boat, cargo-ship, fighting ship, are progressively more difficult to manoeuvre. εὐθὺς ὡς: possibly an example of ὡς with an adverb that is felt to be extraordinary: LSJ s.v. A III b.

2.1 The Athenians have deliberately chosen to degrade their hoplite forces to the point where they are inferior to the enemy, but still sufficient to control the allies and secure their cash tribute. This continues the theme of the relations with the allies from the previous section and begins a theoretical discussion of the greater advantages of sea power over land power. For the parallels with Thucydides on sea power: cf. Frisch (1942) 63–87, and de Romilly (1962).

Τὸ δὲ ὁπλιτικὸν αὐτοῖς ... οὕτω καθέστηκεν 'their hoplite force has been (deliberately) constituted in this condition (i.e. a poor condition).' (Moore (1975) 41: 'is based on the following principle'); cf. κατὰ τύχην 'constituted by chance' below. There is no other evidence that the Athenians deliberately neglected their hoplites. Pericles indicates on the eve of the Peloponnesian War that they had 29,000 hoplites in good condition: Thuc. 2.13.6. *Mem.* 3.5 has Pericles the Younger lament the poor condition of later fifth-century hoplites, but there is no suggestion that the *demos* has deliberately let them go to seed; Socrates suggests that they have let themselves go to seed, and only need improved leadership. However, it was readily admitted that a naval policy did not require anything much more than defence of the walls and cavalry sallies: Xenophon, *Hipp.* 7.4: ἢν δὲ ἡ μὲν πόλις τρέπηται ἐπὶ τὰ ναυτικὰ καὶ ἀρκῆι αὐτῆι τὰ τείχη διασώιζειν. ἥττους ... καὶ ὀλείζους 'weaker and fewer'. The relatively unusual ὀλείζους is found in Homer and Attic inscriptions such as the Tribute Decree: *IG* 1² 63 = *IG* 1³ 71, Meiggs and Lewis (1988), no. 69, lines 17, 21. Lapini (1997) 151–2 reads μὴ μείζους, which would make the description a denial in response to those who thought that the hoplites should be more numerous. The 'enemy' are contrasted with the 'allies' and both remain unidentified, but the Corinthians and Spartans were the main enemies of Athens in the late fifth century. τὸν φόρον: the payment of imperial tribute dates the work to before the abolition of tribute in 413 BC (Thuc. 7.28.4).

2.2–8 The natural advantages of sea power are described. The first point is that land powers need large land forces because the smaller *poleis* they rule can gather their forces into one place, but islanders ruled by sea cannot do the same. The sea power controls *poleis* on the mainland too because the large ones fear her, the small ones need her, because they all export and import, and she is in control of the seas (2.2–3). The contrast between the land and sea power is reflected in balanced contrasts in sentence structure τοῖς μὲν κατὰ γῆν ἀρχομένοις ... τοῖς δὲ κατὰ θάλατταν ἀρχομένοις. Five more areas of natural advantage are then introduced, three beginning with ἔπειτα (2.4, 2.5, 2.6), another with the conventional formula 'if it is right to mention smaller matters' (2.7), and a final ἔπειτα (2.8).

2.2 καὶ κατὰ τύχην ... καθέστηκε 'it has been constituted also according to chance'; cf. 2.1. συνοικισθέντας: 'gathering together'; this need not imply the 'synoecism' that consists in the formal creation of a federation of *poleis*, as at Thuc. 1.58.2 (the cities of Chalcidice) and 3.2.3 (the *poleis* of Lesbos). θαλασσοκράτορες: manuscripts agree on the Ionic σσ- here, as at 2.14 and ἄσσα at 2.17; cf. Hdt. 5.83.2, Thuc. 8.63; the author normally uses the Attic ττ- for σσ- (cf. *Hell.* 1.6.2); perhaps the Ionic form was imported into Attic speech. See Caballero López (1997) 8–11.

2.3 ὁπόσαι ... αἱ μὲν ... αἱ δέ: partitive apposition: *GG* 914.

2.4 The sea power can also more easily damage the land of those stronger than itself by using the greater mobility of its fleet. The land power has no such mobility. τέμνειν τὴν γῆν τῶν κρειττόνων explains the sense of ποιεῖν ἅπερ τοῖς (sc. ἄρχουσι) τῆς γῆς. ἐνίοτε: the point of the qualification may be that the sea powers can do *all* the time what land powers can do only 'sometimes'; see 1.5, 11 for other effects of the restriction to 'some'. Land powers can only sometimes ravage the land of those who are stronger because they need a victory beforehand, whereas the sea power does not. παραπλεῖν: this means 'to sail along the coast' at 2.5, but here just 'come by sea to land'. ὁ πεζῆι παραβοηθῶν 'the one who comes by land', again without a necessary implication of coastal movement; contrast Thuc. 2.90.3 ἔπλει παρὰ τὴν γῆν καὶ ὁ πεζὸς ἅμα τῶν Μεσσηνίων παρεβοήθει.

2.5 The sea power has the speed to cover a greater distance than the land power. The latter has problems of supply because of its slower progress, and must either go through friendly territory, which may mean a detour, or fight for its passage, whereas the fleet can pass by areas where they do not have the advantage. Thuc. 1.15.2 has the basic theory. It has been argued that this cannot have been written after the expedition of Brasidas who marched overland to Thrace on 'a journey of many days through another's land' (Thuc. 4.85.4); but perhaps the exception just proves the rule: Gomme (1940) 225. Agesilaus (*Hell.* 4.3.3–9) nicely illustrates the permanent application of the theory; he had to fight his way through hostile territory on his overland march back to Greece from Asia in 394 BC. τοῖς μὲν κατὰ θάλατταν ἄρχουσιν οἷόν τ' . . . τοῖς δὲ κατὰ γῆν οὐχ οἷον: a balanced series of contrasts begins. ὁπόσον βούλει πλοῦν 'as great a sailing distance as you like'; the use of the second person is almost colloquial; compare its use at 1.8–12. σῖτον . . . πολλοῦ χρόνου 'food for a long period of time', a genitive of measure: *GG* 1085.5. πεζῆι ἰόντα 'if he goes by land'; the participle agrees with the omitted subject of ἔχειν. διὰ φιλίας (sc. χώρας). οὗ δ' ἂν μὴ ἦι, μὴ ἀποβῆναι ταύτηι τῆς γῆς: Kalinka's transposition of C's text gives good sense. 'In this part of the land' better suits the situation where landing is not possible.

2.6 The sea power also enjoys advantages in its food supply: crop failure is worse for a land power, which depends on its own land, than for one that controls the sea and imports from the four corners of the earth. The transition to this new area of natural advantage may be provoked by the previous reference to the problems of supplying land armies.

οὐ γὰρ ἅμα πᾶσα γῆ νοσεῖ: *Poroi* 4.9 refers to *poleis* which 'are sick with crop failures or war' (νοσήσωσιν . . . ἢ ἀπορίαις καρπῶν ἢ πολέμωι). ἐκ τῆς εὐθενούσης (sc. γῆς). ἀφικνεῖται has 'crops' as its understood subject.

2.7 εἰ δὲ δεῖ καὶ σμικροτέρων μνησθῆναι: the next natural advantage of sea power is that it can import luxuries. The conventional formula highlights the notions it introduces rather than apologizing for them: cf. *Hell.* 2.4.27 when it introduces the notable achievement of an engineer, and *Cyr.* 1.4.27, which introduces the 'kiss-story' that proves the attractions of young Cyrus. ἐπιμισγόμενοι ἄλληι ἄλλοις: 'mingling' means growth and power in Thuc. 1.2.1–2, and lack of it means the opposite in Hdt. 1.65.1, but here it characteristically just satisfies the appetites of the *demos*. ὅ τί . . . ἡδύ . . . ταῦτα πάντα 'whatever delight there is . . . all these': the singular focuses on each speciality of the localities listed, while the plural emphasizes their multiple availability at Athens; for a similar list of exotic imports from Carthage to the Black Sea, from Syracuse to Syria, see the comic poet Hermippus in

Kassel-Austin *PCG* 5 63 (= Athen. 1.27e–28a). Thuc. 2.38.2 describes the same flow of goods toward Athens ἐκ πάσης γῆς τὰ πάντα. ἤθροισται 'have been gathered' and are available.

2.8 φωνὴν πᾶσαν ἀκούοντες ἐξελέξαντο τοῦτο μὲν ἐκ τῆς, τοῦτο δὲ ἐκ τῆς 'hearing every language, they have selected this item from that (language) and that from this'; the article has demonstrative force: *GG* 983b. The intention of this very early piece of evidence about Attic speech (cf. Hdt. 1.56–8 for another) is to criticize the *demos*. The Athenians were naturally exposed to the speech of their markets, which included foreign speech: Willi (2003a) 198–225, but the law that kept the Persian youth away from the 'cries and vulgarities' of traders indicates that imitation was undesirable (*Cyr.* 1.2.3). Their 'selection' reflects Herodotus' idea that people actively borrow or reject others' customs: 1.135, 4.76.1. Their pleasure in everything impure accounts for their selection of what is base. There is no evidence to prove or disprove what *Ath.* says: Meillet (1965) 244–5. Thuc. 7.63.3 offers a different view from our author when he says that those who adopt the manners and language of the Athenians share their prestige. ἰδίαι μᾶλλον καὶ φωνῆι καὶ διαίτηι καὶ σχήματι χρῶνται 'they have their own speech and habits and appearance to a greater extent (than the Athenians)' – but the nouns have a range of meanings; φωνή means any sort of sound and could involve pronunciation or vocabulary, even loudness; δίαιτα covers eating, drinking and sexual habits (*Mem.* 1.3.5–8); σχήματα covers appearance, clothing, gestures, even dance-steps (*Symp.* 2.16, 9.5). Hdt. 1.57–8 also recognizes the pure Greek of the Hellenes, contrasting it with the barbaric Pelasgian speech of the original Athenians; but Spartan purity was connected with ignorance, isolationism and corruptibility (Thuc. 1.77.6).

2.9–10 The consumption of luxury food leads to the consideration of the advantage that the *demos* secures from their religious arrangements. Their poverty limits their private sacrificial feasting, so they adopt the same principle as in their arrangements for athletics and make religion a public affair with public feasts. They also pursue sensual pleasure in gymnasia, baths, and changing rooms; previously the private possessions of some of the wealthy, they are now built at public cost for the use of the many, and the wealthy, being fewer, have a lesser share. There were public baths at Athens by the time of Aristophanes: Kassel-Austin *PCG* 3.2 fr. 125. Bathing in private houses is of course a ritual as old as Homer's account of the bathing of Odysseus as a guest on Phaeacia and Ithaca.

2.9 θυσίας introduces a list of accusatives of respect which are the focus of the sentence but have a loose grammatical connection with it. These generally are related to the verbal ideas that follow: to sacrifice, to feast, to establish shrines, to inhabit a fine and large *polis*. κτᾶσθαι ἱερά 'establish shrines'; cf. Hdt. 2.42.2: ἔκτηνται ἱρὸν; *contra* Brock and Heath (1995) 564–6. πόλιν οἰκεῖν καλὴν καὶ μεγάλην 'to inhabit a beautiful and great *polis*'. *Hiero* 11.2 had Simonides consider this an important ingredient of happiness too, but his buildings improved the security and economy of the *polis* as well as its religious life. ἱερεῖα πολλά 'many sacrificial animals' are needed to feed 'the many'. ἔστι δὲ ὁ δῆμος ὁ εὐωχούμενος καὶ διαλαγχάνων τὰ ἱερεῖα: for the participial construction, cf. 1.2; this emphasizes their enjoyment and (equal) share of the sacrificial food.

2.10 τοῖς μὲν πλουσίοις ἔστιν ἰδίαι ἐνίοις: the restriction of the private possession of these goods to 'some rich people' suggests that what was previously a rare pleasure even for the rich is now a common pleasure for the many. παλαίστρας πολλάς, ἀποδυτήρια, λουτρῶνας: *asyndeton* conveys the rapid acquisition of numerous establishments; cf. the καί-connected establishments of the rich. The author may also convey their abundance in using different words for the buildings in question; but on the possible differences between the gymnasium (for general athletics) and the palaestra (purely for wrestling): Glass in Raschke (1988) 155–73.

2.11 Their control of the sea also ensures that Athens alone can build warships, which perpetuates their control. The wealth of the world flows there, particularly the raw materials for shipbuilding: wood, iron, bronze, linen, wax. The significance of the passage for the characterization of the author is discussed on pp. 54–5. There is a good discussion in Gabrielsen (1994) 139–42.

Τὸν δὲ πλοῦτον μόνοι . . . τῶν Ἑλλήνων καὶ τῶν βαρβάρων 'the wealth of the Greeks and non-Greeks' as well as 'alone of the Greeks and non-Greeks'. The acquisition of the wealth of the whole world is characteristic of the *demos* of *Ath.* and so is their unique concentration of wealth. The argument is that various *poleis* (barbarians could be included among them) have forms of wealth (εἰ γάρ τις πόλις πλουτεῖ), which they must send on to Athens. This provides a parallel for their importation of delicacies from all parts of the world in 2.7. ποῖ διαθήσεται: the first of a sequence of rhetorical questions in *anaphora* to emphasize their control of the movement of materials for shipbuilding. This may have been the purpose of official agreements, such as that between Athens and Macedon (*IG* i² 71 = *IG* i³ 89). *SEG* 10 (1949) 86, line 23 refers to an oath sworn by Perdiccas of Macedon: καὶ οὐδένα κο]πέας ἐχσάγεν ἐάσο ἐὰμ μὲ Ἀθε[ναίοις (Gabrielsen (1994) 141–2). τί δὲ: a lively question: cf. *Hiero* 1.22 τί γάρ. ἐξ αὐτῶν μέντοι τούτων καὶ δὴ νῆές μοί εἰσι, παρὰ μὲν τοῦ ξύλα, παρὰ δὲ τοῦ σίδηρος . . . 'from these very materials moreover there are ships for me, wood from this place, iron from that . . .'; the article is demonstrative as at 2.8; the repetition conveys the vast resources at the command of the Athenians.

2.12 ἄλλοσε ἄγειν οὐκ ἐάσουσιν οἵτινες ἀντίπαλοι ἡμῖν εἰσιν 'they will not permit those who are opposed to us to take (their wealth) elsewhere (or if they do, they will not be using the sea to do it)'. The argument so far has been that *poleis* have to *persuade* Athens to allow their ships to move, which means that they use friendly means. The new point here concerns their enemies; ἀντίπαλοι. The author again identifies his interests with those of the Athenians when he refers to 'us'. The lack of permission refers to the informal military pressure of the Athenian fleet. Lapini (1997) and Bowersock (1966, 1968) read οἵ τινες and have the Athenians prevent the goods being taken 'to the place where there are any enemies'. καὶ ἐγὼ μὲν οὐδὲν ποιῶν ἐκ τῆς γῆς πάντα ταῦτα ἔχω διὰ τὴν θάλατταν 'though producing not one (of these materials) from the land (of Attica), I have them all on account of the (control of the) sea'; the focus on materials for shipbuilding continues. The author is representative of the Athenian collective who live off the produce of the empire. He 'owns' ships in this sense. ἄλλη δ' οὐδεμία πόλις δύο τούτων ἔχει: the contrast of 'ego' with 'no other *polis*' confirms that the speaker represents 'the Athenian *polis*'. Hdt. 1.32.8 has Solon say that a *polis* will always lack one of any two given products. οὐδὲ τἄλλα δύο ἢ τρία μιᾷ πόλει, ἀλλὰ τὸ μὲν τῆι, τὸ δὲ τῆι 'nor with respect to the other materials are there two or three for one *polis*, but one for this *polis*, another for that'.

2.13 reverts to the sea power's ability to coerce the mainland, last mentioned at 2.3–6, with a special spin on promontories, islands and channels. This time the fleet anchors offshore to inflict damage. ἀκτὴ προύχουσα: Thuc. 4.3.3 discusses the advantages of seizing 'a jutting promontory': headlands such as the promontories of Pylos/Coryphasion. νῆσος προκειμένη: Hdt. 7.235.2 discusses the advantages of seizing 'an island lying off the coast' such as Cythera. στενόπορόν τι: *Hell.* 1.6.22 exemplifies the advantages of mooring in 'some narrow channel'.

2.14 The focus on promontories, islands and channels leads into the consideration, from the point of view of advantage to the *demos*, of the famous disadvantage of Athens, that she is not an island: Thuc. 1.143.4–5. The author outlines the fears from which they would be freed if they were an island, but then shows that the *demos* secures an advantage even in spite of this. The best men farm the land and are exposed to enemy invasion, but the *demos* does not own land and lives without fear. Fear of loss of property is here characteristically presented as a major barrier to happiness.

μηδὲ τμηθῆναι τὴν ἑαυτῶν γῆν μηδὲ προσδέχεσθαι τοὺς πολεμίους: the infinitive constructions continue to depend on ὑπῆρχεν ἄν. νῦν refers to the real situation, in which they are not an island (again in 2.15). ὑπέρχονται 'court', a source of unhappiness to most (even if not to Spartan Kings: *Lac.* 8.2) because it is submissive and born of fear. The *demos* makes others approach them in this manner (1.18). καὶ οὐχ ὑπερχόμενος αὐτούς: καὶ = καίπερ.

2.15 'In addition they would have been relieved of another fear . . . that the town might sometime be betrayed by a few and that the gates be opened and that the enemy storm inside . . . and that a party stir up revolution against the *demos*'; the accusative and infinitives (μηδέποτε προδοθῆναι etc.) are dependent on the notion of freedom from fear in δέους ἀπηλλαγμένοι (*M&T* 807); μή is customarily added to infinitives dependent on negative main verbs. πῶς γάρ: the lively rhetorical question interrupts the sentence structure; cf. *Hiero* 6.14. στασιάσαιεν and στασιάσειαν: the subject is the wealthy few; the Aeolic optative is used alongside the Attic (*GG* 732) apparently for variation; these forms are found in Homer and Herodotus: Caballero López (1997) 42. καὶ ταῦτ' ἄν ἀδεῶς εἶχεν αὐτοῖς 'these circumstances too would be/have been without fear for them'.

2.16 The *demos* deals with the threat of invasion by removing their property to the islands, merely looking on while Attica is ravaged. The passage finds echoes in Thucydides' account of the evacuation of Attica during the Peloponnesian War (2.14–16), but *Ath.*'s *demos* moves its goods merely to preserve them, whereas Thucydides' *demos* wishes more broadly to maintain its empire. See pp. 57–8 for the implications for dating.

τὴν μὲν οὐσίαν: Thuc. 2.14 mentions property such as farm animals and house contents in the evacuation of Attica. εἰ αὐτὴν ἐλεήσουσιν: this indicative in the protasis of a future condition conveys the threat of giving way to their softer feelings: *GG* 1405. Pericles argues that the Athenians should lament not for houses and land, but for bodies lost in fighting for them (τήν τε ὀλόφυρσιν μὴ οἰκιῶν καὶ γῆς ποιεῖσθαι, ἀλλὰ τῶν σωμάτων: Thuc. 1.143.5), but the *demos* in *Ath.* loses no bodies, and withdraws pity from the land only in order to secure other 'greater goods'.

2.17 The Athenians also profit from their arrangements for international alliances and sworn agreements. Their collective voting means that, unlike oligarchs, they have no individual responsibility, but can renege whenever they want to without incurring opprobrium, and can blame others for bad outcomes while taking credit themselves for good ones. Aristophanes, *Ecc.* 797f. gives a parallel for the about-turn: ἐγᾦδα τούτους χειροτονοῦντας μὲν ταχὺ ἅττ' ἂν δὲ δόξηι ταῦτα πάλιν ἀρνουμένους. *Hell.* 1.7.35 has the *demos* renege on its decision about the generals of Arginusae and blame Callixenus, who proposed the motion. Good government required to the contrary that the *demos* 'remain in the laws' to which they had agreed: *Lac.* 14, *Hell.* 2.4.42.

†ᾗ ὑφ' ὅτου ἀδικεῖ†: the meaning is clear in spite of the corruption; in an oligarchy, if they do not keep to their agreements or if any injustice occurs, the names of those few citizens who made the agreement are known. The next sentence contrasts, first, how members of the *demos* escape blame being cast on their names. 'Whatever the *demos* agrees, it is possible for it, by transferring blame to a single individual (the one who proposed the motion and put it to the vote), for these others to make a denial to the effect that . . .' 'The *demos*' is in a kind of apposition to 'these others' and is distinguished from the named individuals (see below). Members of the *demos* can deny individual responsibility because they are anonymous and they can blame the speaker and proposer because their names alone were recorded on Athenian decrees: 'Person A proposed the motion. Person B put it to the vote.' ἅσσα: the Ionic-σσ-. τοῖς ἄλλοῖς: the dative is in apposition (Frisch 1942): 'possible for the people, i.e. the others apart from the proposer . . .'

The text of the rest of the sentence is corrupt. ἔμοιγε (Kirchhoff) produces a more interesting, first-person form of denial. '*I* was not there, these things do not please me . . .' The sense seems to be that they deny responsibility for the agreements even if they learn of them at a full assembly, i.e. even if they were all there when the agreements were made. συγκείμενα: cf. Thuc. 5.47.8, κατὰ τὰ ξυγκείμενα 'according to the agreements'. τοῦ μὴ ποιεῖν ὅσα ἂν μὴ βούλωνται: the infinitive depends on προφάσεις 'a million arguments against doing whatever they do not wish to do'. ἐξηύρηκε: brings attention to the ingenuity of the *demos* and their notorious desire to do whatever they liked. αἰτιᾶται . . . τὴν αἰτίαν ἀνατιθέασι 'blames' in the one case, 'take credit' in the other, showing that they not only want to break their agreements and escape abuse, but acquire praise for any good thing they do. διέφθειραν: charges of corrupting the *demos* generally implied bribery: Lysias, 28.9; the *demos* was susceptible to bribery (*Ath.* 3.3). **2.18** Transference of blame from the collective to individuals is the purpose of their arrangements regarding comedy as well. They do not allow comic writers to abuse the collective, but they encourage them to abuse individuals, knowing that these will be the rich and powerful, and those who want to prevail over the *demos*, who are not δημοτικοί in any case. The 'advantage' is not to hear the abuse that *Hiero* 1.14 defines as a pain, and to enjoy inflicting pain on the wealthy.

Κωμωιδεῖν δ' αὖ καὶ κακῶς λέγειν: comedy is seen as a genre of abuse (Plato, *Laws* 935d–e banned comedy from the ideal state because of its abusiveness). οὐκ ἐῶσιν ... ἰδίαι δὲ κελεύουσιν: the sentence balances lack of permission against positive encouragement, and the *demos*, which has a public identity, against private individuals. 'Privately' is used where τοὺς ἰδιώτας is expected. 'Permission' and 'encouragement' need not refer to formal decrees; public opinion would have this effect, as in their abolition of athletics at 1.13. Halliwell (1991) 54–6 lists references to formal decrees that gagged comic writers, but they do not directly protect the *demos* from attack as in *Ath.*, nor do they encourage attacks on individuals. The formal ban on mockery of named individuals might constitute a reaction to such attacks, however. Sommerstein (1996) 331–3 finds a context in Cleon's threat to prosecute Aristophanes for slandering the *polis* in *Babylonians*, 426 BC and parallels with *Ach.* 503, 631. *Knights* 424 BC also personified and abused the *demos*.

οὐχὶ τοῦ δήμου ἐστὶν οὐδὲ τοῦ πλήθους ὁ κωμωιδούμενος ... ἀλλ' ἢ πλού-σιος ἢ γενναῖος ἢ δυνάμενος: two words for the *demos* balance the triple designa-tion of their opposition to reinforce the class division; cf. τῶν πενήτων καὶ τῶν δημοτικῶν below; the genitives are partitive: *GG* 1094.7. The targets of comedy did include the ostentatiously rich, but also those who persecute the rich: Sommerstein (1996) 337. ὡς ἐπὶ τὸ πολύ: 'generally'; for ὡς with adverbs, cf. ὡς ἀληθῶς below (2.19). διὰ πολυπραγμοσύνην: Isocrates 13.20 also links *polypragmosyne* with unjust *pleonexia*. Thuc. 6.87.3 represents it as characteristic of Athenians. ἄχθονται takes the accusative and participle 'they are not annoyed either that such people as these are the target of their abuse'. Annoyance is an indication of the displeasure that the *demos* seeks to avoid.

2.19 φημὶ οὖν ἔγωγε: the intrusion marks a particularly important theme. The measures regarding comedy prove that the *demos* can distinguish the bad from the good; otherwise they would not have wanted to protect the (unworthy) *demos* from attack and encourage attacks on the (worthy) oligarchs; but they have deliberately chosen to foster their own kind. Four types of people are then distinguished: the many who are bad and democratic; the few who are good and undemocratic; those who belong to the many but have the *prohairesis* of the few; those who belong to the few but have the *prohairesis* of the many; and their choices of constitutions are assessed.

οὐ γὰρ νομίζουσι τὴν ἀρετὴν αὐτοῖς πρὸς τῶι σφετέρωι ἀγαθῶι πεφυκέναι 'they do not think that virtue was born in them (the rich) for their own (the *demos*') advantage'. ὄντες ὡς ἀληθῶς τοῦ δήμου 'though they truly belong to the *demos*'. The author does not explain why their nature has not run true to their genes. The genitive 'of the *demos*' could mean 'taking the side of the *demos*' (Bowersock 1968; contrast Moore 1975); but τοῦ δήμου in 2.18, 20 means 'belonging to the *demos* by birth'.

2.20 συγγιγνώσκω . . . συγγνώμη: the author expresses 'understanding' for the self-interest that drives the *demos* toward democracy, but not for that of the better classes who deliberately choose their system. In this context, as one of these better classes, he reasserts his own *prohairesis* against democracy. See pp. 54–5 on the implications of the passage for the politics of the author.

ὅστις δὲ μὴ ὢν τοῦ δήμου εἵλετο οἰκεῖν . . . ἀδικεῖν παρεσκευάσατο καὶ ἔγνω: the words emphasize the deliberate choice and deliberate preparation for a life of crime in the one 'not belonging by birth to the *demos*' who chooses democracy; the author is not concerned about the few who happen to find themselves in a democracy, if they have not made such a deliberate choice and have no *prohairesis* for the system. μᾶλλον οἷόν τε διαλαθεῖν κακῶι ὄντι 'that it is more possible for a man to escape attention as a criminal' in the democracy because he would be inconspicuous among that vast number of criminals, whereas his criminality would be conspicuous among the good few in oligarchy. The author is thinking of corruption in office and refers again to his idea about the accountability of oligarchy (2.17). Herodotus' constitutional debate also has Darius characterize the democracy as a cover for undetected crime (3.82.4).

3.1 restates significant ideas in the introduction, omitting the reference to deliberate choice of constitution and the promotion of the base over the good because these have already been fully restated in 2.19–20. The author introduces another area of apparent error: the enormous amount of business that the democracy generates through the council and courts and the delays this causes. He proves this nevertheless to be vital to their preservation.

ἐνίοτε . . . ἐνιαυτὸν καθημένωι ἀνθρώπωι: 'sometimes' restricts the rather astonishing assertion that a man may sit for a whole year waiting to conduct business through Council and Assembly. χρηματίσαι . . . χρηματίσαντες: the author is familiar with the proceedings of the Council and their language; this characteristic word, along with διαπράττειν and διαδικασία and ὅσα ἔτη (below) are found in the Tribute Decree, *IG* I² 63 = *IG* I³ 71 (Meiggs and Lewis (1988) 69, lines 15, 18–20, 35–7). The delays were also due perhaps to the bouleutic calendar year, where if business was not completed before the end of the year, it had to be started all over again: Rhodes (1972) 63, 224–9.

3.2 explains the delays as the result of the number of business-free festival days, as well as the great amount of business, particularly judicial business. οὐδὲν δι' ἄλλο ἢ διὰ τὸ πλῆθος τῶν πραγμάτων οὐχ οἷοί τε: the sense is clear even if there is a missing conjunction 'for no other reason than on account of the amount of business – they are unable . . .'; for constructions on ἄλλο: LSJ s.v. III.2. δεῖ ἑορτάσαι ἑορτάς: festivals are no longer seen in terms of the desire of the *demos* for free feasts (2.9–10), but in terms of their pressure on the calendar: Rhodes (1972) 30; these 'holy days' were normally considered the product of piety. διαπράττεσθαι: middle (as at 1.1) or passive: 'that anyone transact any of the affairs of the *polis*' or 'that any affairs of the *polis* be transacted'; cf. πολλὰ διαπράττεσθαι (3.3). δίκας καὶ γραφὰς καὶ εὐθύνας: three types of lawsuit: (a) private cases where the injured party acted as prosecutor; cf. the trials of the allies (1.16–18), which brought the *demos* such profit; (b) public prosecutions, which were matters of greater public interest; (c) the renderings of accounts by officials leaving office, of obvious interest to a *demos* alert to the possibility of fraud. πολλὰ μὲν περὶ τοῦ πολέμου, πολλὰ δὲ περὶ πόρου χρημάτων 'many matters' is repeated five times in *anaphora* to emphasize the amount of business; 'war and revenues' were standard agenda items for the Council (Rhodes (1972) 88–122), and two key areas of success for any community. The article implies no reference to a specific war. Dem. 4.36 uses 'the war' alongside 'revenues' without reference to specifics: περὶ τοῦ πολέμου . . . περὶ χρημάτων πόρου. περὶ νόμων θέσεως: the *demos* took this out of the hands of the rich (cf. 1.9). περὶ τῶν κατὰ πόλιν ἀεὶ γιγνομένων is in contrast with καὶ περὶ τῶν ἐν τοῖς συμμάχοις (sc. γιγνομένων). φόρον δέξασθαι 'to receive tribute'; this confirms (with 2.1) that the work was composed before its abolition in 413 BC, pp. 57–8. νεωρίων ἐπιμεληθῆναι καὶ ἱερῶν: ἐπιμεληταί looked after the docks, naval sheds and triremes (Rhodes (1972) 117–20, 154–5); see Rhodes (1972) 122–34 on the care of shrines. ἆρα δή: an unusual particle combination that expects a negative response: *GP* 46.

3.3 λέγουσι δέ τινες addresses the objection that things could happen faster if there was more bribery. The author continues to characterize the *demos* by its desire for profit, but maintains that it cannot transact business more rapidly *even* when there is money in it. He returns to the theme of bribery at 3.7, with special reference to the courts. ἀργύριον 'silver coin', the magic word, music to the ears of the *demos*. διότι 'namely that'; cf. 1.12. πᾶσι διαπρᾶξαι . . . τῶν δεομένων: the partitive genitive on 'all' has been defended (by a special case: Arist. *Pol.* 1275b16 τούτων γὰρ ἢ πᾶσιν ἢ τισίν; and by a textually challenged passage: Plato, *Laws* 774c πᾶσι τῶν ἐν ταύτηι πόλει in OCT); but a lacuna could be filled by διὰ τὸ πλῆθος *vel sim.* ὁποσονοῦν χρυσίον καὶ ἀργύριον 'as much gold and silver as you like'; the previous mention of 'silver' is now partnered by gold to indicate that no money in the world could secure the more rapid transaction of business.

3.4 lists further items in the annual round of business, particularly the settlement of judicial disputes. διαδικάζειν: the technical sense is 'to resolve a dispute between two parties' about rights and obligations; *Hell.* 5.3.10 addresses this process within a divided community. εἴ τις τὴν ναῦν μὴ ἐπισκευάζει 'if any (trierarch) does not repair his ship'; the trierarch could lodge a protest against liability for repairs and go to court: Rhodes (1972) 120–1, 153–8; ἢ κατοικοδομεῖ τι δημόσιον 'or if anyone builds a public building'; the Council investigated buildings it had commissioned, and if it found fault in the contractors, took them to court: Arist. *Ath. Pol.* 46.2; there could also be a reference to buildings that obstructed the public ways: *Ath. Pol.* 50. εἰς Διονύσια καὶ Θαργήλια καὶ Παναθήναια καὶ Προμήθια καὶ Ἡφαίστια: the main festivals of the Athenians required numbers of liturgists, and necessitated a great deal of legal business because the liturgists could challenge their selection: Arist. *Ath. Pol.* 56.1–5. The Dionysia was the major dramatic festival in March, and the liturgists funded tragic, comic and dithyrambic choruses. The Thargelia was held in May for Artemis and Apollo, with dithyrambic choirs of adults and girls and the ritualistic driving out of the scapegoat (*pharmakos*). The Panathenaea was held in August and included athletic and musical productions. The Promethia and Hephaestia were noted for their torch races. See Wilson (2000). ὅσα ἔτη 'throughout as many years as there are'; an adverbial use: Ar. *Thes.* 624; cf. ὁσημέραι 'daily': Thuc. 7.27.5 and in the Tribute Decree *IG* 1² 63 = *IG* 1³ 71 (Meiggs and Lewis (1988) 69, line 18); compare ἑκάστου ἐνιαυτοῦ 'within each calendar year'. τετρακόσιοι: 400 trierarchs captain 400 ships, but Thuc. 2.13.8 speaks of 300 ships as 'ready for sailing' (πλωίμους) in the early years of the Peloponnesian War, perhaps implying 100 others that were not. καὶ τούτων τοῖς βουλομένοις δεῖ διαδικάσαι 'it is necessary to settle disputes for those of these (the trierarchs) who want to (register them)' i.e. those trierarchs who challenged their appointment in the procedure of *antidosis*: Dem. 4.36. ἀρχὰς δοκιμάσαι καὶ διαδικάσαι 'to examine credentials and determine challenges to the holding of offices': Rhodes (1972) 171–8. καὶ ὀρφανοὺς δοκιμάσαι καὶ φύλακας δεσμωτῶν καταστῆσαι 'to put orphans to scrutiny' and 'to establish guards for prisoners'; these two groups are mentioned together also in Arist. *Ath. Pol.* 24.3. The authorities checked that orphans were truly of Athenian parents whose fathers had died in the wars, then gave them guardians: cf. Thuc. 2.46.1; *Poroi* 2.7.

3.5 The next business is not what is done annually but διὰ χρόνου 'at intervals' throughout the year. Because these are unexpected and irregular, they add particular pressure to the calendar.

στρατηγικάς sc. δίκας: the transmitted text στρατιᾶς makes no sense. Trials involving commanders (Lipsius) are more serious than mere desertion or failure to answer the call-up (Brodaeus: ἀστρατείας); cf. Brock and Heath (1995). πολλὰ ἔτι πάνυ παραλείπω: the rhetorical strategy (*praeteritio*) of declaring that the main points are enough to prove your case even without going into further detail. αἱ τάξεις τοῦ φόρου 'the calculations of the tribute'. The Tribute Decree (*IG* 1² 63 = *IG* 1³ 71, Meiggs and Lewis (1988) no. 69, lines 17–20) shows how urgent this business could be; the decree required continuous sessions of discussion until it was complete. ὡς τὰ πολλὰ δι' ἔτους πέμπτου: the Greeks used inclusive reckoning, so that 'through the fifth year' means every fourth year; this is qualified 'generally' to allow for exceptions; for example, the assessment of the Tribute Decree itself. φέρε δὴ τοίνυν 'come now then' marks the end of the description of business and begins a very lively but imaginary confrontation with the audience about the conclusions to be drawn from it (εἰπάτω γάρ τις . . . φέρε δή . . . τοίνυν).

3.6 χρὴ χρῆναι διαδικάζειν . . . χρῆν . . . διαδικάζεσθαι . . . χρῆναι διαδικάζειν: repetition insists on the necessity of settling such disputes. The tyrant Hiero also felt the pressure of business: *Hiero* 8.9–10. δι' ἐνιαυτοῦ 'year-long'. ὑπάρχουσιν 'are they numerous enough'. ὑπὸ τοῦ πλήθους τῶν ἀνθρώπων 'because of the large mass of men': *GG* 1219.1c. This could refer to the large juries (Arist., *Ath. Pol.* 53.2, 68.1: 101,

201, 401, 501, and even 1501 strong), but a reference to the large number of people applying to the courts is more in keeping with the central preoccupation on the amount of judicial business in this section.

3.7 ἀλλὰ φήσει τις: the critics accept the need for the trials, but want fewer jurors. ὥστε καὶ διασκευάσασθαι ῥάιδιον ἔσται . . . καὶ συνδεκάσαι πολὺ ἧττον δικαίως δικάζειν 'so that it will be easier to use deception on a few jurors and bribe them to judge far less justly'. Arist. *Ath. Pol.* 41.2–3 addresses the ease with which smaller numbers in the Council could be bribed. δικάζειν conveys the purpose for which money is given (*M&T* 772); compare οὐκ εἶχον ἀργύριον ἐπισιτίζεσθαι (*An.* 7.1.7).

3.8 returns to the festivals as an obstacle to business. καὶ ἄγουσι μέν . . . 'And they *do* have (twice as many festivals as other cities)'; a confirmation of 3.2. ἀλλ' ἐγὼ μὲν τίθημι (sc. τὰς ἑορτὰς) ἴσας τῆι ὀλιγίστας ἀγούσηι πόλει: 'But (for the sake of argument) I count only the number of festivals equal to (those held in) the city that holds the fewest'; an instance of brachylogy; cf. *Hiero* 1.38. μέν *solitarium* begins a curious rhetorical strategy in which the author asks the reader to consider again, in addition to the business he has described, the number of festival days on which business is not done, which is where his argument started (3.2), but then concedes a minimal assessment of their role in the delays, and continues: 'Even in this case, I say . . .' as if the business he has now just mentioned is for him a self-sufficient explanation even without numerous festivals. Hdt. 7.190.1 admits the smallest estimate of wrecked ships for similar rhetorical effect: 'In this toil, they say, those who give the fewest number, that no fewer than 400 ships sank.' Since the smallest estimate is already large, the reader is left to imagine what the highest might have been. So here, one argument is minimized to enhance the magnitude of the others in isolation. τούτων τοίνυν τοιούτων ὄντων: the author sums up the case. There can be small changes made, but nothing major without destroying the democracy, which it has been their aim from the beginning to preserve. τὸ μὲν ἀφελεῖν τὸ δὲ προσθεῖναι 'to remove this and add that'; the article is demonstrative: *GG* 981. There is a suggestion of the constitution as an organism. [Hippoc.] *Regimen* 1.2–3 relates the idea of 'adding' and 'taking away' to the balance that secures health in humans. ὥστε μὴ οὐχί: cf. *GG* 1616 for the negative after a negative main verb.

3.9 This section contains one single periodic sentence. 'It is possible to find many measures that result in improvement of the constitution, but it is not easy to find measures sufficient to achieve this improvement while the democracy still remains intact, except, as I said earlier, by removing or adding the odd detail.'

ὥστε μὲν γὰρ βέλτιον ἔχειν τὴν πολιτείαν: making the constitution 'better' moves toward the 'best' constitution of 1.8. ὥστε μέντοι ὑπάρχειν μὲν δημοκρατίαν εἶναι, ἀρκούντως δὲ τοῦτο ἐξευρεῖν: μέντοι answers the opening μέν, while the next μέν . . . δέ balances the continuance of the democracy against its sufficient improvement in the direction of the best constitution; the two prove incompatible. προσθέντα ἢ ἀφελόντα agree with 'a man', the unstated subject of the infinitive ἐξευρεῖν.

3.10 Δοκοῦσι δὲ Ἀθηναῖοι καὶ τοῦτό μοι οὐκ ὀρθῶς βουλεύεσθαι: the author becomes his own opposition by suggesting a further area in which the *demos* makes an error: in choosing to support the 'worse' people in *poleis* experiencing revolution. In response to his own argument, he points out that to support the better people is to support their natural enemies, to their own detriment. This confirms their earlier choice even in *poleis* not undergoing revolution (1.14–15). αἱροῦνται . . . ᾑροῦντο . . . ᾑροῦντ' ἄν . . . αἱροῦνται: continuing emphasis on their deliberate choice; cf. αἱρεῖσθαι . . . εἵλοντο . . . εἵλοντο below. οἱ γὰρ ὅμοιοι τοῖς ὁμοίοις εὖνοί εἰσι: cf. 1.6, 1.14–15. Thuc. 3.47.2 has Diodotus agree that *demoi* support the *demos* in the allied *poleis*.

3.11 Three examples are given (Boeotia, Miletus, Sparta) where they chose to support the better classes, but the local *demos* suffered, and so did the Athenians. *Ath.* has already noted that enslavement would be the fate of the Athenian *demos* too, under the *eunomia* of their betters (1.8–9). The three instances date from the middle of the fifth century, and their details are not well known. It is inferred from Aristotle, *Pol.* 1302b29 that the Athenians chose to support oligarchies in the Boeotian *poleis* between 457 and 447 BC because their democracies favoured the federation proposed by the Thebans (Gomme (1971) 318). Inscriptions suggest that they also supported the oligarchs at Miletus 450–449 BC: Meiggs (1972) 209. They certainly supported the Spartans against the Messenians in 462 BC: Thuc. 1.101–103.3. This is conceived as support for the best men because the Spartans stand in relation to the Messenians as the best classes to the *demos*; see Isocrates *Panath.* 12.177–80. The three revolutions are not chosen at random, but demonstrate three different ways in which the *demos* suffered: by enslavement (ἐδούλευσεν), massacre (κατέκοψαν), military conquest (καταστρεψάμενοι), with the additional result in the latter case that the Spartans then went to war against the Athenians themselves. These early *exempla* might suggest a date of composition in the 440s, when the memory was still fresh, but they are the most glaring examples where the Athenians preferred the better classes in any era, and paid for their choice. In the fourth century Isocrates still draws on *exempla* from the Peloponnesian War: *Paneg.* 4.100 (the massacre at Scione); *Panath.* 12.89 (the massacre at Melos). ἐντὸς ὀλίγου χρόνου 'within a short time' exaggerates in the case of the Messenians, since that was a ten years' war, but their ten years of 'preservation' still appears short in comparison with the long life of the Athenian democracy. ὁ δῆμος ἐδούλευσεν ὁ ἐν Βοιωτοῖς: the *demos* is seen as one mass in each of the *poleis* of Boeotia. τοῦτο δὲ . . . τοῦτο δέ 'on another occasion . . . and on another': *GG* 1010. τὸν δῆμον κατέκοψαν 'they chopped down the *demos*', a fate even worse than enslavement. καταστρεψάμενοι Μεσσηνίους ἐπολέμουν Ἀθηναίοις: a grand finale, in which the best men actually turned to war against those who chose them.

3.12–13 Ὑπολάβοι δέ τις ἄν: the destruction of the *demoi* in other *poleis* suggests the threat to the Athenian democracy from those unjustly deprived of rights; this is a fitting finale for a work that has argued that the *demos* 'well preserves the constitution on which it has resolved'. However, the argument is curious in several respects. Lysias

25.11 assumes that all those who lose rights favour revolution, but *Ath.* considers that the threat comes only from those unjustly deprived. The other curious point is that the author appears to consider only those who lose rights as a result of corruption in office (below). ἠτίμωται: 'loss of rights' can mean exile, but also other lesser penalties: Andoc. 1.73–6; cf. the ἀτιμία of the coward at *Lac.* 9.4–6. τῶν ἐπιθησομένων 'people who purpose to attack'. ἐπεί τοι καὶ οὕτως ἔχει 'since surely this is the case, that . . .'; the idea is explained in the following accusative and infinitive. οὐδὲν ἐνθυμεῖσθαι ἀνθρώπους οἵτινες δικαίως ἠτίμωνται, ἀλλ' εἴ τινες ἀδίκως: the relationship of the accusative to the infinitive is debated, as well as the meaning ('that men do not plot who' or 'that there is no reason to consider men who'), but the sense is clear: that only those who have been unjustly deprived of rights should be considered a threat to the democracy. πῶς ἂν οὖν ἀδίκως οἴοιτό τις ἄν . . . : the argument is that (the?) many are not unjustly deprived of rights because the *demos* rules; loss of rights comes from corruption in rule; therefore, those deprived pose no threat to the system. The first thought makes best sense if 'the many' are not 'most of those deprived' but 'the entire *demos*' in its political sense (cf. 1.4), since in that case 'the many' are by definition not unjustly deprived of rights because they are the rulers of the democracy. The second thought then follows: that they lose these rights only if they are corrupt in exercising them, which means they are justly deprived. And so they pose no threat, to the author's way of thinking. The unspoken contrast is that in an oligarchy the many were unjustly deprived of rights because only the few ruled. The author thinks of political corruption as the main source of loss of rights because he has been writing an intensely political work.

APPENDIX I
THE IRONIC READING OF *HIERO*

Strauss (1947/1963) 35–66, particularly 41–5 = (2000) 36–65, esp. 41–5, gives a less straightforward reading of *Hiero* than the one presented in this edition. He exploits the lack of stated motivation for the characters, the openness of the dialogue form and the possibility of enmity in the relationship in order to read Hiero's fear of the contrivances of the wise (5.1–2) as his fear that Simonides is intent on securing the tyranny for himself. In this reading, Hiero wants to hold on to power, and his argument against tyranny is insincere, since he is merely attempting to dissuade Simonides from taking it. Hiero is relieved of his fear of the wise only when Simonides fails to encourage him in his final admission in the first part of the dialogue that he might as well hang himself.

As the commentary on *Hiero* 5.1–2 has indicated, this is not a likely reading of that passage, nor does any other passage indicate that Hiero's unhappiness is insincere. Nevertheless, the dramatic form should certainly be kept in mind when assessing the arguments offered by the characters. The wise man has to trim the sails of his free speech. Hiero speaks as a victim blind to any advantage in his tyranny, self-pitying and prone to exaggeration. His arguments should never be considered other than a product of his very particular state of mind.

Strauss (1947/1963) 67–79 = (2000) 66–77 also found Simonides' instruction inferior because it did not secure freedom for the citizens, so that his apparent endorsement of good government is indeed only apparent. There is admittedly less direct reference to freedom than might be expected from a more abstract work, but indirect reference is guaranteed by the work's equation of friendship with freedom. *Hiero* aims above all to establish friendship between the ruler and the ruled, and the connection between freedom and friendship is taken for granted not only in Xenophon's other paradigms, where friends serve each other freely and without compulsion, but also by negative implication in Plato, *Republic* 576a: ἐλευθερίας δὲ καὶ φιλίας ἀληθοῦς ἡ τυραννικὴ φύσις ἀεὶ ἄγευστος ('the tyrannical nature is ever untasting of freedom and true friendship'). Aristotle considered friendship between the rulers and the ruled an impossibility because they were not equals,[1] but Simonides goes out of his way to encourage Hiero to bring himself down to the level of his subjects in his reform, by offering kindnesses that any citizen is capable of (8.1–4). This levelling effect is characteristic of his other representations of the friendship of rulers, for instance in his observation that it was no wonder that Cyrus could outdo his subjects in material benefits, but what was more wondrous was how he looked to the interests of friends in small ways, such as through gifts of food (*An.* 1.9.24; see the same thought in *Cyr.*

[1] See Konstan (1997) 53–92 on the importance of friendship in the classical world, with Schofield (1999) 82–99 for a more philosophical point of view. Konstan (1997) 105–8 discusses the possibility of friendship between the rulers and the ruled in the Hellenistic world.

8.2.13). Hiero certainly desires friendship as a relationship between equals who serve each other freely and without compulsion (1.37; 3.1–2). This is already evident where he says that he does not enjoy the praise of his citizens because it is subject to compulsion (1.14–15) and Simonides agrees that only praise from those who are 'most free' gives pleasure (1.16). He identifies that same lack of freedom as a barrier to his genuine pleasure in his sexual relationships with his community (1.26–38) and in the honour he receives (7.5–8), and since this is his own diagnosis, it is most unlikely that he will not wish to make his citizens free if he can, in order to secure the happiness he wants. Simonides implicitly endorses the free society when he envisages that the citizens will 'willingly' give Hiero their love and praise once he serves their common good (11.8–12). It does not mean that he will not be their ruler; he will maintain the initiative in the relationship, but the initiative will also be open to them to serve him, defend him, delight in him and reveal to him whatever wise or fine or good thing that they have to give him. They are in one sense at his mercy, but because of his inner desire to be loved, this mercy will always be with them.

Nor does it seem that Simonides produces only a limited kind of virtue in his citizens when he encourages competitions in 'valour in warfare' and 'justice in commercial dealings' (9.6). Other paradigmatic rulers use competitions as a straightforward way of improving the ruled (see the commentary on *Hiero* 9.1–11, *Lac.* 4.2). Simonides says that they will encourage many to 'make an inquiry into the good': τὸ σκοπεῖν τι ἀγαθόν, and consider what is 'useful' (9.10), which in philosophic discourse means the pursuit of virtue. The non-ironic Hiero certainly places no qualification on his admiration of the brave, wise and just (5.1–2) whom he positively desires to use in his administration of the *polis*, and whom these competitions will encourage. He also laments his own enforced injustice without qualification (4.10–11, 7.12–13) and expresses a positive desire for the honour that is given for the virtue that consists in serving the common good (7.9). Simonides shows him how to attain this in his reform, and make mankind sincerely 'hymn his virtue' (11.8).

Strauss (1947/1963) 71 = (2000) 69f. finds hidden meaning even in Simonides' instruction to Hiero to enrich his friends, increase the *polis*, consider his land his household, his citizens his comrades, his friends his children and his children his soul (11.14). Comrades, he suggests, can still be slaves, to treat people as children is to make them inferiors, and to treat the *polis* as an *oikos* is to appropriate its goods. Yet, rather than wanting slaves as comrades, Hiero wants to escape this unnatural compulsion (5.2, 6.5). His friends will benefit from being treated as his children, since parents in other paradigms always serve the best interests of their children. This is why people called Cyrus father (*Cyr.* 8.2.9: τοῦτο δὲ τοὔνομα δῆλον ὅτι εὐεργετοῦντός ἐστι μᾶλλον ἢ ἀφαιρουμένου). Agesilaus is also loved as a father in Asia because of his benefits (*Ages.* 1.38) and he treats his fellow citizens as a father too, chastising their faults, but praising their virtues, standing by them in misfortune, wanting to see the good in them rather than the bad (*Ages.* 7.3). Mothers and fathers indeed both serve their children's interests (*Mem.* 2.2.3–6, 9–10). Those populations who called Cyrus father because he indulged their appetites for food and drink and other material pleasures are exemplifying true irony, because they do not realize that he was seeing to it that 'they would continue always without dispute in slavery to him' (*Cyr.* 8.1.44). Other paradigms show also that to treat the *polis* as an *oikos* is to increase its worth rather than steal its goods (*Oec.* passim and *Symp.* 8.25 in the comparison of the one who rents and the one who owns an estate). Certainly, nothing sinister can be made of the injunction to treat his children as his 'soul'. Hiero believes the soul to be the seat of *eudaimonia* (2.4), and will seek *eudaimonia* for his children as he does for his soul.

Another sinister reading would take Aristotle's recognition of the two faces of tyranny (*Pol.* 1313a34–1315b10) and have Simonides' reforms merely dupe the citizens into thinking that they are free. The bad tyrant keeps his subjects humble and divided, eliminating nobles, using spies, keeping the people poor so that they have no time to plot, enforcing public works and taxes, making constant war, the friend of flatterers, the enemy of the free. The good tyrant champions the people, conserves the public funds, has personal self-control, adorns the *polis*, bestows honours in person, but delegates punishments, and so on. Yet both seek to maintain their power. Hiero's suspicion of the brave and wise and self-controlled and his desire to eliminate them (5) is an aspect of the first stereotype, whereas his realization that he will have no one left to rule if he eliminates them entirely (6.12–16) is an aspect of the second. The essential objection to the sinister interpretation is that Hiero seeks friendship rather than power, as is indicated in his memory of his greater previous happiness as a non-ruler (6.1–6) and in Simonides' acceptance of this lack of friendship as the diagnosis of his unhappiness – unless we dismiss what both characters agree, which neither the dramatic situation nor the quality of the utterances, nor Xenophon's other paradigms would encourage us to do.

APPENDIX 2
TOPOI OF TYRANNY

It has been observed that ideas in Plato's account of the unhappiness of the tyrant in the *Republic* are also found in *Hiero*. Luccioni (1947) 18–20 attributed them to the common teaching of Socrates, but they have been seen as 'borrowings' (usually on the assumption that Xenophon borrowed from Plato, though the date of neither work can be fixed).[1] Yet Greek literature worked with *topoi*, and Plato makes it plain that the stereotype of the tyrant was already entrenched in political thought.[2] This means that those who wrote about tyranny were bound to examine the same themes regardless of their relationship. Stobaeus 4.8.1–13 in his 'Accusation of Tyranny' includes passages from Euripides and Sophocles that already portray the tyrant as the enemy of the good, isolated and afraid. Herodotus' constitutional debate (3.80–2) also has many of the commonplaces.[3]

Xenophon should be judged then by what he does with commonplaces, rather than his mere use of them, and this is a matter of literary presentation and the reworking of the ideas. The suffering of the tyrant is a major theme for him. This suffering is made more effective because Xenophon's choice of the dialogue form brought personal interest and dramatic tension to the development of the commonplaces. His range of argument and emotional language show how much he wanted to give the tyrant an effective human voice.

Herodotus' meetings of the wise and powerful, such as Croesus and Cyrus (1.29–33), do have the potential for conveying suffering, but mainly focus on the ignorance of the tyrannical condition. Herodotus' constitutional debate makes nothing of this suffering either, as is shown by a comparison of its use of the commonplaces of tyranny with *Hiero*. For instance, Otanes portrays the sole ruler as one who envies the best men while they live and rejoices in the worst (3.80.4), but *Hiero* makes this an emotional and unacceptable dilemma for the tyrant (5.1–4). Otanes' tyrant is never satisfied with the praise he hears either, because it is either too little or sounds like flattery (3.80.5); *Hiero* finds this a source of pain (1.14–15). Herodotus addresses the *topos* of the tyrant's inability to escape from his tyranny in Maeandrius, who did not think it just to rule equals and decided to liberate his people, on condition that they grant him certain privileges; but when prominent citizens held him accountable for his tyranny, he decided to rule them by force rather than be condemned for his crimes (3.142–3).

---

[1] Adam (1938/1965), vol. 2 on *Rep.* 579e, assumed the priority of the *Republic* and called the *Hiero* 'a diluted commentary on' a single sentence in Plato's image of the tyrant as a master of many slaves, isolated from the support of his community. The relations between Xenophon and Plato continue to provoke argument. Huss (1999) 13–18 discusses their respective dates, and 449–55 lists resemblances between their *Symposia*.

[2] Plato refers to the tyrant's method of acquiring a bodyguard as τὸ δὴ τυραννικὸν αἴτημα τὸ πολυθρύλητον (*Rep.* 566b), as if he has read Herodotus' account of Pisistratus (Hdt. 1.59.4–5).

[3] Pelling (2002) offers a recent discussion of this famous debate.

Hiero 7.10–12 cuts off both escape routes; Hiero sees that he can never settle his account with the citizens, but cannot abide his current unhappiness, and sees suicide as his only way out.

Plato in contrast did not let the tyrant speak, nor even the wise man, but merely reported the findings of a wise judge who entered the heart of the tyrant to investigate his condition (*Rep.* 577b). His description of the unhappiness he found is brilliant, but his tyrant is a creature of melodrama, his wise man is devoid of character, and there is no dramatic exchange. *Republic* 576a ('the tyrannical nature is always untasting of freedom and true friendship') recognizes the lack of friendship that is the tyrant's main problem, but Hiero makes an emotional feature of it, through contrasts of his happy memories of private life and his current unhappiness as a ruler, and in sections such as 1.35–6 and 6.1–4, where the language is highly wrought and the sentiments piteous. *Republic* 579d summed up the paradox of the ruler who seems most free but is most enslaved: ὁ τῶι ὄντι τύραννος τῶι ὄντι δοῦλος, but Xenophon's Hiero insists throughout in his own voice that he is compelled to do what he does to preserve his life, while it is the citizens who are free. Plato described the condition of the tyrant as that of a man surrounded by hostile slaves (*Rep.* 578a), but *Hiero* uses a more sustained metaphor of the tyrant at war with his community throughout the work. This begins with his warlike relations with his *eromenos* (1.34–6), continues in his contrast of the constant misery of this unrelenting war against his subjects with the more joyous and more sporadic wars of his citizens (2.7–18), and reaches a climax in his metaphor of the fear that dwells in his heart and ruins his enjoyment of anything else (6.4–8). Some resemblances are merely the result of good writing, such as Plato's description of the tyrant as 'envious, untrusting, unjust, friendless, unholy' (*Rep.* 580a) and Hiero's description of the honoured man: 'without fear and without envy and without danger and in happiness' (*Hiero* 7.10).

Hiero also innovates in the second half of the work, by showing how the common-place miseries of tyrannical rule can be corrected. So, in response to the complaint that the tyrant must eliminate the best men and be left with the worst (*Rep.* 567d–568a, *Hiero* 5.1–4, 6.15), Simonides finds ways to encourage the best men into service, both to the tyrant and the common good (9). In response to the idea that the tyrant needs a bodyguard to protect his person against his citizens (*Rep.* 567d, *Hiero* 2.8, 8.10), but knows it is more of a threat to his person than a protection (6.11), Simonides frees Hiero of his need to keep a bodyguard for himself, and shows how it can keep the worst citizens from running riot and as a military force be directed to serve the common good of the citizens (10). Xenophon develops some of the commonplaces inventively and matches them with an inventive solution. Thus he develops the *topos* of the tyrant's lack of pleasure in his lack of freedom to travel to see the sights (*Hiero* 1.11–13, Plato, *Rep.* 579b-c), by extending his lack of enjoyment to the sights he sees at home, as well as those abroad. The development prepares for Simonides' deconstruction of the *topos* in his vision of reform, where Hiero will be free to travel if he likes, but will be equally happy if he remains at home, since his court will be itself a place of constant 'festival' of those who wish to show him something clever or good or fine (11.9–10).

The idea that these constitute 'borrowings' would mean that Xenophon borrows from himself. For example, he adapts the *topos* of the inability to travel abroad to define the condition of the rich man in the democracy rather than the tyrant in his rule, and in this adaptation identifies the freedom to travel ironically as the condition of the poor (*Symp.* 4.30–1). The rich man cannot travel because he is a slave to the demands of the *demos* and his fear of burglary. A pair of *topoi* not found in Plato show what different effects Xenophon can achieve with the one *topos*: *An.* 7.4.7–11 and *Hell.* 6.4.37. In these, a tyrant is about to kill a young boy and is asked to spare him. In the first, Seuthes is on the rampage and is about to kill a young boy when Episthenes, who has gathered an army of such boys and loves them dearly, asks Xenophon to intervene; he does so and Seuthes spares the boy after discovering that Episthenes would die for him, and the boy would not let Episthenes die for his sake. Alexander of Pherae, in a different context, is about to incarcerate his own beloved boy when his wife intervenes (*Hell.* 6.4.37); but Alexander does not relent even though the favourite was his own and the intervention comes from his wife, whom he should love most of all; instead of merely imprisoning him, he kills him. The different responses of the tyrant-figures to the same situation send different messages about the characters involved. The first highlights Xenophon's influence with Seuthes and empathy with Episthenes, as well as the empathy between the lover and beloved. The second shows the lack of true friendship in Alexander's relations with members of his household he ought to love most (Hiero himself laments that such friendship is non-existent in the household of the tyrant: *Hiero* 3.6–8).

APPENDIX 3
LAC. 14

One of the enduring problems of *Lac.* is that after describing Lycurgus' laws over the first thirteen chapters, the fourteenth chapter says that the Spartans have lost the success they once had because their harmosts have succumbed to the corrupting effects of empire overseas. 'I know that previously Spartans chose to live at home with one another living on moderate means rather than being corrupted through playing the harmost in the cities and being the objects of flattery.' Further, 'I know that previously they drove foreigners out and did not allow people to live abroad, so that the citizens would not be filled with laziness from contact with foreigners, but now I understand that those who have the top reputations make it their pursuit never to cease playing the harmost abroad.' These harmosts cause the rejection of Spartan leadership of which the chapter goes on to speak because they impress the allies as unworthy leaders.

Questions have been asked whether this chapter is authentic, whether it is in its intended position in the text, and whether it was written subsequent to the rest.[1] The first controversy seems virtually settled since, as already noted, its authenticity seems beyond question.[2] On the second point, though the chapter has seemed to disrupt a natural integrity in chapters 13 and 15 (because these describe the privileges of the kings in war, then in peace),[3] the idea that the kings remain obedient to the law within the *polis* makes a nice contrast with the preceding account of the disobedience of the harmosts outside the *polis*, and the idea that the Greeks have rejected the Spartan ἀρχή (14.6) contrasts neatly with the idea that the Spartans have not rejected the ἀρχή of kingship.

This leaves the idea that Xenophon originally wrote the work in praise of the Spartans, then decided that the praise was undeserved, and added the chapter without tidying up the contradictions.[4] The objection to this is that the subject of the work as stated in the introduction is not praise of the Spartans for obeying the laws, but praise of Lycurgus for inventing them, so that the criticism of their lapses does not

---

[1] MacDowell (1986) 8–14 reviews these problems.

[2] See p. 20 n. 36.

[3] For reasons like these, Ollier (1934) moved it to the end of the work, Chrimes (1948) to the beginning, MacDowell (1986) proposes further dislocation, and Lipka (2002) 27–31 considers the work unfinished.

[4] Ollier (1934) xiii calls the main part of the work 'un très vif éloge de Sparte et de ses institutions' in favour of the continuance of their hegemony; cf. Tigerstedt, vol. 1 (1965) 161–9. It follows that the fourteenth chapter must contradict the rest of the work. Tigerstedt, vol. 1 (1965) 169 formulates this in its starkest terms: 'In his preceding account he has praised Sparta precisely for its obedience to the laws of Lycurgus . . . now he explains that this obedience . . . belongs to the past . . . It is a complete palinode.' His change of heart is said to have been caused by their unjust seizure of the Cadmea of Thebes in 383 BC or when he went to Sparta and saw for himself that the laws were no longer respected: MacDowell (1986) 13 –14. Strauss (1939) argues that the whole work is in fact veiled criticism, but see p. 14 n. 20.

contradict that praise but offers a further rhetorical proof of it; for the body of the work argues that they gained their success through obedience to these laws and this chapter says that they lost it as a result of their disobedience.[5] This is the converse of Aristotle's proof that the laws were defective because the Spartans lost their success even while obeying them (*Politics* 1333b21–6). It seems likely that such a strong proof of the excellence of the laws occurred to Xenophon before he began to write rather than during or afterwards. He writes a similar 'epilogue' for *Cyropaedia*, praising Cyrus in the introduction, then describing the customs he introduced, but in the epilogue declaring and proving that contemporary Persians have lost their power because they have abandoned them (8.8.1–27). It is hard to accept that in both works he had a change of heart about what he had written and added palinodes without tidying up the contradictions.[6] Another parallel may be found in the assertion of the complete corruption of Critias and Alcibiades once they escaped the control of Socrates (*Mem.* 1.2.24–8). Both reinforce the excellence of the original controlling paradigms (pp. 13–14).

The idea that the fourteenth chapter does not contain a contradiction of the rest of the work is supported by the impression throughout the work that the laws belong to the past. The first thirteen chapters describe them as Lycurgus introduced them in the past. This allows the narrator to introduce a reader to ask whether they are still in force at 14.1 – indicating that this reader has not taken the description to refer to anything but the past. In one instance even in the main text a contrast is drawn between previous and current practice (12.3). The introduction admires Lycurgus in the present tense because he remains admirable for inventing the laws, even if they do belong to the past.

The use of the present tense in some descriptions of the effects of the laws has been used to support the idea of their continuing currency. Yet the present tense often only describes phenomena that are contemporary with the time of their introduction in the past, as in *Lac.* 4.3: 'How [Lycurgus] *engaged* them, I will now explain. The ephors *choose* . . .', or 1.9, where the motives for the many past agreements are explained in the present tense. Elsewhere, the present tense could be a vivid re-creation of what life was like in past times, or a momentary lapse by the author into the dream of the ideal.[7]

---

[5] Luccioni (1946) 167–9 recognizes this central point, but still does not see the epilogue as an integral part of the work.

[6] There are as many interpretations of the epilogue to *Cyropaedia* as of that in *Lac.*, but the coincidence favours the interpretation of Due (1989).

[7] Momigliano (1936) followed by Bordes (1982) 198–203 and Carlier (1984) 252–4, resolved even the glaring inconsistency between the statement that they are most obedient to the laws 'in Sparta' (8.1) and the statement that they no longer obey the laws (14.1, 7), by arguing that 'in Sparta' means 'under the ideal system that Lycurgus introduced'. Chrimes (1948) 4–6 is also inclined to read the present tense as ideal, while allowing that some customs may have still been current at the time of writing. The present tense could also be contemporary with Xenophon's original reflection on the laws, before he reflected on their abandonment, or appropriate to the timeless application of politeia-literature. Bordes (1982) 202: 'ils ne se rapportent pas à l'époque

However, the role of the fourteenth chapter as a rhetorical proof of the excellence of Lycurgus' laws means that it certainly uses exaggeration. There is other evidence even in Xenophon that the Spartans continued to obey the laws down to as late as 360 BC. A speaker in *Hellenica* argues for their separate leadership by land and sea in 370 BC, asserting that they still most of all obey their rulers by land, as the Athenians obey theirs by sea (*Hell.* 7.1.8). *Agesilaus* supports the idea that the laws continued to be obeyed down to the King's death, since it praises him for his view that the happiness of the Spartans continued to depend on their observation of the laws: 'he clearly reckoned that if they remained unmovingly in the laws their homeland would be ever successful' (*Ages.* 7.3).

The extension of the corruption of the harmosts to the entire population is another exaggeration, perhaps to be explained by the principle that rulers determine the character of the ruled. The epilogue to *Cyropaedia* spells this out in a similar context after extending the corruption of contemporary Persian governors (their impiety and injustice) to the entire population of Asia: 'the characters of the rulers become those of people under them in most cases' (8.8.5). The principle is also asserted in *Poroi* 1.1: 'constitutions become of the same characters as their rulers'.

Xenophon's other evidence about harmosts proves that he exaggerates their corruption to achieve his rhetorical effect. Lysander attracted a following in the cities of Asia (*Hell.* 3.4.7–8) that provoked other Spartiates to say that he was lawless (παράνομα ποιοίη) in usurping the privileges of the king, but Dercylidas, though he liked spending time abroad (4.3.2), was an admirably uncorrupted harmost of Abydus (4.8.3–5). Thibron was distracted by pleasures, but Diphridas was not (4.8.22). Phoebidas was flattered into taking Thebes contrary to the instructions he received from the ephors and people (*Hell.* 5.2.25–32), but he was not a harmost, whereas Teleutias, who was, gave scrupulous service in spite of his unfortunate death (5.2.37–5.3.7). Sphodrias was bribed by the Thebans (*Hell.* 5.4.20), but he was acquitted on account of his perfect obedience to the laws prior to that (5.4.32). *Hell.* 5.4.1 condemns Spartan impiety and injustice toward the Greeks, but not as a product of the corruption of the harmosts. It says that they transgressed their international oaths, but not as a product of their neglect of Lycurgus' laws. *Anabasis* does not support *Lac.* 14 either. Clearchus secured a commission from the ephors after the Peloponnesian War, refused their summons to come home when they changed their minds, and was condemned to death by them for disobedience, but his 'corruption' was merely being too devoted to war (*Anab.* 2.6.1–15). The Spartans were intent on ruling others and when Xenophon's popularity made him a candidate for supreme leadership, he stood aside because they would not brook his challenge (*Anab.* 6.1.26–8, 6.6.12, 7.1.26–7). But none of these harmosts are corrupt in the way of *Lac.*

où Xénophon fit le raisonnement qu'il livre à son lecteur; ils échappent au temps et à l'histoire, ce qui est le propre de toute politeia "l'âme de la cité", unique et spécifique . . .' Polybius also switches between past and present tense in his ideal account of constitutional change: Hahm in Laks and Schofield (eds.) (1995) 34–6.

The views in *Lac.* 14 are indeed commonplaces. Pausanias the victor of the Persian Wars was the model of the Spartan overseas who abandoned the established customs, alienated the allies and made them reject Spartan leadership (Thuc. 1.130.1): 'Being previously held in great esteem by the Greeks for his leadership at Plataea, he was at that time elevated much higher and was no longer capable of living in the established fashion' (οὐκέτι ἐδύνατο ἐν τῶι καθεστῶτι τρόπωι βιοτεύειν). He wore Median clothing, ate in the Persian style, had a bodyguard and was unapproachable, and for these reasons, the Greeks who were subject to his rule thought him oppressive and defected to the Athenian alliance (1.130.2). The laws still prevailed at home, however, since he was condemned for contraventions of τῶν καθεστώτων νομίμων (1.132.2). The Spartans learned from his example not to send their people abroad because their characters would deteriorate (1.95.7). This lesson was apparently forgotten in the case of Xenophon's harmosts.

Isocrates' *Peace* of 355 BC also attributes general Spartan decline to the acquisition of empire abroad in exaggerated and rhetorical terms similar to those of *Lac.* (8.95–103): 'In place of their established habits of life (ἀντὶ γὰρ τῶν καθεστώτων παρ' αὐτοῖς ἐπιτηδευμάτων), it filled individuals with injustice, laziness, lawlessness, love of money, and filled the community of the city with contempt for their allies, desire for the goods of others, despite of their oaths and compacts' (ὀλιγωρίας δὲ τῶν ὅρκων καὶ τῶν συνθηκῶν): 96. 'They no longer kept the laws they received from their ancestors, nor did they remain in the values they had previously, but thinking that they could do what they liked, they fell into utter confusion': 102–3. Isocrates' *Areopagiticus*, also of 355 BC, extends the commonplace to the Athenians when it describes how such decline alienated the allies of the Athenians in a way that is strikingly similar to Xenophon's account of the alienation of the Spartan allies (*Areop.* 7.79–81; *Lac.* 14.6): 'I tell you that the Greeks so trusted those who lived under that constitution that most of them willingly put themselves in the hands of the *polis*' (80); 'whereas now affairs have come to such a pass that some hate the city and others despise us' (81). Compare *Lac.*: 'I tell you that the Greeks previously used to go to Lacedaemon and ask them to be leaders against those who seemed to do wrong, whereas now many of them exhort each other to prevent them ruling . . .'

We should not read *Lac.* 14 as a careful statement of realities. The rhetorical proof is more concerned with persuasive generalities than with truthful specifics, and so is much political thought. If we find the tone and content of *Lac.* 14 anywhere else, it is in the rhetoric that Xenophon has the Thebans deliver when they call on the Athenians to put an end to Spartan rule at the outbreak of the Corinthian War in 395 BC. There they specifically emphasize Spartan greed and injustice and the oppression of their harmosts (*Hell.* 3.5.10–15). The novelty of *Lac.* is perhaps that the commonplace about their corruption was being used for the first time to reinforce the praise of the paradigm of Lycurgus, rather than diminish it. This paradigm was a higher truth to which specific truths could happily be sacrificed, as in all persuasion. The ironic readings of *Lac.* fail to recognize the positive force of this rhetoric.

The fourteenth chapter does challenge the perfection of the system that Lycurgus devised, since it leaves him open to the objection that he did not secure it against the corruption of empire overseas, but this does not diminish the excellence of the paradigm, if the parallel of the corruption even of the pupils of Socrates after they had escaped his influence and control is rightly adduced, as outlined above. The lesson is merely that virtue is an activity that needs constant practice and surveillance.

BIBLIOGRAPHY

Adam, J. *The Republic of Plato*, 2 vols. (Cambridge 1938, 2nd edn. 1963–5, D. A. Rees).

Amit, M. *Athens and the Sea* (Brussels 1965).

Anderson, J. K. *Military Theory and Practice in the Age of Xenophon* (Berkeley 1970).
Xenophon (London 1974).

Arnaoutoglou, I. *Ancient Greek Laws. A Sourcebook* (New York 1998).

Arrigoni, G. 'Donne e sport nel mondo greco. Religione e società', in Arrigoni (ed.)
(1985) 55–201.
(ed.) *Le donne in Grecia* (Bari 1985).

Azoulay, V. *Xénophon et les grâces de pouvoir. De la charis au charisme* (Paris 2004).

Beck, F. A. G. *Greek Education 450–350 BC* (London 1964).

Bell, J. M. 'κίμβιξ καὶ σοφός Simonides in the anecdotal tradition', *QUCC* 28 (1978)
29–86.

Berve, H. *Die Tyrannis bei den Griechen*, 2 vols. (Munich 1967).

Bianco, E. 'Il capitolo XIV della "Lakedaimonion Politeia" attribuita a Senofonte',
Mus. Helv. 53 (1996) 12–24.

Boedeker, D. and D. Sider (eds.) *The New Simonides. Contexts of Praise and Desire* (Oxford
2001).

Bordes, J. *Politeia dans la pensée grecque jusqu' à Aristote* (Paris 1982).

Bowersock, G. W. 'Pseudo-Xenophon', *HSCP* 71 (1966) 33–55.
Constitution of the Athenians, in Xenophon, *Scripta Minora* (Cambridge, Mass. 1968)
459–507.

Brock, R. and M. Heath, 'Two passages in Pseudo-Xenophon', *CQ* 45 (1995) 564–6.

Buffière, F. *Eros adolescent* (Paris 1980).

Burkert, W. *Greek Religion*, trans. John Raffan (Oxford 1985).

Caballero López, J. A. *La lengua y el estilo de la República de los Atenienses del Pseudo-Jenofonte*
(Amsterdam 1997).

Calame, C. 'Iniziazioni femminili Spartane: stupro, danza, ratto, metamorfosi e morte
iniziatica', in Arrigoni (ed.) (1985) 33–54.
Choruses of Young Women in Ancient Greece, trans. D. Collins and J. Orion (Lanham
1997) = *Les Choeurs de jeunes filles en Grèce archaïque* (Rome 1977).

Campbell, D. *Greek Lyric*, 5 vols. (Cambridge, Mass. 1982–93).

Canfora, L. *Studi sull' 'Athenaion Politeia' pseudosenofontea* (Turin 1980).

Carey, C. 'Comic ridicule and democracy', in Osborne and Hornblower (eds.) (1994)
69–84.
'Rape and adultery in Athenian law', *CQ* 45 (1995) 407–17.

Carlier, P. *La Royauté en Grèce avant Alexandre* (Strasbourg 1984).

Cartledge, P. A. 'Did Spartan citizens ever practise a manual tekhne?', *LCM* 1 (1976)
115–19.
'Spartan wives. Liberation or licence?', *CQ* 31 (1981) 84–105.

Agesilaos and the Crisis of Sparta (Baltimore 1987).

'The Socratics' Sparta and Rousseau's', in Hodkinson and Powell (eds.) (1999) 311–37.

Spartan Reflections (London 2001).

Cartledge, P. A., P. Millett and S. von Reden (eds.) *Kosmos. Essays in Order, Conflict and Community in Classical Athens* (Cambridge 1998).

Chrimes, K. M. T. *The Respublica Lacedaemoniorum Ascribed to Xenophon. Its Manuscript Tradition and General Significance* (Manchester 1948).

Connor, W. R. (ed.) *Aspects of Athenian Democracy* (Copenhagen 1990).

Croiset, A., *Xénophon, son caractère et son talent* (Paris 1873).

Dalby, A. *Siren Feasts* (London 1996).

David, E. 'Sparta's kosmos of silence', in Hodkinson and Powell (eds.) (1999) 117–46.

De Romilly, J. 'Le Pseudo-Xénophon et Thucydide', *Rev. de Phil.* s. 3: 36 = 88 (1962) 225–41.

La Loi dans la pensée grecque (Paris 1971).

Denniston, J. D. *Greek Prose Style* (Oxford 1952).

The Greek Particles (Oxford 1954).

Deuling, J. K. and Cirignano, J. 'A re-appraisal of the later ABS family of manuscripts of Xenophon's *Hiero* tradition', *Scriptorium* 44 (1990) 54–68.

Diels, H. and W. Kranz *Die Fragmente der Vorsokratiker¹²*, 3 vols. (Dublin–Zürich 1966–7).

Dover, K. J. *Greek Homosexuality* (London 1978, rev. edn. Cambridge, Mass. 1989).

Due, B. *The Cyropaedia. Xenophon's Aims and Methods* (Aarhus 1989).

Edwards. M. J. *Lysias: Five Speeches* (London 1999).

Faure P. *Parfums et aromates de l'antiquité* (Paris 1987).

Finley, M. I. *Ancient Sicily* (London 1968).

Fisher, N. R. E. *Slavery in Classical Greece* (London 1993).

'Gymnasia and the democratic values of leisure', in Cartledge, Millett and von Reden (1998) 84–104.

Flensted-Jensen, P. et al. *Polis and Politics. Studies in Ancient Greek History* (Copenhagen 2000).

Fontana, M. J. F. *L'Athenaion Politeia del V secolo a.C.* (Palermo 1968).

Foucault, M. *History of Sexuality*, vol. 3, trans. Robert Hurley (New York 1986).

Foxhall, L. and A. D. E. Lewis (eds.) *Greek Law in its Political Setting* (Oxford 1996).

Frisch, H. *The Constitution of the Athenians. A Philological-Historical Analysis of Pseudo-Xenophon's Treatise De Re Publica Atheniensium* (Copenhagen 1942).

Gabrielsen, V. *Financing the Athenian Fleet* (Baltimore 1994).

Gagarin, M. *Drakon and Early Athenian Homicide Law* (New Haven 1981).

Early Greek Law (Berkeley 1986).

Gargiulo, T. 'Tre note all' Athenaion Politeia pseudosenofontea (1.11; 1.14; 2.11)', *Eikasmos* 10 (1999) 63–81.

Gauthier, Ph. and M. B. Hatzopoulos, *La Loi Gymnasiarchique de Beroia* (Athens 1993).

Gautier, L. *La Langue de Xénophon* (Geneva 1911).

Gera, D. L. *Xenophon's Cyropaedia. Style, Genre and Literary Technique* (Oxford 1993).

Gigante, M. and G. Maddoli (eds.) *L'Athenaion Politeia dello Pseudo-Senofonte* (Naples 1997).

Glass, S. L. 'The Greek gymnasium. Some problems', in Raschke (1988) 155–73.

Goldhill, S. and R. Osborne (eds.) *Performance Culture and Athenian Democracy* (Cambridge 1999).

Gomme, A. W. 'The Old Oligarch', *HSCP* Suppl. 1 (1940) 211–45.

A Historical Commentary on Thucydides, vol. 1 (Oxford 1971).

Gray, V. J. 'Xenophon's *Hiero* and the meeting of the wise man and tyrant in Greek literature', *CQ* n.s. 36 (1986) 115–23.

'Images of Sparta: writer and audience in Isocrates' *Panathenaicus*', in Powell and Hodkinson (eds.) (1994) 223–72.

The Framing of Socrates (Stuttgart 1998).

'Xenophon and Isocrates', in Rowe and Schofield (eds.) (2000) 142–54.

(a) 'Le Socrate de Xénophon et la démocratie', *Les Études philosophiques* 2 (2004) 141–76.

(b) Review of C. Nadon, *Xenophon's Prince*, in *Ancient Philosophy* 24 (2004) 193–6.

(c) 'A short response to David M. Johnson. "Xenophon's Socrates on law and justice"', *Ancient Philosophy* 24 (2004) 442–6.

Review of V. Azoulay, *Xénophon et les grâces de pouvoir. De la charis au charisme*, in *CR* 56 (2006) 43–5.

'The evidence in Xenophon, *Respublica Lacedaemoniorum* for Spartan women', in Ellen Millender (ed.) forthcoming.

Guarducci, M. *Inscriptiones Creticae*, 4 vols. (Rome 1935–50).

Hahm, D. E. 'Polybius' applied political theory', in Laks and Schofield (eds.) (1995) 7–47.

Halliwell, S. 'Comic satire and freedom of speech in classical Athens', *JHS* 111 (1991) 48–70.

Haltinner, D. O. and E. A. Schmoll 'The older manuscripts of Xenophon's *Hiero*', *Revue d'histoire des textes* 10 (1980) 231–6.

Harrison, A. R. W. *The Law of Athens*, 2 vols. (Oxford 1968, 1971).

Harvey, F. D. 'Two kinds of equality', *C&M* 26 (1965) 101–46.

Herman, G. *Ritualized Friendship and the Greek City* (Cambridge 1987).

Hicks, R. D. *Diogenes Laertius*, 2 vols. (Cambridge, Mass. 1925).

Higgins, W. E. *Xenophon the Athenian* (Albany 1977).

Hindley, C. 'Xenophon on male love', *CQ* 99 (1999) 74–99.

Hodkinson, S. 'Inheritance, marriage and demography: perspectives upon the success and decline of Classical Sparta', in Powell (ed.) (1989) 79–121.

Property and Wealth in Classical Sparta (Cardiff 2000).

Hodkinson, S. and A. Powell (eds.) *Sparta. Past Perspectives* (London 1999).

Holden, H. A. *A Commentary on Xenophon's Hiero* (London 1888).

Hornblower, S. '*The Old Oligarch* (Pseudo-Xenophon's *Athenaion Politeia*) and Thucydides. A fourth century date for the Old Oligarch?', in Flensted-Jensen et al. (eds.) (2000) 363–84.

Hunter, R. L. *Theocritus and the Archaeology of Greek Poetry* (Cambridge 1996).

Huss, B. *Xenophons Symposion* (Stuttgart 1999).

Jackson, D. F. 'Correction and contamination in Xenophon's *Hiero*', *SIFC* 6 (1988) 48–76.

'A new look at the manuscripts of Xenophon's *Hipparchicus*', *CQ* 40 (1990) 176–86.

'Manuscripts of Xenophon's *Poroi*', *SIFC* 8 (1990) 166–79.

Jackson, R. *Doctors and Diseases in the Roman Empire* (London 1988).

Jeanmaire, H. *Couroi et courètes* (Lille 1939, repr. New York 1975).

Johnson, David. 'Xenophon's Socrates on law and justice', *Ancient Philosophy* 23 (2003) 255–81.

Jones, A. H. M. *Athenian Democracy* (Oxford 1957).

Jones, J. W. *The Law and Legal Theory of the Greeks* (Oxford 1956).

Jordan, B. *The Athenian Navy in the Classical Period* (Berkeley 1975).

Kalinka, E. *Die PeudoXenophontische Ἀθηναίων Πολιτεία. Einleitung, Übersetzung, Erklärung* (Leipzig 1913).

Kennell, N. M. *The Gymnasium of Virtue. Education and Culture in Ancient Sparta* (Chapel Hill 1995).

Konstan, D. *Friendship in the Classical World* (Cambridge 1997).

Kunstler, B. L. *Women and the Development of the Spartan Polis* (diss. Boston 1983).

Laks, A. 'The laws', in Rowe and Schofield (eds.) (2000) 258–92.

Laks, A. and M. Schofield (eds.) *Justice and Generosity* (Cambridge 1995).

Lana, M. 'Xenophon's *Athenaion Politeia*: a study by correspondence analysis', *Journal of Literary and Linguistic Computing* 7.1 (1992) 17–26.

Lanzillotta, E. (ed.) *Problemi di storia e cultura spartana* (Rome 1984).

Lapini, W. *Commento all' Athenaion Politeia dello Pseudo-Senofonte* (Florence 1997).

Lazenby, J. F. *The Spartan Army* (Warminster 1985).

Leduc, C. *La Constitution d' Athènes attribué à Xénophon* (Paris 1976).

Lefèvre, E. 'Die Frage nach dem ΒΙΟΣ ΕΥΔΑΙΜΩΝ. Die Begegnung zwischen Kyros und Kroisos bei Xenophon', *Hermes* 99 (1971) 283–95.

Lefkowitz, M. *Lives of the Greek Poets* (London 1981).

Leverenz, L. 'The Descendants of Laurentianus 80.13 in Xenophon's *Hiero*', *SIFC* 7 (1989) 12–23.

Lipka, M. *Xenophon's Spartan Constitution* (Berlin 2002).

Lissarrague, Fr. 'Publicity and performance: *kalos* inscriptions in Attic vase-painting', trans. Robin Osborne in Goldhill and Osborne (1999) 359–73.

Loraux, N. *The Invention of Athens. The Funeral Oration in the Classical City*, trans. Alan Sheridan (Cambridge, Mass. 1986).

Luccioni, J. *Les Idées politiques et sociales de Xénophon* (Paris 1946).

Hiéron (Paris 1947).

Luppino Manes, E. *Un progetto di riforma per Sparta. La 'Politeia' di Senofonte* (Milan 1988).

MacDowell, D. M. *Athenian Homicide Law in the Age of the Orators* (Manchester 1963).

Spartan Law (Edinburgh 1986).

Meiggs, R. *The Athenian Empire* (Oxford 1972).

Meiggs, R. and D. Lewis *A Selection of Greek Historical Inscriptions to the End of the Fifth Century* BC (Oxford 1969, rev. edn. 1988).

Meillet, A. *Aperçu d'une histoire de la langue grecque* (Paris 1965).

Millender, Ellen (ed.) *Unveiling Spartan Women* (Cardiff 2007).

Missoni, R. 'Criteri eugenetici nel κόσμος licurgico', in Lanzillotta (ed.) (1984) 107–19.

Mitchell, L. G and P. J. Rhodes (eds.) *The Development of the Polis in Archaic Greece* (New York 1997).

Molyneux, J. H. *Simonides. An Historical Study* (Illinois 1992).

Momigliano, A. 'Per l'unità logica della 'Λακεδαιμονίων Πολιτεία' di Senofonte', *RFIC* n.s. 14 (1936) 170–3.

The Development of Greek Biography (Cambridge, Mass. 1971, expanded edn. 1993).

Moore, J. M. *Aristotle and Xenophon on Democracy and Oligarchy* (California 1975).

Morrison, D. R. *Bibliography of Editions, Translations, and Commentary on Xenophon's Socratic Writings, 1600-Present* (Pittsburgh 1988).

'Xenophon's Socrates on the just and the lawful', *Ancient Philosophy* 15 (1995) 329–58.

Muratore, D. *Studi sulla tradizione manoscritta della Costituzione degli Spartani di Senofonte* (Genoa 1997).

Nadon, C. *Xenophon's Prince* (Berkeley 2001).

Nafissi, M. *La nascita del kosmos. Studi sulla storia e la società di Sparta* (Naples 1991).

Navia, L. E. *Antisthenes of Athens* (Westport 2001).

Nevett, L. C. *House and Society in the Ancient Greek World* (Cambridge 1999).

Norden, E. *Die antike Kunstprosa*[6], 2 vols. (Darmstadt 1971).

Ober, J. *The Athenian Revolution* (Princeton 1996).

Political Dissent in Democratic Athens (Princeton 1998).

Ollier, Fr. *Le Mirage spartiate* (Paris 1933/43, repr. New York 1973).

Xénophon. La République des Lacédémoniens (Lyons 1934, repr. Illinois 1979).

Orizio, R. *Talk of the Devil. Encounters with Seven Dictators*, trans. Avril Bardoni (London 2003).

Osborne, R. 'Law and the laws. How do we join up the dots?', in Mitchell and Rhodes (eds.) (1997) 74–82.

Osborne, R. and S. Hornblower (eds.) *Ritual, Finance, Politics. Athenian Democratic Accounts Presented to David Lewis* (Oxford 1994).

Palmer, L. R. *The Greek Language* (London 1980).

Parke, H. W. 'The development of the second Spartan empire (405–371 BC)', *JHS* 50 (1930) 37–79.

Parker, R. *Miasma. Pollution and Purification in Early Greek Religion* (Oxford 1983).

Pelling, C. 'Speech and action: Herodotus' debate on the constitutions', *PCPS* 48 (2002) 123–58.

Persson, A. W. *Zur Textgeschichte Xenophons* (Lund 1915).

Pierleoni, G. *Xenophontis Opuscula* (Rome 1937).

Pomeroy, S. B. *Goddesses, Whores, Wives and Slaves. Women in Classical Antiquity* (New York 1975).

Xenophon Oeconomicus (Oxford 1994).

Spartan Women (Oxford 2002).

Ponting K. G. *A Dictionary of Dyes and Dyeing* (London 1980).

Powell, A. (ed.) *Classical Sparta. Techniques behind her Success* (London 1989).

Powell, A. and S. Hodkinson (eds.) *The Shadow of Sparta* (London 1994).

Pritchett, W. K. *The Greek State at War*, 5 vols. (Berkeley 1971–85).

Ancient Greek Battle Speeches and a Palfrey (Amsterdam 2002).

Purvis, A. *Singular Dedications* (New York 2003).

Raaflaub, K. A. 'Contemporary perceptions of democracy in fifth-century Athens', in W. R. Connor (ed.) (1990) 33–70.

Raeder, I. (ed.) *Collectionum Medicarum Reliquiae*, 5 vols. (Amsterdam, 1964).

Raschke, W. J. (ed.) *The Archaeology of the Olympics* (Madison 1988).

Rebenich, S. *Xenophon. Der Verfassung der Spartaner* (Darmstadt 2000).

Redfield, J. 'The women of Sparta', *CJ* 73 (1977/8) 146–61.

Reinmuth, O. W. *The Ephebic Inscriptions of the Fourth Century* BC (Leiden 1971).

Rhodes, P. J. *The Athenian Boule* (Oxford 1972).

A Commentary on the Aristotelian Athenaion Politeia (Oxford 1981).

Richards, H. 'The minor works of Xenophon', *CR* 11 (1897) 133–6, 229–37.

Richardson, N. J. 'Homeric professors in the age of the sophists', *PCPS* 21 (1975) 65–81.

Richer, N. *Les Éphores* (Paris 1998).

'*Aidos* at Sparta' in Hodkinson and Powell (eds.) (1999) 91–115.

Roscalla, F. 'Περὶ δὲ τῆς Ἀθηναίων πολιτείας . . .', *QUCC* 50 (1995) 105–30.

Rowe, C. and M. Schofield (eds.) *The Cambridge History of Greek and Roman Political Thought* (Cambridge 2000).

Ruschenbusch, E. 'PATRIOS POLITEIA. Theseus, Drakon, Solon und Kleisthenes in Publizistik und Geschichtsschreibung des 5. und 4. Jahrhunderts v. Chr.', *Historia* 7 (1958) 398–424.

Schofield, M. *Saving the City. Philosopher Kings and Other Classical Paradigms* (London 1999).

'Approaching the Republic', in Rowe and Schofield (eds.) (2000) 190–232.

'Plato and practical politics', in Rowe and Schofield (eds.) (2000) 293–302.

Serra, G. 'La tradizione manoscritta della *Costituzione degli Ateniese* dello Pseudo-Senofonte', *Atti e Memorie – Accademia Patavine* 91 (1978/9) 77–117.

Sokolowski, F. *Les Lois sacrées de l'Asie Mineure* (Paris 1955).

Les Lois sacrées des cités grecques (Paris 1969).

Sommerstein, A. H. 'How to avoid being a *komodoumenos*', *CQ* 46 (1996) 327–56.

Sordi, M. 'Lo Ierone di Senofonte, Dionigi e Filisto', *Athenaeum* 58 (1980) 1–13.

Strauss, L. 'The spirit of Sparta and the taste of Xenophon', *Social Research* 6 (1939) 502–36.

On Tyranny (Ithaca 1947, repr. Cornell 1963, rev. edn. Victor Gourevitch and Michael S. Roth (eds.) Chicago 2000).

Szegedy-Maszak, A. 'Legends of Greek lawgivers', *GRBS* 19 (1978) 199–209.

Tatum, J. *Xenophon's Imperial Fiction* (Princeton 1989).

Thomas, R., 'Written in stone? Liberty, equality, orality and the codification of law', in Foxhall and Lewis (eds.) (1996) 9–31.

Tigerstedt, E. N. *The Legend of Sparta in Classical Antiquity*, 3 vols. (Stockholm 1965–8).

Tuplin, C. 'Xenophon, Sparta and the *Cyropaedia*', in Powell and Hodkinson (eds.) (1994) 127–81.

Van Wees, H. 'Tyrtaeus' *Eunomia*. Nothing to do with the Great Rhetra', in Hodkinson and Powell (eds.) (1999) 1–41.

Wehrli, F. 'Les Gynéconomes', *Mus. Helv.* 19 (1962) 33–8.

West, M. L. *Iambi et Elegi Graeci (IEG)*, 2 vols. (Oxford 1989, 1992).

Whitehead, D. *The Ideology of the Athenian Metic* (Cambridge 1977).

Willi, A. (a) *The Languages of Aristophanes. Aspects of Linguistic Variation in Classical Attic Greek* (Oxford 2003).

(b) 'New language for a New Comedy', *PCPS* 49 (2003) 40–73.

Wilson, P. *The Athenian Institution of the Khoregia. The Chorus, the City and the Stage* (Cambridge 2000).

INDICES

These indices note authors cited and items deemed to be substantial; references to works include the commentary on those works and are in italics, page numbers are plain (*H.* = *Hiero*).

INDEX OF NAMES

229

INDEX OF SUBJECTS